AF263612

FIRST EDITION:
ANNINA NOSEI, ITA/ENG, Arte e Critica, Roma (Italia), 2023

EDITORS-IN-CHIEF
Daniela Bigi, Roberto Lambarelli

RESEARCH EDITOR
Daniela Bigi

ASSISTANT RESEARCH EDITOR
Tabea Badami

EDITING
Tabea Badami, Alessia Coppolino, Dominic McElwee

TRANSLATIONS
Dominic McElwee, Claudia Vincenti

THANKS TO
Paulina Jakubowski
Richard Milazzo
Elizabeth Fiore
Lee Ortega Robert
Edelmann Ken Smith
Joe La Placa
Mario Campo
Stefano Fontebasso De Martino
Tommaso Lambarelli

DESIGN
Matteo Perra **matteoperra.com**
Organ organcreative.com

ANNINA NOSEI

ROBERTO LAMBARELLI

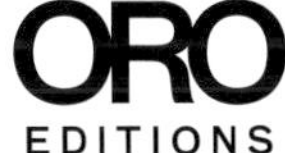

ORO EDITIONS

ORO EDITIONS
PUBLISHERS OF ARCHITECTURE, ART, AND DESIGN
GORDON GOFF: PUBLISHER

www.oroeditions.com
info@oroeditions.com

Published by ORO Editions

Author: Roberto Lambarelli
Book Design: Matteo Perra
Project Manager: Jake Anderson

10 9 8 7 6 5 4 3 2 1 First Edition

ISBN: 978-1-961856-73-8

Prepress and Print work by ORO Editions Inc.
Printed in China

ORO Editions makes a continuous effort to minimize the overall carbon footprint of its publications. As part of this goal, ORO, in association with Global ReLeaf, arranges to plant trees to replace those used in the manufacturing of the paper produced for its books. Global ReLeaf is an international campaign run by American Forests, one of the world's oldest nonprofit conservation organizations. Global ReLeaf is American Forests' education and action program that helps individuals, organizations, agencies, and corporations improve the local and global environment by planting and caring for trees.

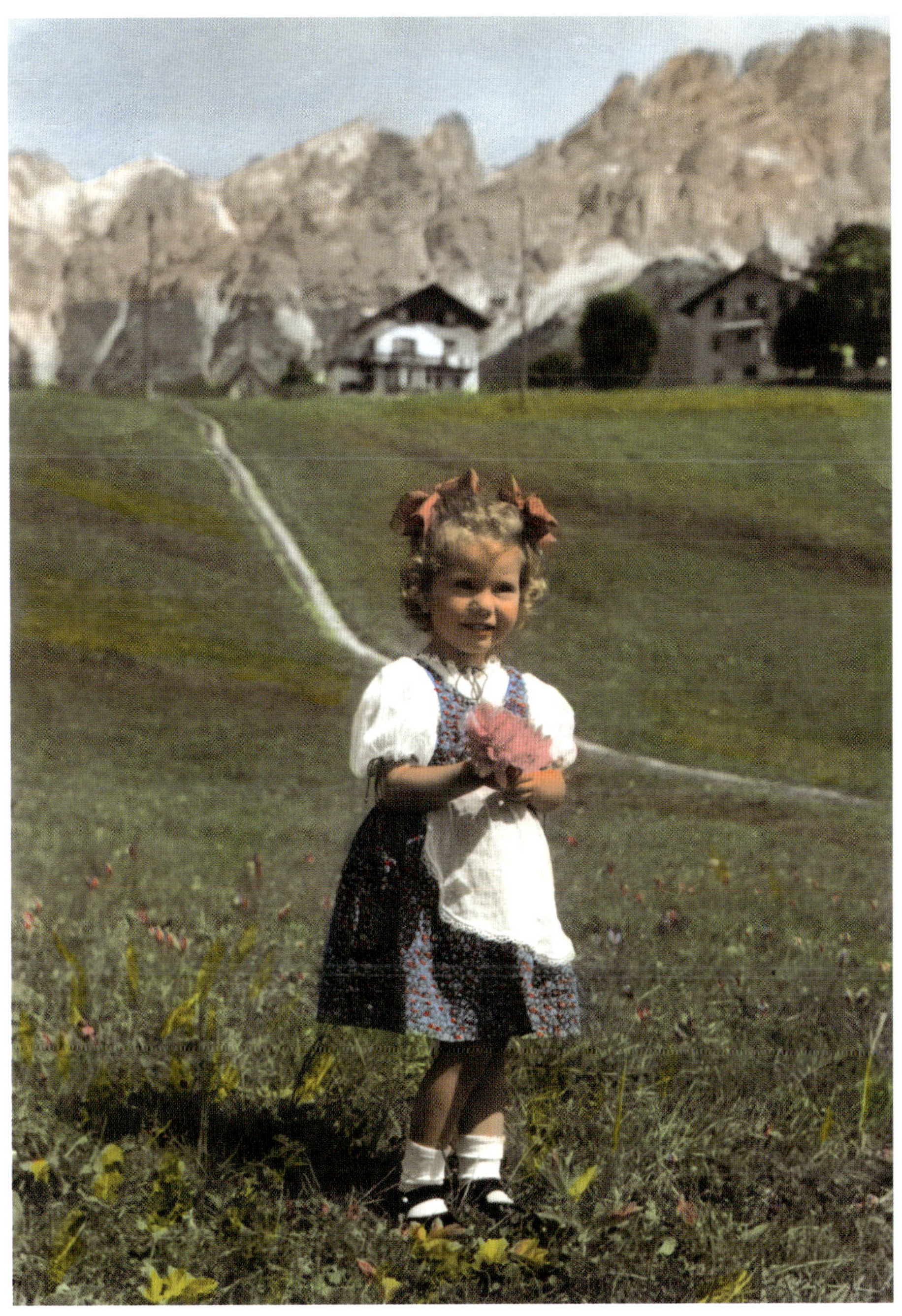

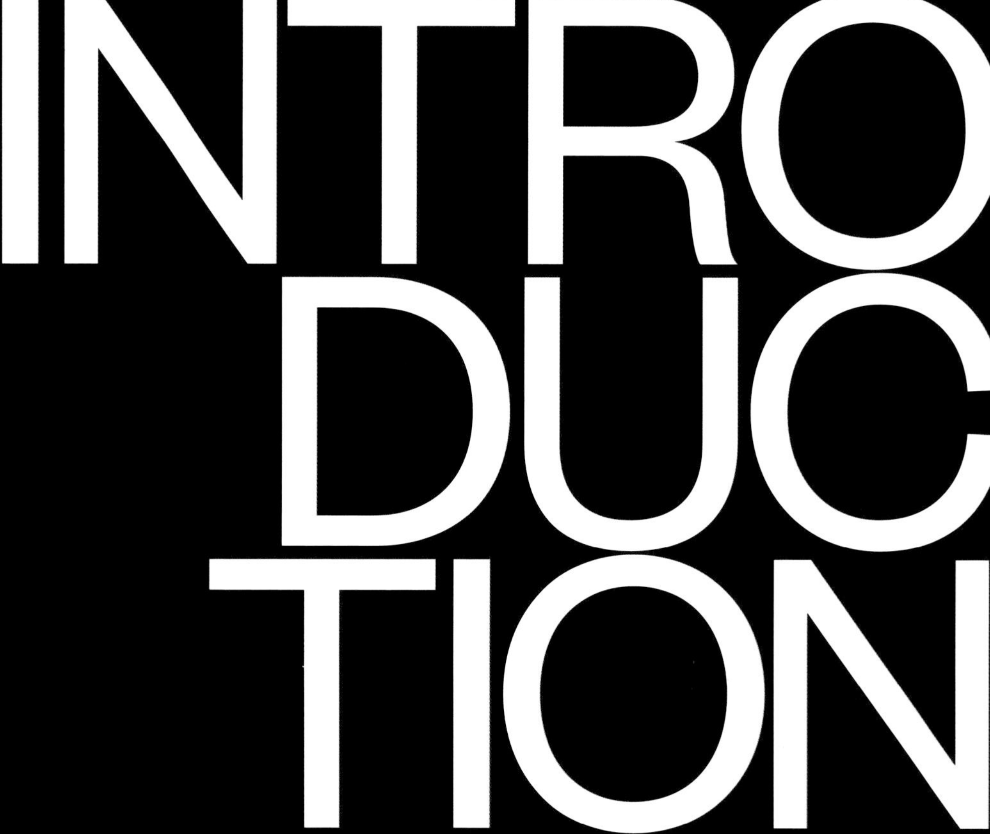
INTRODUCTION

1. Roberto Lambarelli, conversation with Annina Nosei, "Il Faut que tu te transforme en argent," *Arte e Critica*, no . 78 (2014): 60-63; and Roberto Lambarelli, conversation with Annina Nosei, "Il Faut que tu te transforme en argent #2," *Arte e Critica*, no. 94 (2019): 46-67.
2. Clement Greenberg wrote to the effect that at the bottom of such cultural phenomena, applicable to such thoroughly different artists, is the pain associated with them: "Why the public is so fascinated by the spectacle of this kind of suffering cannot be discussed here. Suffice it to say that the completeness with which Pollock appears to have exemplified the syndrome of the *artiste maudit* has invested his legend with a resonance like that of Van Gogh's and Modigliani's." Clement Greenberg, "The Jackson Pollock Market Soars," *The Collected Essays and Criticism, Volume 4: Modernism with a Vengeance, 1957-1969*, ed. by John O'Brian (The University of Chicago Press, 1993), 107-114 (114).

The idea of this book arose out of two conversations published in *Arte e Critica*. The first of these originated in a desire to record Annina Nosei's account of her activities in the New York art scene of the 1980s. The second, arriving some time later, served to recount her formative years and her professional beginnings.[1] This second conversation was prompted by Nosei's irritation at an unsettling recent development. In an interview that had appeared in precisely that period, a noted art-world personality had expressed opinions that misrepresented her relationship with Jean-Michel Basquiat. It does not require great familiarity with the vicissitudes of art to know that a fully-fledged *mythos* has arisen around the figure of Basquiat, a late addition to those myths that every so often cement themselves in the art world. Just as it would suffice to skim through the vast mass of publications fuelling that myth to affirm the importance of Annina Nosei's role in the painter's meteoric rise.

The fact remains that in the declarations of that noted personality there once again echoed the old cliché of the artist of genius, the artist at the margins of society, who at some point encounters the bad guy (in this case the white woman) who proceeds to exploit him.[2]

In Basquiat's case, the only substance underpinning such a fanciful interpretation is the brutal fact of his story's epilogue, his tragic death at only 28. But despite the grimness of that end, and while acknowledging the undisputed proof of his talent, one cannot help but recognize that the aspects of his story that have always taken center stage, often speciously, are those best serving the construction of his myth.

The point, however, is that myths fade over time if they are not constantly reinvigorated, continually retold. As Annina knows very well, hailing as she does from a family of philologists, the Greek word *mythos* means "word" or "story". For Basquiat, the mainstream press has nurtured and continues to nurture this story, incessantly feeding it while feeding upon

it in turn. But if common sense alone is enough to hint at the source of
and reasons for certain narrations, then their restatement by anyone
sufficiently versed in the dynamics of the art world – above all those that
regard the relationships between artist and dealer, dealer and dealer, or
dealer and collector – cannot but be tinged with doubt. Perhaps within
certain stories there hides only a core of rivalry and conflict, buttressed
by the nine-figure values attained by Basquiat's works which seal and
corroborate the myth's ongoing renewal.

These were the essential motivations that gave rise to our second conversation: the unmasking of the often perverse, always tacit, machinations
that direct certain art-world behaviours. Annina's story did not begin with
Basquiat's 1982 solo show, however, nor with his inclusion in her *Public
Address* group show the year before, alongside artists soon to see their
names in lights throughout the international panorama. It did not even
begin in 1980, with the opening of her New York gallery in its space on
100 Prince Street. It began long before, at the dawn of the sixties, with her
participation in Happenings organized by Rome's Ken Dewey-directed
ACT collective – a branch of the San Francisco group – and with her
successive recruitment to Ileana Sonnabend's Paris gallery. During our
second encounter, while Annina recalled her background, her training
and her first immersion in art between Rome and Paris, her old passion
gradually resurfaced. Her irritation waned and her narrative lent ever-
more space to the artistic affairs of a generation bound to the moment
of modernity's furthermost extension.

When it came time to choose a title, I felt it significant to refer to Marcel
Duchamp's exhortation to a very young Nosei on the occasion of their
first meeting in Rome in 1963: "Il faut que tu te transforme en argent." An
enigmatic assertion, characteristic of the French master's style and work.
Even sibylline, if we imagine it addressed to a young graduate to whom
it might have seemed more facetious than instructive. But Duchamp's

thought proceeded along symbolic and metaphoric lines, not easily deciphered; Annina understood only afterward that those words' meaning dwelled beyond reach of common sense, in the esoteric and alchemical culture in which Duchamp exalted, which would only later come to significant critical attention.[3] His assertion meant something quite different to what the words seemed to imply. He referred to a spiritual order, to the transmutation of matter, and in some manner he invested Annina with the mission – so I prefer to imagine it – of transforming currency into radiant gold.

On the subject of money, of markets, Duchamp had wilfully kept art in a constant and fragile balance between symbolic dimension and material value, almost as if to reflect on the social function of art, without ever losing sight of his ultimate, inalienable objective of the cultivation of knowledge.[4] This constitutes another waymark toward casting Annina's journey in the proper light. Courtesy of her bachelor's thesis, dedicated to Duchamp himself, Annina knew very well that the artist's methods assigned great importance to *behaviour*, the result of a complex vision of the relationship between art and life, between ethics and aesthetics. Thus, on the occasion of this second conversation, we decided on a book that would convey Annina's experiences at the heart of that crucial historical period: the moment that so emblematically encompasses both the apex of modernity's advance and its final crisis. Indeed, Annina's story is interwoven with that of an entire generation, the bridge-generation that took the first steps of the long "post-war years", that is, the period of collective enthusiasm surrounding the foundation of the Italian Republic.[5] Against a backdrop of heightened industrial expansion, Annina's peers passionately embraced everything arriving from overseas, beginning with art. That generation was to witness many radical transformations between the sixties and the nineties, from avant-garde elitism to social activism, from the presiding European-North American dynamic to globalization

3. Maurizio Calvesi, *Duchamp invisibile: Un'estetica del simbolo tra arte e alchimia*, 2nd edition (Maretti Editore, 2016). First published in 1975, this was the first systematic study to interpret the artist's work from the perspective of alchemical knowledge. As the author himself acknowledged, Breton had already referred to alchemical codes in 1929's *Second Manifesto of Surrealism*. The presence of such codes in Duchamp's work was left implicit in the works of some authors, such as Michel Sanouillet; others declared them explicitly, such as Robert Lebel in 1959, although without exploring their significance. The first edition of *Duchamp invisibile* was published in 1975 in Rome by Officina Edizioni. The author saw to it that a copy reached Annina Nosei in New York, accompanied by a note of thanks for her translation (from French into Italian) of Marcel Duchamp, *Marchand du Sel*, ed. by Michel Sanouillet (Paris: Le Terrain Vague, 1959). The collection's first Italian edition appeared in 1969, published by Rumma Editore and accompanied by an introduction by Alberto Boatto.
4. At the beginning of the sixties, Duchamp's relationship with the market became increasingly apparent. At the same time that he came to be recognized by an entire generation as modern art's defining master, it became evident that many of his works, including the most celebrated, were no longer traceable, having been abandoned and forgotten by the artist himself. In 1964, Arturo Schwarz took on the task of producing replicas of Duchamp's most notable readymades. The underlying idea of this assignment was twofold: on one hand, to reconstruct the lost works of art; on the other, to cultivate awareness of the artist's work among a wider public.
5. *Dopo-dopoguerra* ("Post-postwar") was the expression by which Jannis Kounellis customarily referred to the protracted postwar condition spanning the duration of 1950s Italy.

and from the foregrounding of innovation to the dominance of the market. Precisely as we reached a promising point in the project, events once more intervened to reawaken that old irritation: the cyclings and recyclings of cultural commentary. The culprit this time was a theatre piece dedicated to Basquiat.[6] Betraying the effects of token press coverage, the piece invoked the same old quadripartite cliché in which the artist remains imprisoned: genius-profligacy-exploitation-tragic ending. A vision which, aside from the genius and – alas – the tragic end, does no justice to the figure of Basquiat. Firstly because it doesn't correspond to the reality of art, upon which – contrary to the Duchampian values underpinning the later artist's practice – money has imposed itself so presumptuously and pervasively that it has come to interfere in the formation of our collective consciousness itself; secondly, because it ignores the social conditions to which Basquiat belonged, his family's comfortable circumstances and his bourgeois upbringing. In any case, if he continues to be reduced to that same mass-media effigy, if we are forced to persist in reducing art to fairy tales, then it will always fall to someone to play the part of the hero and to someone else that of the villain, regardless of the truth of the matter. One thing is certain. Annina has been allotted the peculiar destiny of forming a part of the Basquiat myth. A destiny indeed assigned to her at the beginning of her story, when she met the artist who pointed the way: "Il faut que tu te transforme en argent." After all, none deny that Duchamp was the true mythic founder of modern art. How, then, can we not surmise that Annina's acquaintances and her choices followed the very trajectory that he signalled for her, in search of the philosopher's stone?

6. *The Slave Who Loved Caviar*, a two act play by Ishmael Reed, directed by Carla Blank. Theater for the New City, New York, 23 December 2021 – 9 January 2022.

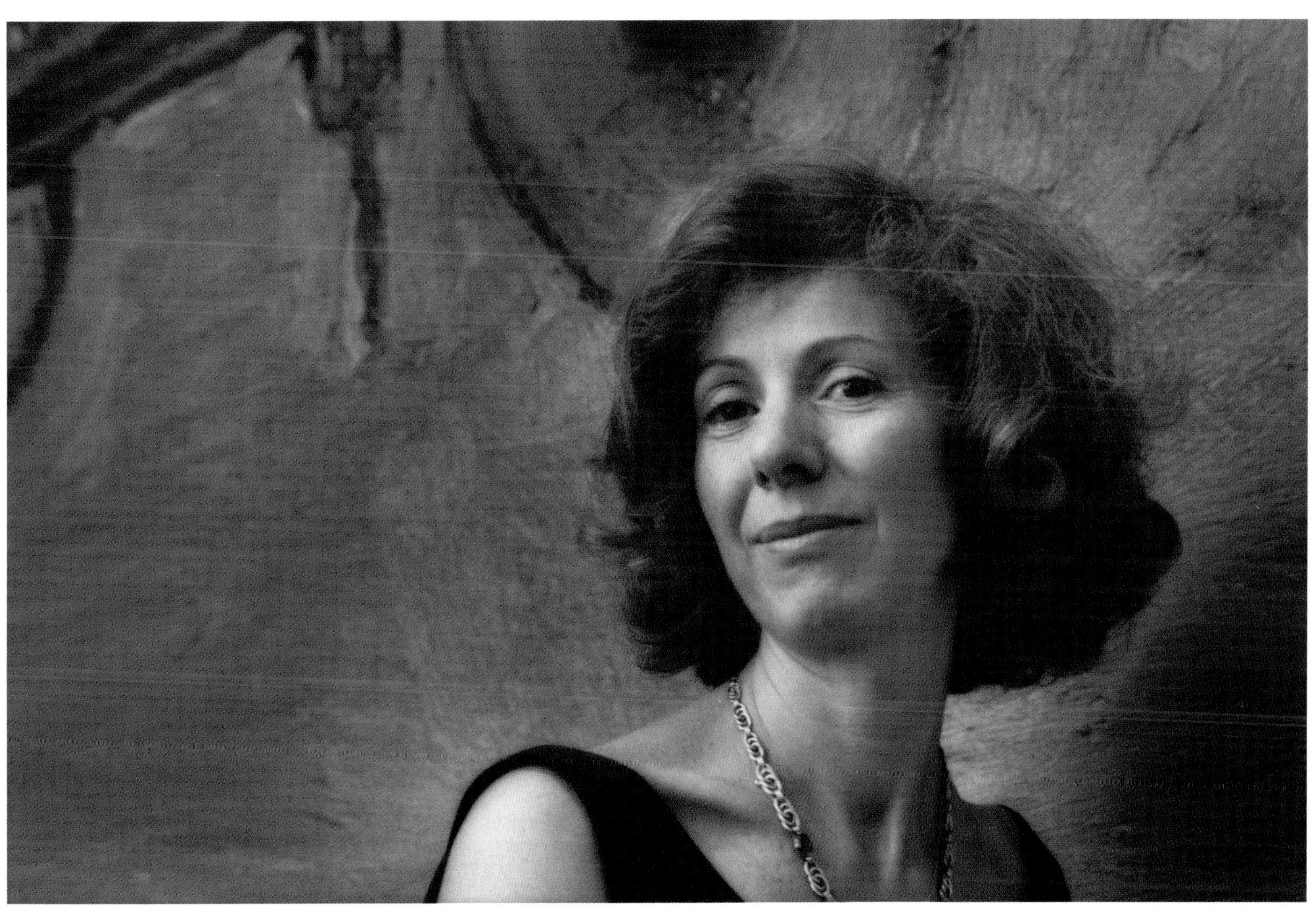

PAOLINA WEBER

TO HER MOTHER

ANNINA NOSEI

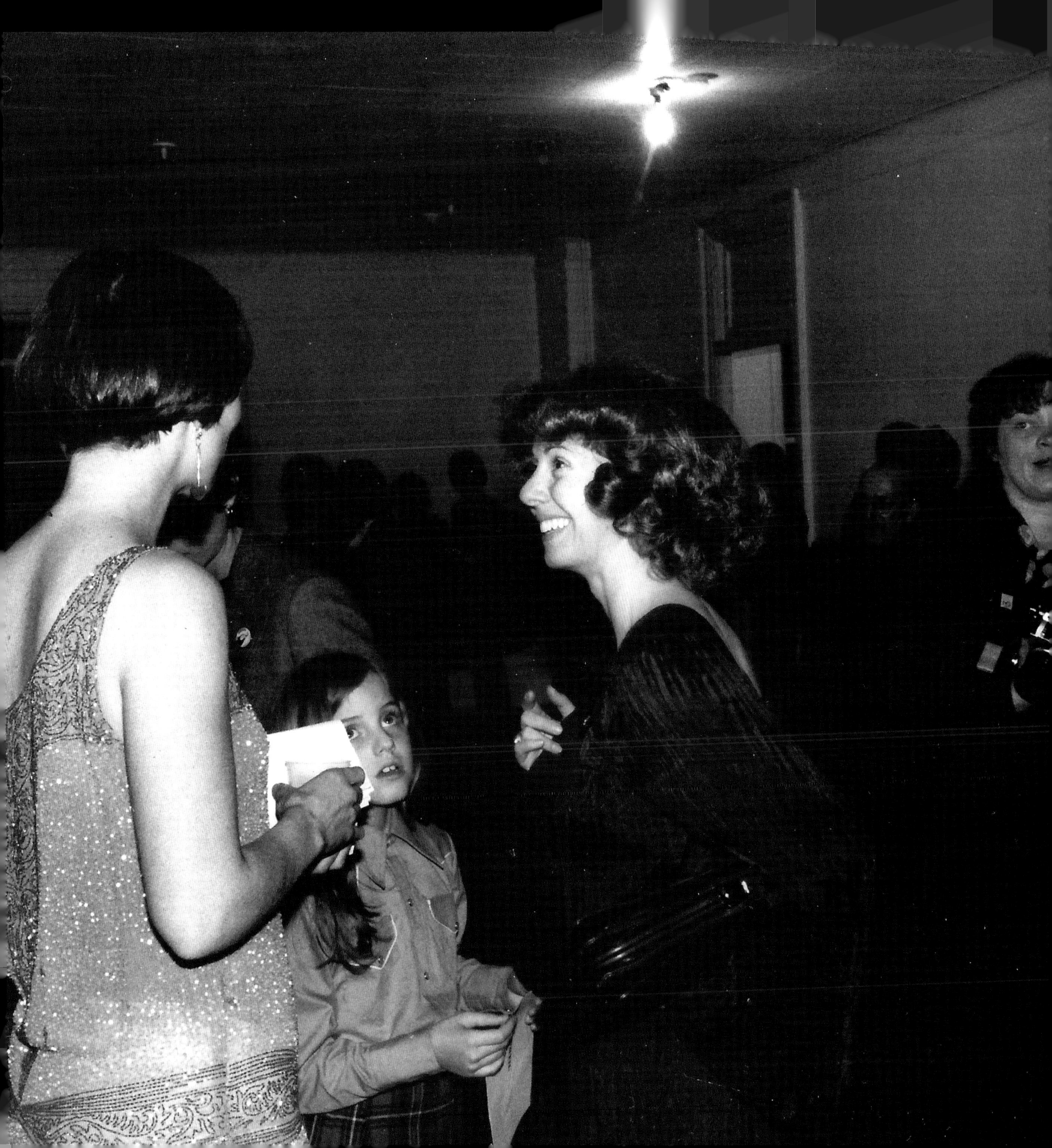

"Was that Merce Cunningham by the way? Marina Abramovic? Sometimes I was really bored. Bored beyond sentences."

There we were. Some landfill that is now Tribeca. My revolutionary mother and that artist. I was the... tag along. Had we been to PS1? Back when it was an empty school. Or were we at some happening on Wooster Street. I remember those (always) red square pillows. Sitting on them on the floor with you watching: naked people bump into each other. No, that one, that was in Venice at the Biennale. This one was a screaming man naked except for a sheep-skin hide (Willem Dafoe). That one, they walked in a square pattern and eventually crashed. Now I understand. Was that Merce Cunningham by the way? Marina Abramović? Sometimes I was really bored. Bored beyond sentences. Another performance in Venice: do you remember the artist that made a fake cow with a seat inside and then he had a bull mount the cow, while he was inside collecting fluid? That was so obscene. I remember you pulled me quickly away, but a bit too late. Some other island in some other factory or church. I was still the tag along. Sleeping on piles of coats at my bedtime, during the parties for the openings. The coats piled in the only room in a loft; back when a loft was just a big space and a wall to divide the loft space from the bed space. Except for your friend who had that crazy big white foam couch like the surface of the moon and a mirror with a man inside it looking back at me. And your car. Our car. The yellow Volkswagen Beetle, driving up the West Side Highway, with the rocks shooting up at me through the little rusted hole in the floor. They hadn't really paved the West Side Highway yet. At least not evenly. I was in my Swiss orthopedic shoes; shoes you said were so elegant (I hated that word) for my knees from the Doctor in Cortina. Blue ankle boots. Driving back up to our apartment. Listening to the radio. I push the buttons. I turn the knob. Our apartment on the River, with the aluminum square cold floor tiles placed like a square. My hopscotch game, a Carl Andre that Daddy left us, along with that work, who made it? Those four funny wheels drilled into each corner on the ceiling! I imagined if the house fell into the river, I would just roll down the

Annina with her daughter Paolina Weber in the 1970s.

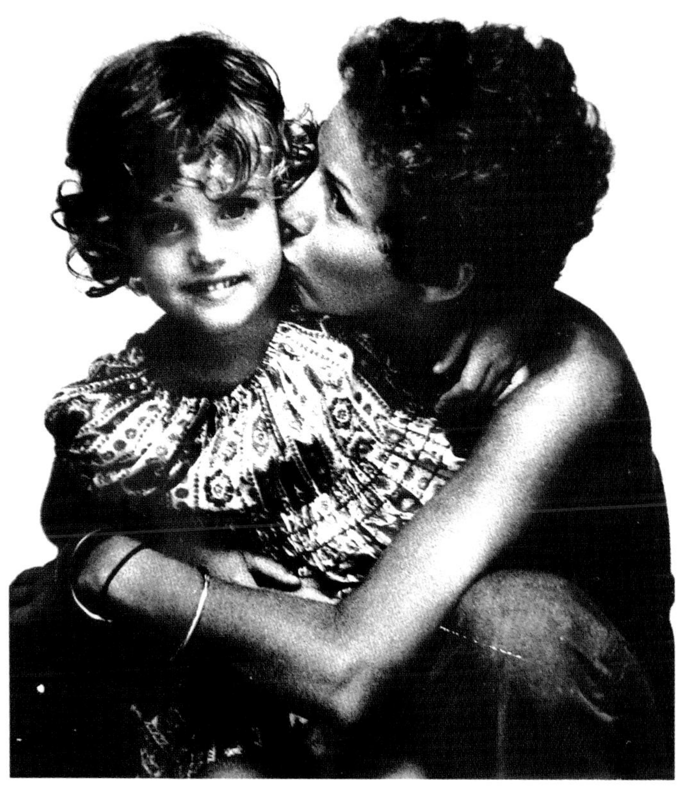

hill, standing on our ceiling. Some conceptual artist. I was seven and I could say the word "conceptual artist." The corner light piece Flavin gave (Untitled, to Paolina) that later you sold. To Paolina. I understand why. Now that I am a mother. You sold it like we buy groceries. What was mine was yours and yours was mine. We were the same body. The "strumming my face with his fingers" song. You wouldn't even have to tickle me, just singing it wiggling your fingers at me; I'd burst into a frenzy of laughter. Jeepers Creepers. The hand in the lagoon. How was it that every car broke down? All those rentals, whether it was in Pisa or in Pennsylvania. Mommy you took me to the *Lightning Field*. I understand now. I saw the *Lightning Field*. The Walter De Maria *Lightning Field* and that log cabin. Walking through those lightening rods. The rain and the field lit up like a grid and the mountains met the sky in the pink darkness. It was the same as the car breaking down. I understand. It was for me to see everything. To pause and look. To pause. The poppies on the side of the road. The landfill off Tribeca. This wall drawing, that dance piece, this word, a definition printed on a canvas, that shoe, this smile, that flag on the George Washington Bridge, this neon tent, that wrapped church, this striped red and white piazza, that artist in linen, this sea of coats, that FREEDOM, this Freedom. Freedom. Freedom. A freedom to bend language and space. You are so beautiful I understand. I was always there. You showed me everything, you gave me everything. Even when you were always looking everywhere else, you had me inside your eyes, looking out. You gave me eyes. When I'm looking from above the graph. Time is not as important as memory. It doesn't have to be flat. We are together.

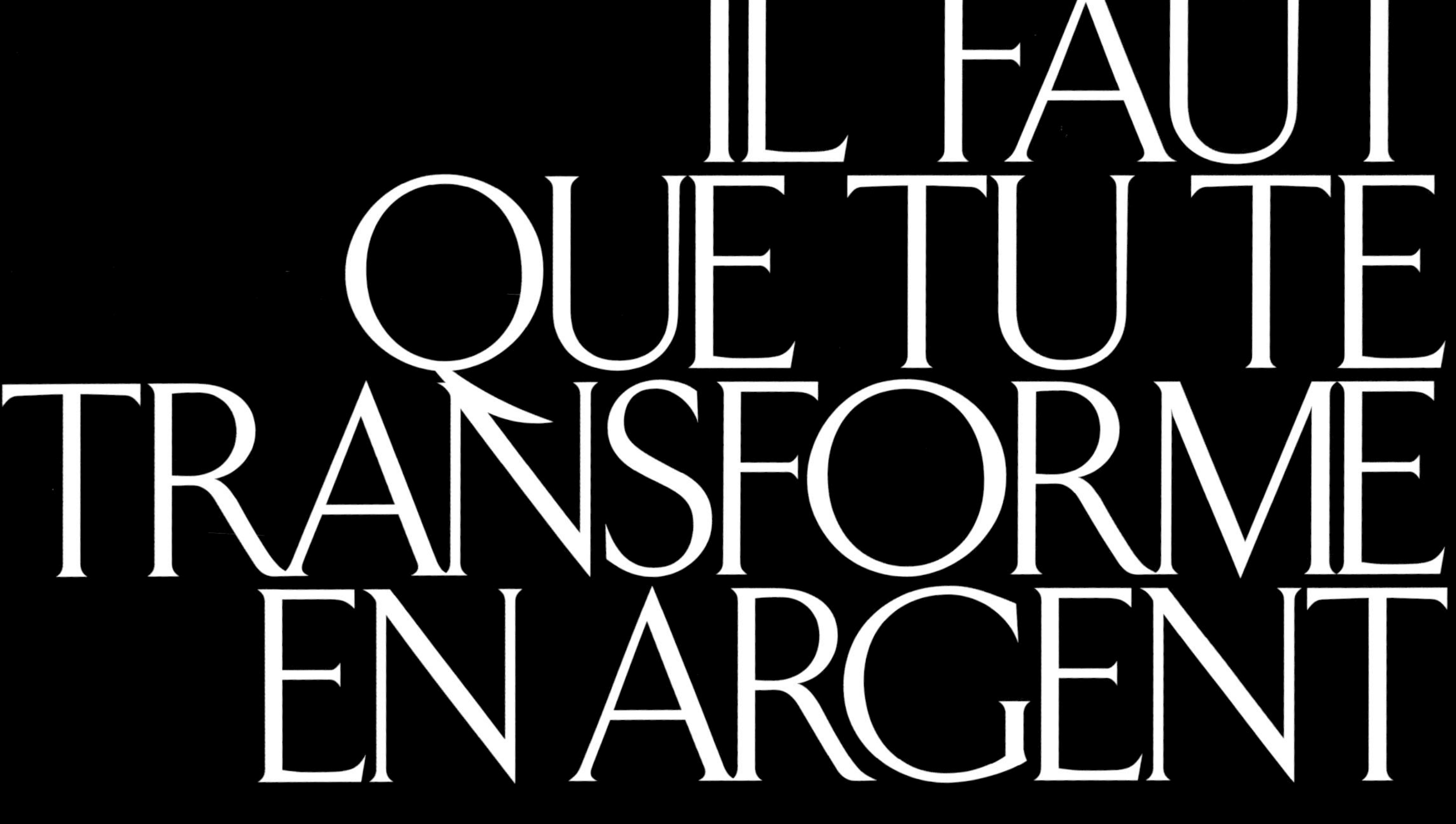

IL FAUT
QUE TU TE
TRANSFORME
EN ARGENT
A CONVERSATION WITH ANNINA NOSEI

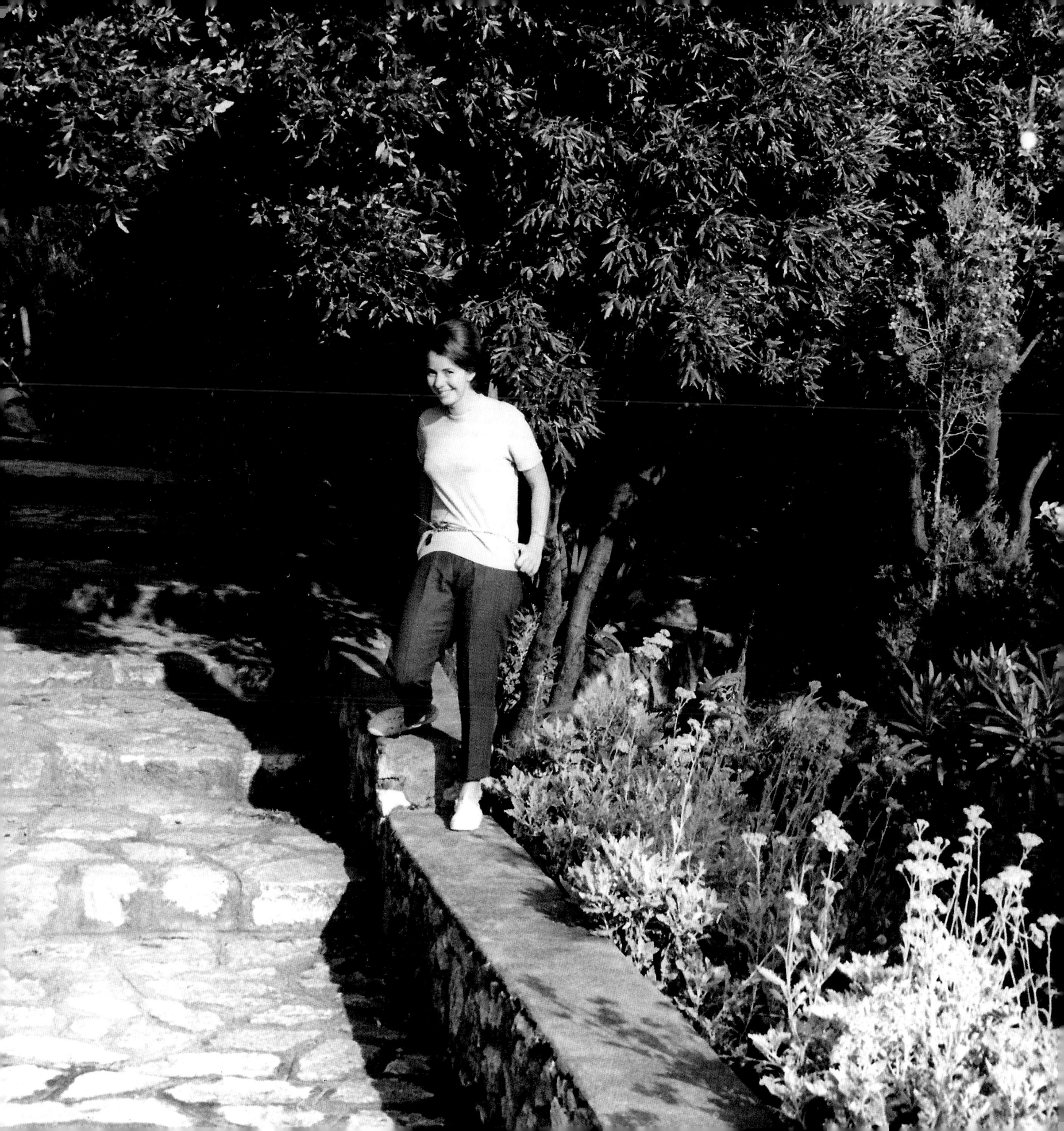

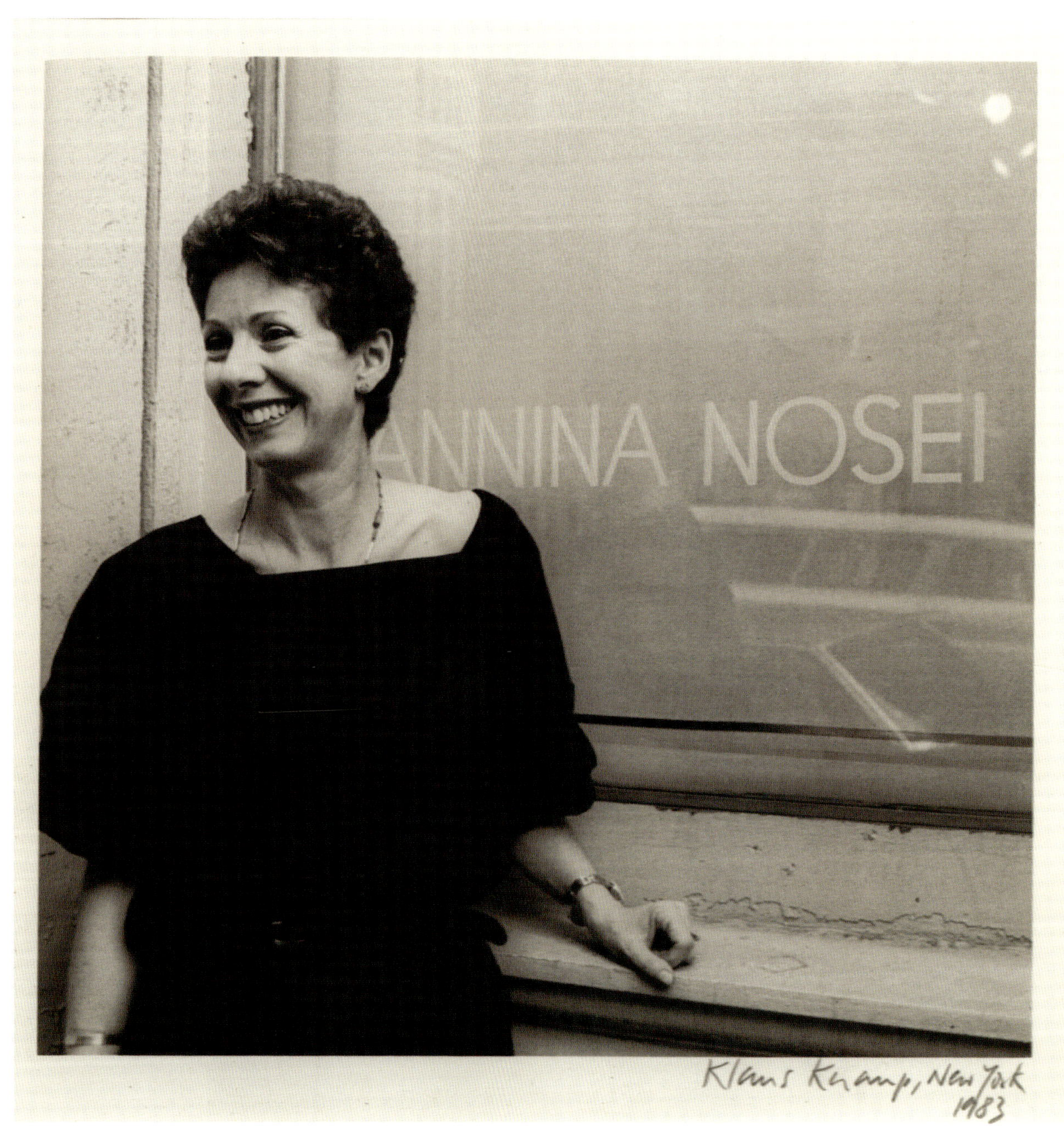

ANNINA IN FRONT OF ANNINA NOSEI GALLERY
NEW YORK, 1983

ROBERTO LAMBARELLI: Annina, you belong to a generation that found itself protagonist of the richest and most exciting phase of the last century. A generation which, starting from the very early 1960s, initiated a process of transformation in the way of conceiving of and dealing with art, producing radical changes that we cannot avoid confronting even to this day. If you don't mind, I'd like to begin with the anecdote you told me some time ago about how in Rome, in the early 1960s, you came into contact with the Living Theatre, successively following it to Paris, if I remember correctly...

ANNINA NOSEI: In reality, things did not go quite like that. At that time I had two friends who were part of the ACT group, which was an experimental theatre group that was also in contact with actors from the Living Theatre. Their names were Carmen Scarpitta, an already well-known and well-established actress, and Rospo Pallenberg. I joined the group and I went with them to Paris in the spring of '63, where we had been invited to participate in a Happening directed by Ken Dewey, entitled *The Gift*. Dewey had chosen some actors from the Living Theatre and some from ACT for this show featuring Chet Baker, for whom I acted as personal translator as well as interpreter on the set. The group was made up of many professional actors and other people who, like me, were just starting out in their careers. I was paired with a Mormon girl. We both participated in minor roles, one of which took place during a change of scene. Since Ken Dewey didn't want interruptions – the action onstage had to go on uninterrupted – he asked the two of us, the youngest of the group, to come up with something. I didn't like the idea of an improvisation done through miming, which was typical of those years, so I thought up an idea and at the scheduled moment I got off the stage and went toward the audience, stopping in front of a couple to whom I introduced myself in a loud voice, saying: my name; my father's name; what he did for a living, a professor of Latin and Greek etc.; who my mother was; with which professor I had studied, Giulio Carlo Argan; and, since I had recently discussed my thesis on Marcel Duchamp, I spoke about my experiences. The couple in question turned out to be Ileana and Michael Sonnabend. At the end of my performance, Ileana said to me very politely: "So when the summer ends, come work in my gallery."

RL: From the postwar period on, great attention had come to be paid to what was happening overseas: from music to theatre to art. Within a few years – even if Paris still managed to amaze with its vitality – Rome had grown very quickly. It soon became an interesting scenario, where the remnants of the jingoistic Strapaese tradition coexisted with the most advanced demands of modern art. Who were you seeing in those years?

AN: Well, I owed my first outings after high school to Franco Angeli. My father, a very strict professor of Latin and Greek, would only grant me permission to go out if Franco was there, because he liked him very much. He found him respectable, kind… and besides, he was a communist. And my father was a communist, too. If he was there, I could go out. I remember putting aside my used nylon stockings, which he needed for his paintings. This also amused my father.

RL: Let's go back to Carmen and Rospo, with whom you participated in the Happenings staged by ACT. Was Carmen the wife of Salvatore Scarpitta?

AN: No, the sister. His wife, indeed his ex-wife, was named Clotilde. I was friends with Carmen, but I also knew Clotilde because my father and I would often meet her at Cesaretto, the trattoria in Via della Croce where we often dined in the evening, which was frequented by writers, artists, and directors. Clotilde Scarpitta threw a lot of parties and I was allowed

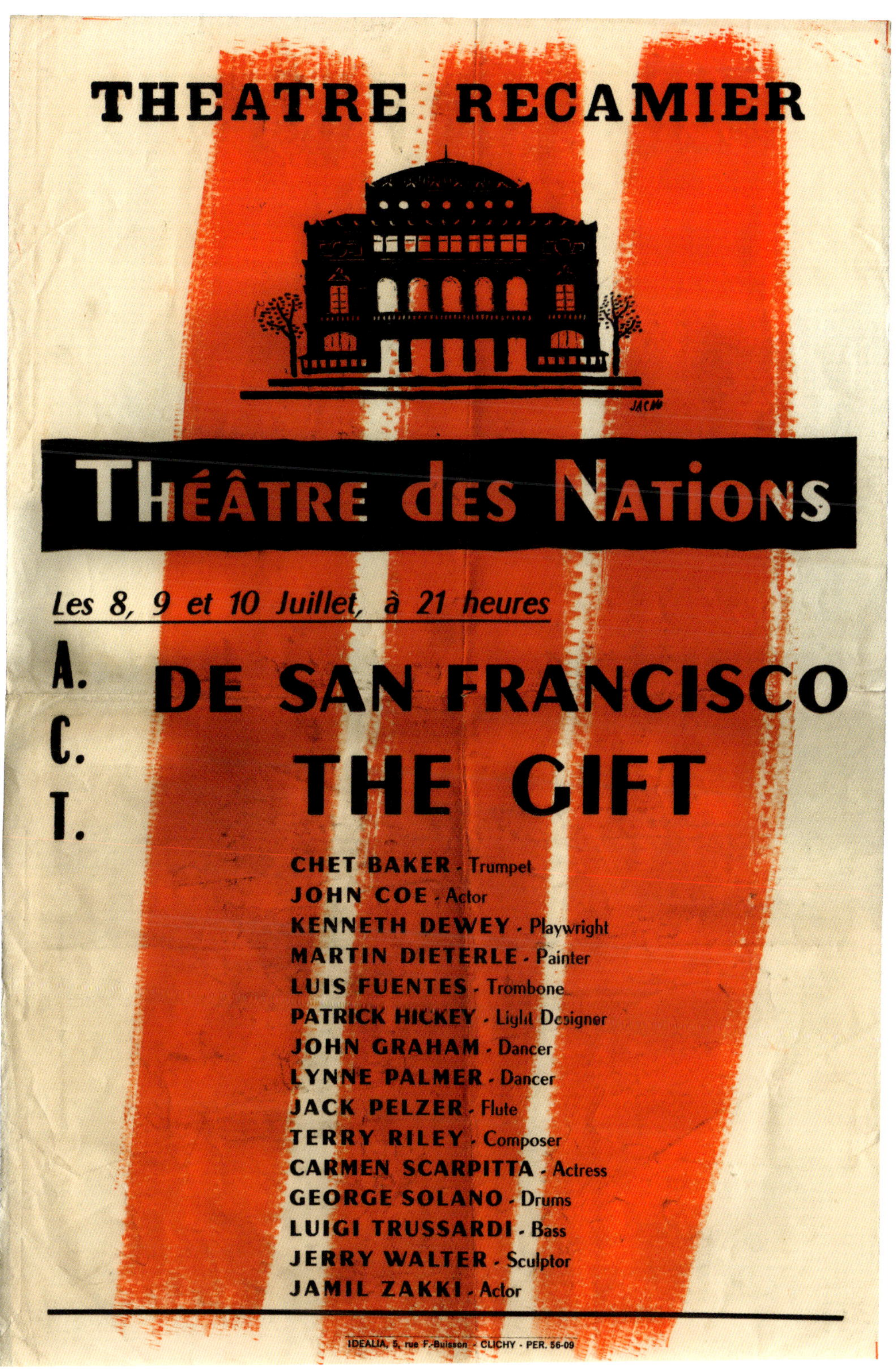

POSTER FOR *THE GIFT* (WRITTEN AND DIRECTED BY KEN DEWEY, ACT SAN FRANCISCO), THÉÂTRE RÉCAMIER, PARIS, JULY 1963.

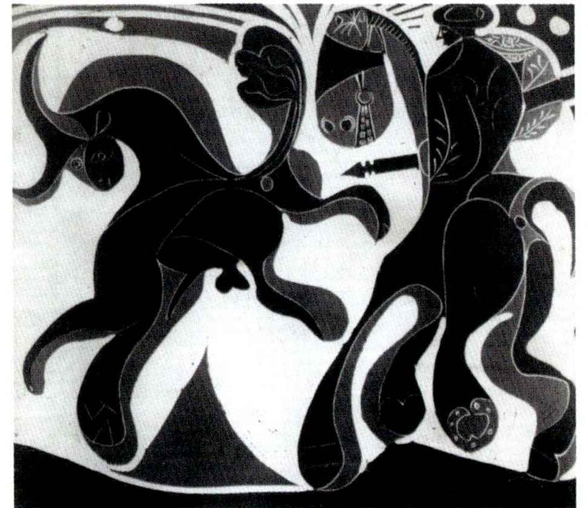

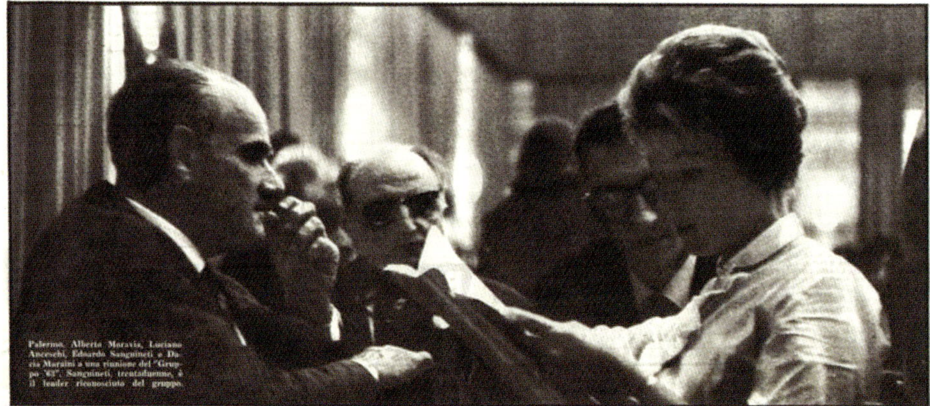

to go there precisely because Franco Angeli accompanied me. At her house I met many of the artists who frequented the Caffè Rosati, friends of Franco. Mario Schifano, Tano Festa, Francesco Lo Savio, and Jannis Kounellis. I also remember a small collection of paintings amongst which a Picasso dominated. Years later, in Los Angeles, I met Lola, the daughter of Clotilde and Salvatore Scarpitta; she showed me a picture of herself as a little girl in her mother's arms and said to me: doesn't it look like the Picasso? True, I replied. Through Clotilde I also met Gabriella Drudi and Toti Scialoja; later on I would also see him from time to time in Paris, where he taught for a period. His digressions on art were very important to me.

RL: Did you frequent the Caffè Rosati?

AN: Yes, my father sometimes gave me permission to go there. Initially only in the afternoon, then also in the evening.

RL: So you socialized with the artists who met there?

AN: Yes, of course – even though I was studying at Cambridge in those years. Before that, while I was at high school, during the summer my mother would send me to study in a college in Switzerland, in Vevey. She would accompany me there. I remember the lake, vast spaces. Once there was also the daughter of the Savoy dynasty, Beatrice. We had double rooms and sometimes my roommate and I would climb over the balcony to join the others in their rooms and chat together.

RL: You had an international education. Just what you needed to bring awareness to your involvement in the new cultural developments of those early 1960s, in Happenings. Earlier you were speaking about Carmen and Rospo and the ACT group in Rome...

Cover of the catalogue for Picasso's exhibition of lithographs at the gallery Il Segno, Rome, 1960.
Right: Newspaper clipping dedicated to the experimentations presented in Palermo by Gruppo 63 during the 4th *Settimana Internazionale di Nuova Musica*, October 1963.

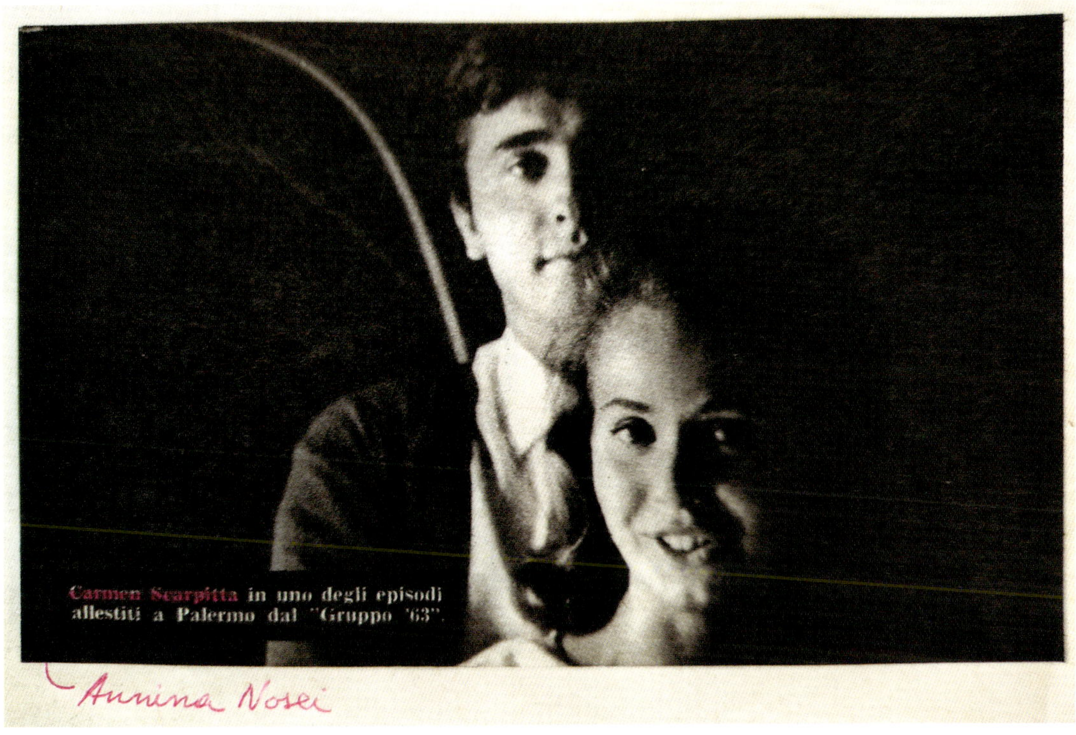

Clipping from the newspaper *Il Punto* with a photograph of Annina and Rospo Pallenberg in Palermo during Alfredo Giuliani's *Povera Juliet*, one of Group 63's performances on the occasion of the *4th Settimana Internazionale di Nuova Musica*, October 1963. The caption erroneously lists Carmen Scarpitta's name instead of Annina's, corrected in pen by Annina's father.

AN: I also participated with them in the first performance of Gruppo 63 in Palermo.

RL: Of that famous evening, in which 11 plays by as many authors were staged, and for which there was talk of a new experimental theatre, what do you remember?

AN: Together with Carmen, I took part in Alfredo Giuliani's *Povera Juliet*, one of the works directed by Ken Dewey. The costume which I used was made of the same fabric as the stage chair. I still have it, I'll show you. Gianni Novak, who was in the audience, laughed to the point of falling out of his chair.

RL: So can we say, albeit jokingly, that your career in the art world officially began in 1963?

AN: No, I had already worked for Panicali in Rome before that.

RL: Carla Panicali?

AN: Yes, I was an assistant at the gallery Il Segno. I remember that one of the first things I did was write addresses on envelopes and put invitations in them. They showed Picasso lithographs, of the Minotaur, which excited me.

RL: How was your relationship with Carla Panicali born?

AN: Claudio Cintoli introduced me to her. We had been friends since high school. I went with him to see the Jackson Pollock exhibition. For me it was fantastic. Claudio had a great passion for art from a very young age.

"I went with him to see the
Jackson Pollock exhibition.
For me it was fantastic.
Claudio had a great passion
for art from a very young age."

RL: We're talking about the '58 exhibition at the Galleria Nazionale d'Arte Moderna, curated by Palma Bucarelli and Nello Ponente… but tell me something about Cintoli.

AN: I had a great friendship with him, he was only a few years older than me but he was already a teacher and a great lover of art. He later became a friend of the family when I married John Weber, who acknowledged the vast breadth of his expertise. Cintoli also wrote about art.

RL: I think he taught, right? Did you have him as a professor?

AN: No, we were just friends. I don't remember exactly how I met him. He was a particular sort of person. He had a small room in his house, not far from Mamiani, where he would paint.

RL: Did you attend Mamiani Lyceum?

AN: Yes.

RL: You went to Mamiani Lyceum and lived at the foot of Via Flaminia.

AN: That's right, it wasn't far.

RL: What memories do you have of lyceum?

AN: Once, in the third year of lyceum, I don't know why, with Renato Mariani (who later became my lawyer) and another classmate, Giorgio Monaco, we brought a cat to class. The literature teacher, who was also the principal's wife, had me suspended from school. I was scared, I dreaded my father's reaction – but actually, despite being a very severe

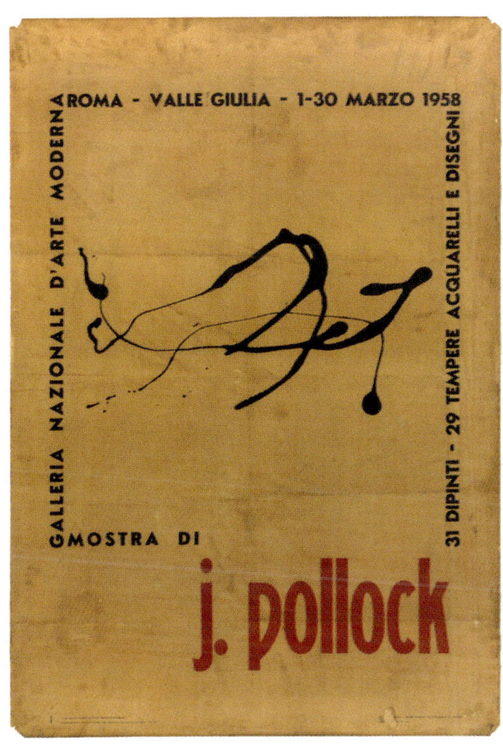

man, he didn't get angry with me that time. The event probably amused him. He brought me along as a guest to his lessons at Virgilio Lyceum, where he taught Latin and Greek; then he made me take mathematics lessons from a teacher who was in Via Nazionale. For Italian he took me to the Treccani Encyclopedia, where he was editor of the Latin section. In the end, my high school exams went well.
I was telling you about Claudio: he had a brother and I believe his father was a soldier. At their home, they had made the maid's room available to him. He painted and made his collages in that little room. And he talked about painting... He was a friend of Carla Panicali and it was he who asked her to let me work at her gallery, Il Segno.

RL: That job brought you closer to the Roman artistic milieu. In what period are wo?

AN: Right at the end of university, in my last year. In that same period I met Carmelo Bene. I don't remember precisely if it was an American actress friend who introduced him to me. Anyway, we became friends and started dating. One afternoon he came to my house; we were in the living room listening to records when my father, who generally went to the Treccani Encyclopedia at that time of day, returned home earlier than usual. Surprised to find me alone with a man, he began shouting verses in Greek, quoting Homer, and, after a couple of lines, Carmelo Bene continued the same passage in Greek. So my father, who was ready for a fight, calmed down, immediately feeling a strong liking for him. Afterwards, however, Carmelo wanted to go out in the evening, but my father, as I was telling you, did not give me permission. I remember once he had another boy call my house – maybe Carlo Lenzi, they were together – asking for me. My father was telegraphic. He told him I couldn't go out and put the phone down annoyed. So then the two came up the steps to our house

Poster for the Jackson Pollock exhibition at the Galleria Nazionale d'Arte Moderna, Rome, 1958.

"My father... began shouting verses... quoting Homer, and, after a couple of lines, Carmelo Bene continued the same passage in Greek..."

and presented themselves at the door.

My father, in his underwear, went to see who it was. I was right behind him, terrified. He swore in Tuscan, something like "Dio Cristo," saying I that I wasn't going out and that was that. And then we heard them leg it, running down the steps... Shortly after, Carmelo Bene staged the performance Cristo '63. I remember that Carla Panicali invited him to repeat the show at her home, in a Happening that once again shocked all the guests, with the actors jumping from the stage into the audience and back again, and so on.

RL: Where did this happen? At Panicali's actual home?

AN: Yes, in a villa a little way out of Rome. Carmelo did all sorts of things, everything he did was theatre. At the time I had a Fiat 600 and once we went to the zoo together. In front of the lion cage, Carmelo, facing a mother with her baby, said: "Now I'm going to take that baby and throw it in," something like that. The mother obviously panicked and started screaming and we, together with another boy (I think it was Lenzi again), had to make a run for it to reach the car and escape. Sometime before, at the Theatre of the Arts, I had seen Caligula, which had been his first show, much discussed... He was on a throne a little off the stage. Camus had authorized them to use his text. I think I went to see that show with Carmen Scarpitta.

RL: Let's return to Claudio Cintoli. We're towards the end of the 1950s, you attend lyceum and meet Cintoli, who was a few years older than you. Did he flirt with you?

AN: No, mostly he flirted with art. He was also a friend of Emilio Villa, of poets. When I went to Paris he wrote me letters...

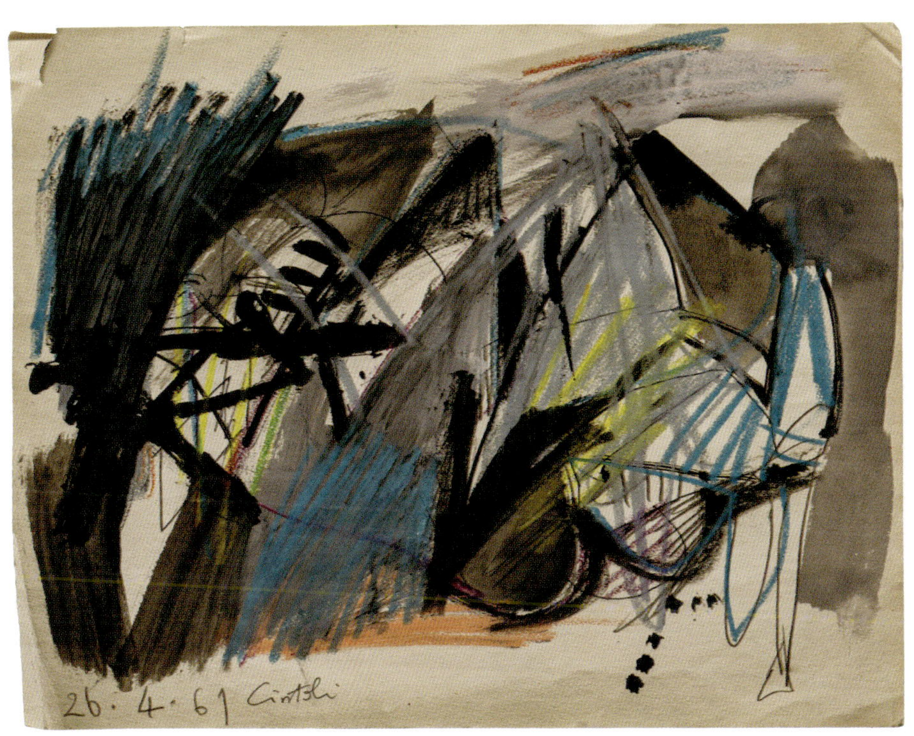

Untitled painting by Claudio Cintoli, 1961.

RL: I'd like to have your account of the Roman cultural climate in the late 1950s and early 1960s.

AN: Actually, I stayed at home and didn't go out often… But I'll tell you about one thing, which is significant. At a certain point, my father took me to Paris and I clearly remember that, in addition to the Louvre and other museums, we went to see the Mark Tobey exhibition at the Musée des Arts décoratifs. I wondered for a long time why he had brought me to see that exhibition, and then I understood. We had gone to see it because my father had surely heard about that artist through Carla Accardi, through her husband Antonio Sanfilippo and through the other members of the Forma 1 group: Giulio Turcato, Piero Dorazio, Pietro Consagra, and Achille Perilli – all of whom often sat at the table next to ours when we went to the trattoria. After all, if you look at the drawings of Carla Accardi or of Antonio Sanfilippo, you can immediately recognize their connection to those of Mark Tobey, who became quite famous in Italy after winning the Golden Lion at the Venice Biennale in '58; although the Forma 1 artists had been influenced by his work well before that accolade.

RL: The trattoria that you went to, was it the Fratelli Menghi, in Via Flaminia?

AN: Yes, exactly. My father and I used to go there for lunch, and often there was also my uncle Gennarino Perrotta, an important Greek scholar and a classical philologist, with his university assistants. As I was telling you earlier, Accardi, Sanfilippo, Consagra always went to Menghi's – and also Scarpitta, from time to time, even though I never met him…

RL: Who knows if these encounters influenced your decision to follow Art History at university and to graduate with Argan, or if you got there

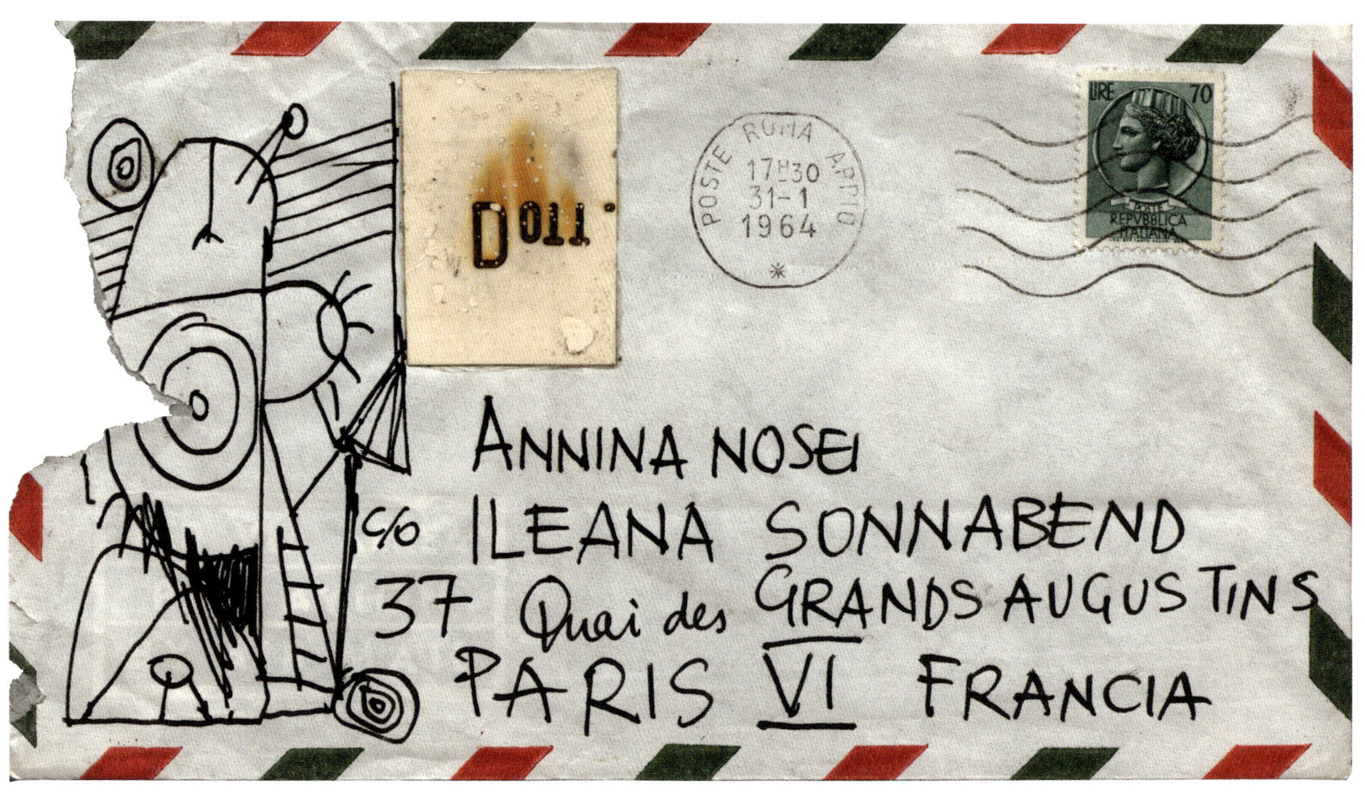

LETTER FROM CLAUDIO CINTOLI ADDRESSED TO
ANNINA CARE OF GALERIE ILEANA SONNABEND IN PARIS
31 JANUARY 1964

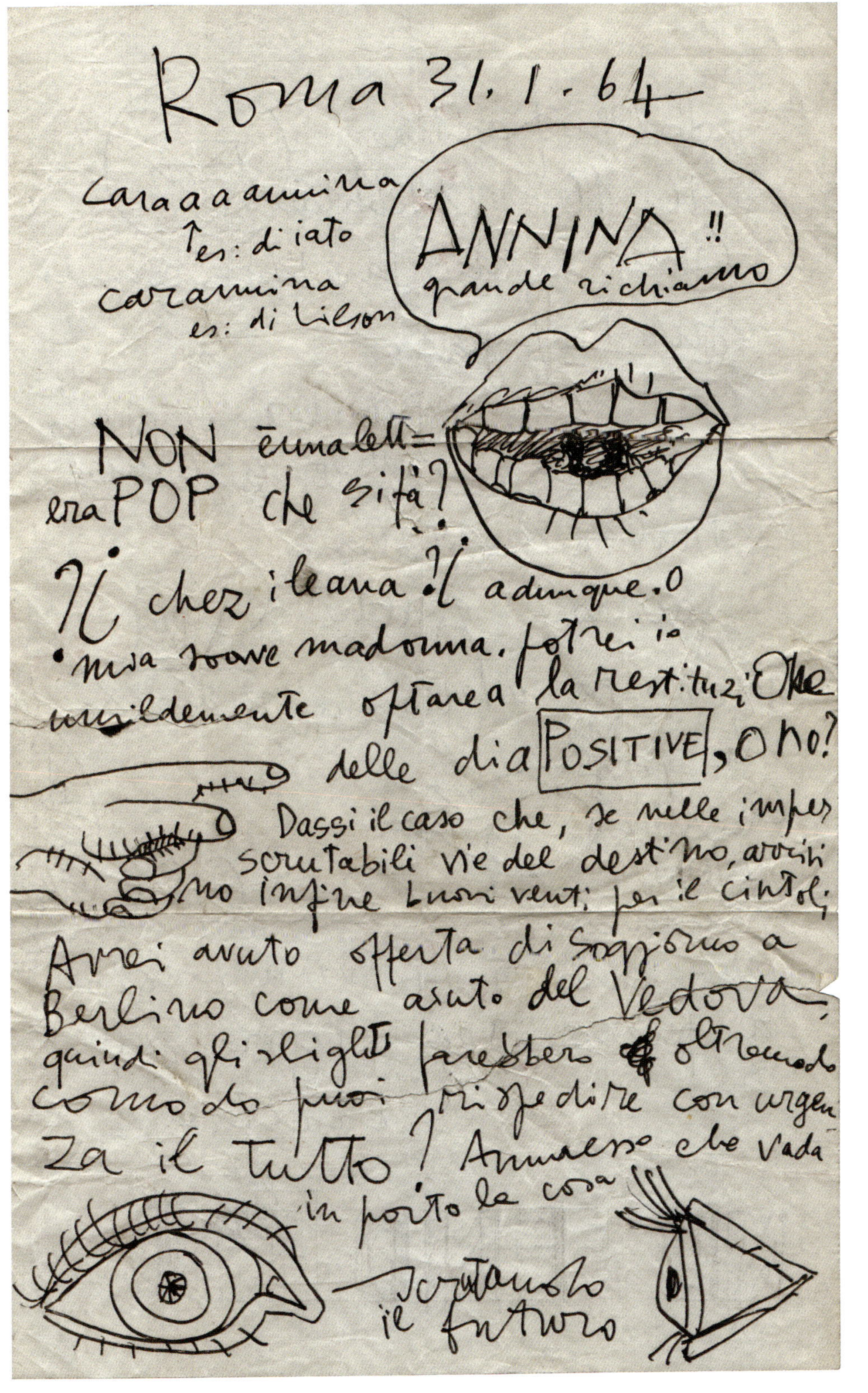

Roma 31.1.64

Caraaaamina.
es: di iato
caramina
es: di Wilson

ANNINA !!
grande richiamo

NON è una lett=
era POP che si fa?

?!(chez ileana ?!(adunque. O
. mia soave madonna. potrei io
umildemente optare a la restituziONE
delle dia POSITIVE, o no?

Dassi il caso che, se nelle imper
scrutabili vie del destino, arrivi
no infine buoni venti per il cintol.

Avrei avuto offerta di soggiorno a
Berlino come aiuto del Vedova,
quindi gli slights farebbero oltremodo
comodo puoi spedire con urgen
za il Tutto? Ammesso che vada
in porto le cose

scrutando
il futuro

thanks to knowing Cintoli, who had introduced you to the world of art?

AN: Cintoli certainly played a decisive role. In fact, in a diary of that period, I later found a drawing in which I had portrayed myself with a ponytail and underneath which I had written: "Girl looking at a work of contemporary art." It's evident that the work I was looking at was a work of Cy Twombly, who at the time had an exhibition at the gallery La Tartaruga. I was 16, I think, and that was perhaps my first real encounter with contemporary art. I also remember exhibitions at the Galleria Nazionale. I went to see that memorable Pollock show with Claudio, but I also saw others after that. I remember, for example, an exhibition of the Macchiaioli, which stuck with me.
It's not impossible that I'd already encountered Tuscan painting through my father's family, which was Florentine, but I was not aware of it in any case. I acquired that awareness with Cintoli, through his discussions about art and through his works, which he sometimes went on to give to me.

RL: What do you remember of your university years? What other teachers did you have besides Argan?

AN: Well, I remember Ettore Paratore, with whom I studied Latin literature, and Ugo Spirito, with whom I learned theoretical philosophy. English liter-ature I learned with Mario Praz and French literature with Gianni Macchia. I also studied the history of religions with Angelo Brelich. But above all, the relationship I had with Giulio Carlo Argan, who was the supervisor of my final thesis on Marcel Duchamp, was particularly important. He would occasionally invite me to lunch at his house, since I had become friends with Paola, his daughter. One summer he rented a house in Ansedonia, where I also had a house. But for my postgraduate course I attended Pierre Francastel's lectures.

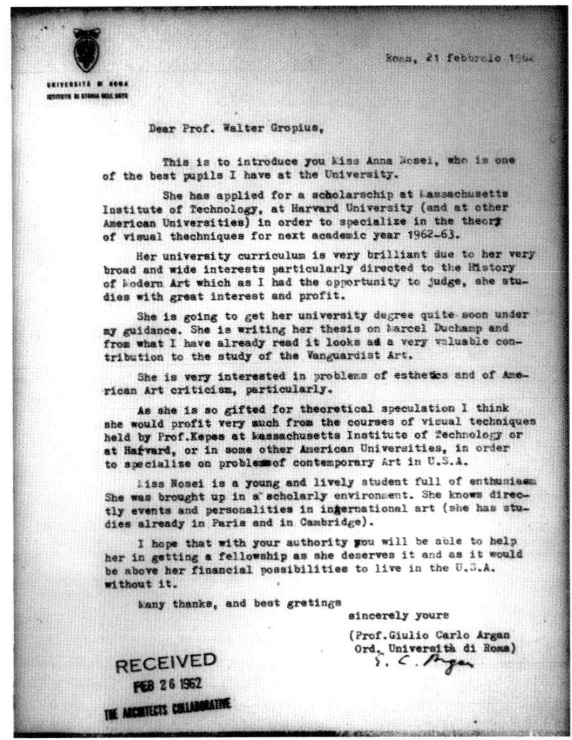

Roma, 21 febbraio 1962

UNIVERSITÀ DI ROMA
ISTITUTO DI STORIA DELL'ARTE

Dear Prof. Walter Gropius,

This is to introduce you Miss Anna Nosei, who is one of the best pupils I have at the University.

She has applied for a scholarschip at Massachusetts Institute of Technology, at Harvard University (and at other American Universities) in order to specialize in the theory of visual thechniques for next academic year 1962-63.

Her university curriculum is very brilliant due to her very broad and wide interests particularly directed to the History of Modern Art which as I had the opportunity to judge, she studies with great interest and profit.

She is going to get her university degree quite soon under my guidance. She is writing her thesis on Marcel Duchamp and from what I have already read it looks ad a very valuable contribution to the study of the Vanguardist Art.

She is very interested in problems of esthetics and of American Art criticism, particularly.

As she is so gifted for theoretical speculation I think she would profit very much from the courses of visual techniques held by Prof.Kepes at Massachusetts Institute of Technology or at Harvard, or in some other American Universities, in order to specialize on problems of contemporary Art in U.S.A.

Miss Nosei is a young and lively student full of enthusiasm She was brought up in a scholarly environment. She knows directly events and personalities in international art (she has studies already in Paris and in Cambridge).

I hope that with your authority you will be able to help her in getting a fellowship as she deserves it and as it would be above her financial possibilities to live in the U.S.A. without it.

Many thanks, and best gretings

sincerely yours

(Prof.Giulio Carlo Argan
Ord. Università di Roma)

RECEIVED
FEB 26 1962
THE ARCHITECTS COLLABORATIVE

Letter of introduction on Annina's behalf from Giulio Carlo Argan to Walter Gropius (21 February 1962).

RL: I find it very interesting that you did your thesis on Marcel Duchamp; both because of the date, so timely in relation to his recognition in Italy, and because it was Argan who assigned it to you…

AN: I still have it, you can read it if you want. My encounter with Duchamp, studying his thought, was very significant for me. It was at the time, and it continued to be in subsequent years. At certain crucial moments in my life, some of his words or ideas have come back to me. I assure you of that. But maybe we've already discussed it in the past…

RL: What about the translation of *Marchand du Sel*?

AN: Exactly. I translated Sanouillet's *La Boîte verte* into Italian. I had talked about it with Marcel Duchamp in person, who had come to Rome. The book was later published by Marcello Rumma.

RL: I know the book well. It is indeed entitled *Marchand du Sel* and it collects the writings contained in *La Boîte verte*. It was published a few years later, in '69, with an introduction by Alberto Boatto.

AN: Maybe I was talking to you about it in connection to something which happened in New York many years later. I was about 40 years old and I was going through a difficult moment, so I decided to go to a psychoanalyst, who told me: "Madam, you don't need psychoanalysis; however, if you want practical help –" I wanted to open my gallery "– go to Barbara Sher." She was a very good motivational therapist, now deceased. She'd help you to accomplish what you wanted out of life, trying to understand your life experiences, your problems with your father, mother, children, ex-husband, etc… but above all she'd seek out your sources of enthusiasm. She'd written a well-known book about it, *Wishcraft: How to Get What You*

"Duchamp came to Rome in '63... as soon as I was discharged, with my stitches still in, I went to see him at Gianfranco Baruchello's house"

Really Want. Eventually I went to her, because I was very disheartened. And she asks me, "Why do you feel like this?" And I tell her, "Nothing's going right, I don't like anyone, I don't like anything." And she says, "Aw, come off it. Don't you like this?" And I say: "No." "You don't like any artist?" And I say: "No, I don't like them anymore." Then she asked me: "Not even Marcel Duchamp?" And I replied: "Not even Marcel Duchamp."

RL: Not even Duchamp. But how? One of the first exhibitions you hung in your gallery was The Door. Was that not a tribute to his work?

AN: Yes indeed. Then I told her about when I had met Marcel Duchamp for the first time, after having agreed to do my thesis on him and while I was translating his book. Duchamp came to Rome in '63. I was in hospital for appendicitis at the time, but as soon as I was discharged, with my stitches still in, I went to see him at Gianfranco Baruchello's house, where he was staying. I was disappointed with the meeting because I hadn't gotten the answers to my questions.

RL: What did you want to know? Something regarding his work, or something else?

AN: At the time I was very young and I thought that meeting him would inspire me, that he would give me ideas on how to move forward in the art world. At one point, he said to me: "Il faut que tu te transforme en argent." Talking to Barbara Sher, I said: "How was I supposed to transform *en argent* if the publisher wouldn't even pay me for the translation?" Upon returning home that same evening, I found a book by Maurizio Calvesi on my doorstep. It had just arrived in the mail and I read that it cited my name, Annina Nosei Weber (I was married to John Weber), explaining in a note that he had used my translation because he had detected alchemical underpinnings in it. My mind suddenly opened up with the realization that what Duchamp had told me when I was 20 he had meant literally; while all of a sudden I understood that the message was now of a different nature, and it was that I had to transform myself, going by that alchemical interpretation, in a spiritual sense – I had to have new ideas, to undergo a transformation. I understood Duchamp's works better, that they function like a mirror in which everyone reflects themselves, and so I realized that at 20 I had been looking for a way to earn some money, while in his words there was a condemnation of money. Now that I was 40 and looking for something else, that phrase no longer spoke to me about money, but rather it revealed new ideas to me. This is what I have found interesting, as well as amusing, in Marcel Duchamp. Just a few days ago, furthermore, the curator Peter Eleey was telling me about the work *Three Mirrors*, which I wasn't familiar with. It's a work that Duchamp created in 1964 by signing mirrors, a readymade that was renewed every time someone looked into it. This goes to show what I've always thought: that in his works everyone reflects themselves. Speaking of The Door, in that one there was the theme of opening... I'll have something more to tell you about that later.

RL: The Calvesi book that you're talking about, was it *Duchamp invisibile: La costruzione del simbolo* (Duchamp invisible: The construction of the symbol)?

AN: Yes. It was the first time that an alchemy-based interpretation of Duchamp was proposed.

RL: I'd like to take a step back. I know nothing about your parents, about your childhood... From the anecdote that you recounted about the time in Paris when you improvised in front of the Sonnabend couple by saying

"He tried once more to persuade my aunts to come to Italy. The Germans were already in Warsaw."

your name, what you'd studied, your father's name, his profession, etc., I assume that they played an important role.

AN: I lived in Rome, where I was born, at 125 Via Flaminia, and I attended the Misericordia elementary school, run by the nuns. It was next to the piazza that housed the Naval Ministry, not far from home. At the age of six, I was already able to walk alone. My mother, Paolina Frydman, worked in the Villa Borghese at the International Institute of Agriculture, which would later become the FAO.

RL: Her surname's not Italian. Where did she come from?

AN: From Poland. Her surname, Frydman, is Jewish, but my mother was Catholic – very Catholic indeed, like all Poles. Her father, Joseph Frydman, had been a businessman and had died in Vienna in the early 1930s. I don't know exactly what kind of business he was involved in, but I found bank statements from British and Swiss banks at home.

RL: How had your mother come to be in Italy?

AN: After having attended university in Krakow, she had come to Italy to study in Venice, at the university for foreigners, Ca' Foscari. There she had made friends with a young Frenchman named Daniel Kaltenbach, who came from a very wealthy family, the producers of the notorious insecticide DDT.
There are photographs of my grandfather with my mother's sisters at Piazza San Marco in Venice, all covered in furs, with the pigeons. There are other photographs of my mother with Daniel and other friends in Portofino, on sailing boats... Daniel at a certain point moved to Rome to work at the International Institute of Agriculture, inside the Villa Borghese.

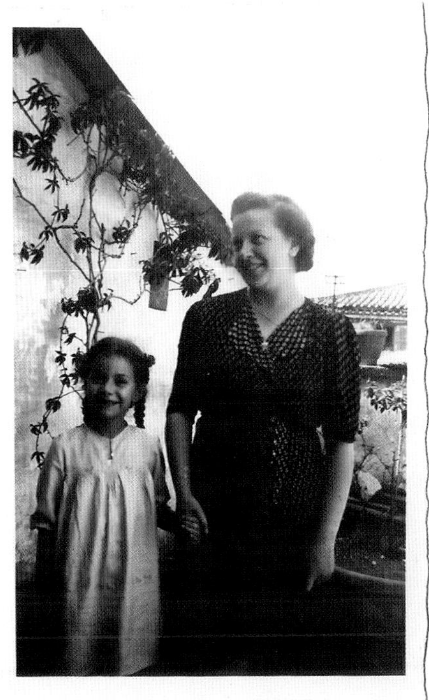

In Rome Daniel befriended my father, Angiolo Nosei, who taught Latin and Greek. They would go for long walks together along the Appian Way to study the ancient ruins. Both were staying, like many other students and young professors, at the then-famous Valentini residence hall, in the vicinity of Via Veneto. After she had completed her university studies, my mother left Venice and came to Rome; Daniel helped her get a job in the library at the International Institute of Agriculture, where he worked. So it was through him that she met my father. And so Daniel married Odette, a young French woman, and my father married my mother, Paolina Frydman. Both of the couples went to live in Via Flaminia, opposite the tennis club (it's no coincidence that I played a lot of tennis during my adolescence). The two apartments were on the top floor, with adjacent terraces overlooking the hill of the Villa Borghese, where the Strohl-Fern villa is located.

RL: What kind of relationship did you have with your mother's family?

AN: In the first months of 1939, two of my mother's sisters came to Rome to see me, because I'd just been born. My father, who'd intuited the unfolding political situation quite clearly, had tried to convince them to stay in Rome. They couldn't believe that what duly happened could really happen and they insisted on going back home. A few months later Germany invaded Poland.
Meanwhile, with the start of the war, Daniel and his wife Odette returned to France and my father went to Warsaw, where he tried once more to persuade my aunts to come to Italy. The Germans were already in Warsaw. On one of those days he was on a tram and some German soldiers boarded as well, checking documents and treating people badly; they also turned their attention to my father, who promptly told them in German that he came from Rome, where the fascists were (even though my father was a communist) – but anyway – he tried to convince my aunts right

Annina with her cousin Giovanna Ukleja after her return from Auschwitz, Rome, 1946.

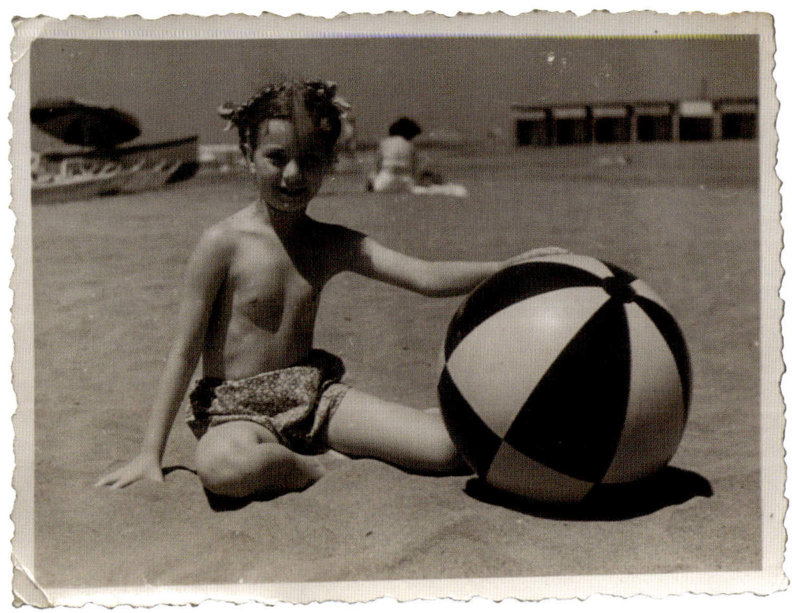

to the very end, he was still urging them even at the station. As he was about to get back on the train, he begged them: "You don't have to worry about your bags, you don't have to worry about anything, just get on the train." But they didn't.

RL: A tragic story… If they had come to Rome they would have been saved.

AN: Instead they were deported to Auschwitz a few years later and never returned.

RL: Do you have any other memories from your early childhood?

AN: I remember, for example, that my mother was friends with a famous Polish painter, Jarema, who frequented the artists' club in Via Margutta.

RL: Ah yes, Jarema, who had founded the Art Club in Via Margutta with Prampolini.

AN: A funny thing: I remember that Jarema had a motorcycle, and I remember having gone with him, when I was a small child, to exactly that artists' club in Via Margutta, sitting between him and mom. My mother was also friendly with Angelo Savelli. I wrote a text for one of his shows in New York a long time later, in the 1970s. At the Art Club there was also another artist friend of my mother's; Riccardi was his name, an Italian who painted portraits and once portrayed my nurse holding my little self in her arms, as if she were the Madonna. His daughter Gemma Riccardi also painted my portrait. With my mother we would also go to Villa Strohl-Fern, which was located inside the Villa Borghese, because her office was near there.

RL: Villa Strohl-Fern housed the studios of many of the leading artists of

Young Annina at the beach.

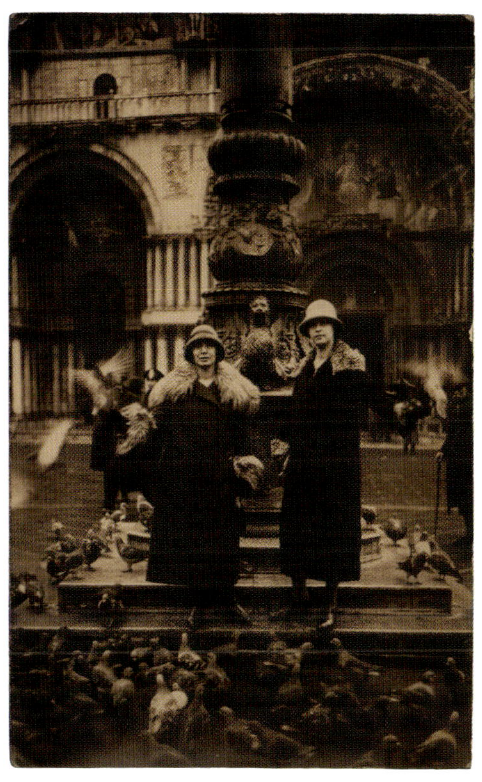

the Roman art scene. Your mother was still working at the International Institute of Agriculture, which later became the FAO?

AN: During the war she had overseen the bulletins published by the International Institute of Agriculture. They had offered her a posting in Washington, but she refused because she didn't want me to become an American teenager. Then she met the Italian Ambassador to Poland, Eugenio Reale, and began to work with him. My mother spoke many languages: she knew Russian and French because she belonged to a wealthy Polish family; naturally she also knew English, she had learned some Spanish, and obviously spoke Italian. I remember that she was always traveling, I always have the image of her packing her suitcase, with all those beautiful clothes. At that time she attended a lot of soirées with the Ambassador, not only in Poland but practically everywhere, which is why she always brought elegant clothes with her. I've found a letter that she mailed to my father in which she sent news to her Jewish friends in Rome concerning their relatives who had remained in Poland. In those years the situation was dramatic. She told me that on one occasion the Ambassador's retinue was invited to a meeting at the British headquarters in Warsaw. At the entrance to the building she had noticed some furniture from Mies van der Rohe's Bauhaus years, which she recognized as his. How had they ended up in that building? In that period, anything could happen...

RL: What Roman circles did your mother move in?

AN: Well, for instance, the stirring image comes to mind of the evening that we went to the Teatro Argentina to listen to Arthur Rubinstein. He was Polish and at the end of the concert, with a few other Poles, we joined him on the stage where he played two or three small pieces just for us. It was

Paolina Frydman (Annina's mother) sisters in Venice in the 1930s.

as if he were playing for a reserved group of friends. It was extraordinary. I remember that during the war years, due to my mother's work for the Ambassador, our house had been granted extraterritorial rights. There was a plaque hanging on our door that certified as much. One day, some German soldiers showed up: my father opened the door and said: "You can't come in, can't you see what's written on the door?" The soldiers apologized politely, in German, and went away. Our porter, who was a fascist, had probably reported us to the authorities; our presence bothered him, but technically our house belonged to a diplomatic mission.

RL: Do you have any other memories of the war years?

AN: I still have very vivid memories of the bombings, of taking shelter in the basement. I also remember that the consequences lingered for a long time. Some time after the end of the war, while my mother was in Geneva, two young people in uniform rang at our door. They were Romano Ukleja and my cousin Giovanna, the daughter of one of my mother's sisters. They had come from Auschwitz. Romano was a filmmaker, an expert in cinematographic techniques, and in the concentration camp, the Germans had entrusted him with a job as a photographer. One day he had seen Giovanna in the line of women destined for the gas chamber, but he had managed to remove her from the line and had hidden her. That was on one of the last days before the liberation. Then they had fled together: walking, taking trains, riding on trucks and finally arriving in Rome. The uniforms that they were wearing had been taken from dead Italian soldiers they had happened upon during the journey. My father recognized them immediately and welcomed them with great enthusiasm, giving Romano some clean clothes and taking Giovanna to my mother's room, where he opened the wardrobe and made her choose one of her dresses. I was very upset, at that moment I was outraged, but then we all went out to

From top left clockwise: Annina with her mother Paolina Frydman, 1939; Annina grandfather Joseph Frydman; Annina in the arms of her nurse Lucia Sales, Rome, 1939; Paolina Frydman identification photograph.

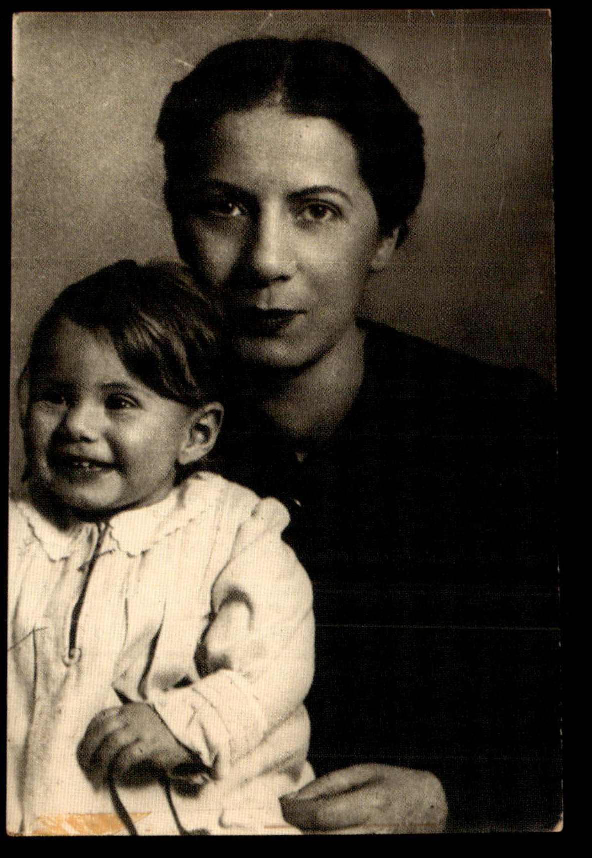

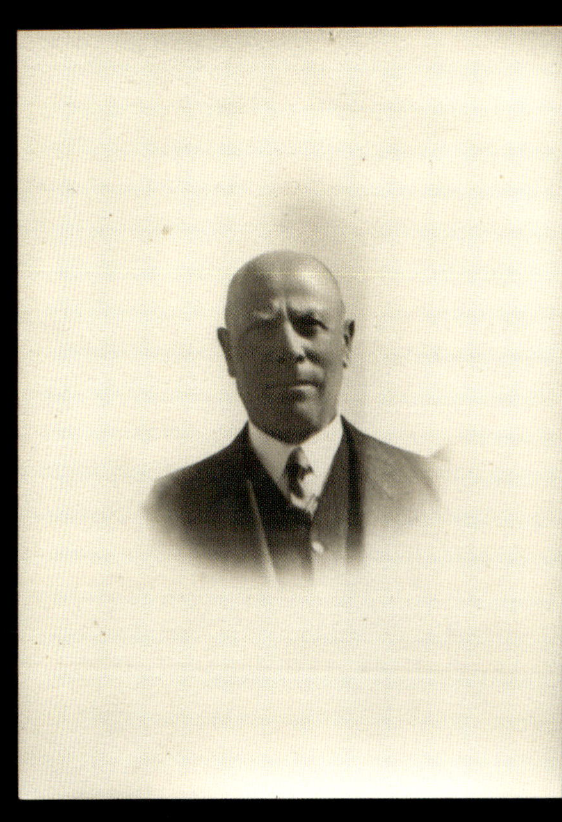

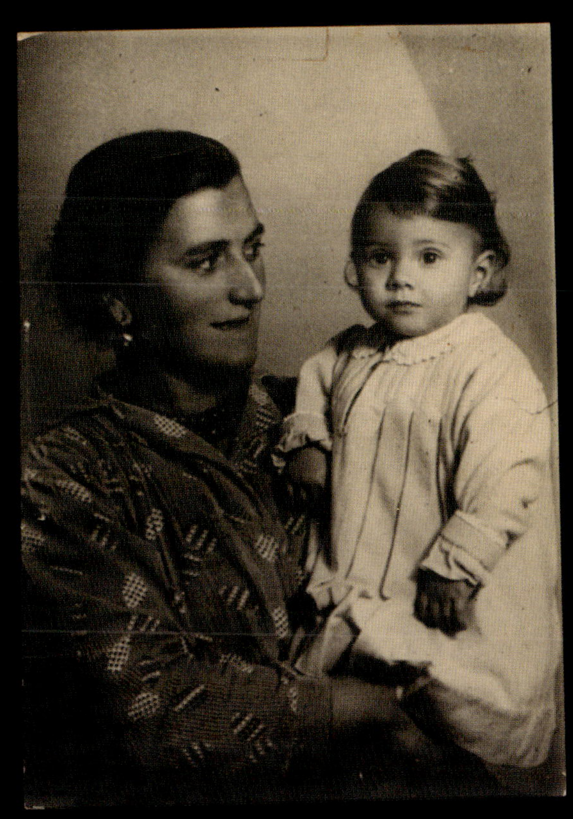

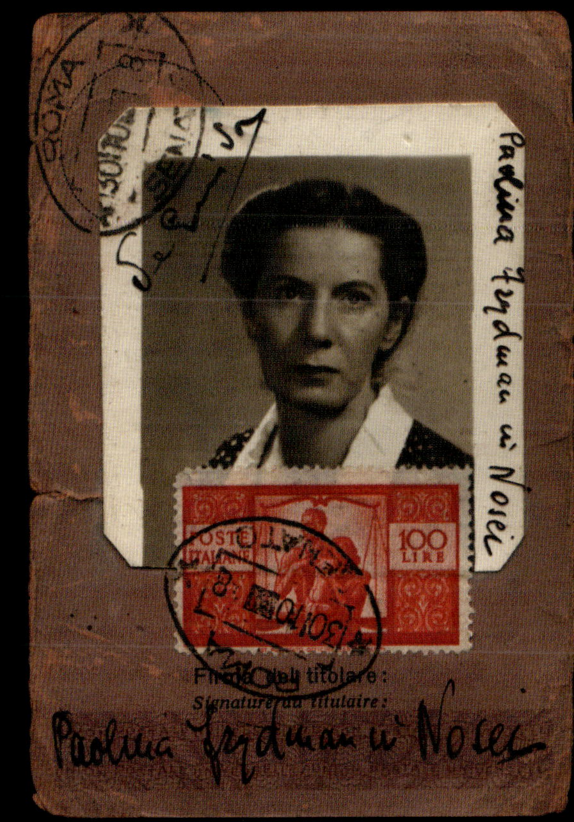
Paolina Frydman w Noee
POSTE ITALIANE 100 LIRE
Firma del titolare:
Signature du titulaire:
Paolina Frydman w Noee

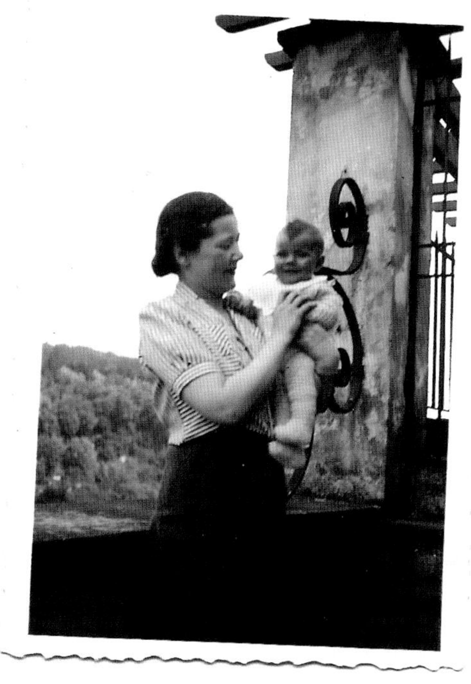

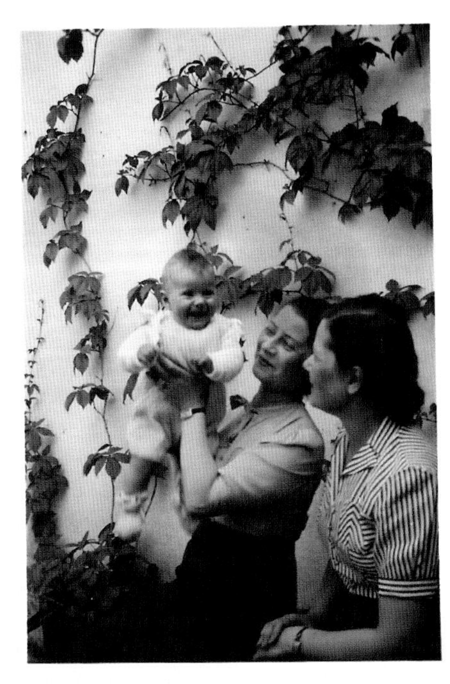

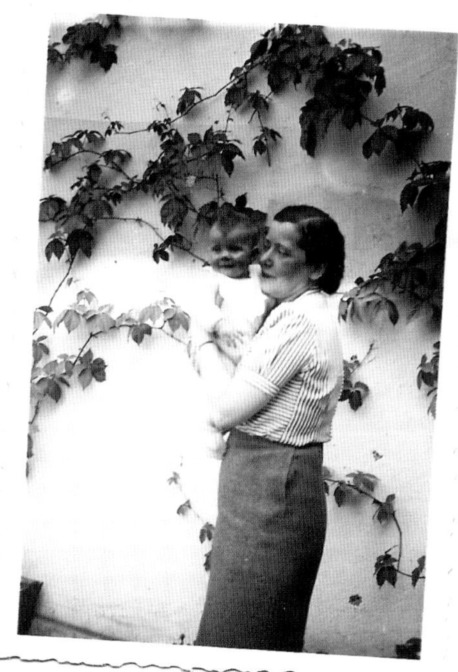

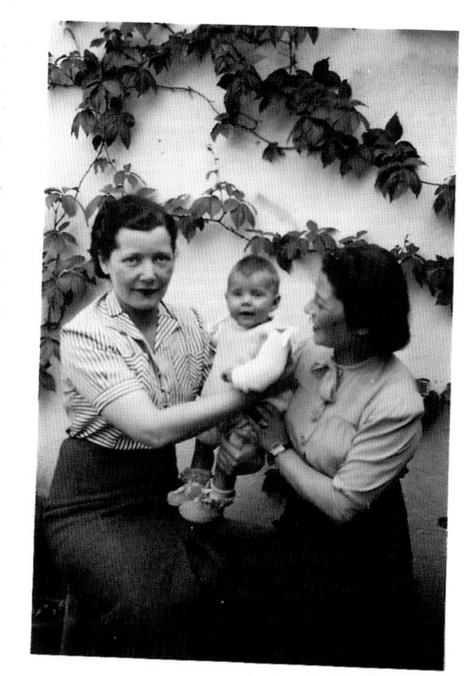

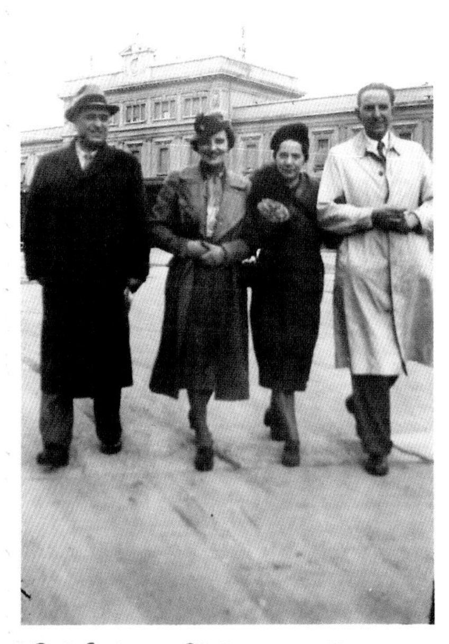

have ice cream in Piazza Colonna.

RL: An incredible story. And what happened then?

AN: Giovanna and Romano were taken in at the Valentini residence hall and they attended the university, where my father had enrolled them, and got married. The 1950s arrived and despite my mother's efforts to persuade them to stay in Italy, they decided to return to Poland. Romano continued to work in cinema there. I remember receiving some magazines that talked about his films. There were also photographs of the two of them at the previews; Giovanna was always elegant. After a few years, however, they decided to move again, but they didn't return to Italy: they would have wanted to go to America for its cinema, but Romano was a communist sympathizer and there was Senator McCarthy there... so in the end they chose Australia. That was their official motivation, at least. In Australia, though, Romano found himself forced to leave the world of cinema and made a living working as a window dresser for Sydney department stores. They had two children: Christopher and Katie, two distinctly Catholic names, of course. Over time, Katie moved to England to study, while Christopher took to traveling the world and eventually arrived in Rome. I was already in America and he went to stay at my father's house in Via Flaminia, making him very happy: for my father, Christopher was like a son.

I remember that one day, many years later, during lunch while she happened to be in New York, Giovanna told me that, on his deathbed, Romano had confessed to her that the real reason they had chosen to move to Australia was not because his films would not have made their way in Hollywood, but for fear of a repetition of what had happened with the arrival of the Germans. He had told her: "Christopher and Katherine are Catholic names, but your mother's surname is Frydman; therefore

Annina's parents and uncles: Paolina Frydman and Angiolo Nosei (right) with Professor Gennarino Perrotta and his wife Adele Nosei (left).
LEFT Paolina Frydman's sisters, who had come to Rome from Poland to meet the newborn Annina - May 1939, Rome.

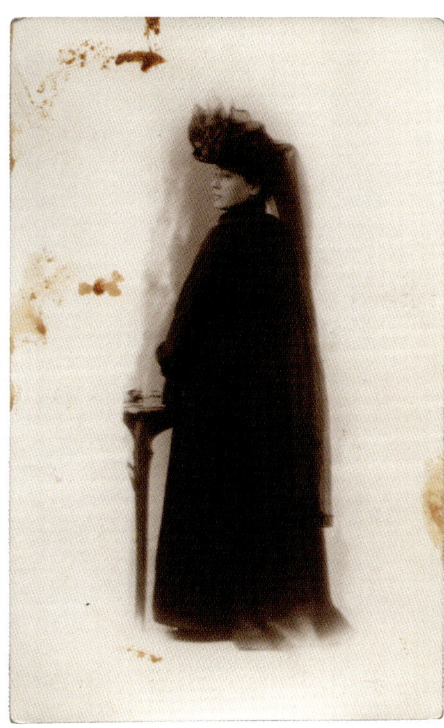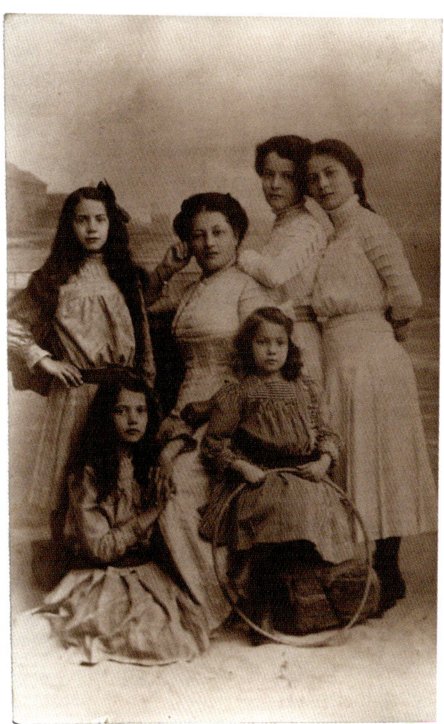

we're considered Jews."

RL: Let's get back to you...

AN: While my mother was traveling, my father and I were in Rome, he went to the University and to the Treccani Encyclopedia. There was a Sardinian maid with us, Gemma. She was the wife of Bruno Atzei, who took care of the tennis courts in Via Flaminia. Bruno's sister Adriana later became my father's assistant and also my daughter's nanny. A great friend of mine.

RL: Tell me something about your father. What's the history of the Nosei family?

AN: You have to understand that my grandfather, Giuseppe Nosei, was also a professor of Latin and Greek. At his home in Florence, those students and scholars who were particularly close to him would often gather for dinner. And then there were his sons and daughters. He had a very large family. One of the best students who attended those get-togethers was Gennarino Perrotta – whom I mentioned earlier with regard to the lunches at the Menghi brothers' trattoria – who married one of my grandfather's daughters, Aunt Adele. And then there was Giorgio Pasquali, who married my father's older sister, Aunt Maria. Pasquali and Perrotta later became two world-renowned scholars of classical philology. Uncle Gennarino Perrotta taught at the University of Rome, while uncle Giorgio Pasquali taught at the University of Florence.

RL: You once told me that your apartment on Corso Vittorio, in which we find ourselves at this moment, is linked to the Pasquali family.

AN: Precisely so. There's also a plaque on the façade, placed there by the

Left: Anna Frydman, Annina's grandmother; Anna Frydman with her daughters.

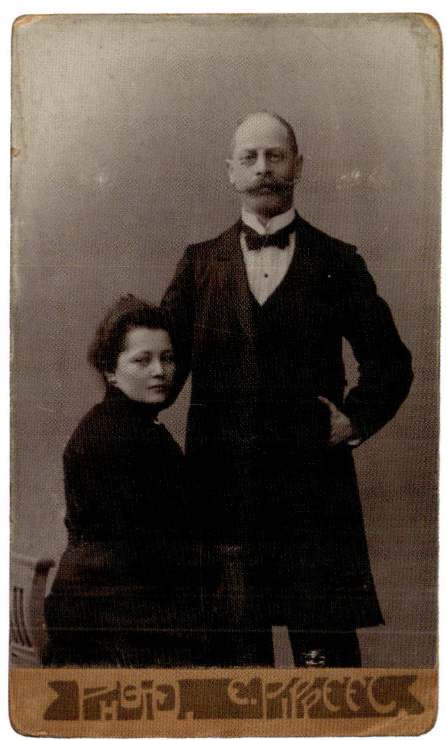
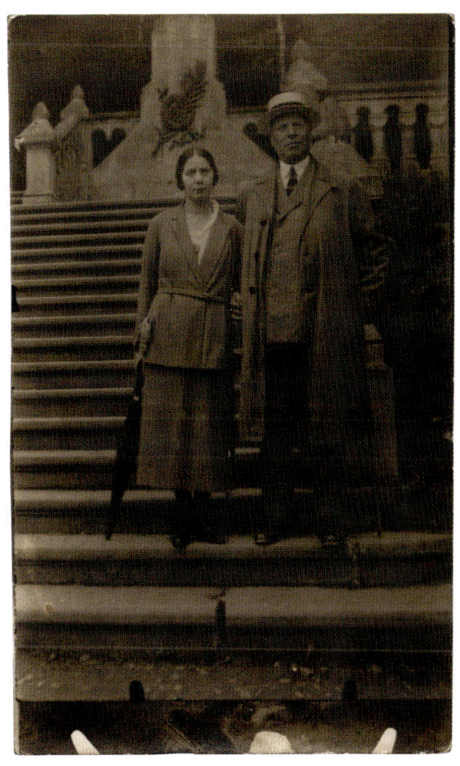

Municipality of Rome about 10 years ago, which serves as a reminder that the great philologist Giorgio Pasquali once lived in this building. I inherited this apartment from my Aunt Maria. It was Uncle Giorgio's family that had had the building constructed. His mother, Marianna Lasagni, was the last descendant of an illustrious family and the niece of Cardinal Lasagni, who was responsible for the construction of the building. Nor is it any coincidence that we're right on St. Peter's doorstep, just this side of the bridge that leads to the Vatican. Uncle Giorgio had studied in Germany, in Göttingen; he had been the pupil of an esteemed philologist, Wilamowitz Möllendorff. World War II broke out in the middle of his time there. Being a scholar of German philology, like other philologists, including my father, he was considered a sympathizer of the fascist regime, but that was not true. There's an essay dedicated to my father and written by a student of the Accademia della Crusca, Yorick Gomez Gane, in which a body of evidence is presented, including my father's correspondence with his brothers-in-law Giorgio Pasquali and Gennarino Perrotta and with other scholars of philology, from which their aversion to Nazi ideology is evident. The war years were very difficult for Uncle Giorgio – he was even taken to a mental health institute in Fiesole, near Florence. The traumas of the war, and in particular the Nazis' atrocious crimes, had caused him to have a nervous breakdown. At that time, I spent my holidays with my family in Zuel, a mountain resort near Cortina, in both summer and winter. That's where I spent most of my time between 2 and 4 years old. For this reason, as a child, I spoke better in Ladin – the ancient Latin-derived language of the Ampezzo valley – than in Italian. Even when the war had ended, Giorgio's nerves continued to cause him problems. I remember his crises well. Once, upon arriving at his apartment in Florence, he lost control to the point of punching himself in the head. It was my father who calmed him down, hugging him and shaking him by the arms. His crises often overtook him in the mountains as well, until something happened

Left: Annina's grandparents Joseph and Anna Frydman; Paolina Frydman with her father Joseph Frydman in Venice, 1929.

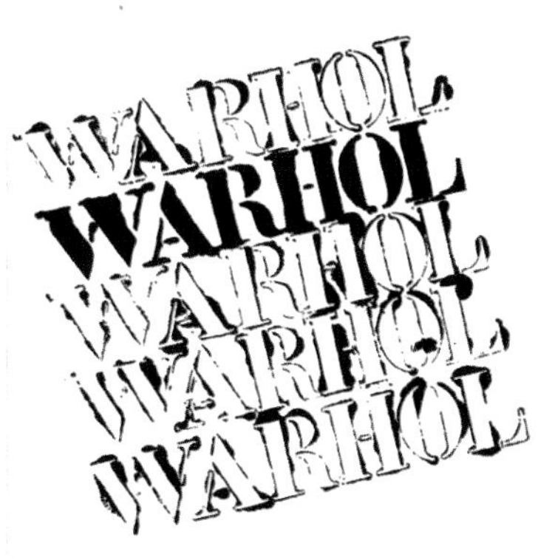

one summer: Uncle Giorgio and I had been left home alone, so we had decided to take a walk. At that time he never wanted to go out anymore, but together with me he did. We walked for a long time and went up to the Zuel ski jump. We spent the whole afternoon up there making faces at the world. He was very good: he would put his hands in his mouth, he would wring his nose; his grimaces were aimed at all those accountable for that damned war, especially the Germans. On our way home, we ran into my aunt, who, not having found us at home, had gotten worried and had come looking for us. But when she saw that Uncle Giorgio was smiling and that I was fine, she was so happy that she hugged me and said: "Thank you very much, Annina: you managed to get him out of the house." That was the day that my uncle overcame his fears. Certain problems can be solved by making faces at the whole world.

RL: At this point I understand why, in improvising in front of Ileana and Michael Sonnabend during Ken Dewey's performance, when you summarized the elements that defined you in a few phrases, you mentioned your father's name and his profession as a Latinist and Greek scholar. For you it was a very precise reference to a cultural identity that you felt in a profound way, a belonging to a cultural sphere of a high order. And finally, in that improvisation, naturally you also inserted your recent studies on Duchamp, which instead represented your independent personal story, the one that you had begun with that very thesis. At this point, then, we can pick right up from that July of 1963 when, during the showing of *The Gift* at the Théâtre Récamier in Paris, you met Ileana Sonnabend. It seems fair to say that certain female encounters have been a significant recurring feature of your formative experiences (before you were talking about Carla Panicali...). So, Ileana asked you to work in her gallery.

AN: Precisely. In her acclaimed gallery on Quai des Grands Augustins,

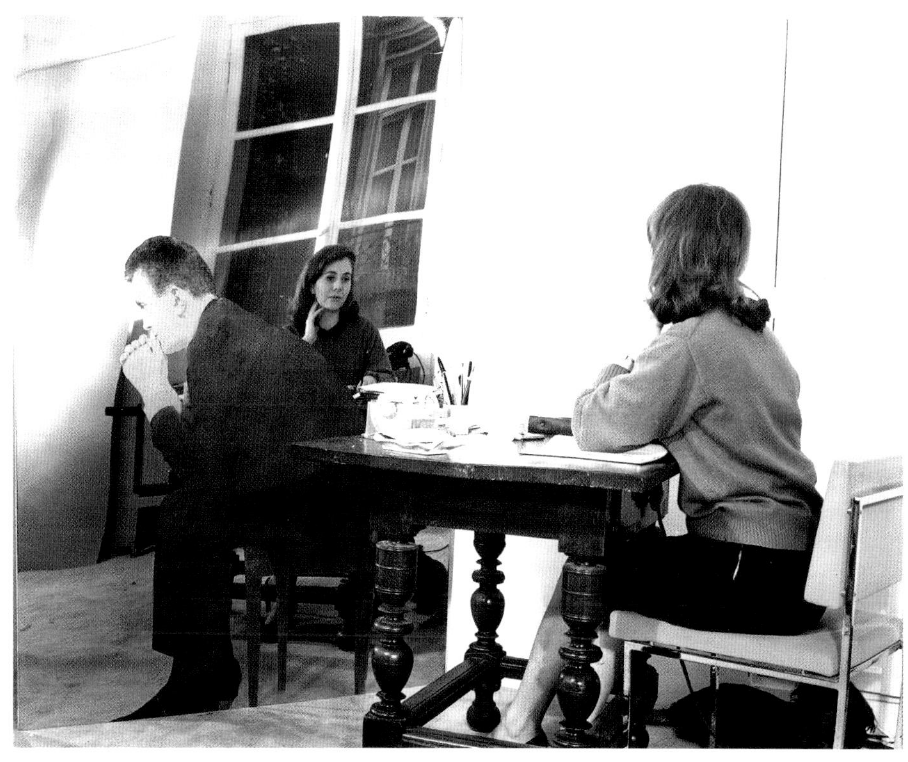

Ileana held extraordinary exhibitions, each more interesting than the one before it. When I arrived, I found a Chamberlain exhibition in her gallery. Then she curated a wonderful one by Rauschenberg, with drawings of the Inferno from the Divine Comedy. I remember that Michael Sonnabend kept reciting Dante's verses in Italian. Once we had to get some of Andy Warhol's works into the gallery. One of them, the purple electric chair, was very large and it wouldn't fit in the stairwell, so it had to be passed through the second floor window. I have an image imprinted in my memory of the painting hanging in the void, whitened by the snow that was beginning to fall quite heavily. Then the work was mounted on a kind of panel behind which the exhibition unfolded, and everything was filmed by Christo. It was Warhol's first exhibition in Europe; it was curated by a friend of Ileana's, the French poet Alain Jouffroy, with texts by Jean-Jacques Lebel and John Ashbery. All the works were inspired by brutality and death. I also remember Pistoletto's first exhibition. He made one of his mirror works from a photograph of me sitting at my desk in the gallery.

RL: Who else did you meet during that period?

AN: Well, for example, on that occasion I met Gian Enzo Sperone, who had come to Paris for the Pistoletto exhibition. Also, I rented the small apartment that Christo had vacated in order to move to New York. Being in that place was like being inside one of his works, it was like one of his Packages. The fabric on the sofa and the bed, the curtain that separated the kitchen from the living room, everything was made from the same canvas that he used for his works.

RL: So basically, you could meet a lot of art people in Paris?

AN: I often saw Piero Manzoni, whom I had already known previously.

Annina sitting at her desk in the Galerie Ileana Sonnabend, reflected in Michelangelo Pistoletto's 1963 mirror work *Uomo seduto* (Paris, 28 January 1964).

"In her acclaimed gallery... Ileana held extraordinary exhibitions, each more interesting than the one before it."

Sometimes we'd go out in the evening. Occasionally he would come to pick me up, or sometimes he would wait for me at the restaurant, where he'd begin to eat in the meantime. Then we'd go to dinner, and at that point he'd eat again, and after the cinema he'd often eat. He was very nice. He would tell me about the new humanism, about his white paintings. In Rome a few years earlier, in a restaurant near San Giacomo where I was having lunch with Franco Angeli, Manzoni had come over to us and asked us to be his works of art. I held out my hand and he signed it; Franco, on the other hand, was smarter than me and had him sign his sneakers, certainly easier to sell...

RL: You were in very good company: I've heard from Aldo Tagliaferri that Emilio Villa was also a living sculpture signed by Piero Manzoni. But let's go back to Paris. How was Ileana Sonnabend at work?

AN: Very interesting. She held extraordinary exhibitions, one more important than the next.

RL: How long did you work for her?

AN: I went to Paris knowing that I'd be working for Ileana over the duration of the exhibition season, from September '63 to June '64. I had recently graduated from college and had won a Fulbright Scholarship at the University of Michigan, which would begin in the fall of '64. Ileana asked me to stay and work with her, but it wasn't possible for me because of the scholarship. I remember that I went to Venice on her behalf in June. Rauschenberg's works were to arrive there from France and America, to then be transported by boat from the Academy to the Giardini. It was the year in which he won the Venice Biennale's Golden Lion. At the Teatro La Fenice, a Merce Cunningham show was also scheduled

Piero Manzoni's certificate of authenticity (having signed Annina on 24 April 1961).

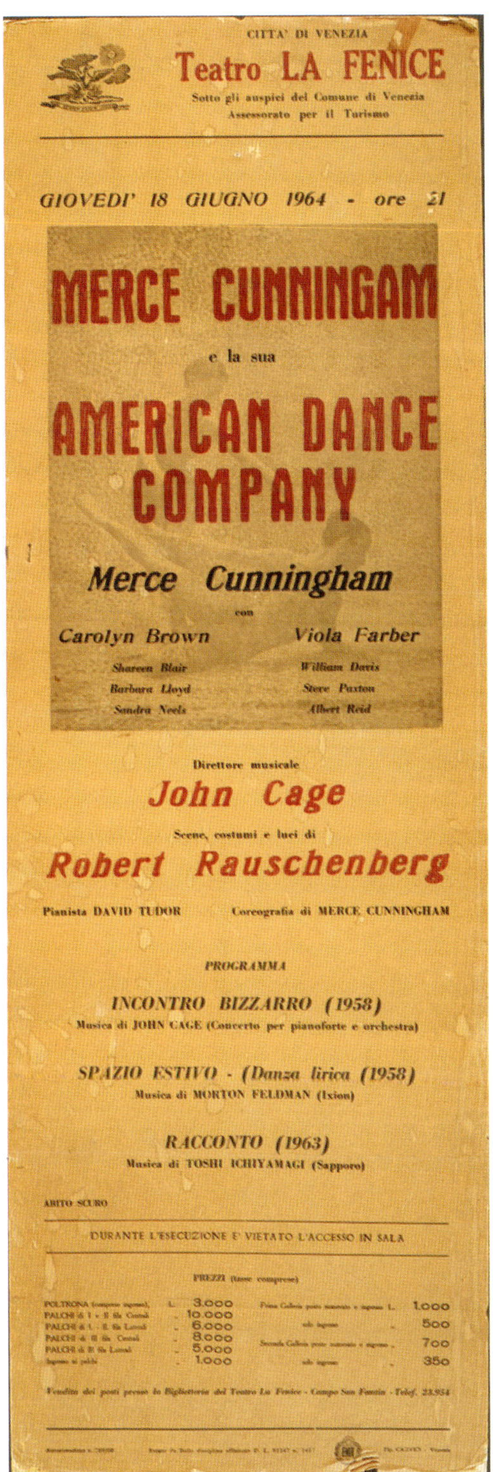

Poster for the performance by Merce Cunningham and his American Dance Company at the Teatro La Fenice, Venice (18 June 1964).

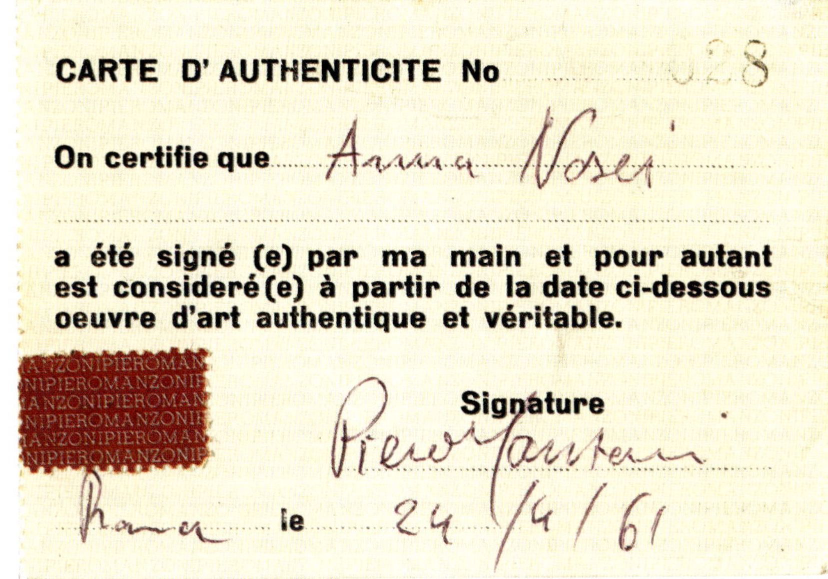

to be held, with his sets and with music by John Cage. I earned my first dollars on that occasion, courtesy of Leo Castelli. My job was to translate Rauschenberg's directions from English: for moving the sets, for the lighting sequences, and for everything else. We were all there for the show's premiere, and I stood close to him in order to translate his instructions for the technicians; I had a sheet in my hand with numbers and letters, which were his notes for moving the lights and the sets. I read the sequence as written, but instead of turning on the light on the right, the way Rauschenberg wanted, the one on the left came on. And so on, for all of the instructions. It was all wrong. We looked at each other in surprise and immediately realized that everything had been written backwards.

RL: How had that happened?

AN: Simply that Rauschenberg had written in an inverse way.

RL: And how was it resolved?

AN: By reversing the indications. The interesting, and also quite funny, thing is that, for John Cage, who had made chance one of the cornerstones of his practice, the chaos that emerged worked perfectly.

RL: So, after that summer, you left for the USA.

AN: Cage had recommended that, on my way to the University of Michigan in September, I try to meet the legendary ONCE Group, an ensemble of directors, musicians, and performers. So I went to meet them when I arrived in Ann Arbor and they immediately invited me to be part of the group. I became friends with filmmaker George Manupelli and composer Robert Ashley in particular. I put on some Happenings of my own devising

ONCE-OFF

THE ONCE GROUP IN A BENEFIT PERFORMANCE AT ANN ARBOR HIGH SCHOOL AUDITORIUM
601 WEST STADIUM BOULEVARD   ANN ARBOR

APRIL 9, 1966   8:30 PM

$2.00 ADMISSION   TICKETS ON SALE AT MARSHALL'S BOOK SHOP, DISCOUNT RECORDS AND AT THE DOOR.   FOR INFORMATION WRITE ONCE—OFF BOX 179 ANN ARBOR, MICHIGAN

and then participated in Kittyhawk, which was held at the Judson Church in New York. I stayed in Ann Arbor for less than a year, from September '64 to the summer of '65. I was hired by UCLA, the University of Los Angeles, in the same year, and during that time I met John Weber, who was director of the Dwan Gallery.

RL: Whom you would then marry... But before that?

AN: Before anything else, I met Carolee Schneemann, who, together with her husband, welcomed me to New York when I arrived on the ship that I had taken in Naples, the *Independence*. I slipped coming down the catwalk; in short, I arrived in the United States on my backside. Carolee was a great artist. We had always been friends. I had met her in Paris, in Ileana's gallery, and we had immediately bonded. I had also taken part in a famous Happening of hers, *Meat Joy*, which was held in Paris and London, and later in New York, at the Judson Church.

RL: Right, that Happening which took place in 1964 as part of the Workshop de la Libre Expression. Schneemann was a standout figure for her work concerning subjectivity, the female body, social questions. So what did you do when you arrived in New York?

AN: For those first few days, before I went to Michigan, Carolee Schneemann hosted me in her loft on 28th Street in New York. I remember that, the morning after my arrival, I went out for a coffee and on my way back a guy followed me all the way into the building. So I grabbed a curling iron and pointed it at him, saying in a firm voice, "This is an Italian gun," and he ran away.

RL: Circling back to John Weber, how did you meet him?

ONCE Group, invitation card to the performance *Once-off* at Ann Arbor High School Auditorium (9 April 1966).

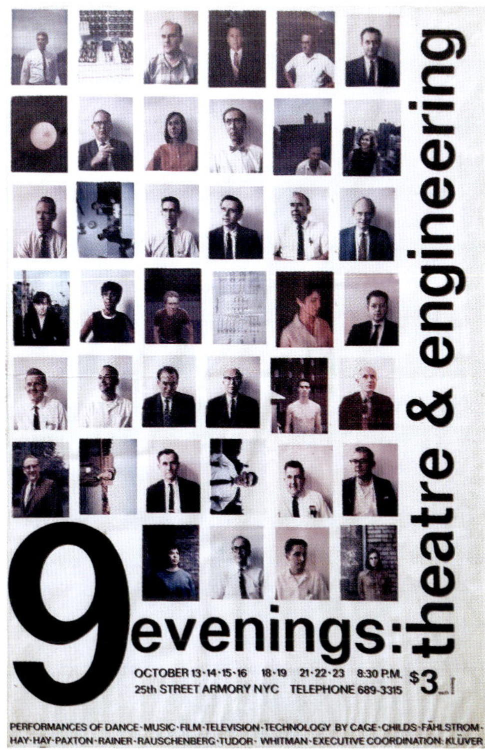

AN: Rauschenberg introduced us. I had gone to visit him in the gallery, where a Mark di Suvero exhibition was in progress. Actually, the first time I went to the gallery, maybe it was an Ad Reinhardt exhibition on show. The paintings were all black and I thought that it was a tribute to Kennedy's death.
I also saw some wonderful Kienholz works and then the exhibitions of Minimal Art and Carl Andre. I became friends with John and met the artists he worked with. We dated for a year and we were married in October of '66. We had gone to Italy during the summer.

RL: Tell me something about the wedding.

AN: We got married in New York. Christo and Jeanne-Claude organized a big party for us at their home. We also attended an important event during those few days, 9 Evenings: Theatre & Engineering, which Rauschenberg and Billy Klüver had organized along with other artists and engineers at Park Avenue Armory on 69th Street. Dancers like Steve Paxton, the Judson Dance Theater, Robert Whitman, Yvonne Rainer and David Tudor participated. You can imagine how that was for me, the same person who'd taken part in the ONCE Group performances in Ann Arbor and who'd taken part in Ken Dewey's *The Gift* in Paris before that; it was a great experience.

RL: While John was organizing important exhibitions at the Dwan Gallery, what were you doing in Los Angeles?

AN: I'd finished my work at the University of Michigan and I'd received an offer to teach at UCLA. I was assistant to a very special professor, Kurt von Meier, who also dealt with music as well as theory and history of art. I held a seminar on Duchamp as part of his course. I was still fresh from

Poster for the performance program
9 Evenings: Theatre & Engineering,
New York, October 1966.

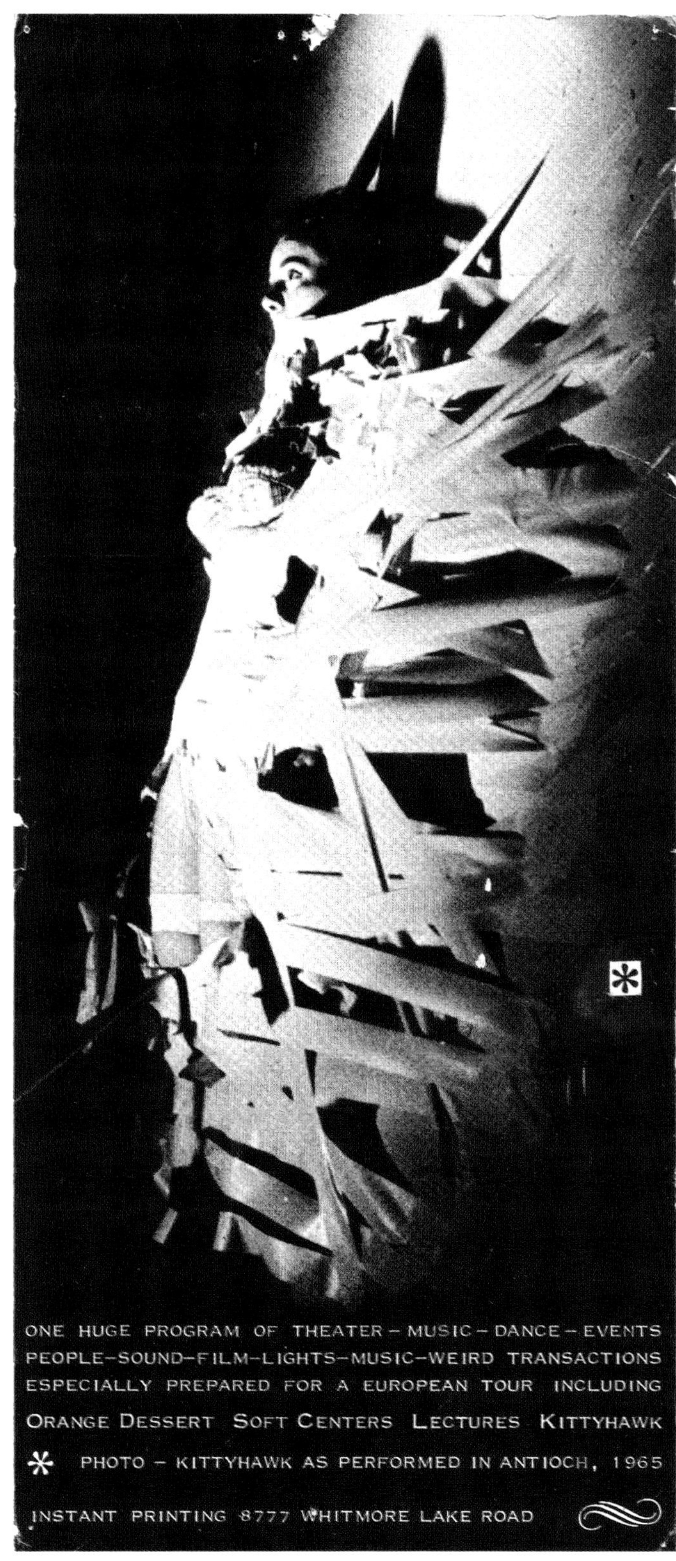

POSTER FOR THE ONCE GROUP'S EUROPEAN TOUR
WITH AN IMAGE FROM *KITTYHAWK*, 1965

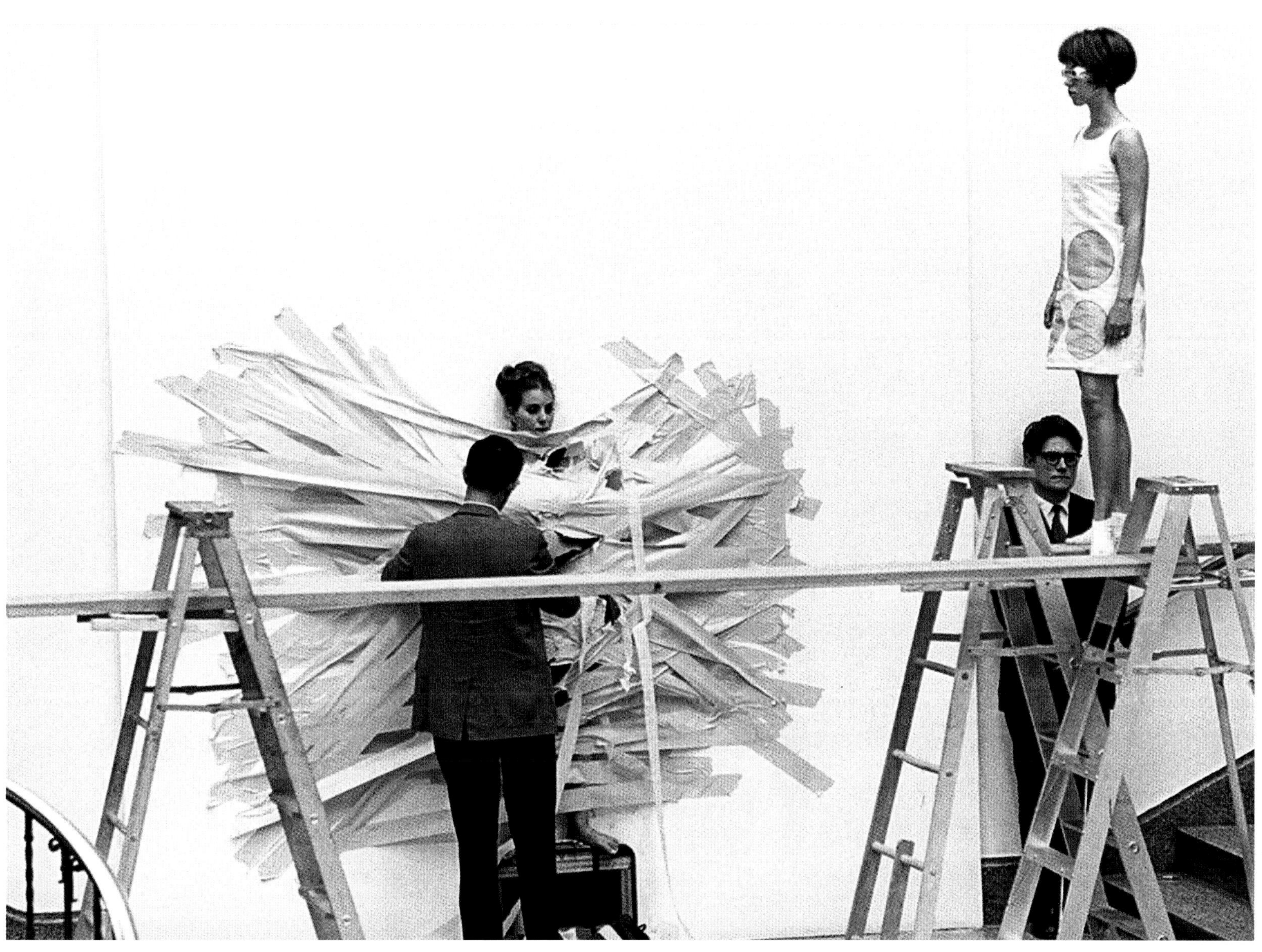

AN IMAGE FROM THE ONCE GROUP'S *KITTYHAWK*, 1965.
FROM LEFT: THE FILMMAKER GEORGE MANUPELLI, ANNINA, THE
MUSICIAN GORDON MUMMA AND ANOTHER PERFORMER

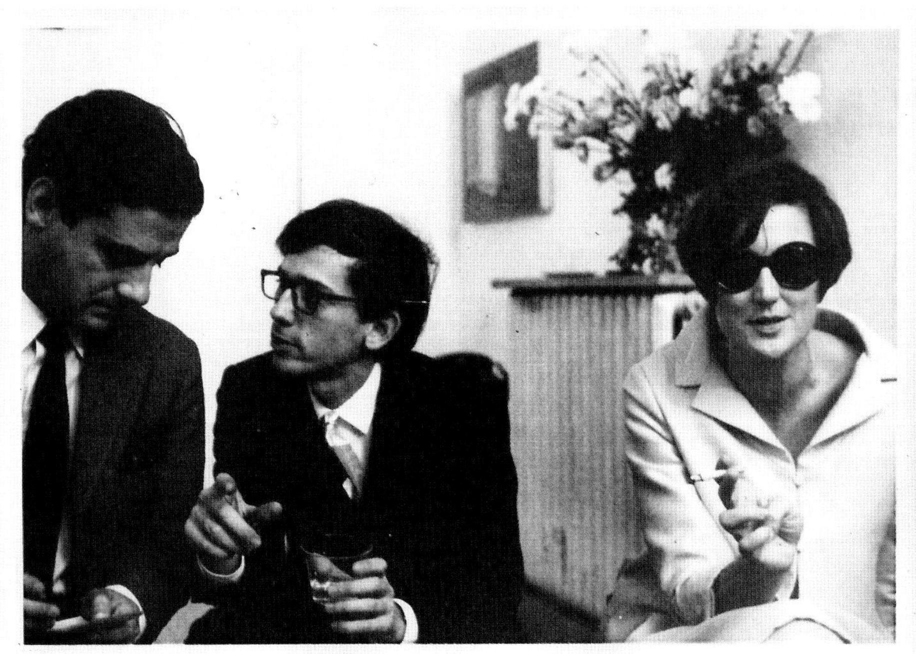

my thesis studies, I knew how important a figure he was in America and, moreover, interest in him had been greatly revived at that time thanks to a big retrospective of his work that had been organized in the fall of '63 at the Pasadena Museum. My offerings were therefore very topical. The seminar went well and at the end of it they awarded me a PhD from UCLA.

RL: Did you follow John's work?

AN: Of course. Through him I knew the young artists who in those same years were having their first exhibitions at the Dwan Gallery: Dan Flavin, Sol LeWitt, Carl Andre, Kenneth Snelson. I remember Robert Smithson's early works. I witnessed the birth of Minimal Art firsthand. Helping them while they set up Carl Andre's solo show was an unforgettable experience, for example. Thanks to Virginia Dwan, we were given the opportunity to rent a private plane to go to Nevada, near Las Vegas, to see Double Negative, created by Michael Heizer; and another time we went with Walter De Maria instead.

RL: You showed me that survey on American art in the magazine *Metro*. Was it during that period that it was published?

AN: That investigation in *Metro* came out in the late 1960s. I'd asked some American artists some questions and I'd even written an accompanying piece. That text is very interesting for me now. When I wrote it, I said that American artists had no relationship with politics or with contemporary civilization. Accustomed to Argan, to artists' political ideas, I hadn't found the same depth of content amongst Americans. Having arrived in the USA, before John introduced me to all these great figures, Minimalists, conceptualists, etc. Having had the example of Giulio Carlo Argan, of my father, of Rome, I'd seen that these artists had no idea about politics. It was

John and Annina's wedding party (Christo at center, Virginia Dwan at right), New York, 1966.

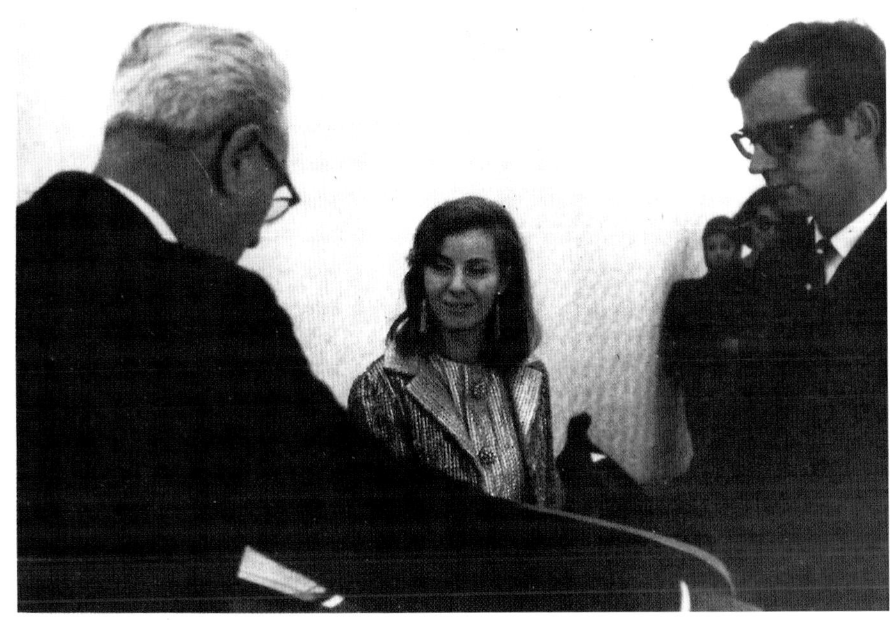

John Weber and Annina Nosei's
wedding by civil ceremony, 1966.

a demanding text and eventually I gave up. It's no coincidence, however, that the first major group show that I organized in my gallery, which I opened in New York several years later, in 1981, was entitled Public Address.

RL: Eventually you and John moved from Los Angeles to New York.

AN: Yes, because John moved the Dwan Gallery there. Or rather, Virginia had decided to close the gallery in Los Angeles and to open an additional location of the gallery in New York, on 57th Street. We moved into an apartment at 190 Riverside Drive, near 91st Street, where our daughter Paolina was born the following year.

RL: When exactly did he open his gallery, the John Weber Gallery?

AN: In 1971, when Virginia Dwan decided to retire. Some time before, she'd taken up storage spaces in a building at 420 West Broadway. Leo Castelli, Ileana Sonnabend, André Emmerich, John and others opened their galleries there in the same period. Mary Boone arrived later on. At that time John was curating the Art & Language exhibition, Robert Ryman, etc. While Leo Castelli had decided to focus on Pop Art, John had settled on Minimalism, which Castelli subsequently began to follow as well. I once went to Robert Morris' studio with the two of them. John already knew him because he'd curated his exhibition in Los Angeles. The studio was flooded with new works made from felts; Castelli thought they were by his wife, Yvonne Rainer.

RL: Yvonne Rainer, the choreographer?

AN: Yes. He thought they were props to be used for the theatre, Robert Morris' previous work had been more geometric, painted gray, and then

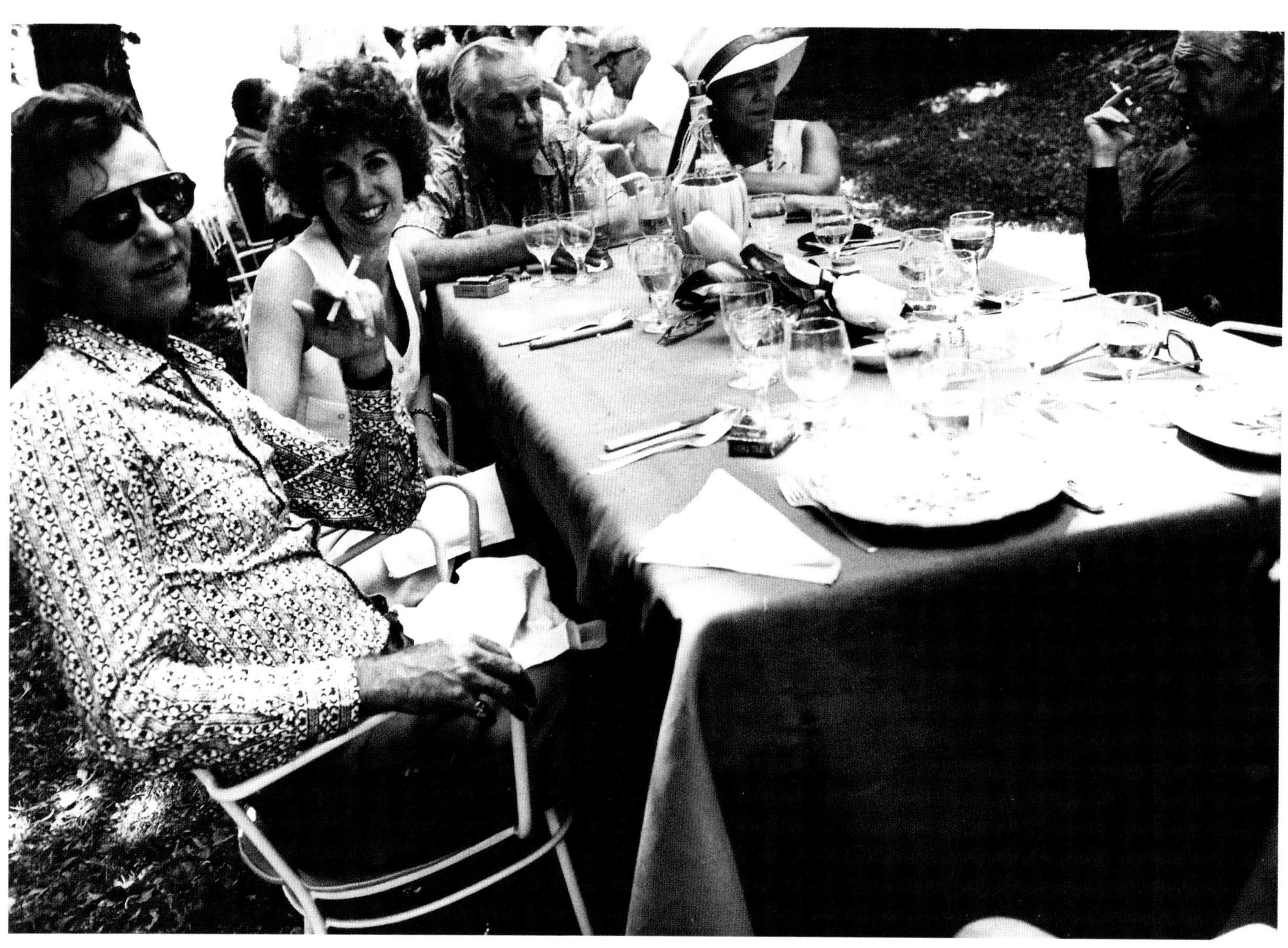

JOHN WEBER AND ANNINA
AT THE VENICE BIENNALE, 1966

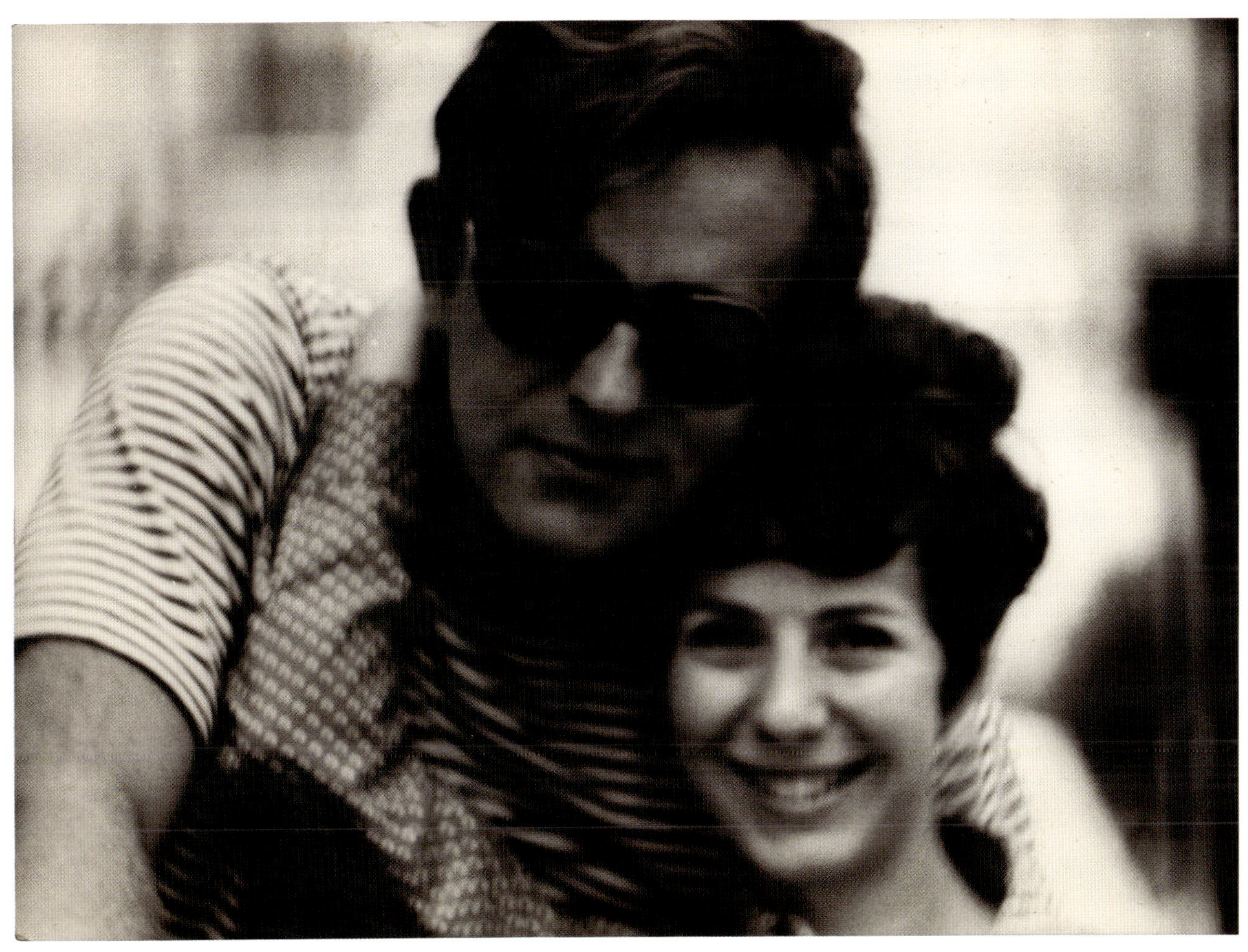

PORTRAIT OF
JOHN WEBER AND ANNINA

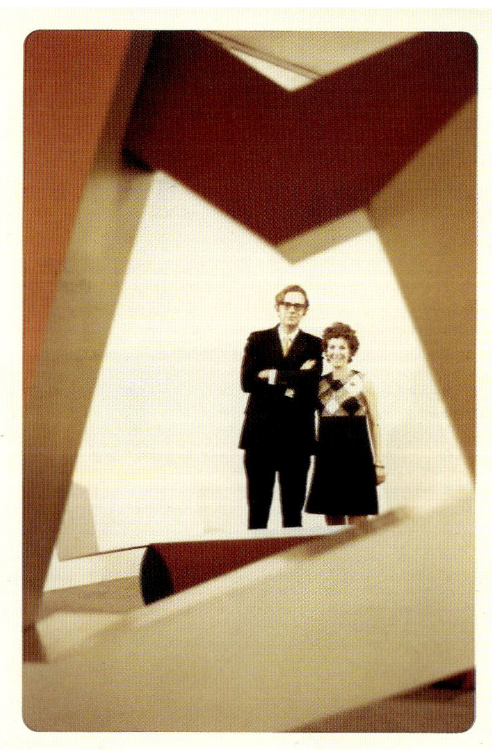
Portrait of John and Annina in the 1960s.

he'd made plaster objects, like boxes; so Castelli hadn't connected them to what was in the studio.

RL: When you left Los Angeles, you also left UCLA. And what did you do in New York?

AN: I kept teaching. First at St. John's University, then at Kingsborough Community College of the City University of New York, in Coney Island, where I also held the position of director of the college art gallery.

RL: Did you work with John Weber?

AN: Let's say that I introduced him to some Italian artists, whom I'd met in Turin through Gian Enzo Sperone during the time that I worked for Ileana Sonnabend: Mario Merz, Alighiero Boetti, and Michelangelo Pistoletto. But John would've gotten to know them in any case... Then we decided to get divorced; regardless, some time later he gave me the opportunity to stage a substantial exhibition in the gallery at Kingsborough Community College, lending me all the works of the artists he'd exhibited in De Europa, which was one of the first exhibitions of the Arte Povera artists in the United States. The exhibition wasn't well received by the university executives and my colleagues, who'd have preferred for me to deal with American artists and who, precisely because of my relationship with John Weber, had hoped I'd secure his gallery's artists for them. I was about to receive tenure at a certain point, in 1975, but they didn't renew my contract or that of my other female colleagues. They said that the university's budget had shrunk, that they had to cut jobs, so of course it was us women whose contracts didn't get renewed. If I'd gotten tenure, my salary would obviously have increased significantly (although I still earned about a third more than what my father was earning at the University of Rome during

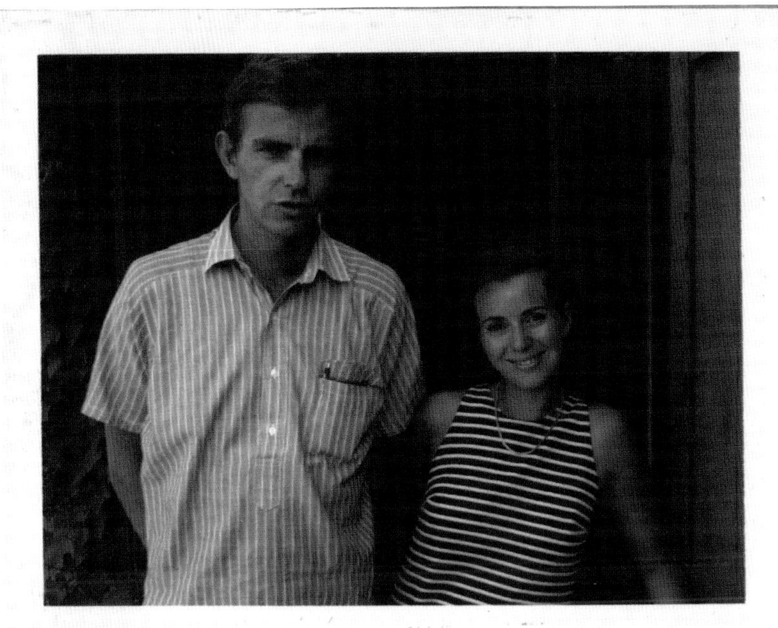

the same period). I sued the university and the union, representing myself, but I wasn't cut out for it and so I lost my case. But that same day, the union lawyer told me that she'd represent me along with the other faculty members who, like me, had been wrongfully terminated, and we won the class action a while after that. A few years had passed in the meantime and I'd gone on to teach at the New York School of Visual Arts. But I was happy to receive the compensation check.

RL: When did you divorce John Weber?

AN: In 1972/1973. I'll tell you something funny, since we talked about Manzoni earlier. While we were getting divorced, John had left the apartment where we were living together and he'd taken a broom and the cat with him. He said he'd need the broom in the other house. Despite our marriage ending, we still remained good friends. We'd often speak on the phone and we had long conversations about how to split our works of art. I remember one discussion in particular: "Ok, that's yours, this one's mine, that one we bought together, no, we bought two of those. So one is mine, one is yours…" At a certain point I said to him: "You're taking everything." "No, Annina, you know that's not true, I'm a gentleman and we're friends." I had just enough time to go into the other room and the phone rang again: it was John. "Did you forget something?" "Yes, I'd like to have the Lichtenstein drawing of the Temple of Apollo." "And what are you going to give me in exchange?" "I'll give you back the Piero Manzoni." "But you don't have any works by Manzoni." "I'll give you back Annina. You're the work by Manzoni."
He was referring to the signature on my hand that Piero Manzoni had given me all those years before, of which I had the certificate; I then donated it to the MoMA, where they were very pleased because they had other works by Manzoni, but not a living sculpture.

John and Annina on the terrace of the house in Via Flaminia, Rome, July 1966.

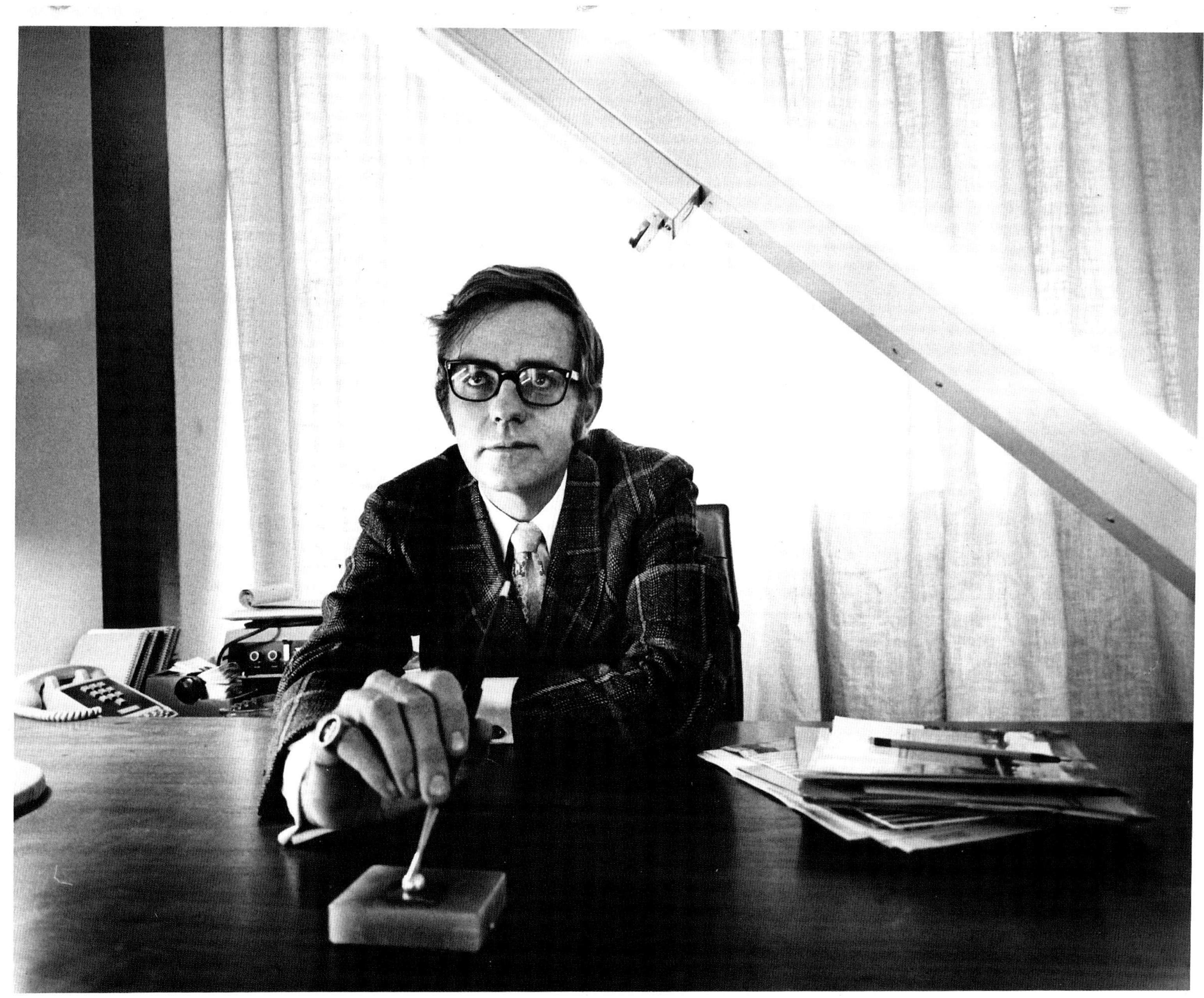

JOHN WEBER AT
DWAN GALLERY, 1966

C SPACE 81 Leonard Street, New York NY 10013
(212)925-3877 964-2093

MEMORY

organized by
ANNINA NOSEI WEBER

Films by CAROLEE SCHNEEMANN

FUSES Color, Silent 16mm (1965-68) 18 minutes
PLUMB LINE Color, Sound 16mm (1969-71) 18 minutes
Selected reels from
KITCH'S LAST MEAL Color, Sound, Super 8 double-screen
(1973-77) 20 minutes each

Screening :
Saturday April 16th 1977 6 PM

The invitation card reads:

C SPACE 81 Leonard Street New York NY 10013
(212) 925-3877 964-2093

MEMORY

organized by
Annina Nosei Weber

Opening: April 2, 4:00-7:00
Exhibition: April 2-April 20

Open 3:00-6:00

Paolo Colombo
Pietro Cicognani
William Childress
Claudia De Monte
Eleanor Dube
Patrick Ireland
Leandro Katz
Carolee Schneemann

RL: The seventies were particularly difficult for everyone. Before opening your gallery in 1980 and thus charting a new course for yourself, what did you do?

AN: Before opening the gallery, I organized group exhibitions in a space called C Space. That's where I organized Memory, for which I also wrote a text. It was a reflection on the function of memory, starting from the centrality that Giulio Camillo gave it in his Theatre of Memory, in Venice.

RL: Which artists did you work with on that project?

AN: I invited Carolee Schneemann as well as Paolo Colombo, Pietro Cicognani, William Childress, Claudia DeMonte, Eleanor Dube, Patrick Ireland, and Leandro Katz. I also wrote a rather challenging text. Then I put on another group exhibition, also at C Space, which showed Sandro Chia's first works, which I hung together with Suzanne Santoro and Paolo Colombo.

RL: Did you also organize the festival at C Space that you told me about?

AN: Are you referring to *Discussions*? No, actually, that was in May of '77, so I organized it at New York University. I'd created a program of meetings in which various contributions from artists were presented – some recorded, others live. A number of conceptual artists participated, such as Joseph Beuys, Joseph Kosuth, Victor Burgin, Carolee Schneemann, Robert Ashley, Lucio Pozzi, David Antin, Ian Wilson, Sarah Charlesworth, and Anthony McCall. Giuseppe Chiari came from Italy. The idea was neither that of a conference with contributions based on themes, nor that of a series of actions; rather, it was precisely that of presenting discussion itself as an art form, as a dialogue between artist and public:

Invitation card to the exhibition *Memory*, curated by Annina at C Space, New York, 1977.

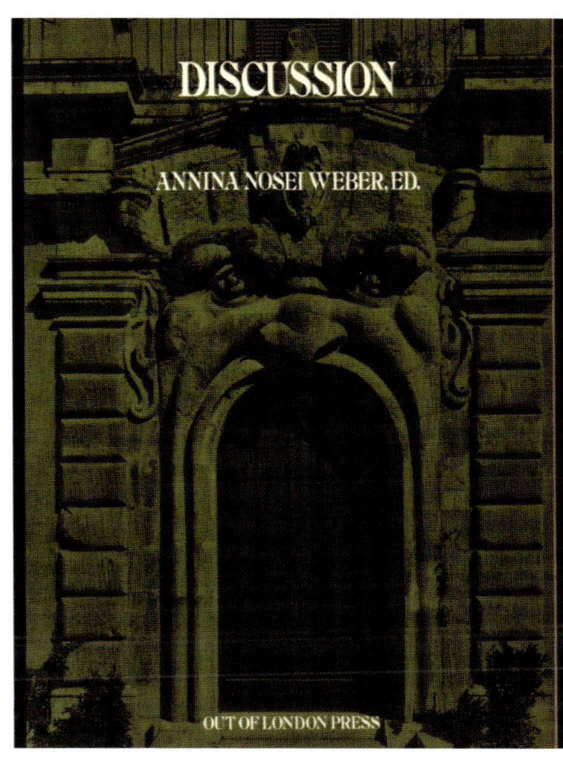

Cover of the book *Discussion*, published by Out of London Press, 1980.

discussion-as-art was what we wrote in the poster.

RL: Do you have any documentation of that project?

AN: Yes. Thanks to Richard Milazzo we published a book with OOLP [Out of London Press], which reconstructed all the discussions. The cover shows an image of the doorway of Palazzo Zuccari in Via Gregoriana, Rome. The book also contains transcriptions of the videotapes.

RL: You made videotapes? Do you still have them?

AN: No, I donated them to the Bard College Library in New York State; it's a good university, which also has a museum.

RL: You'd also put together another interesting exhibition, dedicated to painting.

AN: Yes, *Painting*, which was shown in a space downtown called the Fine Arts Building. I'd invited a number of artists active at the time, including Carolee Schneemann once again, Daniel Buren and others.

RL: What year was it?

AN: It was in January of 1976.

RL: From the activities that you undertook as an independent, it seems to me that your need to analyze the dynamics and mechanisms behind the thought and creation of art comes through clearly.
I haven't asked you yet if you had any contact with Andy Warhol in those years...

DISCUSSIONS

AN EXHIBITION OF TYPES OF DISCUSSION ON VARIOUS TOPICS WILL BE HELD AT NEW YORK UNIVERSITY AT WASHINGTON SQUARE FROM MAY 9 - 20. THE EXHIBITION IS ORGANIZED BY ANNINA NOSEI WEBER AND SPONSORED BY THE DEPARTMENT OF ART AND ART-EDUCATION AT N.Y.U. MAY '77

PROGRAM

Mon
May 9 **JOSEPH BEUYS : "PUBLIC DIALOGUE"** *, videotape
1977   6:00 - 10:30 pm , Loeb Student Center , outside of south lobby .
WILLOUGHBY SHARP , producer , will be present to discuss the tape .

Tues.
May 10 **LUCIO POZZI : a continuous discussion**
6:30 - 10:00 pm , Lassman Hall , 50 W 4th St .

Tues. - Fri.
May 10,
11, 12, 13 **SARAH CHARLESWORTH, JOSEPH KOSUTH & ANTHONY McCALL : videotape**
VICTOR BURGIN : videotape *** produced by Paul Tschinkel and Inner-Tube Cable T.V.
6:00 - 10:30 pm , Loeb Student Center , outside of south lobby .

Fri.
May 13 **DAVID ANTIN** at Lassman Hall , 7:30 pm. 50 W 4th St.

Sat
May 14 **CAROLEE SCHNEEMANN : "ABC - WE PRINT ANYTHING - IN THE CARDS"**, a performance - text
Loeb Student Center , Room 310 at 7:00 pm .

Tues.
May 17 **GIUSEPPE CHIARI** ** at Lassman Hall , 7:30 pm . 50 W 4th St.

Wed. & Thurs.
May 18, **IAN WILSON** at Loeb Student Center
19 Room 408 on Wed.   Room 513 on Thurs.   2:00 - 6:00 pm

Fri.
May 20 **ROBERT ASHLEY** at Lassman Hall , 8:00 pm. 50 W 4th St.

* Joseph Beuys' PUBLIC DIALOGUE is a 2 hour, unedited video document of Beuys' first American work - a social sculpture - executed at The New School , N.Y.C. in 1974 . This tape was produced by Willoughby Sharp and shot by Andy Mann in collaboration with Ronald Feldman Fine Arts, N.Y.

** in collaboration with Renzo Spagnoli Gallery , Florence   *** interviewed by Tom Wolf

DISCUSSIONS IS AN EXHIBITION BASED ON THE IDEA OF DISCUSSION AS AN ARTFORM . The discussion , not as performance , not as a panel discussion , but as the artist's public dialogue , is a specific form of art expression .

From the early John Cage pieces to Beuys' current ideological forum , the interaction of public and artists as a carrier has been used in cases where artistic activity finds its main justifications in social ideologies (Kosuth , Burgin , Haacke) or in theoretical speculation (early Art and Language) as well as in Ian Wilson's epistemic discussions in which the research for a common , meaningful topic legitimizes the coming together of artist and public. This direct interaction is the best shortcut to the purpose of art .

The discussion as a type of art expression is different from panel discussions in which many artists are called to discuss issues of art and culture. However , the frequency of these panels certainly indicates that the meeting of artist and public in a dialogue is a format of pressing interest. Without intending to draw a strict line between what IS art and what IS ABOUT art , the discussion-as - art should be signaled as one of the forms of the dematerialization of art ; the only form which substantiates the participatory mode and phase of art .

PAINTING,

EVRIAH BADER	JANUARY 17-27 3-6PM TUE - SAT
DANIEL BUREN	JANUARY 17 3-8PM OPENING
RALSTON FARINA	JANUARY 17 4-7PM DANIEL BUREN
RON GORCHOV	"IN SITU" PART I*
ERNEST GUSELLA	JANUARY 23 8PM CAROLEE SCHNEEMAN
MARCIA HAFIF	"FUSES"
ELLEN PHELAN	JANUARY 24 6PM ERNEST GUSELLA
JUDY RIFKA	"VIDEO TAPE"
CAROLEE SCHNEEMAN	
TOM WOLF	

organized by   ANNINA NOSEI-WEBER

THE FINE ARTS BUILDING
105 HUDSON STREET NYC

*Daniel Buren in collaboration with Art & Project, Amsterdam where Part II will be

"I should have been vainer: my portrait by Andy Warhol would be worth well over that amount today."

AN: Sure. Let me tell you about when Candy Darling, the transgender superstar from Andy Warhol's Factory, stayed with Maxime de la Falaise, the designer who was living in the apartment next to mine on New York's West Side. Candy was a beautiful woman, but she suffered from an incurable disease. She spent long periods with Maxime, during which Andy Warhol also visited her. After visiting Maxime, Andy would usually drop by to say hello to me too. John Weber and I had already divorced at that point and we'd divided up our works of art. Among those left to me was an important sculpture by Carl Andre made from copper tiles; it was right in the entrance to my apartment. One evening I got a call from Warhol: he wanted to take me to dinner. We went to a Chinese restaurant that he liked a lot, not far from the MoMA. There were other people from the Factory with us too. Andy Warhol wasn't a great talker: he didn't speak much during dinner, but at a certain point he told me that he wanted to paint my portrait. At that time – in the mid-1970s – contemporary art wasn't selling particularly well. So I replied that I couldn't afford to have him paint my portrait, but Warhol made me a counter-proposal: he didn't want money, he wanted the Carl Andre sculpture that he'd seen in my apartment. I was certain that I could have sold that work for at least $30,000 – which in due course I did, when I let it go to the art collector Francesco Pellizzi, a friend of mine. Needless to say, that was a really big mistake; I should have been vainer: my portrait by Andy Warhol would be worth well over that amount today.

RL: Did you organize other independent exhibitions in those years?

AN: Yes, there's another story linked to that period. One day, in the gallery of Ivan Karp, a former colleague of Leo Castelli, I saw some drawings by Cy Twombly and I wanted to buy them. He'd been one of the first artists who had interested me, actually. There was a problem though: someone else was already interested in buying those drawings – Larry Gagosian. We didn't know each other, but I knew how to track him down, so I called him and told him, "If we keep trying to buy the same works, we'll only succeed in driving their prices up." I don't remember how it ended with Twombly (we probably bought a few each) but we were friends from then on and started doing business together. At one point, Larry proposed to me that we buy a loft together in New York to use as an office, but I didn't feel like buying a property and so I proposed that we rent instead: we split the rent on a loft at 421 West Broadway. Larry lived in Los Angeles and I lived on Riverside Drive – that loft was our office. It was across the road from the famous 420 West Broadway, the building I was telling you about earlier, which housed the galleries of John Weber, Leo Castelli, Ileana Sonnabend and others.

RL: What did your collaboration with Larry Gagosian consist of?

AN: We were constantly on the phone. I remember once that I had to leave the cinema because Larry Gagosian absolutely wanted me to close the sale of a Frank Stella, which I did as soon as I was able to get home… Or I'd heard about a Jasper Johns that was available and he sold it; or he'd found a sculpture by Twombly that I then sold to Francesco Pellizzi. Another time, Larry brought in an immense Donald Judd sculpture. This was what defined our collaboration: a series of very intense interactions between him and me. Only I was in New York and he was in Los Angeles. We had an assistant, Kim Gordon, who later became the leader of the band Sonic Youth. After a while I thought of organizing exhibitions in that space, with Larry Gagosian's approval. I put works by Troy Brauntuch, David Deutsch, Donald Newman, and David Salle on show in that loft. One day, looking out of the window, I saw some Robert Mangold works on display in the John Weber Gallery across the street. Although the

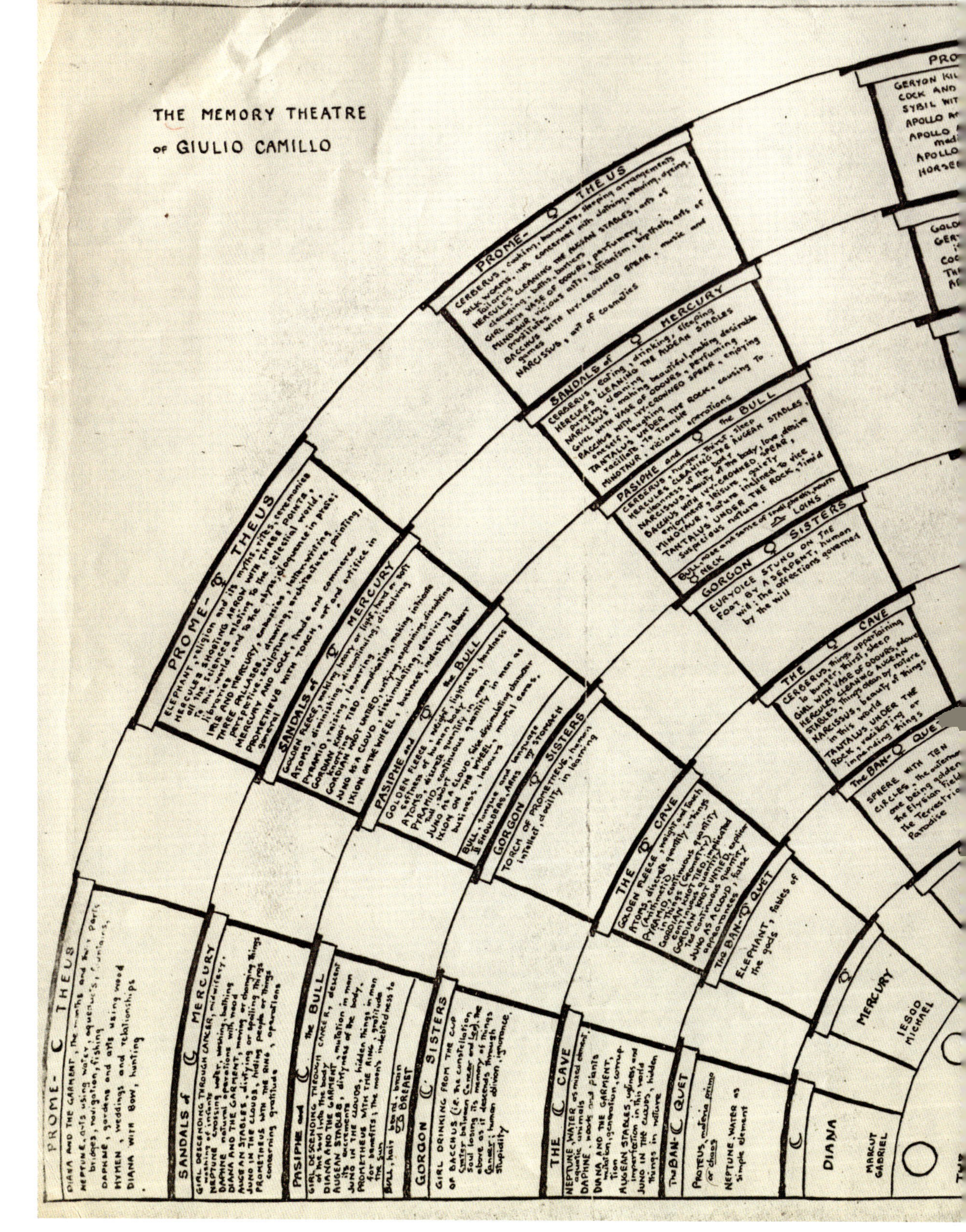

The Memory Theatre of Giulio Camillo

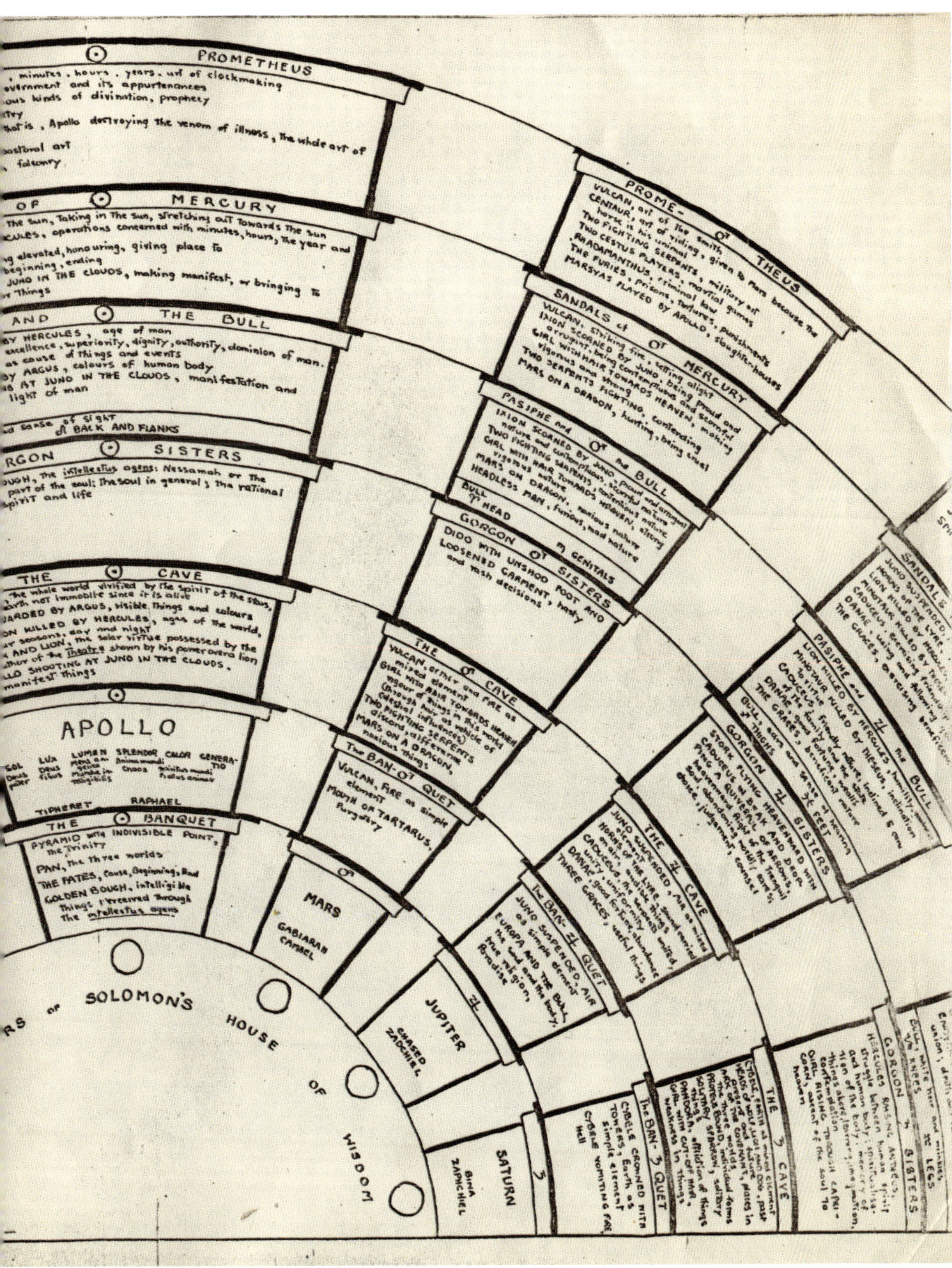

GIULIO CAMILLO'S THEATRE OF MEMORY,
USED IN THE POSTER FOR THE EXHIBITION
MEMORY AT C SPACE
(drawing by Cynthia Chapin)
New York, 1977

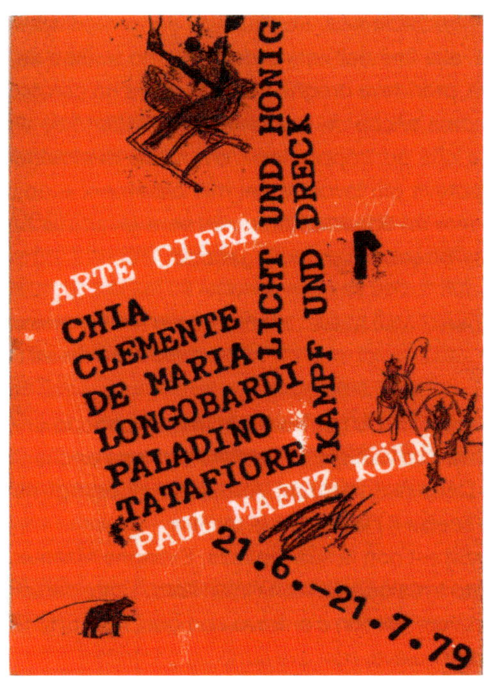

works were very different – Mangold's were characterized by lines and geometries, Salle's were dominated by female nudes – they harmonized perfectly on a chromatic level.

That coincidence amused me so much that I decided to organize a solo exhibition of Salle. A lot of people came to the opening and everything sold. It was a success. Mary Boone also came and asked him if he wanted to work with her, to be represented in her gallery. I still didn't have my own gallery. David Salle then promised me that, if I were to open my own space, he'd give me an exhibition; when I opened in due course, the Mary Boone Gallery, with great fairness, immediately sent me all his works without asking for any commission.

RL: From what you're saying, it sounds as if you had a good relationship with Mary Boone.

AN: Absolutely. What other gallerist would've behaved that way, without asking me for any commission? Anyway, everybody liked that Salle exhibition, it sold out.

RL: So over what period did you collaborate with Larry Gagosian?

AN: 1978, 1979...

RL: In the exact same years that the art scene was undergoing rapid changes, with new artists emerging. When did you organize the David Salle exhibition? What was it that attracted you?

AN: Between '79 and '80. At that point I was interested in artists who dealt with ideological content through conceptual strategies, so when I mounted Salle's exhibition, I didn't want to concentrate on the painting, but rather

Cover of the catalogue for the exhibition *Arte Cifra* at Paul Maenz gallery in Cologne, June 1979.

I was focused on the ambiguity of the imagery in his work. In the case of Donald Newman, I was interested in the way that his work incorporated the photographs by making them pictorial again. I never considered him a traditional painter but rather, like Salle, an artist who'd established a new emotional ambiguity between the medium and the image.

RL: Were you still teaching when you began working with these young artists?

AN: In the beginning, yes. Then I stopped and, in the spring of 1980, I decided to open my own gallery. In September, with the beginning of the season proper, I organized a group show first of all, then a solo exhibition of Mimmo Paladino immediately after that, after which I opened the David Salle show.

RL: Did you have any interest in Italians at that time?

AN: My primary interest, in reality, wasn't directed so much toward Italian art as toward what was coming out of California – in particular, from the California Institute of the Arts, CalArts, where John Baldessari taught. The artists who emerged from there belonged to a kind of American New Figuration, exactly like David Salle. When I went to Italy in the summer, I became interested in the Italian New Figuration, which at the time was called Arte Cifra, and I approached those artists through Lucio Amelio and invited them to take part in some group shows. Clemente, Chia, Cucchi, Paladino, even Tatafiore – I included all of them in the *Drawings and Paintings on Paper* exhibition together with American artists like Mike Glier, Robert Longo, David Salle, Julian Schnabel, and others.

RL: *Arte Cifra* was the title of the exhibition that Paul Maenz organized in

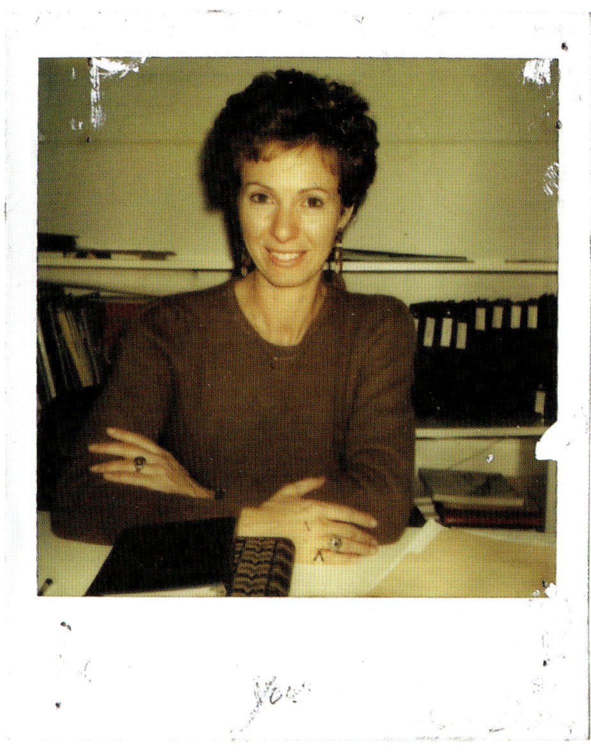

his gallery in Cologne, in agreement with Lucio Amelio I believe...

AN: Yes, it was.

RL: What did you appreciate about Paladino?

AN: For me, he represented the typical Italian artist. His drawings reminded me of Sironi, reminded me of Italic art.
Maybe that was a bit of a stretch, but my father was a Latinist and a philologist, so I was always looking for the etymology in all languages, visual, or musical. Regardless of his formal qualities, I especially liked the Italianness of Paladino.

RL: In a more general sense, what interested you in the new generation of artists that was sweeping in?

AN: In the work of the Italians, I was very interested in the question of the subject. The legacy of Italian culture was tangible in their work, which was full of poetic images cultivated through feeling. At that moment I saw that the Italians were searching for their own personal syntheses between past and future. I was also interested in the Germans, including those of the previous generation (such as Hödicke or Koberling), but especially in the Berliners: they were painters who were really focused on the issues of painting itself – of color, of the subject. If their work was often linked to the Expressionism of the turn of the century, it was due to a new sense of protest that was somehow linked to the same freedom and intensity of performance. And then, as I told you, I was very interested in the Americans.

RL: In those early years, many artists passed through your gallery who'd

Annina in the early 1980s.

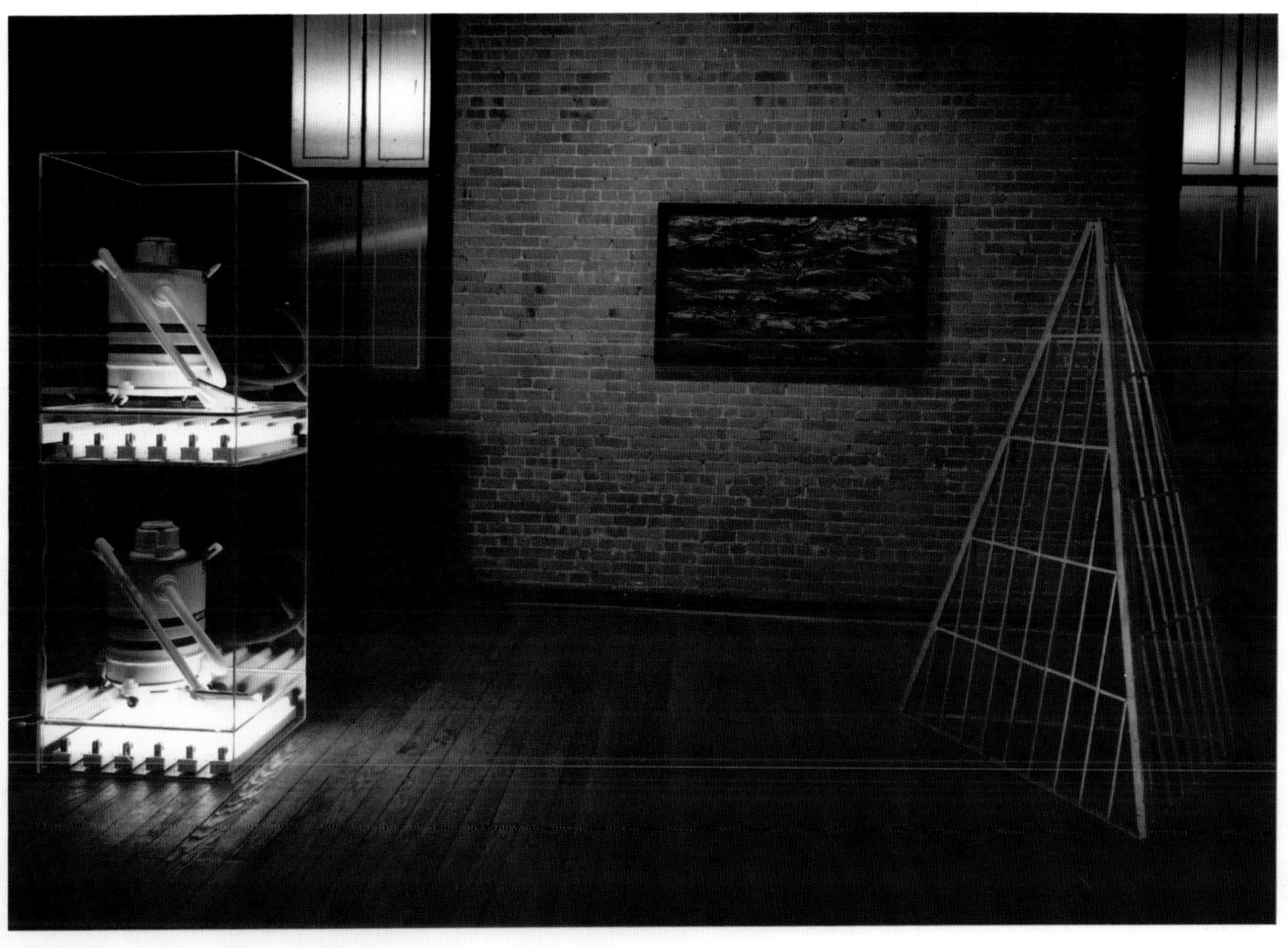

INSTALLATION VIEW OF THE GROUP SHOW
ORGANIZED IN MARCH 1981 AT ANNINA NOSEI GALLERY
(FROM LEFT, WORKS BY: JEFF KOONS, NEIL JENNEY, RONNIE CUTRONE)
Photo D. James Dee

“He had an educated family behind him and he spoke several languages.”

later become famous; in addition to David Salle, you exhibited, for example, Jeff Koons…

AN: I certainly did. I exhibited one of his works in a group show that I put on in 1981. It was an interesting piece, made up of two plastic cubes, which called Larry Bell to mind, with two vacuum cleaners inside, which reminded me of Oldenburg. Koons wrote me a letter after the exhibition. He wanted to know what my intentions were for his career. I replied with a letter in which I told him that I wasn’t even concerned about my own career, how could I be concerned about his? I suggested that he find himself another gallery to show in. Jeff Koons was very bright as an artist, but his works didn’t interest me.

RL: What bound you to Basquiat, however? What did you find in his work?

AN: Jean-Michel Basquiat was very young but also very, very intelligent. He had a great curiosity about the meaning of things, about ideas, about culture, and he read a lot. His mother had taken him to museums as a child, so he’d often visited the Brooklyn Museum as well as the MoMA. He had an educated family behind him and he spoke several languages. His father Gérard was a very kind, elegant gentleman from Haiti, who was an accountant. His sisters attended one of the most prestigious schools in New York, Saint Ann’s School in Brooklyn. His father and his partner Nora had luxurious cars.
When we inaugurated *Public Address*, they arrived before the opening still wearing their tennis gear because they were returning from one of the most exclusive sports clubs in the city, the tennis club in Forest Hills. They were far from poor. And they also had a loving relationship with him. I remember that Jean-Michel gave a painting from the show to his sister Jeanine.

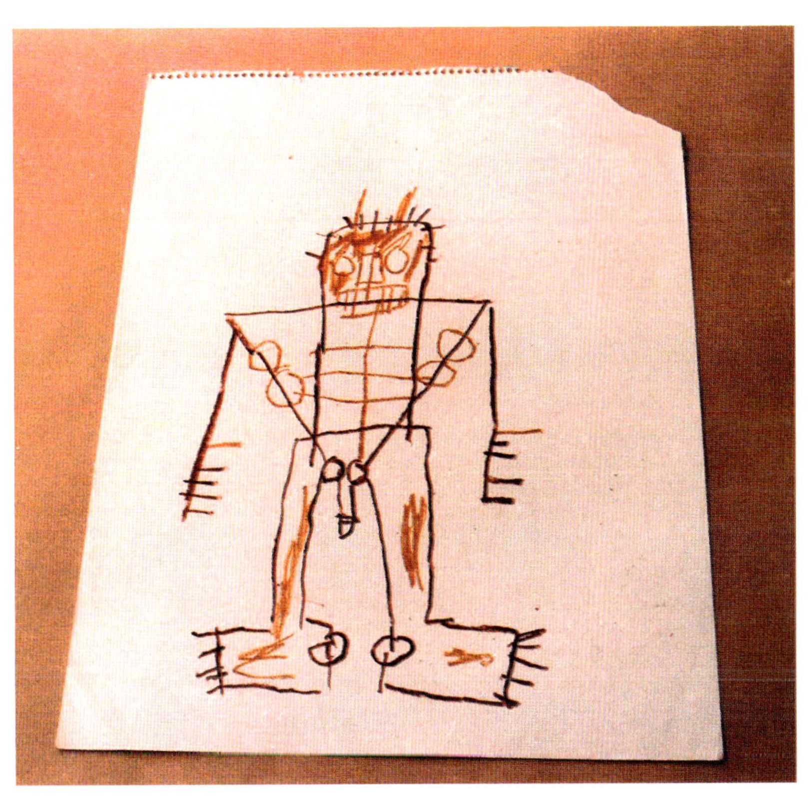

EARLY BASQUIAT DRAWING

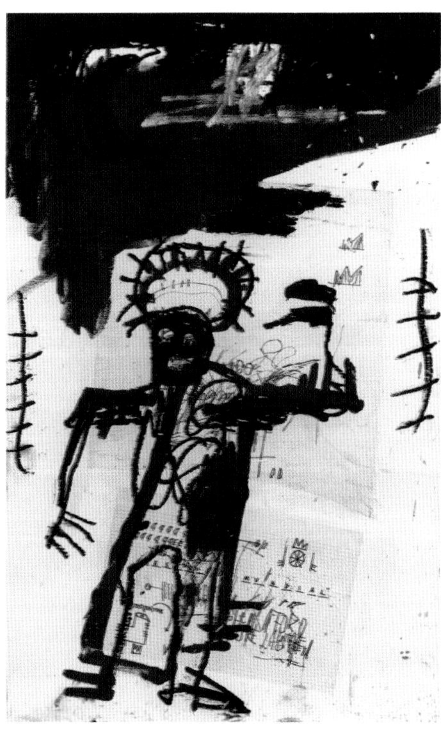

RL: And regarding art?

AN: With regard to art, he was curious, eager to learn. When I saw his work, I immediately drew a comparison with Twombly. Maybe Basquiat knew who he was, but if so he didn't know him well. I was the one who gave him Twombly's catalogue raisonné, because I felt that there was a connection between their bodies of work. And if you look at Jean-Michel's first paintings, you'll recognize that the black strokes you see are those of Franz Kline. I also thought there was brilliance in Basquiat's affinity with modernist painting, with Matisse, for example, with his paintings of Algiers at the MoMA. There's a distinct likeness, even in the structure. Also, I liked the fact that you could find New York, the society of New York, in his paintings, but that there was also Caribbean culture in it. His way of painting was always direct, never illustrative. I was interested in its immediacy, its instantaneous conceptuality. As in jazz, his works were improvised but they had a robust structure underneath; his images and their conceptual references appeared instantly.
Jean-Michel wrote on the canvases, but he didn't just write the words – he wrote the painting. His graffiti was like concrete poetry on the wall, not like that of the so-called graffiti artists, who were of a previous genera-tion. He had an extraordinary, instinctive power that I've never found in any other artist.

RL: How did you settle on the idea of putting on a solo exhibition?

AN: I saw his work for the first time at PS1, in a group show curated by Diego Cortez and entitled *New York/New Wave*, which featured over 100 artists. I asked the director, Alanna Heiss, if I could see the exhibition privately on a day when the museum was closed to the public, because I wanted to look at the works calmly. I had it in mind to include some

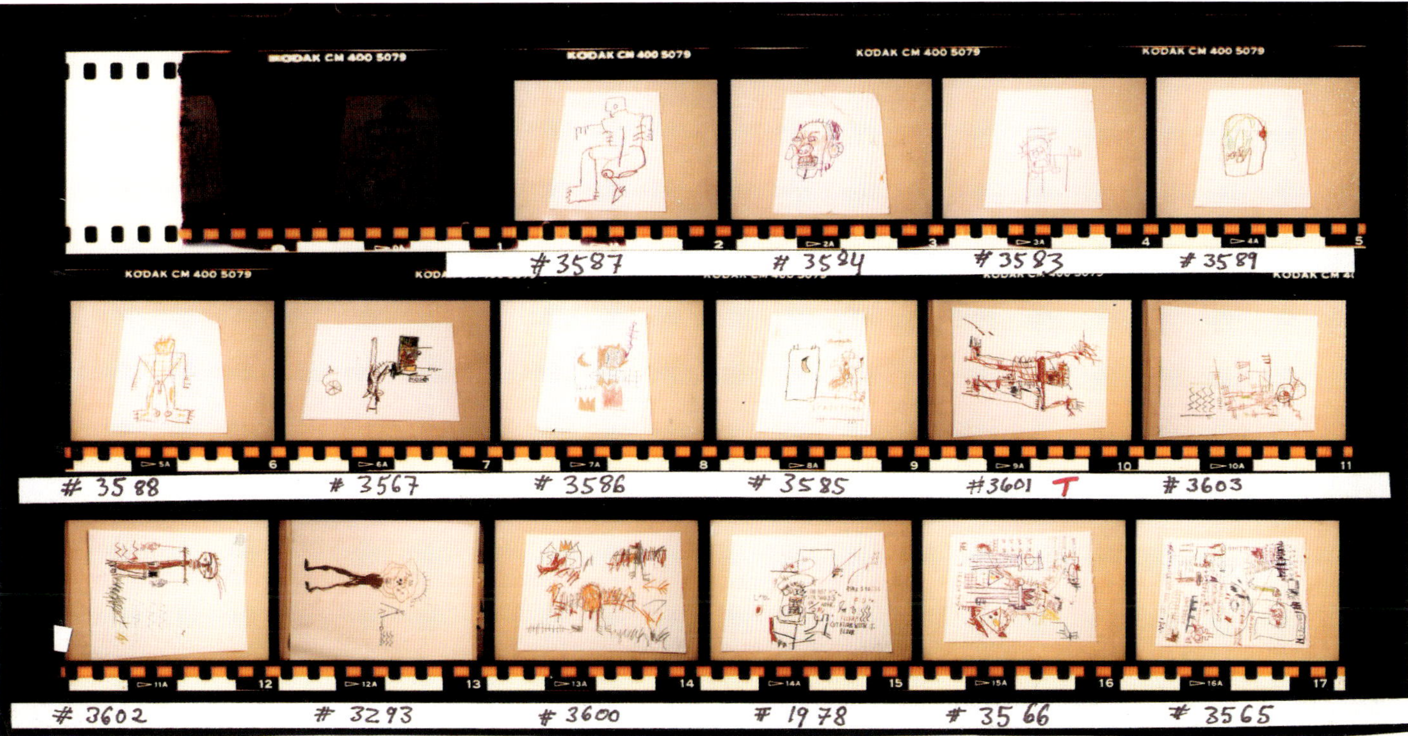

Early Jean-Michel Basquiat's drawings on paper.

young American artists in my gallery, New Yorkers, after having exhibited foreign artists. There were two artists who particularly interested me in the PS1 exhibition; one was Jean-Michel Basquiat and the other Roberto Juarez. Their works struck me by their authenticity because they mixed a great sense of painting with Latin iconography – one Caribbean, the other Mexican – that belonged to their cultures of origin. They made me think of Wifredo Lam. Their sense of color and painting was very close to my interests, to my passions.

RL: Did you also work with Juarez in those years?

AN: No, not much. Roberto Juarez was already working with Robert Miller's gallery, so I could only slip him into a group show. But I'd have given him a few more exhibitions if I could have.

RL: What struck you about Jean-Michel Basquiat in the exhibition at PS1?

AN: He had some small works on display and I liked those a lot. I was interested in the fact that the images were made with concrete symbols, like the tangible poetry of the ancient Greeks. They were like an alphabet of signs. So I thought I should meet him. I looked for his number in the telephone book and I called his father's house, leaving a message for Jean-Michel, but then he called me back without catching me. I was teaching at the School of Visual Arts at the time and I know that he tried to reach me there too. Anyway, we eventually met at the opening of an exhibition at the Brooke Alexander Gallery on 57th Street and we arranged to go see his work at his then-girlfriend Suzanne Mallouk's apartment on the Lower East Side. So I went. It was mostly drawings, lots of drawings, and I was intrigued by all of them. We went for a coffee and started talking. He insisted on exhibiting in my gallery. I told him

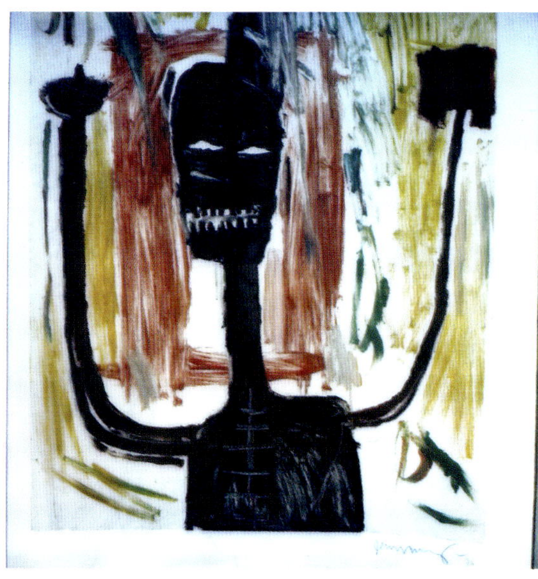 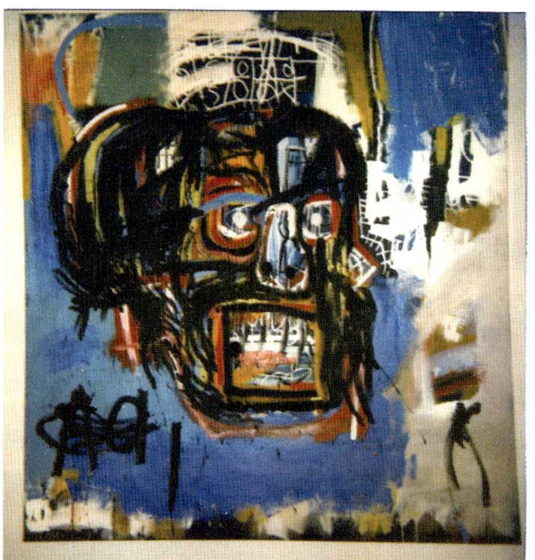

that there was no possibility of that right away, that I'd already finalized
the program for the year. He asked me to at least include him in a group
show and I tried to explain to him that I couldn't do it because my first
group show was centered around the idea of *Public Address*, while he
was doing self-referential works relating to himself. My interests were in
another direction, to the effect that I'd invited artists like Barbara Kruger
and Jenny Holzer. He argued that his work actually did have a lot to do
with the public dimension, that it was political.

RL: And so he convinced you to include him in the exhibition?

AN: Yes, but there was a problem, because he didn't have any works
ready for the show; he only had his drawings, so I gave him $400 to buy
what he needed to make his pieces for the exhibition. A few days later
he brought two paintings to the gallery for me to look at, but it was late.
I didn't want to stay in the gallery after closing time, and above all I was
worried that if I didn't like them I'd find myself in trouble, so I suggested
that we go see them at Sandro Chia's studio.
Once we were there, he unrolled them and I liked them a lot. He told me
he didn't have enough space to paint, so I offered him the studio below
the gallery to work in. It was a space with a skylight and two large windows.
In the meantime I bought the canvases he'd shown me, so he asked me:
"And what do I show in the exhibition?" So I answered him: "Some doors."
And so I got hold of some panels the size of doors. My reference was a
nod to Marcel Duchamp, who'd used his door to demonstrate the mind
games inside and outside of art.
Few people are aware that Jean-Michel's doors came out of Duchamp's
door. If you agree to it, I'd like this book that we're working on to have
something to do with the door in its title, because so much stems from
Marcel Duchamp.

Polaroids of early Basquiat work.

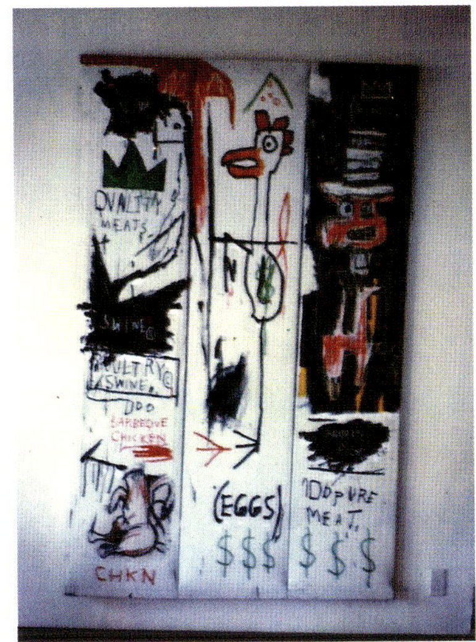 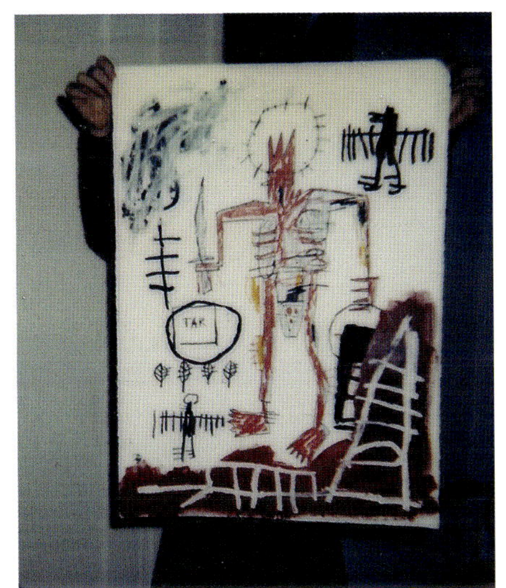

RL: It's already possible to note the idea of a public dimension in this Basquiat-Duchamp connection of yours, actually...

AN: And I have to say, there are elements in the paintings shown on that occasion that many people have subsequently interpreted precisely in the light of this public dimension. The works that Basquiat created for the exhibition, about ten of them, were all hung together in the back room while the other artists – Keith Haring, Barbara Kruger, Jenny Holzer, Mike Glier, etc. – were in the front room.

RL: Alright, we'll come back to that later. We're in the very earliest years of your gallery's operation, but when exactly?

AN: I opened *Public Address* on October 31, 1981.

RL: So the first time you showed Basquiat, it was in a group show. And those were the first canvases he'd done, because previously he'd only worked on paper, yes?

AN: No, he'd painted some pictures in Modena for Mazzoli. Diego Cortez had acted as intermediary. They were large paintings, which I bought and sold with Jean-Michel's consent. We opened his first major solo exhibition in my gallery in March of 1982, however. It was a great success and all the paintings sold, both to important collectors and to institutions.

RL: Basquiat had used the gallery basement as a studio while he prepared the works shown in *Public Address*, right? I think you gave him a great opportunity. I remember that when I came to New York with Pizzi Cannella and Nunzio a few years later, we stayed in your loft on Wooster Street, near the gallery, where they worked toward the show. In short, it was a

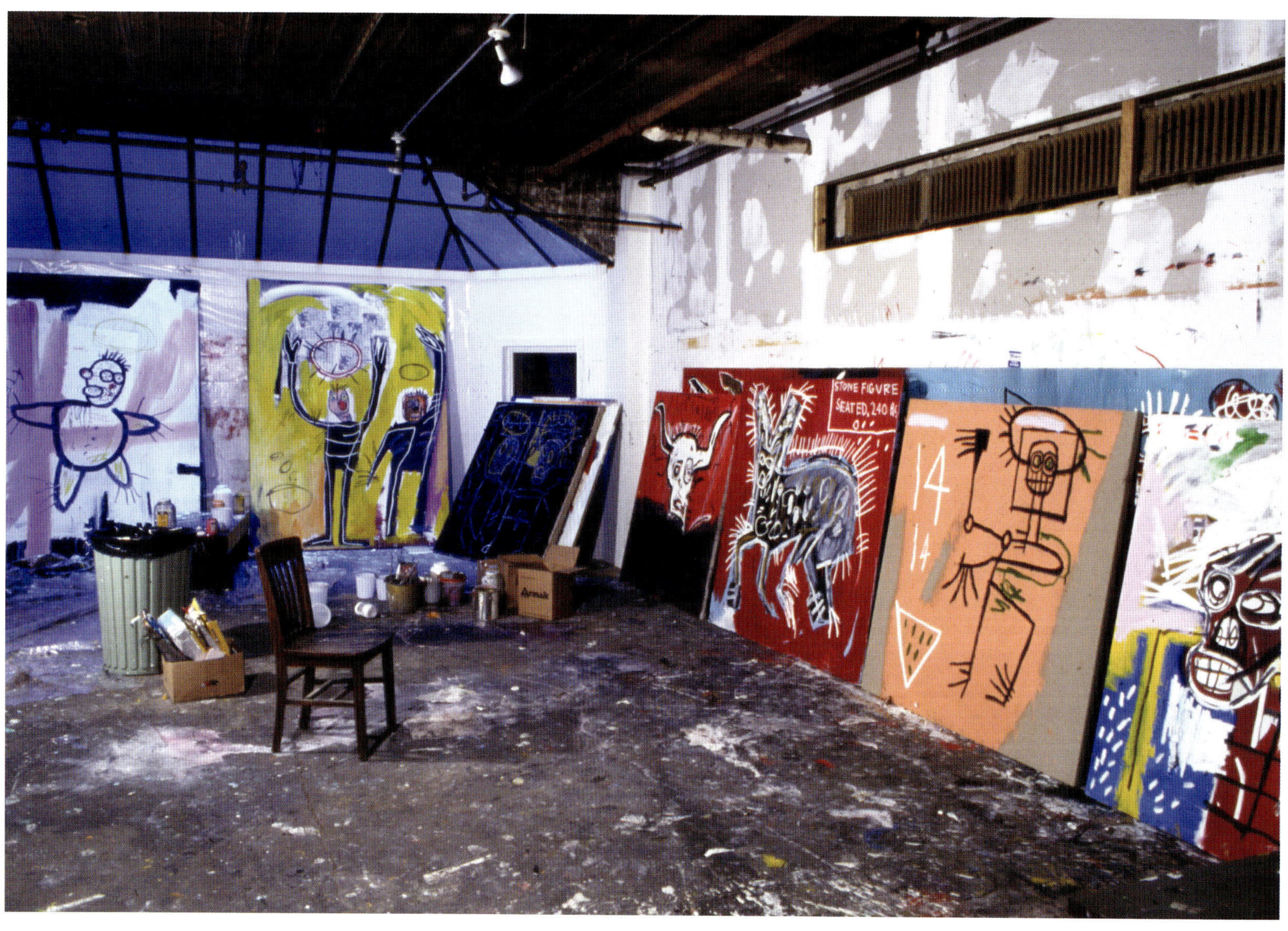

THE BASEMENT OF ANNINA NOSEI GALLERY
WHERE JEAN-MICHEL BASQUIAT WORKED
BETWEEN 1981 AND 1982

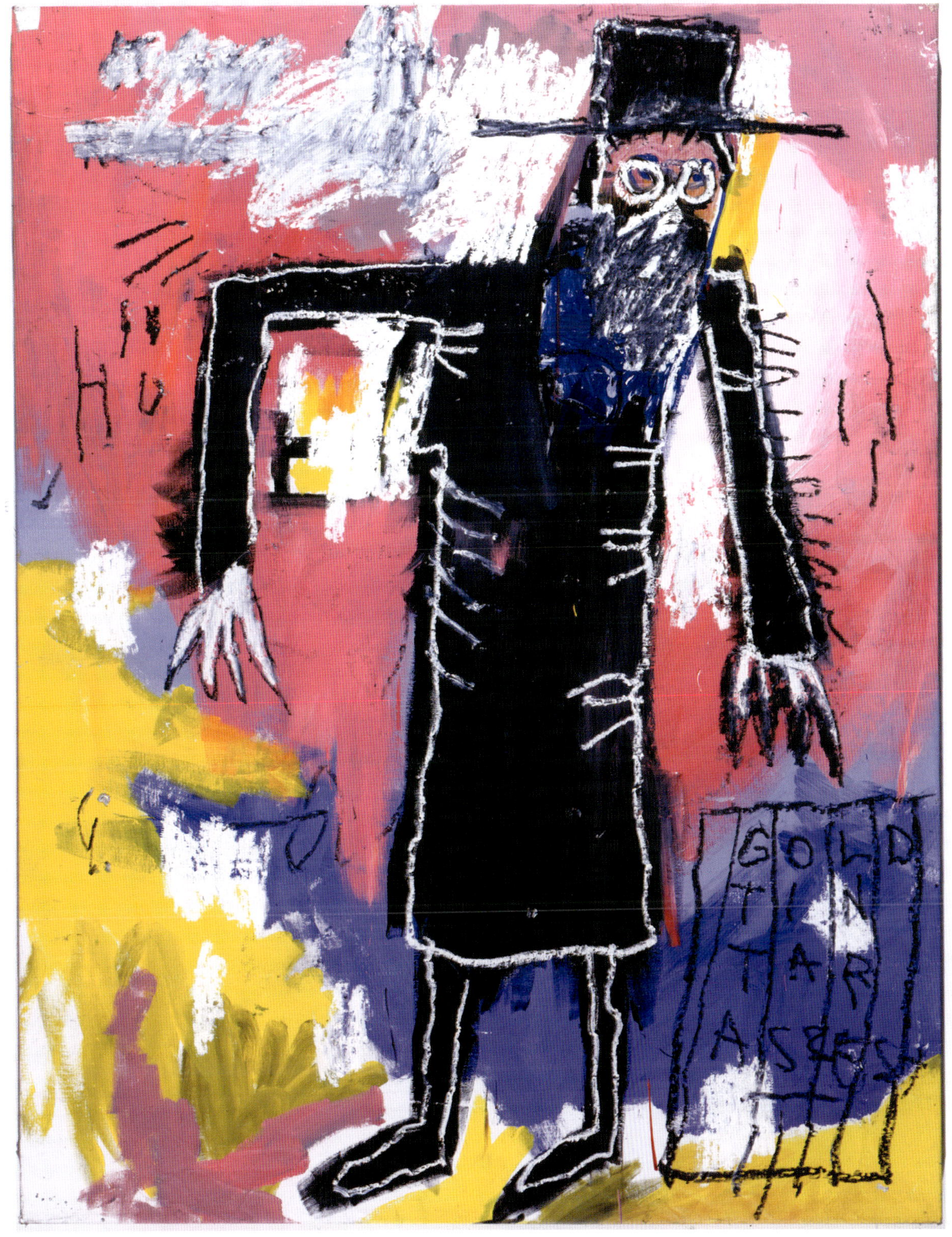

JEAN-MICHEL BASQUIAT
THE JEW, 1981

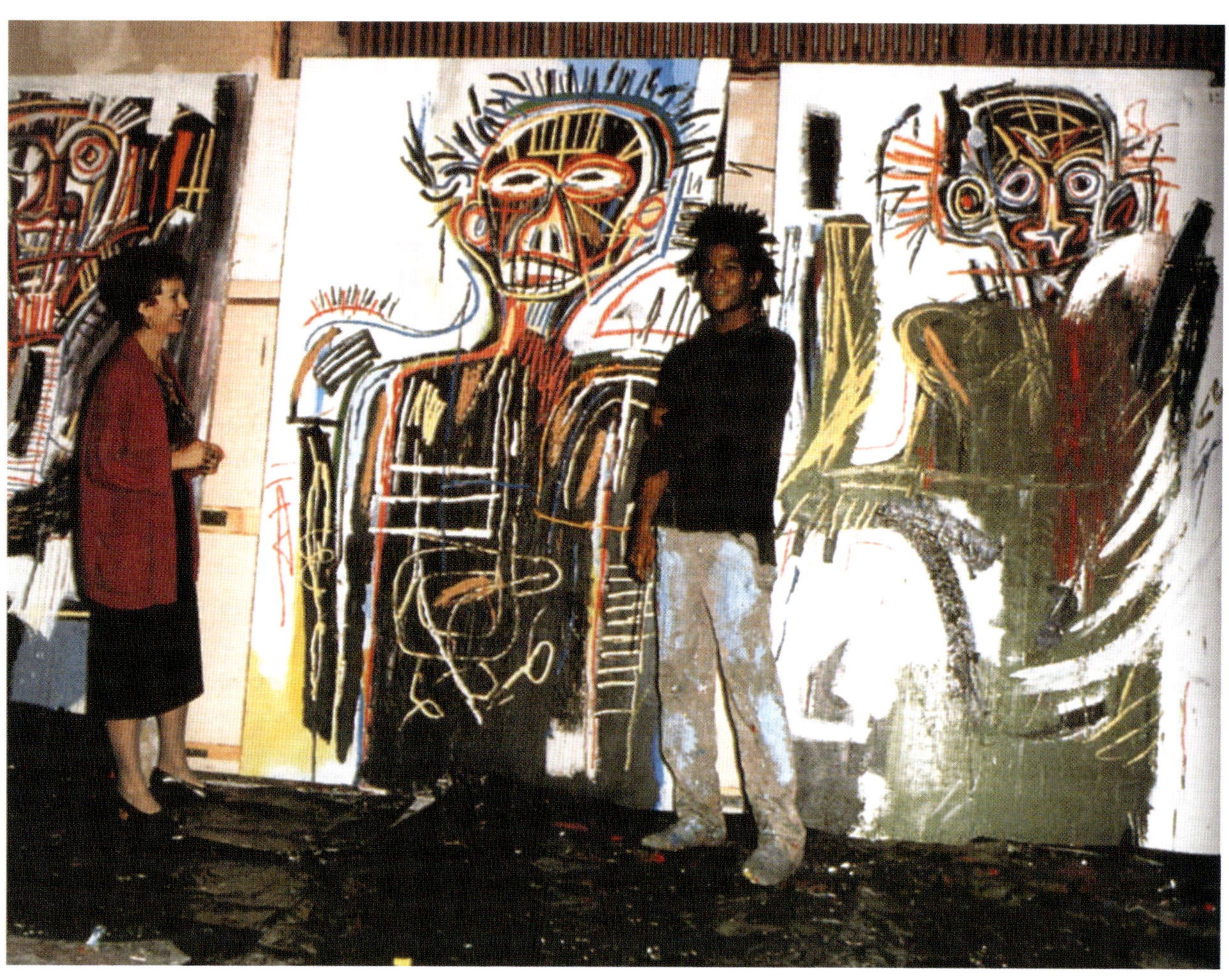

ANNINA AND BASQUIAT IN THE BASEMENT OF ANNINA NOSEI GALLERY
WHERE JEAN-MICHEL BASQUIAT WORKED BETWEEN 1981 AND 1982

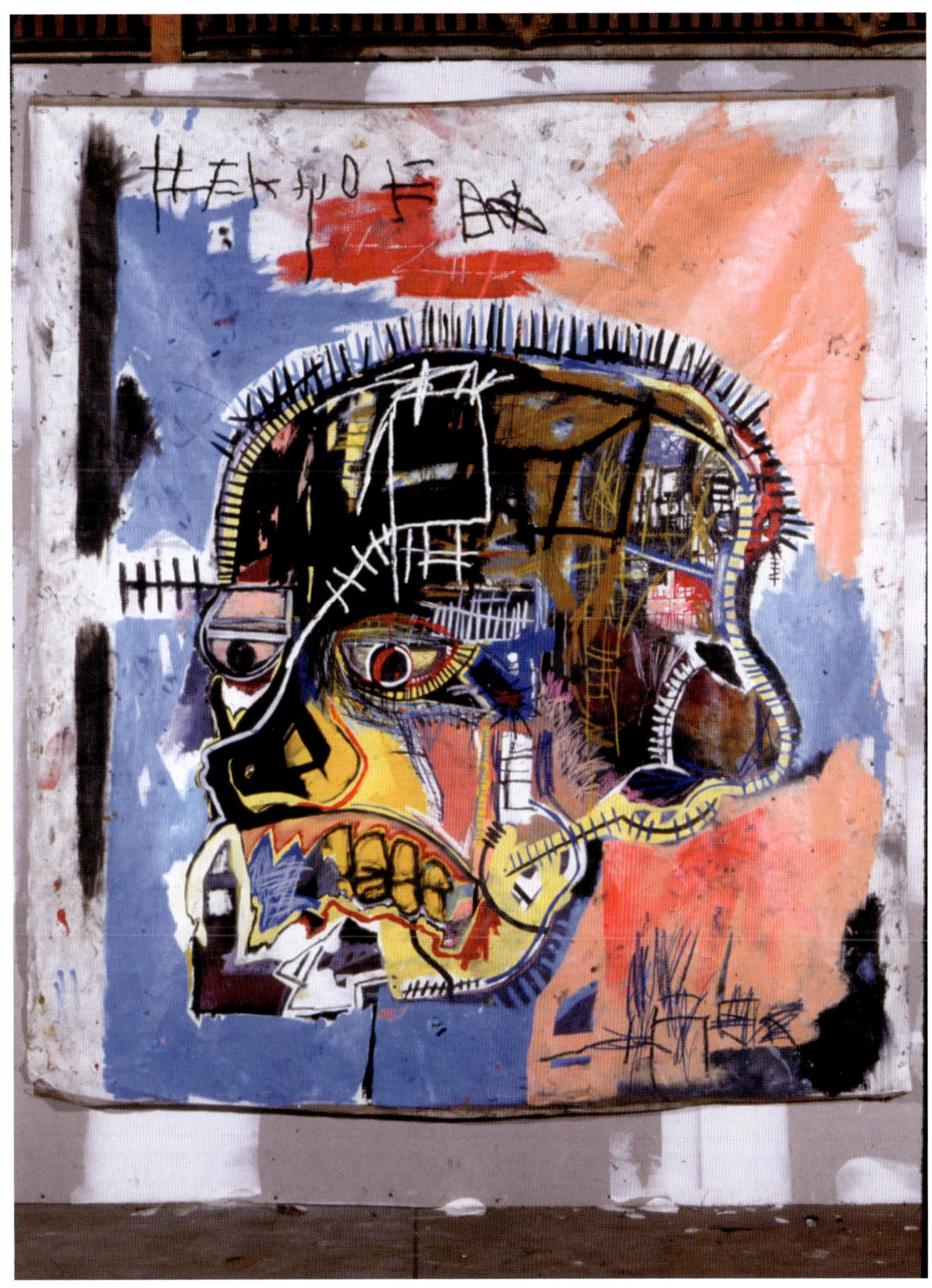

JEAN-MICHEL BASQUIAT *UNTITLED (SKULL)*, 1981
IN THE BASEMENT OF ANNINA NOSEI GALLERY, NEW YORK

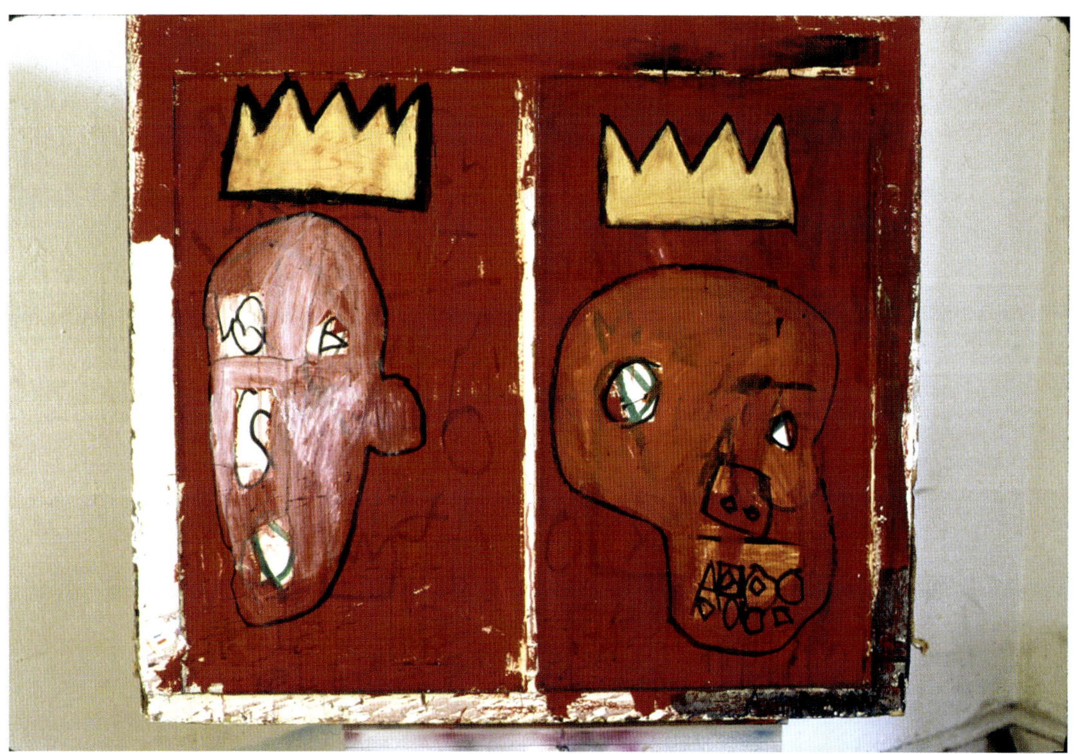

normal thing to do. And yet it seems to me that a lot of misunderstandings have arisen around the Basquiat affair.

AN: Yes. Jean-Michel was very enthusiastic about the opportunity, but some people began to say that he was in a place where a white woman was holding him prisoner, who was giving him drugs to make him paint and things like that. Obviously that wasn't true. Jean-Michel answered these polemics by saying that, if he'd been white, everyone would've simply called him an "artist in residence". And just so, as you yourself recall, when after that I put many artists up in both the basement and the Wooster Street loft – artists like Julio Galán, Helmut Middendorf, Massimo Kaufmann, and various others – nobody ever talked about imprisonment. When there were very large paintings that I couldn't fit through the stairway down to the basement, I took them to a room in the Wooster Street loft. Once, while Lia Rumma was a guest there, a small fire broke out and a work by Bruno Ceccobelli caught fire. She was thoroughly startled by it, but luckily there were no consequences and the insurance paid for everything.

RL: How was it living with Jean-Michel Basquiat? I mean, how did he behave during the period that he stayed in the basement?

AN: Jean-Michel was a person who'd never do anything he didn't want to do. I'll tell you something else, he arrived very punctually at the gallery each morning. He was already there by opening time at 10, like the secretary, and if by chance he couldn't be punctual at 10, he'd apologize when he did arrive. I explained to him that he could arrive when he wanted, that he didn't have to work to the gallery's timetable. He'd often bring cappuccinos and croissants that he bought from Dean & DeLuca and he'd eat them at my desk. Then he'd go downstairs, put on Ravel's "Bolero" – which he'd listen to all the time – and he'd paint all day. Sometimes we went to the

Jean-Michel Basquiat, *Red Kings*, 1981.

Odeon for lunch together. He'd often receive friends or critics like Rene Ricard, for example, who in that same period wrote an important article in Artforum entitled "The Radiant Child," which talked above all about Basquiat and Haring.

RL: Rumors circulated around the collectors too.

AN: It was rumored that I'd bring them all down to the basement and that it irritated Jean-Michel. But it wasn't like that. He'd receive visitors all the time, including the collectors Herbert and Lenore Schorr, but that was because they'd become friends; some people also said that I was selling off his unfinished works, but in reality it was Lenore Schorr who said, "When this painting's finished, I'll take it." Mick Jagger came to the gallery one time during those months and he bought a work by Carlo Maria Mariani. He wasn't interested in Basquiat. But that didn't matter to Jean-Michel, who was thrilled all the same because the singer from The Rolling Stones had come to the gallery where he himself was working. So it's hard to imagine him as a prisoner. For that matter, I remember that on my birthday he gave me a book on Duchamp and wrote me a dedication in it.

RL: He produced a lot of important works in that period.

AN: Yes, he made some interesting and beautiful paintings which in turn met with great success. His work represented something completely new to the history of American art in the twentieth century, after Expressionism, Minimalism, conceptual art. Each image he created had to do with society, with life, and expressed his relationship with the state of that moment. I saw a tight bond between his work and his person while at the same time, as an African American artist, he maintained a position of both adhesion to and distance from the society of the eighties. He was young but he

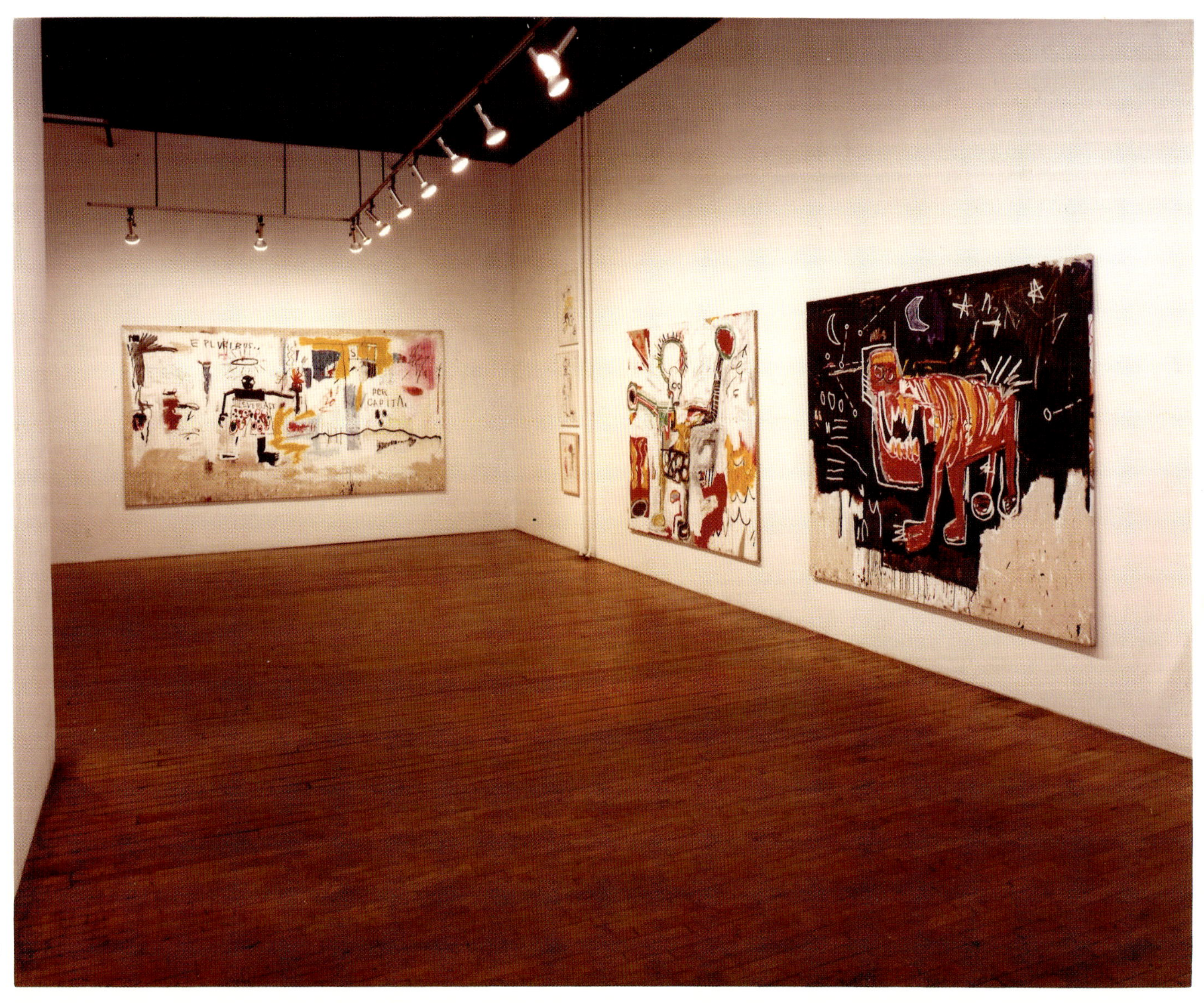

INSTALLATION VIEW OF JEAN-MICHEL BASQUIAT'S
FIRST SOLO EXHIBITION AT ANNINA NOSEI GALLERY
MARCH 1982

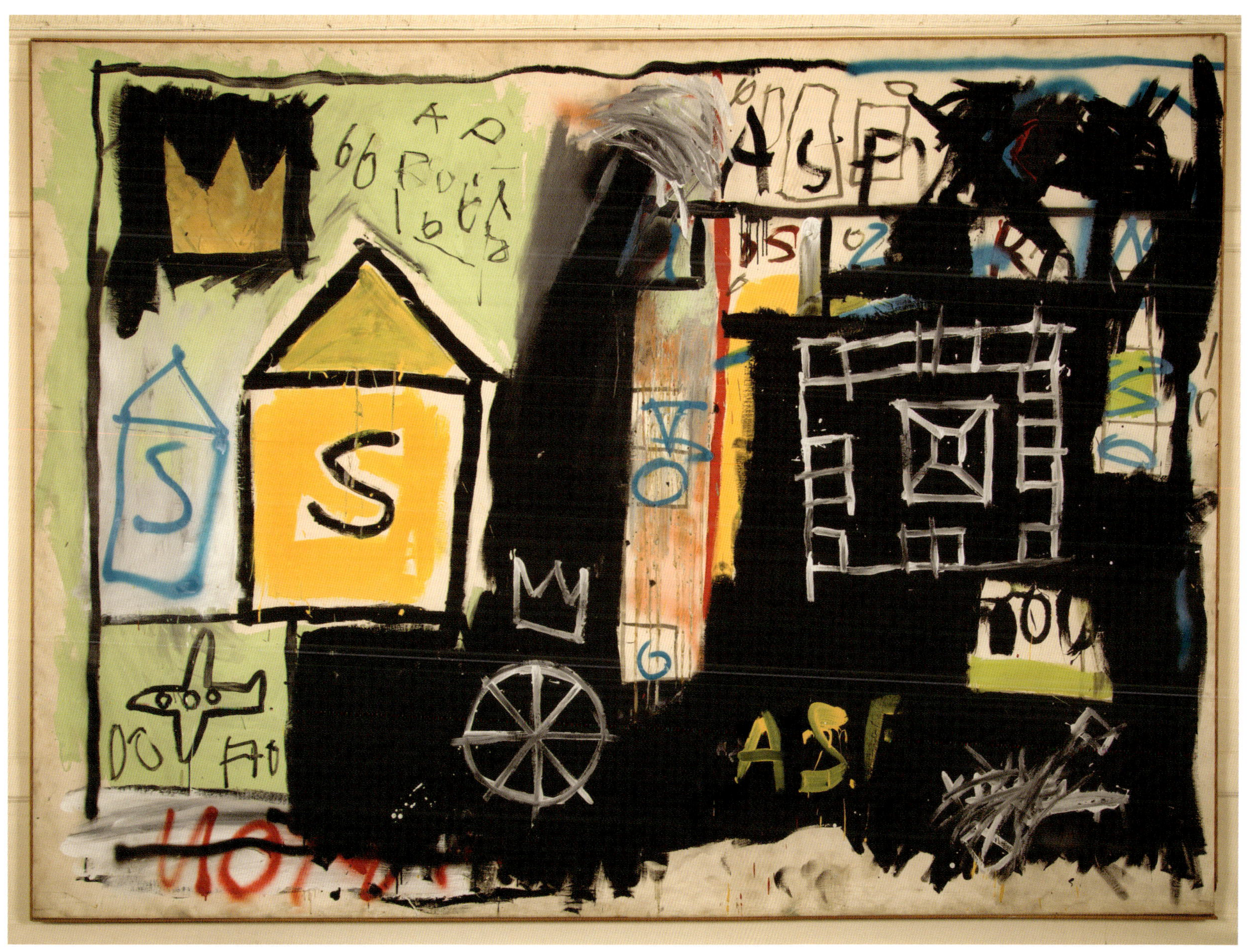

JEAN-MICHEL BASQUIAT, *UNTITLED*, 1981.
ANNINA NOSEI GALLERY, NEW YORK

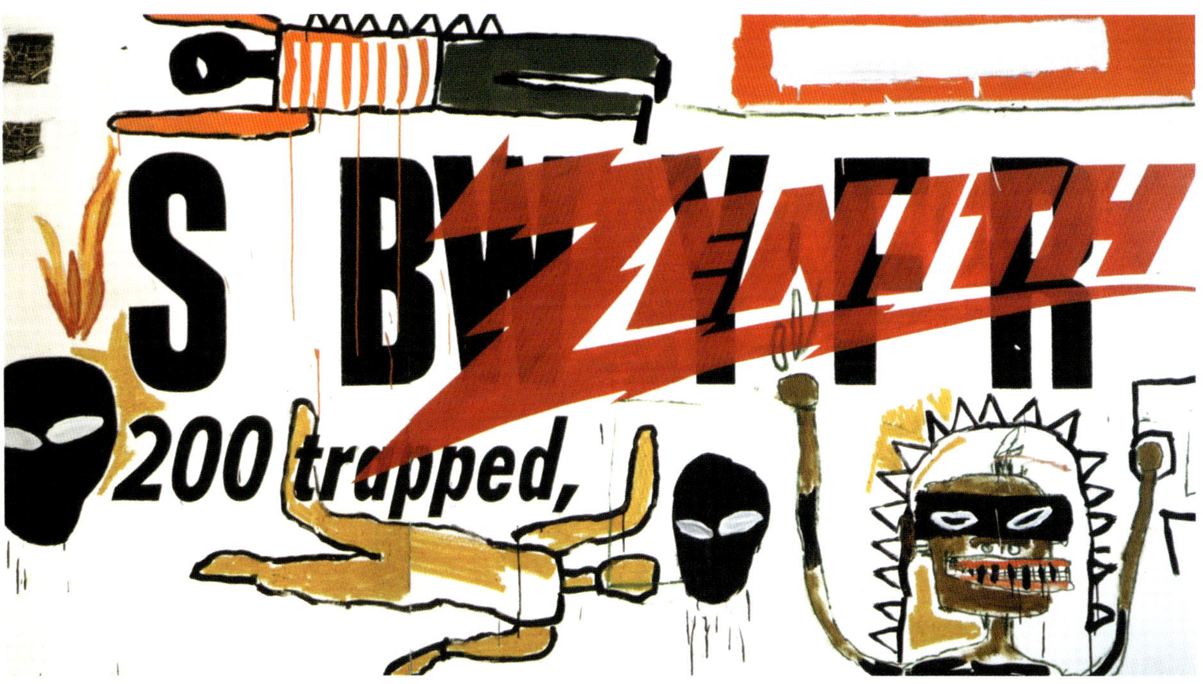

knew plenty. He'd read a lot.

At a certain point, though, things changed. I returned to New York from Italy and saw Basquiat in front of the gallery with a young man, a certain friend of his. I immediately understood that Jean-Michel was on drugs and so I asked him, "What are you doing? Do you do drugs now?" And he replied, "Don't tell my father." He knew that I'd be seeing his father Gérard, who would sometimes invite me to lunch. I told him that I'd certainly be telling his father, because he was still a teenager, but that the problem wasn't whether I'd tell his father or not, but that he'd kill himself doing that stuff. And when I asked him who that friend of his was, he replied that he was his agent and that he was going to help him organize an exhibition on the Lower East Side that he cared about a lot. I told him that he could have done it through me and that I could have given him advice. I was worried about him, so I suggested that we meet with John Weber, because I thought that he might have listened to an older and more serious gentleman. John accepted and came to the gallery, then Jean-Michel arrived, bringing his friend with him. They exchanged a few words and John took in the situation.

When they went out for a coffee, John said to me, "Annina, what are you doing? I know you, I know your father and your aunts in Florence, I know your family well. What are you doing? We have a teenage daughter together. What do you think you're doing with these people?" It seemed to me that he was right. I didn't want to be dragged into certain kinds of problems. And so I explained to Jean-Michel that he'd have to leave the basement, but I told him that I'd find him another place. Sure enough, I rented him a big loft on Crosby Street straight away, acting as guarantor. Just a few days ago I happened upon the lease I signed for him. After a while Suzanne Mallouk went there too, but she left only a few months later because she didn't want to be involved with heroin either. Eventually her account of the whole story was recorded in a book.

Basquiat & Warhol *Collaboration No.19* - Executed in 1984-1985.

RL: He was free to do what he wanted. Didn't he have a contract with you?

AN: Of course he was free, so much so that he exhibited at Patty Astor's Fun Gallery. I went to see the exhibition and bought some works by Basquiat, but he never got his cut. And when he learned that I'd resold one of those paintings, he asked me for his share, but I told him that I'd paid the gallery owner for the work and so I owed him nothing. That experience disappointed him. I'd told him to exhibit through me, but he'd wanted to do it himself. He also showed at the Galerie Delta in Rotterdam around that time. When the director who selected works for the show came to the loft, I was the one who brought him there. A lot of people went to visit him. I had nothing to do with those relationships, he could do whatever he liked. We didn't have a contract.

RL: When was it that Basquiat came into contact with Mary Boone?

AN: At a certain point Bruno Bischofberger invited him to Switzerland and tried to promote him — he was the one who organized the exhibition for Basquiat at Mary Boone's. I think she put on a couple. Then Bischof- berger organized that famous exhibition with Warhol and Basquiat at Tony Shafrazi's gallery. But it wasn't very successful. His paintings weren't as beautiful as the ones before. He'd lost his authenticity. He'd gone from immediacy to style.

RL: Can you tell me the backstory of the cut paintings?

AN: One day I arrived at the gallery and found my assistant very worried. He told me that Basquiat had cut some of his pictures with a knife. A lot of people later said that he'd ruined all my paintings of his, but that wasn't true – he'd only damaged two of them, the two paintings with the prophets.

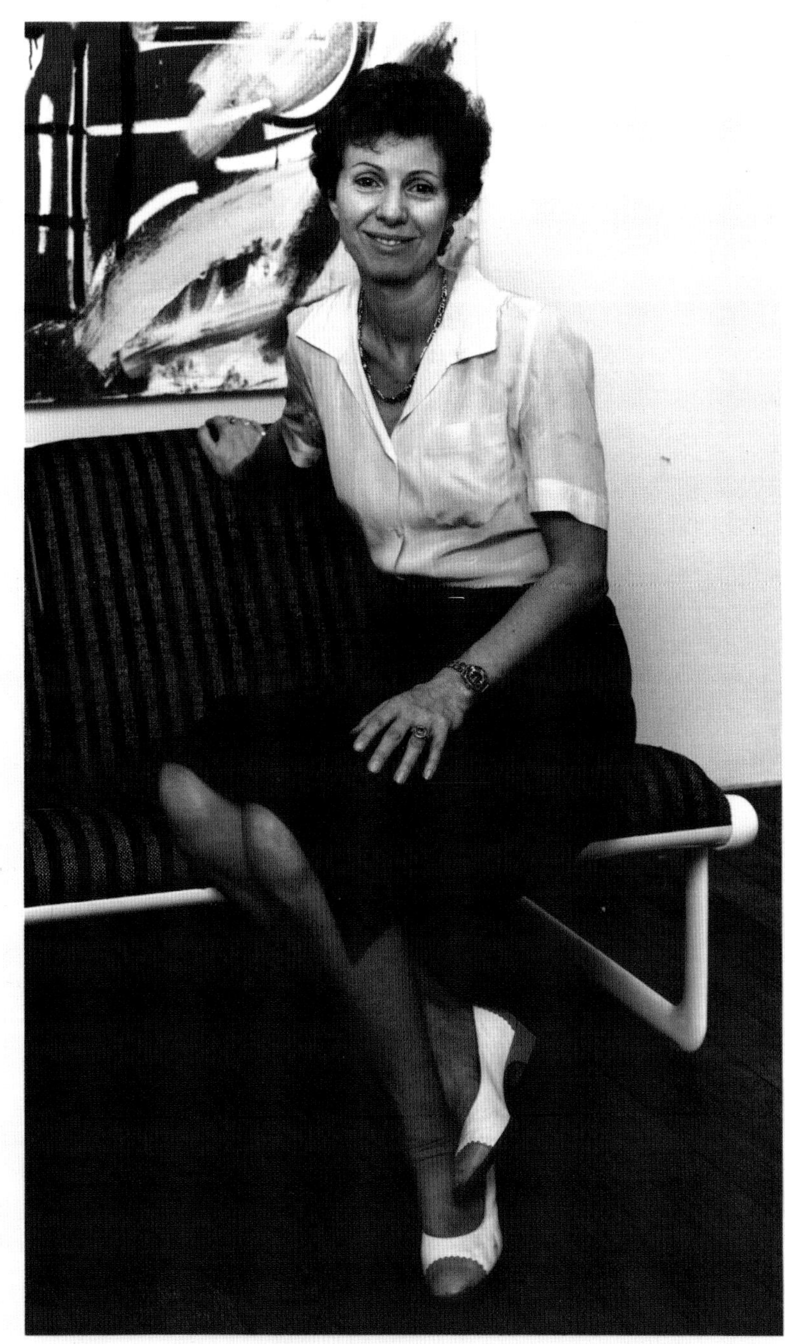

ANNINA IN HER GALLERY BEFORE
A WORK OF JEAN-MICHEL BASQUIAT
NEW YORK, 1982

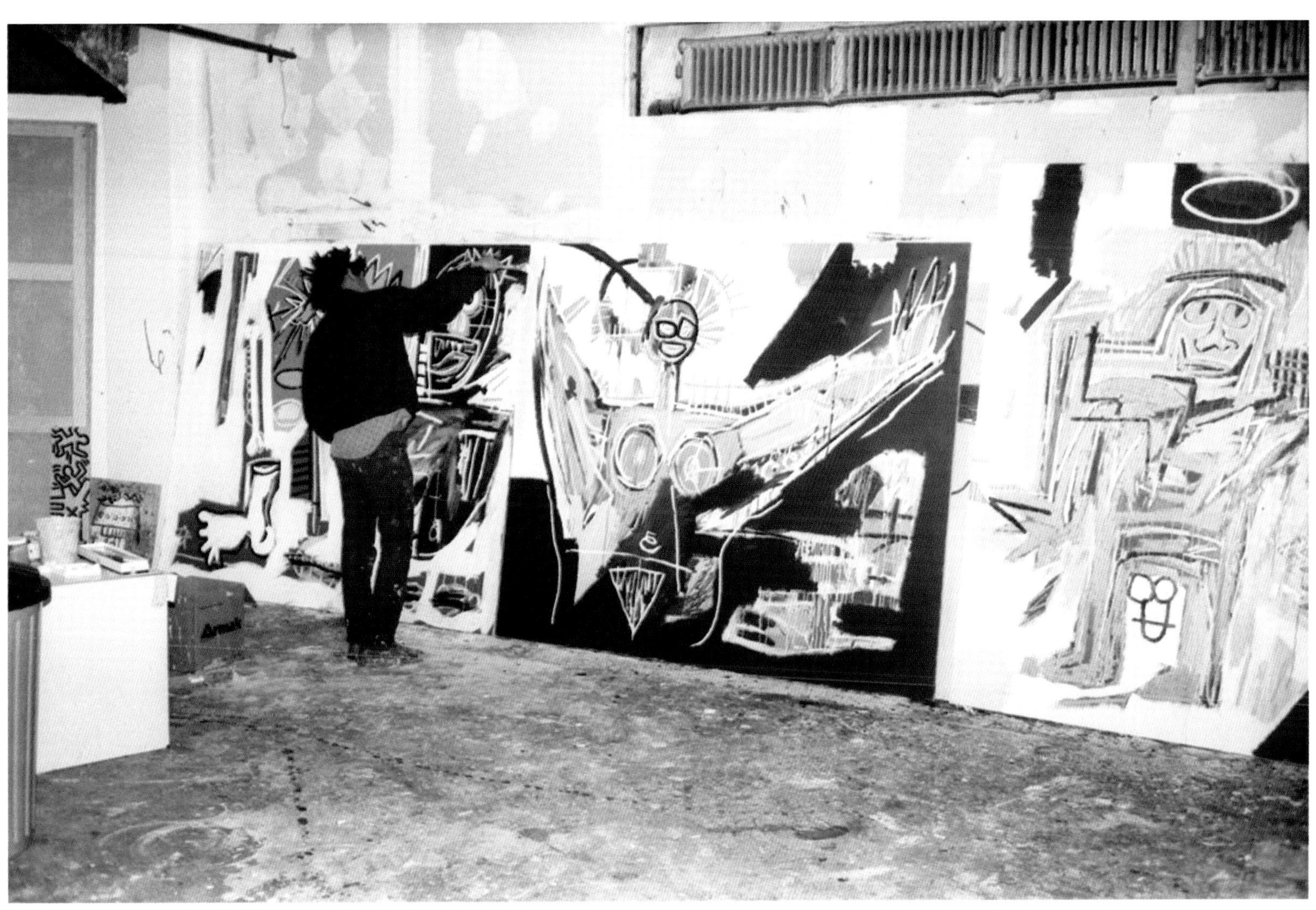

JEAN-MICHEL BASQUIAT AT WORK IN
THE BASEMENT OF ANNINA NOSEI GALLERY

"I'd told him to quit drugs. He also gave me a small sculpture; it was touching..."

There's a photograph of the two of us smiling in front of those two works that's been published often. "Why did you cut them?" I asked him, and he replied, "Because I didn't like them." "But if you didn't like them, you could have repainted them, what with all the money that the canvases cost." And he said, "No, because their ghosts would have come back." *To Repel Ghosts* was indeed a title that he gave to a lot of self-portraits. Which is something that I also found in a painting that I sold to Pino Calabrese, which I told him was a self-portrait because it looked like Jean-Michel sitting on a throne, and then there was that title... Only after seeing the Basquiat exhibition organized by Gianni Mercurio in Milan did I realize it wasn't a self-portrait. A photographer who'd gone to see that same exhibition said that the painting was just like the photographic portrait he himself had made of the artist Jack Walls wearing a chain with a cross. So I went looking for the artist and went to see him in Hudson, where I ascertained that he was indeed the subject of the painting, he had the same chain and had other photos by the same photographer hanging on the wall. Jack Walls was disappointed, too, because he'd thought I was coming to his studio to buy some paintings, when I'd come to bring clarity to the self-portrait issue.

RL: Let's go back to Basquiat's transformation.

AN: Things got worse and worse. Suzanne Mallouk later recounted that the situation was degenerating and that she'd left Jean-Michel because she ultimately chose life.
It occurs to me that Basquiat was deeply affected when Warhol died. I went to see him with that in mind. He was complaining about those terrible people who always came to see him to take away all his work. He said that since Warhol had died there was no one left who could understand him. He felt alone. I remember him saying, "See, I'm taking vitamins and

drinking orange juice like you told me." But above all I'd told him to quit drugs. He also gave me a small sculpture; it was touching, but also sad. During that period he spent a lot of time in Hawaii... He said he wanted to try to get clean, but it wasn't easy. In the spring of 1988 he held a huge exhibition at Baghoomian. He contacted all of his old friends for the exhibition, his father, me. He was so glad that we were all there. We all went to dinner together at Mr. Chow. He gave me a poster of the exhibition with the dedication "W/ love." Yet it was patently obvious that he wasn't well... He'd made some paintings that were a premonition of his death, which occurred shortly thereafter. In fact, the most important painting in the exhibition was entitled Man Dies. And then there was Riding with Death, which depicted the skeleton of a horse with a human skeleton riding it, calling Rembrandt to mind.

RL: How did you hear about Jean-Michel's death?

AN: I remember well how I found out he'd died. I was in Ansedonia. Vincent Gallo called me one day...

RL: Oh, Vincent Gallo. I wrote a text for his exhibition at your gallery in 1985. At that time, before he embarked on his career as a filmmaker and an actor, he was an artist and, as such, quite tuned in to art-world issues.

AN: Him specifically, Vincent. That August, having uncharacteristically remained in New York, he called me and said, "I have to give you some very sad news," and he told me that he'd gotten a phone call from Jean-Michel. "He probably couldn't reach anyone else and so he had to talk to me," he said. The two of them had known each other since they'd collaborated on the experimental band Gray. So Vincent had gone to pick up Jean-Michel and he'd driven him around the city in his car to help him pass the

Invitation card for the *Memorial Exhibition* that Annina dedicated to Jean-Michel Basquiat after his death.

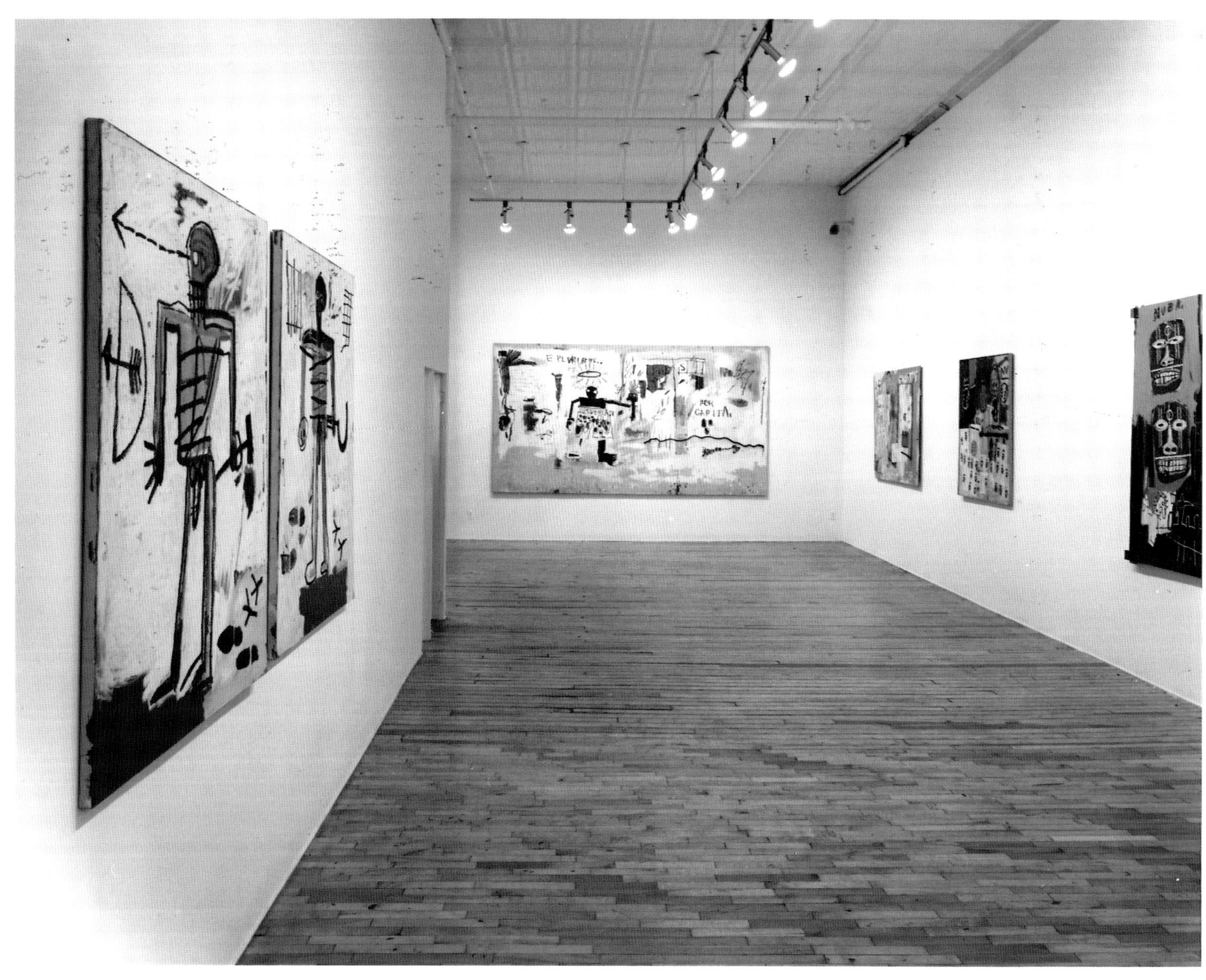

TWO INSTALLATION VIEWS OF THE MEMORIAL EXHIBITION THAT
ANNINA DEDICATED TO JEAN-MICHEL BASQUIAT AFTER HIS DEATH.
ANNINA NOSEI GALLERY, NEW YORK,
DECEMBER 1988

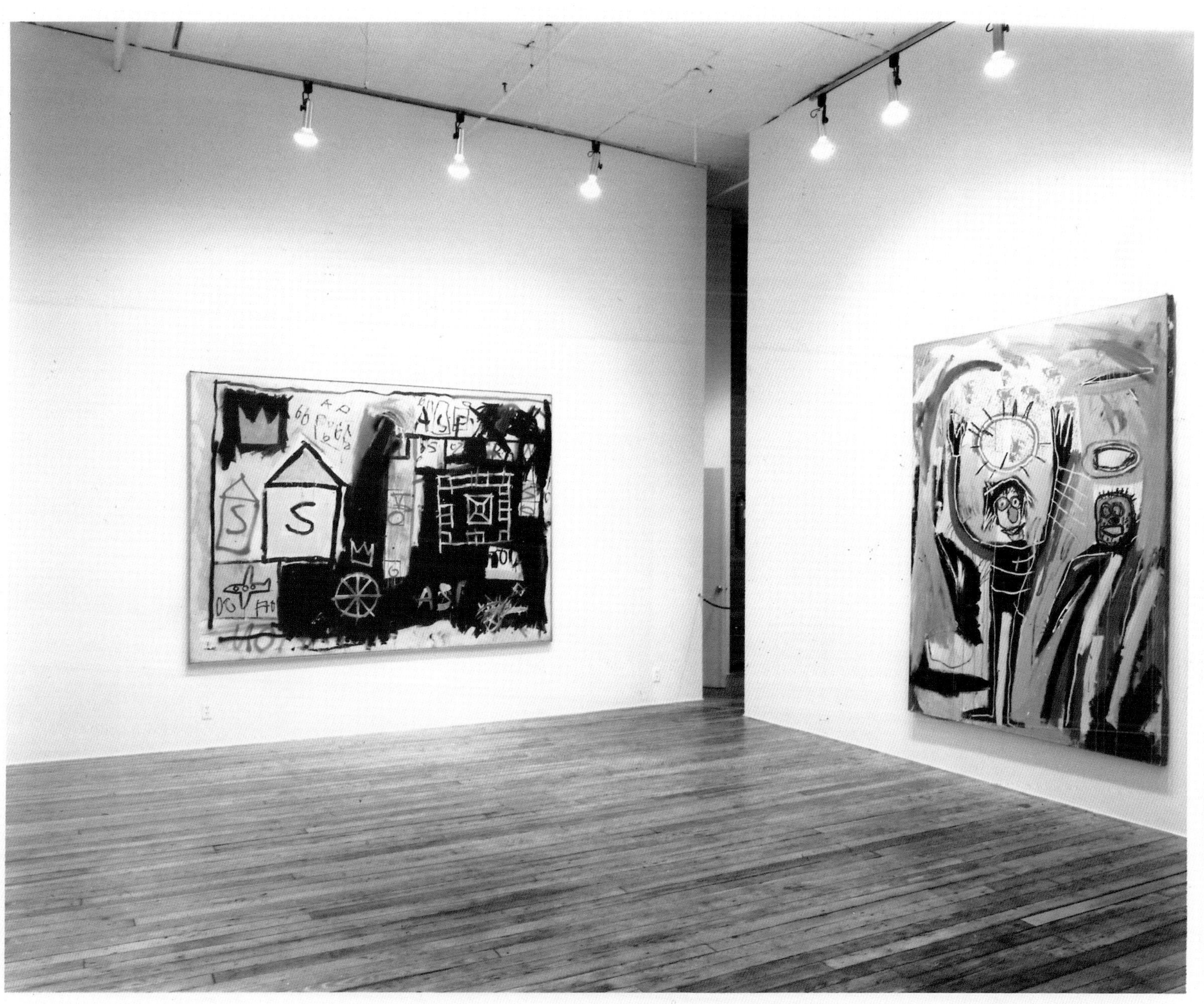

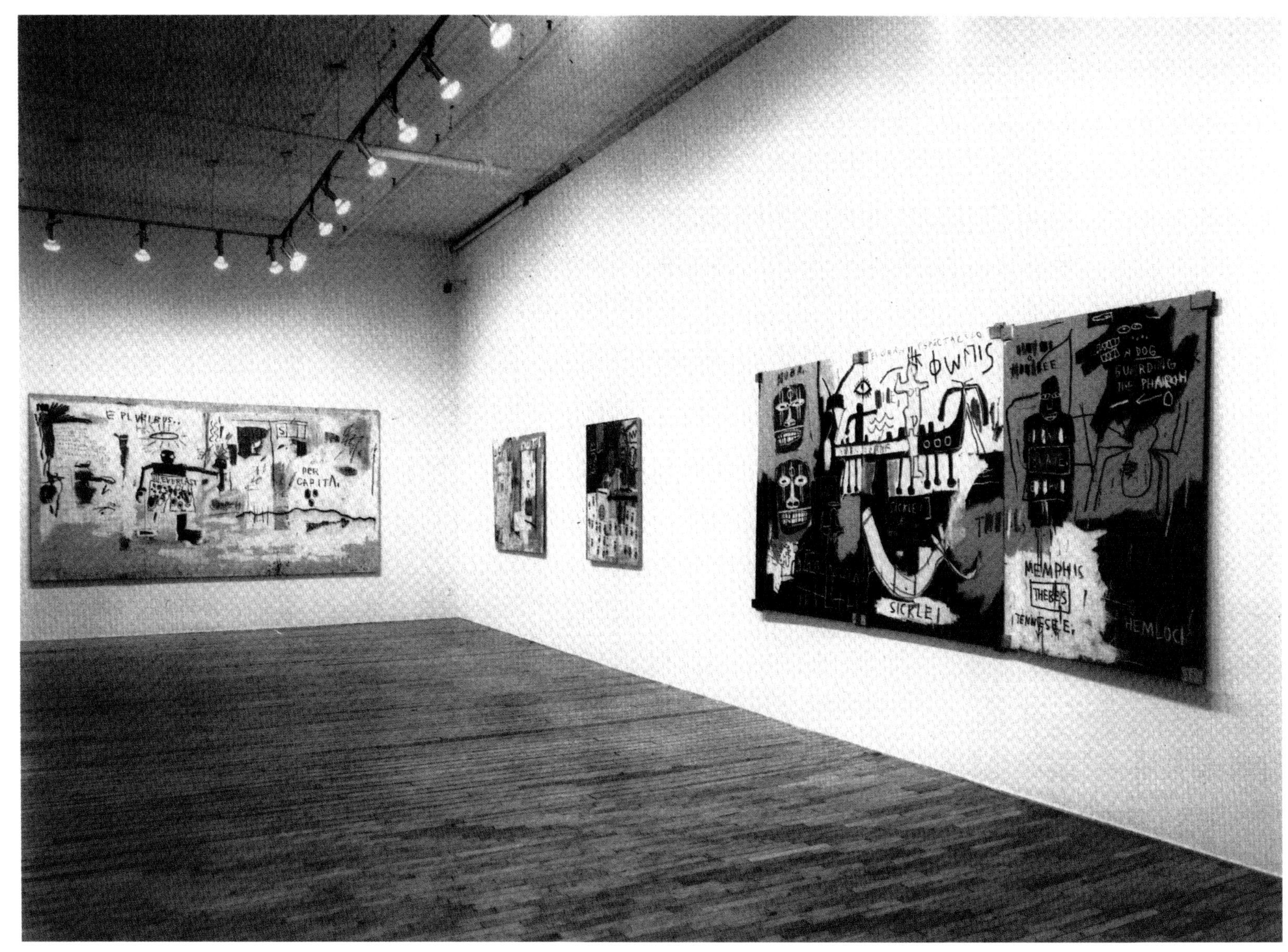

INSTALLATION VIEW OF THE MEMORIAL EXHIBITION THAT
ANNINA DEDICATED TO JEAN-MICHEL BASQUIAT AFTER HIS DEATH.
ANNINA NOSEI GALLERY, NEW YORK
DECEMBER 1988

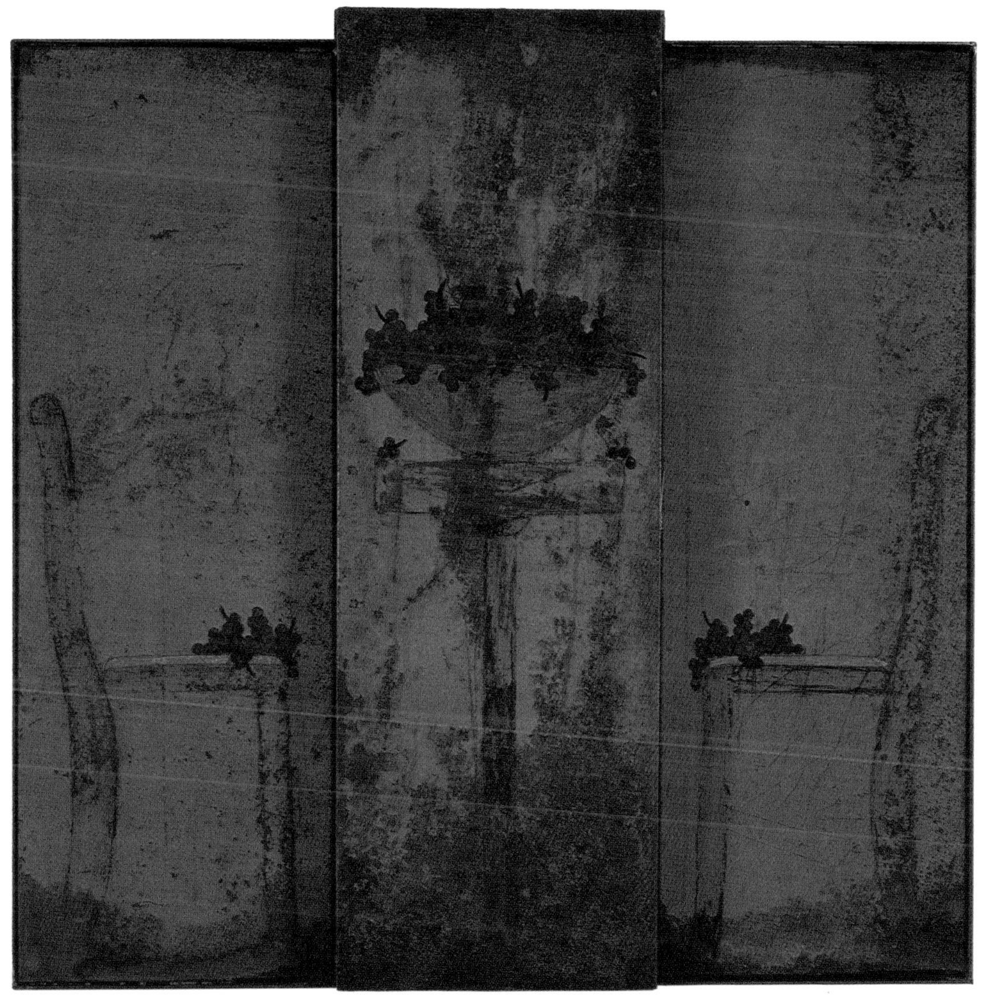

VINCENT GALLO, *NO MORE PAPA AND MAMA*, 1983
ANNINA NOSEI GALLERY, NEW YORK

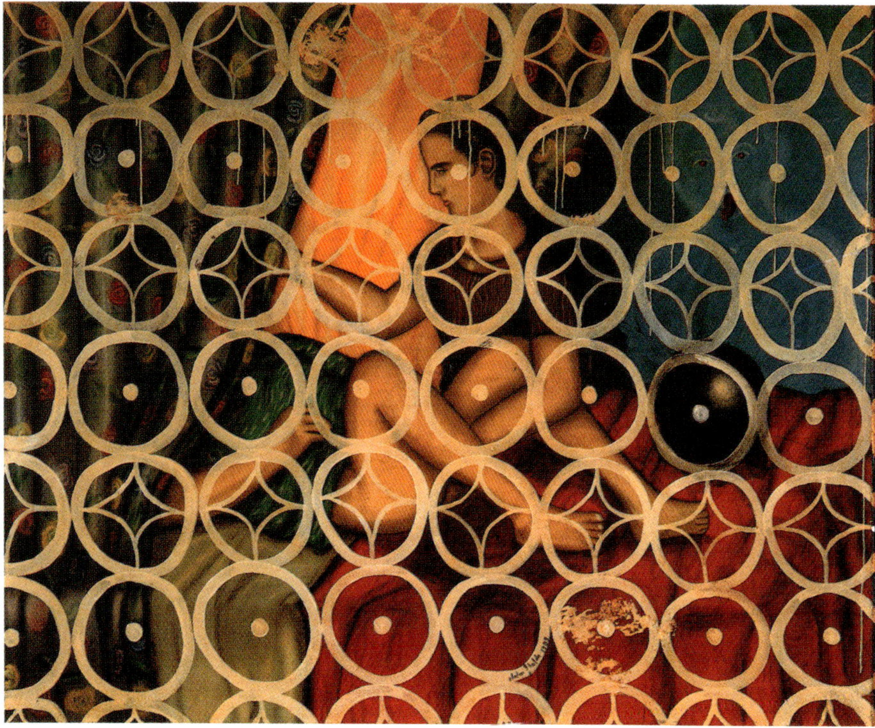

day. He went on to say, "I talked to him about life, I told him to give up the drugs, to think about beautiful women, about beautiful things, about places and travelling. So on and so on, all day." Vincent was very fond of cars, so much so that the first time he came to pick me up he'd showed up in a Lamborghini. My secretary had been amazed. Vincent liked cars and so did I. Then he told me that he'd brought him home late: "I was tired, it was time to go to sleep and I was sure that Jean-Michel would go to sleep too, after that entire beautiful day spent together. And so I left. I'm so sorry Annina" – he went on – "but it looks like he went back out again in the night, bought who knows what and took it. He died that same night." I was speechless, but alas I'd been expecting it.

RL: We've jumped a long way ahead in the story. Let's go back to the early years, to the gallery's launch in 1980...

AN: Yes, I opened the gallery at 100 Prince Street with a group exhibition, where there were also Italian artists, including Mimmo Paladino, as I told you.

RL: You launched the gallery while still teaching at the School of Visual Arts. Was there a connection between these two activities? Did you include any former students in your lineup?

AN: Not many. I only invited Clegg & Guttmann, who'd been my students, to a double solo exhibition with Lynn Hershman in February of 1981. And one of my best students, Joe La Placa, was my assistant in the gallery for a time – he arrived just around the time when Basquiat was working in the basement. Joe took care of attending to Basquiat, of listening to him, of providing everything he needed. It seems to me that he was also there that time in Chia's studio.

Julio Galán, *El encantamiento 3*, 1989
Annina Nosei Gallery, New York.

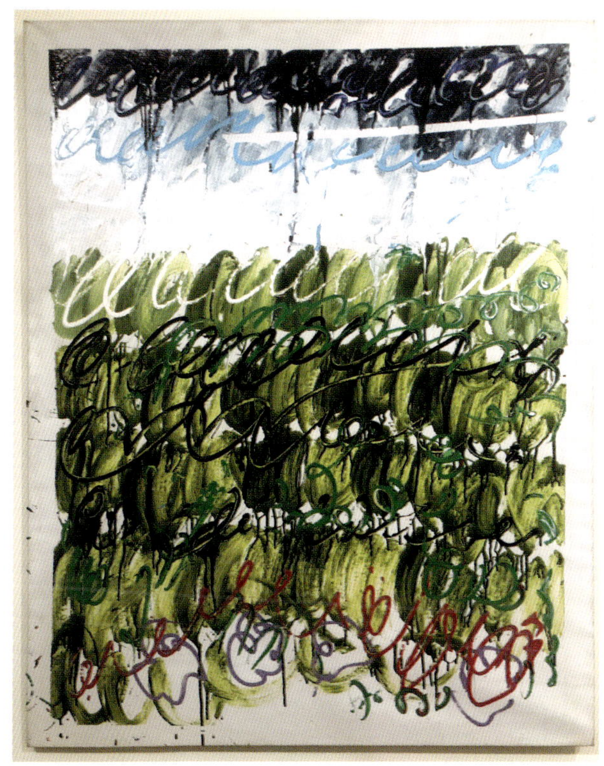

Mario Schifano, *Orto botanico*, 1982.
Annina Nosei Gallery, New York.

And one time, instead of teaching in the classroom, I had my students come to the gallery and the lesson was held by my accountant. He was very interested in art and John Weber had introduced us. He talked to the students about the difference between being really interested in art rather than just in the business of it. He was a real enthusiast, so he accepted works in payment for keeping my accounts. Once, for example, he took three works by Franco Angeli that he liked very much. Kenny Scharf was my student as well, but I never showed him. I remember that he had a show with Shafrazi at the time.

RL: On another occasion you spoke to me with enthusiasm about the exhibitions that you'd dedicated to Mario Schifano and Julio Galán. You enjoyed their paintings a lot.

AN: Yes, I think those were the two truly great exhibitions of painting that I held.

RL: Let's talk about Schifano.

AN: I organized an exhibition for Mario Schifano in January of 1983. He'd been famous since the 1960s and was considered something of an Italian Andy Warhol. Ileana Sonnabend had gone to Rome to meet him right at the beginning of that decade with the intention of organizing an exhibition, but their negotiations had gone nowhere. I think Ileana had been convinced that Schifano would offer her those fantastic abstract paintings that he'd been producing in those years; but he'd presented her with other works, inspired by the blending of materials like plastic and photographs. Ileana had probably been quite disappointed, but the fact remains that the exhibition in New York fell through. Anyway, I was in Italy in the spring of 1982 and I asked Mario Schifano if he wanted to show in

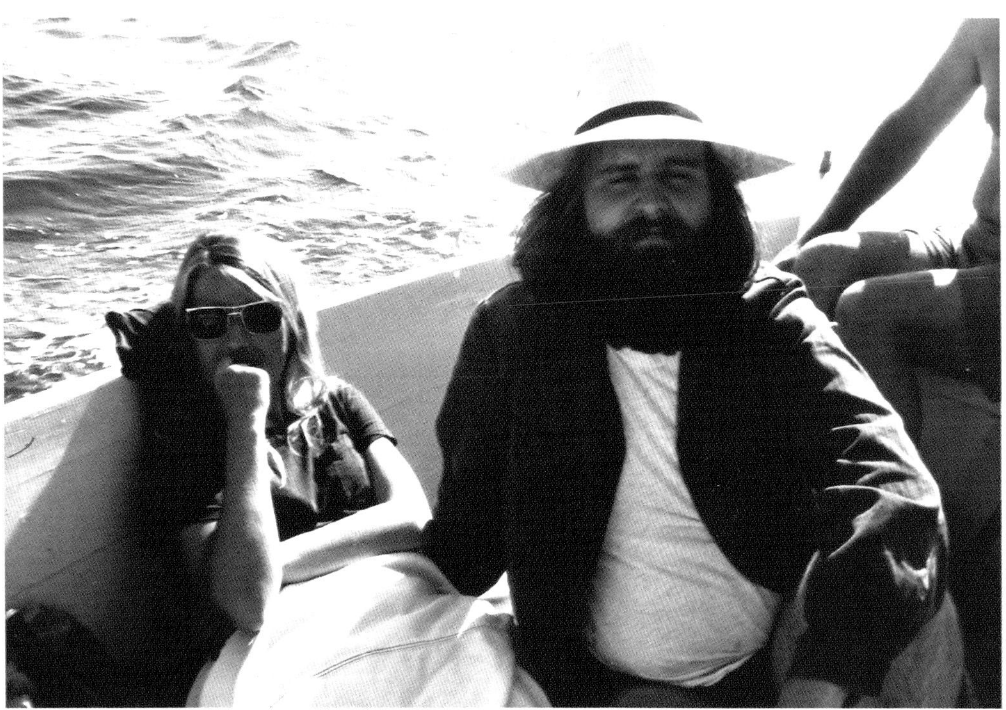

my gallery. He rented a house in Ansedonia, not too far from mine, and he produced a lot of paintings, many of them inspired by the botanical gardens located near his studio in Rome. He worked on those paintings all summer or even into early autumn. I stayed longer in Ansedonia that year too because I'd had a car accident, and he was a great support: he constantly sent his doctor to visit me and his assistant came over with lunch. Then when I returned to New York in the fall, just as I was about to begin installing the show, I heard that Schifano had been arrested at a gas station for drug possession and was being held in Frosinone prison. It was his partner who sent me all of his works, and so I curated the exhibition by myself. Ileana Sonnabend was immediately very interested in the exhibition and we went to lunch together, over which we also talked about the time she'd spent in Rome in the sixties.

The exhibition was a success: I sold all the pieces except one from the *Botanical Gardens* series that I kept for myself. I remember that on the day of the opening I received a phone call from Schifano directly from prison. I told him about the great success at the opening and he was delighted. He told me that he'd become very good friends with the warden and he'd even painted his portrait! When I asked him what the food was like, he replied, "Annina, I'm in Frosinone. The food here's delicious even in prison!"

RL: The villa in Ansedonia often resurfaces in your stories.

AN: Yes, because many artists have passed through that Tuscan house of mine; before, during and after my marriage to John Weber. Many were friends of John, such as Walter De Maria, Sol LeWitt, or Carl Andre; many others were artists who'd shown in my gallery. Sandro Chia and Franco Angeli also stayed there and they actually paid their rent with paintings – the same ones that the accountant I mentioned earlier took for himself. Sabina Mirri also stayed at my home in Tuscany for a long time. Among

Carl Andre and a friend boating in Ansedonia, late 1960s.

the many people who passed through Ansedonia, I remember Karel
Appel with particular pleasure. We'd met in New York, where I'd curated
an exhibition of his in the gallery in 1984, a solo exhibition, and I'd also
invited him to participate in the group exhibition *The Door* in 1985, which
I'd like to tell you about. We'd become friends right away: myself, Karel,
and his wife Henriette. I think he was interested in my gallery because I
exhibited Jean-Michel Basquiat. One summer Karel and his wife arrived
in Ansedonia in a white Rolls-Royce. I was quite surprised by that visit: I'd
taken particular interest in his work over the course of that year, in the
production of CoBrA, and I'd even talked about it with Jean-Michel. Then
some time ago, in 2013, in the catalogue for an auction at Farsetti in Prato,
I saw a painting by Asger Jorn that had been valued at between 65 and
95,000 euros and which bore a strong resemblance to a Basquiat painting
from 1982, *Dust Heads*, which had been auctioned by Christie's, also in
2013, with an asking price of 25-35 million dollars, but which then sold
for 47 million dollars. The connection between the two works is blatantly
apparent: the white brushstrokes in the center, the two heads... When I'd
spoken to Basquiat about CoBrA I'd shown him that exact Asger Jorn.

RL: You talk often about your country house in Hudson, too.

AN: Yes, because I like it a lot. I bought it in the early nineties. Actually,
I'll tell you how it happened. One day I was the guest of some friends
in the countryside and I got a call from John Weber. He begged me to
come over because he'd hit his head while he was lighting the fireplace
and he'd hurt himself. So I left my friends and headed over to him. While
we were there, he told me that he'd made an appointment with an agent
for the next day to go and see a house in a nice area and suggested that
I purchase it. I told him that I had no intention of buying a house in the
country, but I liked the idea of going to see this place that he was talking

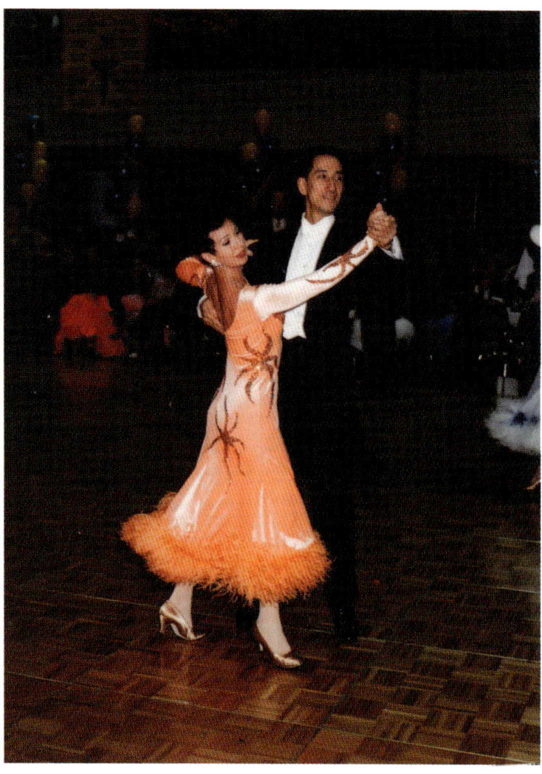

about so enthusiastically. We went to see it the next day and I liked the place immediately; it also had a paddock out front, which, since I was horseback rider, made it even more appealing to me. So I suggested to the agent that I leave him a deposit and, since I had to go to the FIAC in Paris shortly thereafter, I told him that I'd give him a definitive answer when I got back. The fair went very well and so, returning from Paris, after balancing the sales and expenses I realized that I had exactly the right amount of money left over to buy the house – down to the dollar – and so I bought it.

A few years later, it must have been in 1994, Irving Blum stayed as my guest in order to visit Ellsworth Kelly's studio nearby in Chatham, Columbia County. When I returned from a long ride on horseback, very tired, he said to me, "Annina, you look overwhelmed. At your age, with your personality, you're likely to fall off the horse one of these days and end up like that actor who found himself living in a wheelchair. Find yourself another sport." I thought it over and realized he was right.

RL: So what did you decide to do with your free time?

AN: By pure chance I found an advertisement at home for free dance lessons at Fred Astaire's studio. I decided to go and they happened to pair me with an excellent dancer, Darius Mosteika, who was Lithuanian champion. After some weeks, Darius invited me to go with him and his wife, who was also a superb dancer, to a dance competition in New Orleans; another pair of Russian champs and a pupil of theirs would be coming with us as well. I won a competition, but most importantly I discovered that this pupil of theirs was a designer, who then bought several works from me. Not only that, but at their dance lessons I also met a rich Russian lady who then started coming to the gallery and buying works. She especially enjoyed those of Stephen Mueller.

Annina at a dance competition.

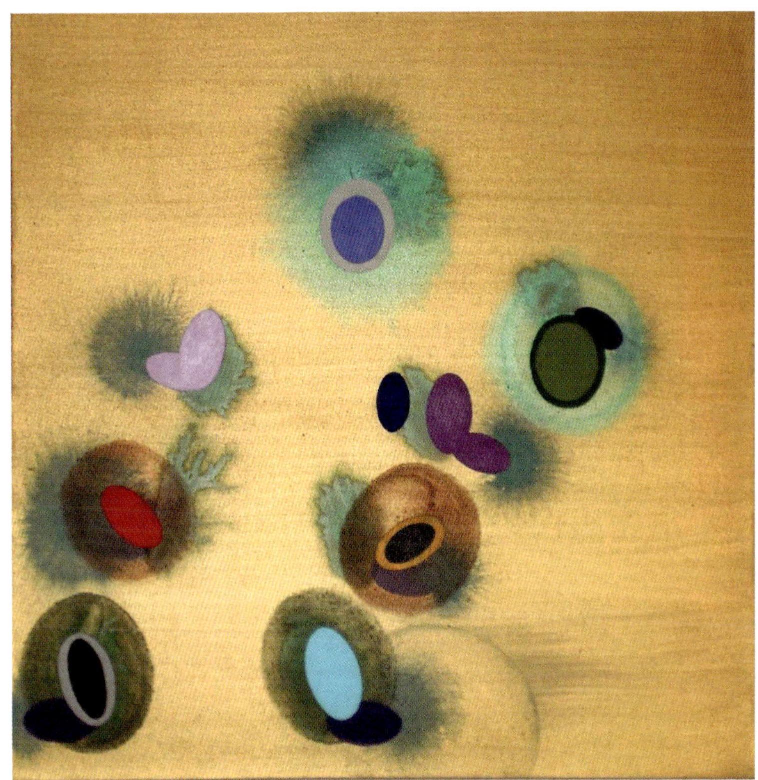

RL: An excellent painter, his work was very interesting but difficult too. I wrote a text for one of his exhibitions at your gallery as well, more or less around the same time as Vincent Gallo's.

AN: Yes, I told myself that I'd found just the right place. I continued dancing for years after that. Some afternoons after leaving the gallery I attended sport dance studios and took lessons with professionals. I mainly studied International Style dancing. I've still got some particularly beautiful dresses that I used for competitions. I had them made by Centini, a famous tailor in Acilia, near Rome.
Over time I won several awards. I received the most important ones, at a world-class level, in 2011 and 2012 while paired with a Ukrainian dancer, Nazar Batih. The last time I danced in Italy, I met Mirko Selli, a great Italian champion who's won a lot of international competitions with his sister Marika. Mirko once proposed that we enter an important international competition in Riccione. We trained, we went and we won. But not as Italians, unfortunately, because I was living in the United States and Mirko was working in Hong Kong... anyway, I've got heaps of photographs – I've done a lot of things in the world of dance.

RL: But this is a whole other, lovely story, Annina, another life, another book. Let's pick up the threads of our discussion on art. Earlier you mentioned the group show *The Door*.

AN: Well, in 1985 I organized an exhibition called *The Door*. In its catalogue, I explained the important metaphorical connotations of the word "door," which coincides with the way that art works in its closing and opening, amplifying the scope of communication and permitting an extension of language. Among the various artists who made their works available for that exhibition – Tàpies, Rauschenberg, Appel, LeWitt (who worked on

Stephen Mueller, *Untitled (Chi Stories)*,
Annina Nosei Gallery, New York.

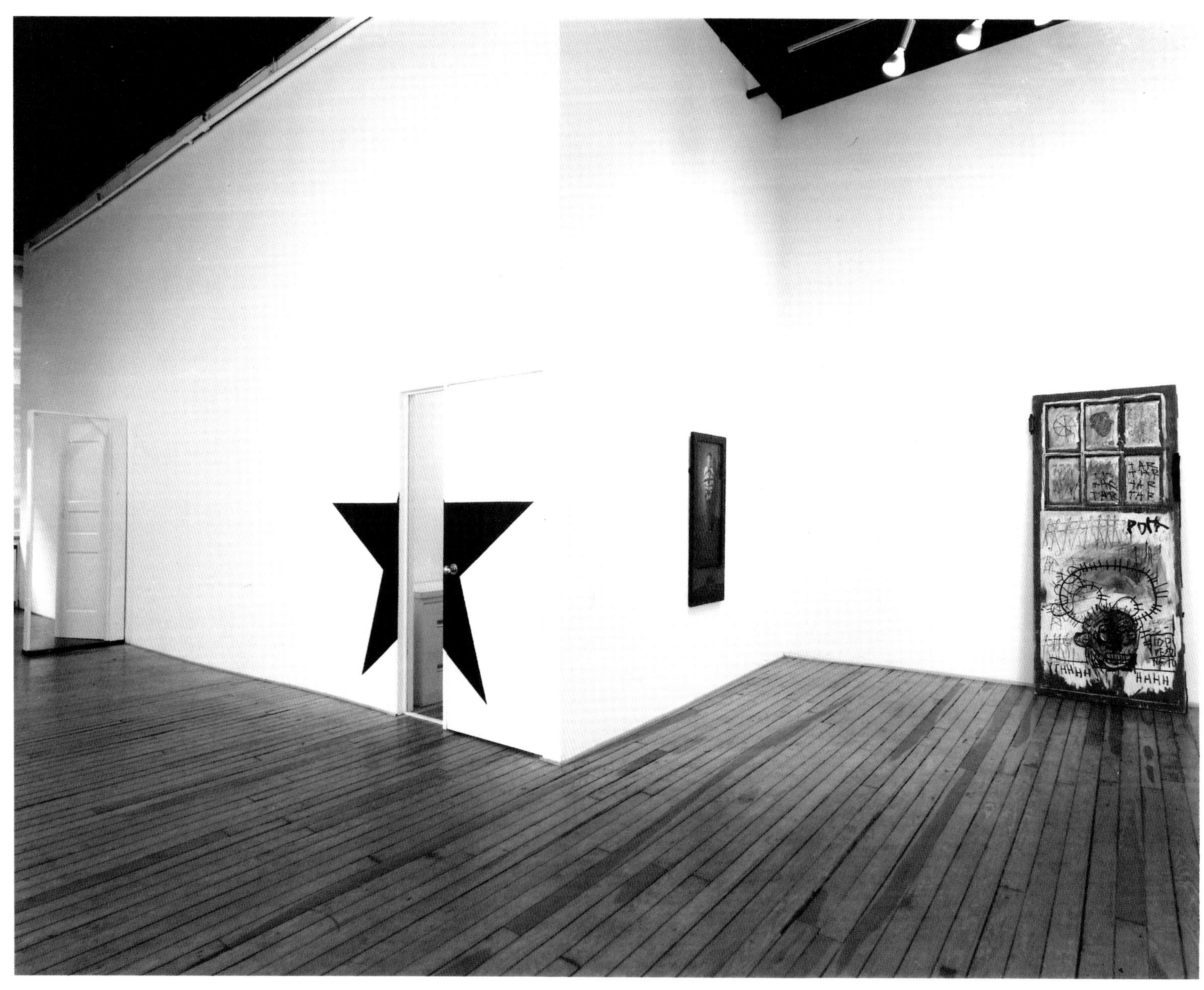

INSTALLATION VIEW OF *THE DOOR*
FROM LEFT: WORKS BY MIKE BIDLO, SOL LEWITT,
CHUCK CONNELLY, JEAN-MICHEL BASQUIAT,
ANNINA NOSEI GALLERY, NEW YORK, 1985

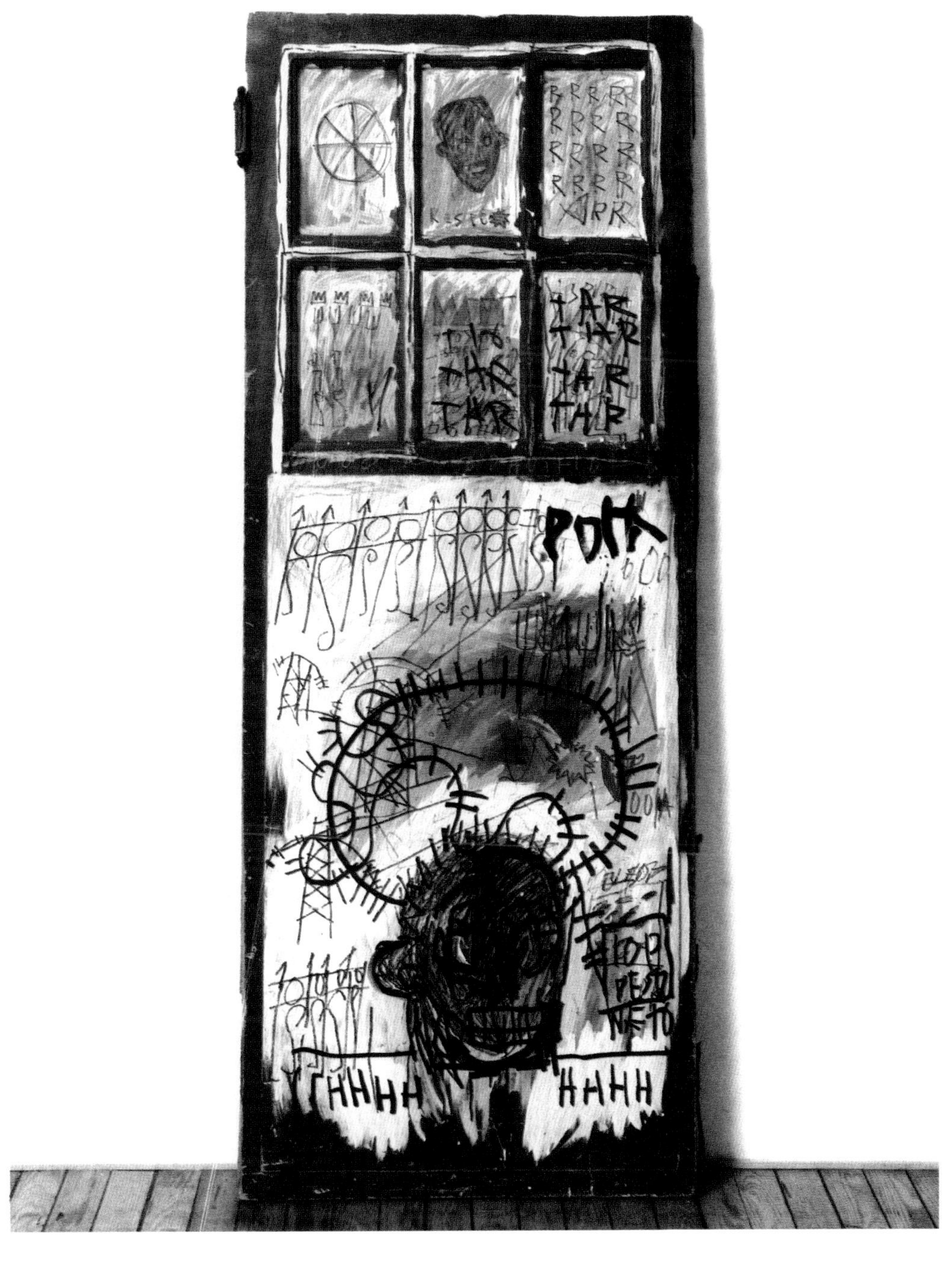

JEAN-MICHEL BASQUIAT, *PORK*, 1981,
INSTALLATION VIEW OF *THE DOOR*,
ANNINA NOSEI GALLERY, NEW YORK, 1985

the office door), Vincent Gallo, Schnabel, Pizzi Cannella – there was also Mike Bidlo, an artist who I've always found particularly interesting. I've admired his work a lot, but I've never organized a solo exhibition with him. I particularly like his Pollocks and I had one at home, but unfortunately I sold it to a collector in Milan. Another work of his that I particularly like is the copy of a sculpture by Brancusi, which I have in my apartment. Bidlo would reappropriate works by artists like Duchamp, Pollock, and Picasso, producing a displacement between the original and the copy. His contribution to the exhibition *The Door* was a reproduction of Duchamp's famous 11 rue Larrey, which simultaneously served the double function of opening and closing; it opened one room while closing another and vice versa in a conjunction of opposites. With his "false authorship," Bidlo establishes the conjunction of the authentic work and the copy. His work lies precisely in the conjunction of fake and original.

RL: Let's talk a little bit more about the eighties. So many things were happening at the beginning of that decade, it was like being trampled by a new enthusiasm.

AN: I'll tell you another story. Once while I was in the gallery in New York, Lucio Amelio came directly from Naples to urge me to go and meet an artist.

RL: You already knew Amelio, of course?

AN: Yes, since the 1960s. It was 1966, the Fulbright regulations required that you return to your home university after two years, but I'd decided to stay in the USA and I needed a visa. For a series of reasons they granted it to me immediately, but I had to go and pick it up from Naples. I went to Italy with John Weber. It was the summer before the wedding and we

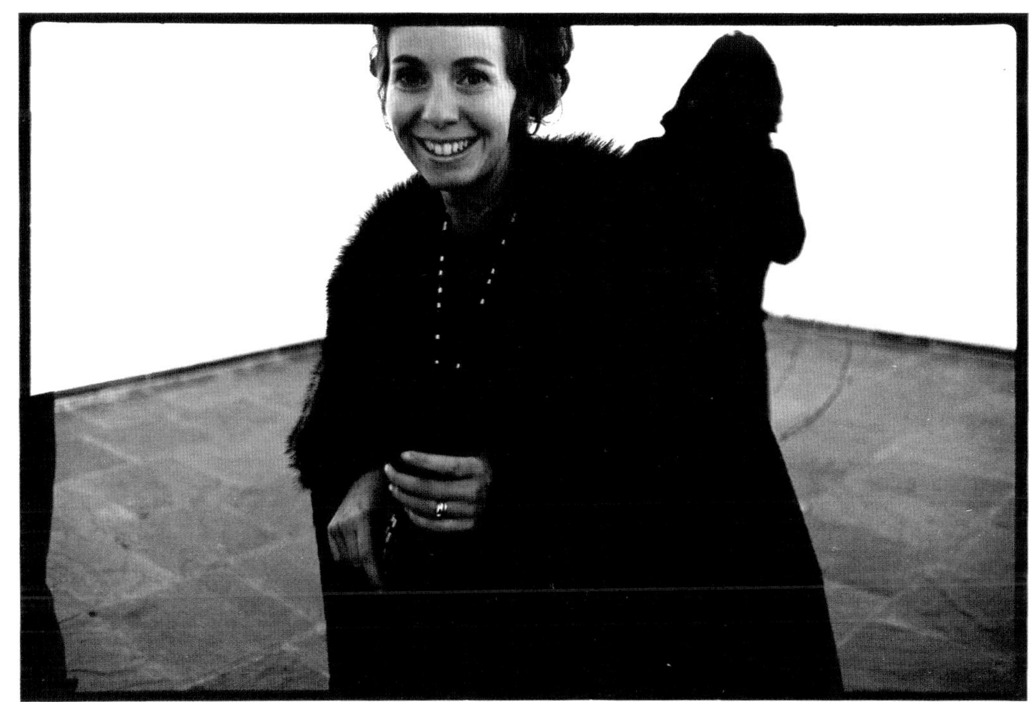

Annina in the 1980s.

went to Naples together. It was on that occasion that we visited Amelio's gallery. I'd then run into him many other times over the years after that. I met Paladino through him and I saw the works of Anselm Kiefer for the first time at his stand at Art Basel. I bought them immediately, before everyone else, and sold them immediately afterwards, unfortunately… That time at the gallery in New York, he asked me if I'd go to Edward Brezinski's studio on the Lower East Side, because Brezinski absolutely wanted to meet me. So I went and it was a disaster: the place, the poverty of this young man who was also a bit strange, with these little paintings all over the place. The only thing I wanted was to get away, but he expected me to be interested in his work and when he realized that I wanted to leave he became even more upset. So, to avoid his feeling too badly, I said to him, "Why don't you loan me a small painting of yours? I'll take it to the gallery." At that point, instead of calming down, he asked me if I'd be coming back to his studio again. I didn't want to come back, but seeing as he was so insistent I told him I'd be back in April, thinking that date would never come. "When?" he asked me. "On the 14th," I replied. A few days later, Brezinski showed up at the gallery with an invitation to an exhibition by Nino Longobardi, an artist who worked with Lucio Amelio. It was the image of a painting of a coffee shop and a skull, very similar to the painting he himself had given me. And he says to me, "I'm going to the gallery and I'm going to kill them all. I'm going to kill Lucio Amelio and the rest of them." I told him, "Calm down. I'll give you 500 dollars, I'll buy the painting from you, but you go home, relax, and don't kill anyone." But then April 14th arrived and Brezinski called me and asked me to come to the studio. "It's April 14th, you said you'd come." He caught me by surprise and I answered that I wasn't coming, then I hung up. A few weeks later I went to the Kenny Scharf exhibition at Shafrazi's gallery. He'd been one of my students, as I said. The paintings on show weren't very large, yet they cost around 15,000 and 20,000 dollars. I couldn't believe it. Anyway,

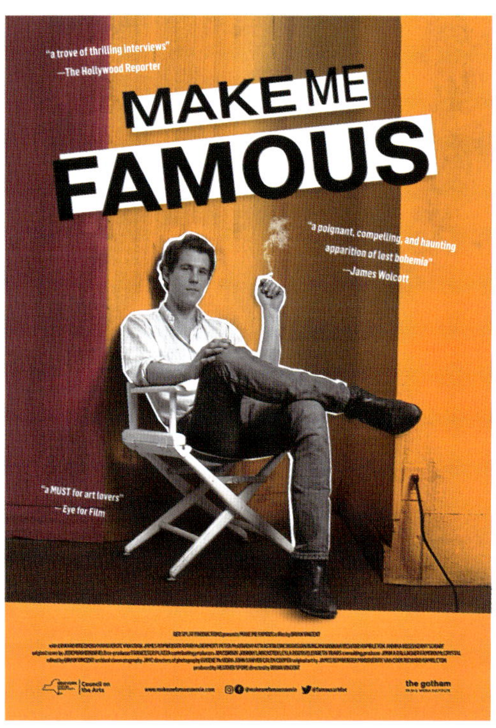

I turned around and amongst the many people there I saw Brezinski with a glass of wine in his hand. He came toward me and threw the wine in my face. I understood the reason for it, I didn't react, and I left. The next day, Milton Esterow, director of the magazine *ARTnews*, invited me to lunch and, while talking about the state of things, I said to him, "Look what's happening in these eighties." I told him about the Kenny Scharf exhibition, my ex-student who was nothing special, who was racking up $15,000-20,000 while poor Brezinski got nothing. "What's the difference between the two? The other night he threw wine in my face" – I explain to him – "and I can understand him, the poor guy. I went to his studio and nothing happened for him and this other character earns all that money." The next day, Milton Esterow did a nice editorial on the story and mentioned my name, Brezinski's, etc. After a little more time had gone by, a strange man came into the gallery saying he absolutely had to meet me. He claimed to be the psychiatrist who was treating Brezinski and he'd come to tell me that Brezinski wanted to kill me. But I told him, "He won't kill me, I bought one of his paintings." "No, no," he insists, "he's dangerous, he even stole money." I asked him to leave, because he hadn't stolen anything from me and I didn't want to hear any more stories about that poor kid. If anything, it was this gentleman who was doing the stealing by taking money for keeping him in psychiatric treatment when that young man didn't have a penny. Then I reflected on the matter: did he want to kill me? So I called the police. I explained the situation and the policeman replied, "Madam, excuse me, I'm very busy, call me when he kills you." At that point I asked my neighbor and friend Mick Jones, who was interested in art and to whom I'd also sold some paintings, if I could use his security guard (he was a member of the band Foreigner). I explained the situation to him and he agreed, but the cost was $350 a day and so I decided to wait a while to understand the situation better. A few days later they called me from Leo Castelli's gallery to invite me to a special, very private party. I

Poster and scene from the film *Make Me Famous.*

called them the next day to find out if I could bring along the director of the Galleria Nazionale d'Arte Moderna in Rome, who was in New York, but they answered that I couldn't because the party was really very restricted. The day of the party arrived, I got myself all dolled up and I left the gallery and headed to the party on Green Street at around 6 pm. And along the way, who do I see coming towards me? Brezinski. Oh my God, I thought, he wants to kill me. So as he comes closer I say to him, "Brezinski, how nice to see you!" I took him by the arm and told him to come with me to a very special party at Leo Castelli's. The first person I see on entering is Larry Aldrich, the director of the Connecticut Museum. A rather elderly man, and Brezinski was very courteous. "Aldrich, let me introduce you to this very good artist: Brezinski." I introduced them and walked away. And that's the end of the story.
Actually, not quite the end. The finale is that Brezinski had an exhibition in The Aldrich Museum in Connecticut a few months later. Those were the 1980s.

RL: Very entertaining. I recognize the spirit of those years entirely. Brezinski's story certainly didn't end with that exhibition. The NewFest film festival in New York recently premiered the film *Make Me Famous*, which tells his quite tragic story as an artist who never won any great success despite circulating among the artists of the Lower East Side during an era in which it seemed everybody could have their proverbial fifteen minutes of fame. That too was a reality of the eighties. It was such an effervescent era, during which, for the first time in avant-garde history, an artist could happen to make a lot of money quickly. It was an era full of oddities.

AN: Speaking of which, let me tell you another story. Last year, in 2020, I decided to go to Cartier on 5th Avenue to replace the battery in my Panthère watch. It's got to be replaced every five years, more or less. The

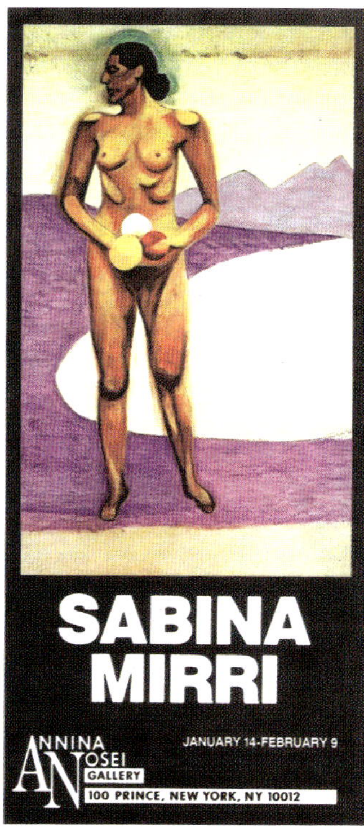

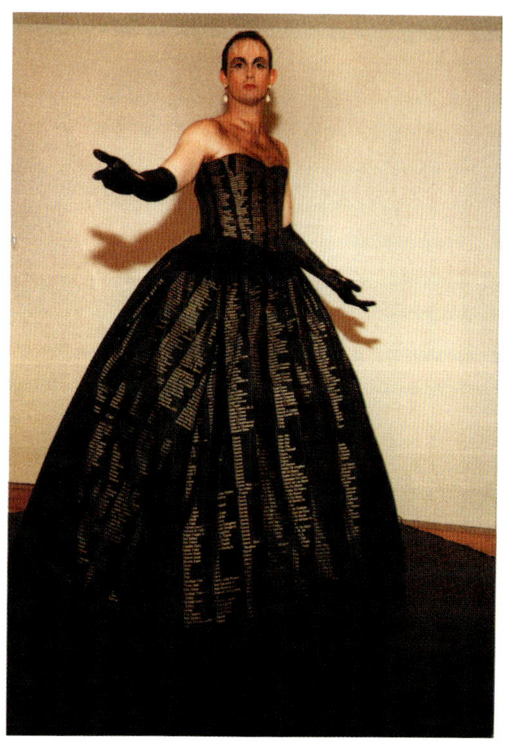

last time I'd done it had been in 2015. I scheduled an appointment and I went. Seeing 5th Avenue completely deserted and the shops closed was striking: it called World War Two to mind and I thought that maybe the Third had begun.

I'd bought the watch in Paris in 1985, as it says on the receipt, which I still have. Over that period I'd given Sabina Mirri the use of my apartment in Via Flaminia, but whenever I returned to Rome I still stayed there regardless. The living room had become her study. Her great friend Gino De Dominicis was often with us. Once we decided to go to Paris together, but Gino didn't take planes and so we went by train. It was during that trip that I decided to buy a Cartier watch, a purchase that was important to me. When we arrived in Paris, we went to Cartier together and I bought it. Back at the hotel, we arranged to meet at noon the following day at a famous café, Les Deux Magots. The next morning I realized that the watch I'd bought wasn't what I wanted. It was a round-faced watch when I wanted a Panthère, a square-faced watch. So first I went to change it and then I went to the midday appointment. We sat down for breakfast and Gino asked me if I was happy with the watch and I told him that I'd replaced it with a Panthère, a square-faced watch. Gino started abruptly in his chair and said to me, "Are you crazy? What've you done? You'll never be able to read the minutes, the hand'll never make it around the corners." But then again, Gino De Dominicis always had a very particular relationship with squares. His famous video *Tentativo di formare quadrati invece di cerchi attorno a una pietra che cade nell'acqua* (Attempt to Form Squares Instead of Circles around a Stone Falling in Water) from 1969 shows him throwing stones into the water for the entire duration in an attempt to form squares instead of circles, which is of course impossible. To Gino, it represented proof of the impossibility of forming squares. The first time he showed it to me, he said to me, "See? You can't create squares, but only and exclusively circles."

A flyer for Sabina Mirri exhibition and Hunter Reynolds aka Patina du Prey, Annina's assistant, early 1990s.

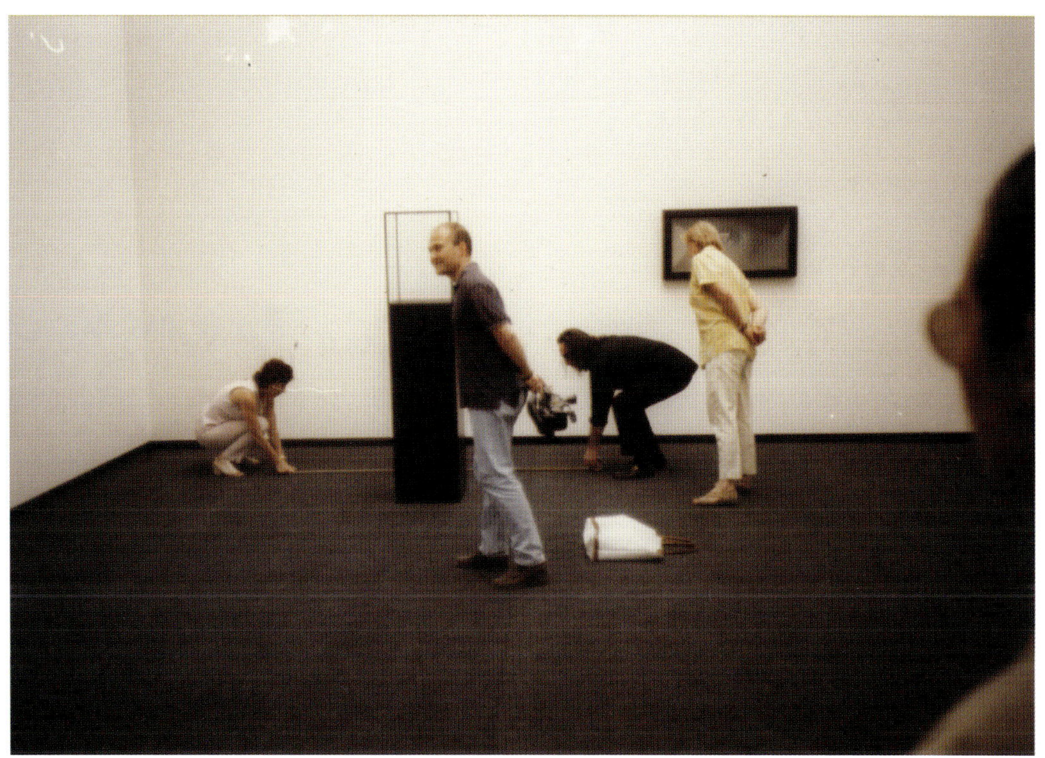

Annina and Gino De Dominicis place a square on the floor around the artist's work during the preview of the Venice Biennale, 1990.

RL: Now that you mention it, I don't know if his was really an aversion to squares. But if so, he also had an aversion toward cubes – I'm reminded of the invisible cube reduced to a square marked on the ground.

AN: Well, continuing to meditate on squares, I recall another episode, linked to one of his works exhibited at the Venice Biennale, I don't remember exactly in which edition. The work consisted of a glass cube with another cube inside it. A work that had something incredible about it, with the second cube floating within the first. I visited the Biennale before it was open to the public. Rosma Scuteri was with me and we went with Gino to see his space. Gino got furious over the fact that the installation had been set up in such a way as people could touch it. A girl, the room attendant, was on the verge of tears, so I told Gino to calm down. I asked a clerk for some duct tape and I laid it on the floor around the cube so that people would understand that it wasn't possible to go beyond that point and therefore wouldn't get too close to the cube. I traced a square, but that time Gino was very happy with it.

RL: The oddities that we talked about with regard to the 1980s stemmed in large part from the attitudes of the artists of the previous generation. Remember when we worked toward a book project on Chuck Connelly?

AN: Of course I remember. By mentioning Connelly, you remind me of an episode involving both him and my assistant at the time, Hunter Reynolds. I don't know if I've ever told you about him. Hunter was an artist who used the stage name Patina du Prey, but I wasn't aware of that artistic dimension to him, of Patina du Prey. With those very elegant women's dresses, he slipped into a fantastic character. Performing as Patina du Prey was his job. Over all the time that he worked in the gallery, he never told me. He was a very tall, muscular man, and from his looks you certainly wouldn't

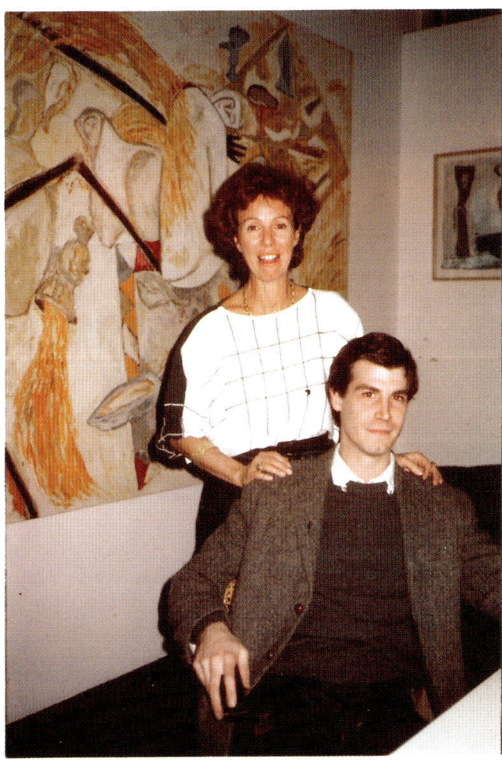

have said that he was also very sensitive.

In the same year that I wanted to publish the book on Chuck Connelly, I'd already photographed many of his works and you'd already outlined the book's structure as well. Chuck was a very difficult artist, probably partly due to his struggle with alcohol. One day I went to his studio with Hunter to talk about the book and choose some more paintings to photograph. He behaved so badly that I decided I didn't want to have anything to do with him. I realized that working with him was going to be really unpleasant and so we left. But I remained quite struck by the way that Hunter reacted to what had just happened. He was such a big strong man. Everyone in the gallery was frightened every time Chuck Connelly showed up, except for him. But as we came out of his studio that day, Hunter, that big, tough guy, began to cry. He'd been really hurt by the artist's behavior.

RL: Did you go to Connelly's studio often?

AN: No, I never actually returned there. But while talking with Connelly and looking at his paintings that time, I told him that they reminded me a lot of *The Night of the Hunter* with Robert Mitchum. Chuck said to me, "You're the only one who's understood that that's where I got my inspiration from." That film had obviously inspired a lot of his paintings: more than one painting showed the scene on the river with the boat drifting away and the two children on board. Seeing his paintings and having seen that movie more than once had allowed me to grasp the connection. I've always found his works interesting, above all because they contain ideas and transmit feelings very much like those you get when you're watching a film.

RL: There's an enduring connection between film and visual culture. It's historically determined and inevitable, but in the USA in the 1980s it was even stronger. In relation to what we're talking out, Downtown 81 comes to

Annina with Chuck Connelly,
New York, 1985.

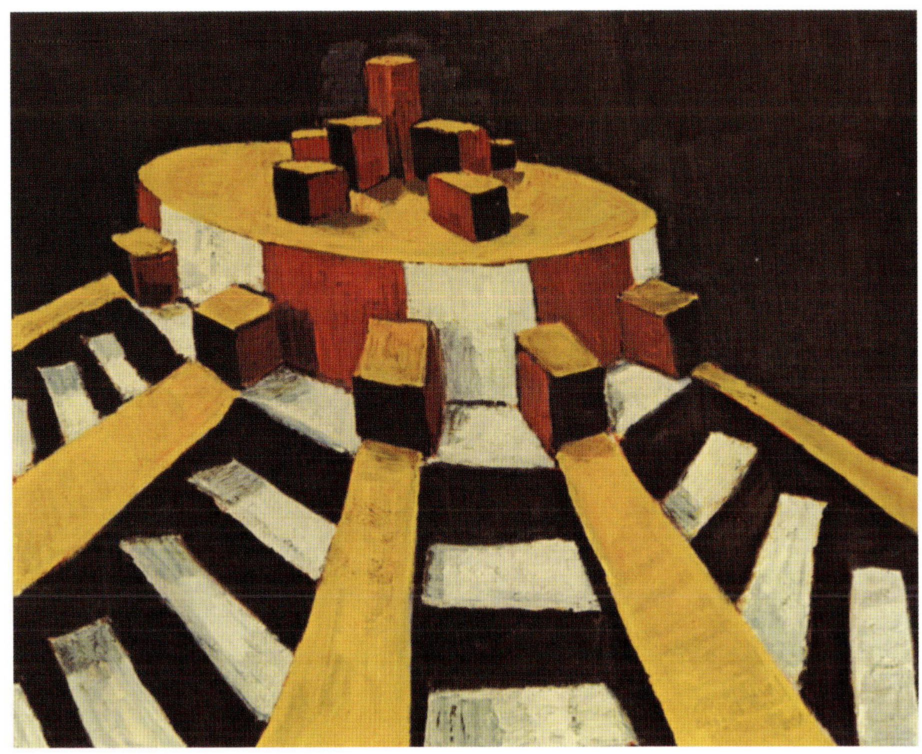

mind, with Basquiat as protagonist. Then we mentioned the documentary on Brezinski and you remembered the Scorsese film inspired by Connelly. A documentary film about him was also released a few years ago, screened at the Los Angeles film festival in 2008. A particular theme emerges from these last two films, that of the always problematic relationship between artists and their careers: Brezinski's failure to succeed and Connelly's noteworthy exit from the market. All told, when the eighties come up, a lot of us often think of money.

AN: Several episodes come to mind in this connection. In 1980, for example, I'd purchased a Julian Schnabel painting from Mary Boone for $2,300. *The Patients and the Doctors*, one of his first paintings with broken plates. Schnabel wasn't yet well known, but I liked his works. In some ways they reminded me of Ossorio. I decided to auction it off at Sotheby's in 1983, asking for a reserve of $60,000. When I told Schnabel that I was selling it, he asked me not to. He cared about that painting and he offered me another one in exchange. I accepted and offered it to Sotheby's, again specifying that I wanted a minimum reserve of $60,000. Anita Reiner bought it for $83,000. In 2017, a work by Basquiat went to auction that I'd sold to collector Phoebe Chasen in the 1980s for around $6,000. Upon her death, her daughters had sold it for $20,000, but it's rumored that the collector who later bought it at the Sotheby's auction paid $110 million for it. Not many years ago, a Jackson Pollock drawing and two Jean-Michel Basquiat drawings went to auction. The Pollock was of great intensity. The two Basquiats came from my gallery. The Pollock went for 2.5 million dollars; my gallery was listed in the provenance of one of the Basquiats, which I'd sold for a few hundred dollars in the 1980s, and it sold for $4.5 million. The other drawing went for 1.5 million dollars. This all makes little sense. Analyzing the paintings from the point of view of artistic worth, there's no comparison between the value of a Pollock

Invitation card to Chuck Connelly's
solo exhibition, Annina Nosei Gallery,
October 1984.

and that of a drawing by Jean-Michel Basquiat.

RL: Often market value doesn't correspond to artistic or historical value. It often happens that the prices of works by the foremost artists of a newer generation are consistently higher than historical ones. But it's difficult to imagine that the market's judgment can be independent of a historical or aesthetic one, or that it can be sustained over time.

AN: Still regarding the market, I could tell you about the Keith Sonnier exhibition that I arranged in the autumn of 1983. It was Leo Castelli who asked me to do it – I was surprised but I accepted. In this sense, too, significant things were happening in terms of the relationship between art and the market. Even though I appreciated Sonnier's neon works very much and the public also liked them, I didn't succeed in selling any. Perhaps that's the reason Castelli offered me the exhibition; he hoped that having him exhibit in my gallery would mean he might infiltrate the younger scene and that somehow the effect of their success could rebound onto him. Anyway, that exhibition was very important to me. I remain a staunch fan of Keith Sonnier, regardless of his success in the market.
That episode reminds me of when Richard Milazzo organized the Salvatore Scarpitta exhibition in my gallery, because he worked with Castelli as well. That time they stole a work of art. You can imagine how angry I got with the gallery assistant. I didn't sell anything from that exhibition, but a piece was stolen!

RL: I know from my own experience that, underneath it all, an artist is happy when one of their paintings is stolen. It's a sign of appreciation in some sense. Paradoxically, we could interpret it as a position, even as a critical act. By the way, returning to the running of your gallery and considering the long succession of exhibitions that you've organized,

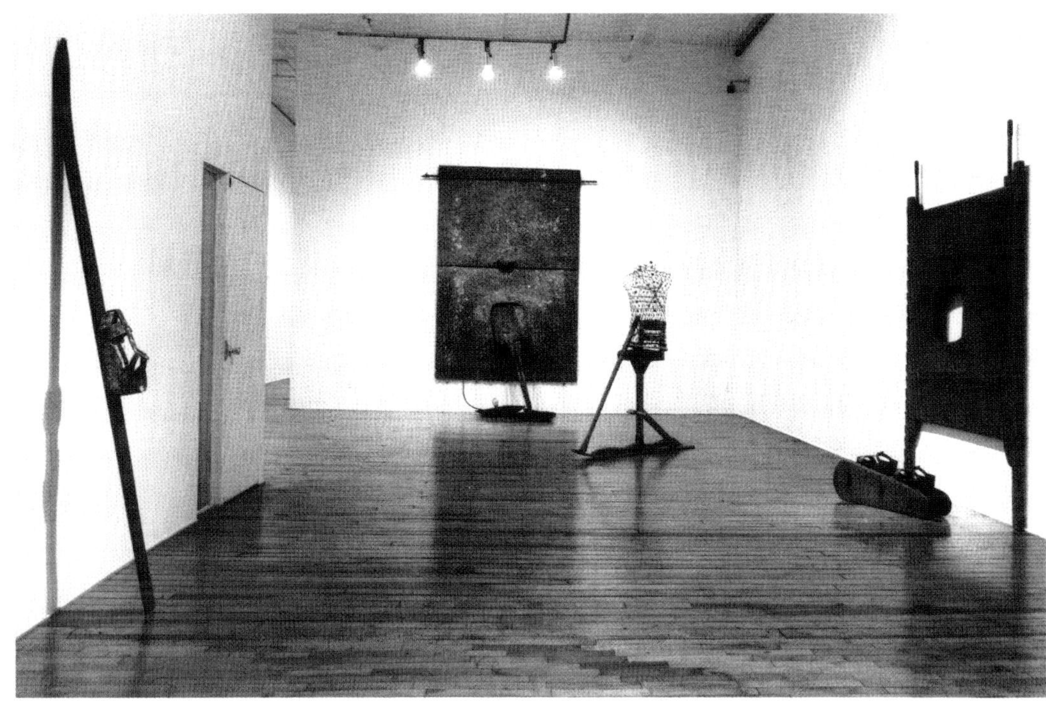

Installation view of the exhibition
Sal Scarpitta: *New Works 1990-1992*, Annina Nosei Gallery, 1992.

even while knowing your approach to selecting artists, I was wondering how certain group exhibitions, or certain two-person shows, were born. Whether around themes or around some kind of affinity.

AN: Usually the exhibitions developed around the works of artists whom I admired, who for me attested to something that I've always considered very important: I'm talking about the profound connection between art and culture. I've organized exhibitions of Mexican, Israeli, Australian, and Argentine artists. Each and every one was also a mirror into the socio-historical substrate of the countries of their origin. Sometimes, however, there were also other elements that motivated me, other ideas. For example, the exhibition of Gary Lang and Nancy Bowen, both Americans, which I put on in 1991, was born from a particular idea. I liked Gary Lang's paintings because of their bright colors and their robust structure while I found Nancy Bowen's sculptures and ceramics extremely interesting, but I felt that something was missing. I wasn't convinced of staging a solo exhibition of either of them. That something emerged splendidly for me when I put the two bodies of work together: both were children of an American art that had its roots deep in the past, specifically in the Arts and Crafts movement born in the second half of the nineteenth century. So I decided to exhibit them in a single show. Once the exhibition was hung, the Gary Lang paintings on the walls interplayed perfectly with the Nancy Bowen works scattered throughout the gallery. Together, they perfectly represented the evolution of American art, it was the result of a trajectory born in the past and transformed over time. Nevertheless, the artists weren't as enthusiastic about it, Gary Lang in particular. Our relations remained good but, following that exhibition, he moved his paintings to another gallery where he'd been offered a solo exhibition. I've still got fond memories of Nancy Bowen, I still have one of her works at my place in Rome – every time I look at it, I think back with satisfaction

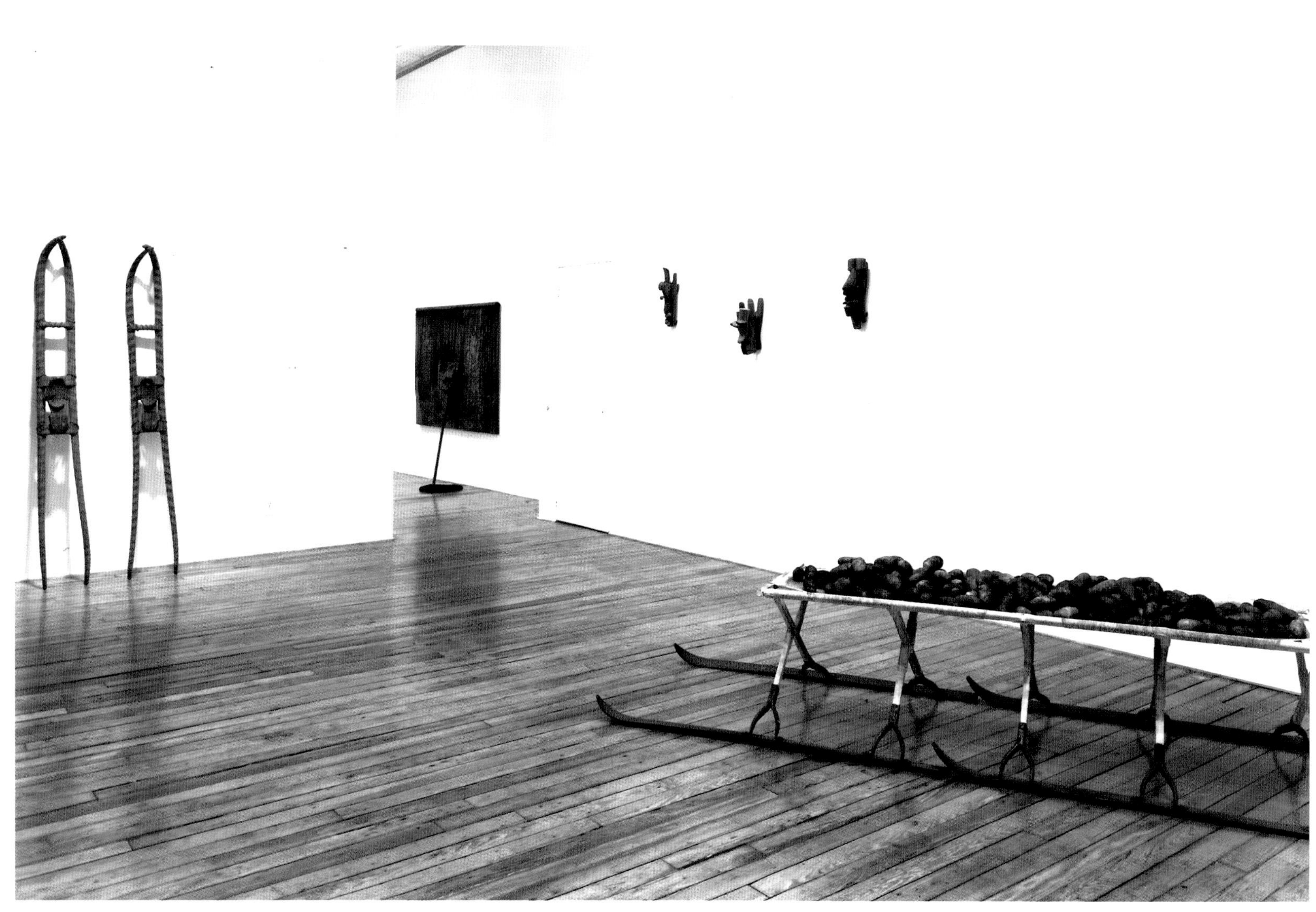

TWO INSTALLATION VIEWS OF THE EXHIBITION
SAL SCARPITTA: NEW WORKS 1990-1992,
ANNINA NOSEI GALLERY, 1992

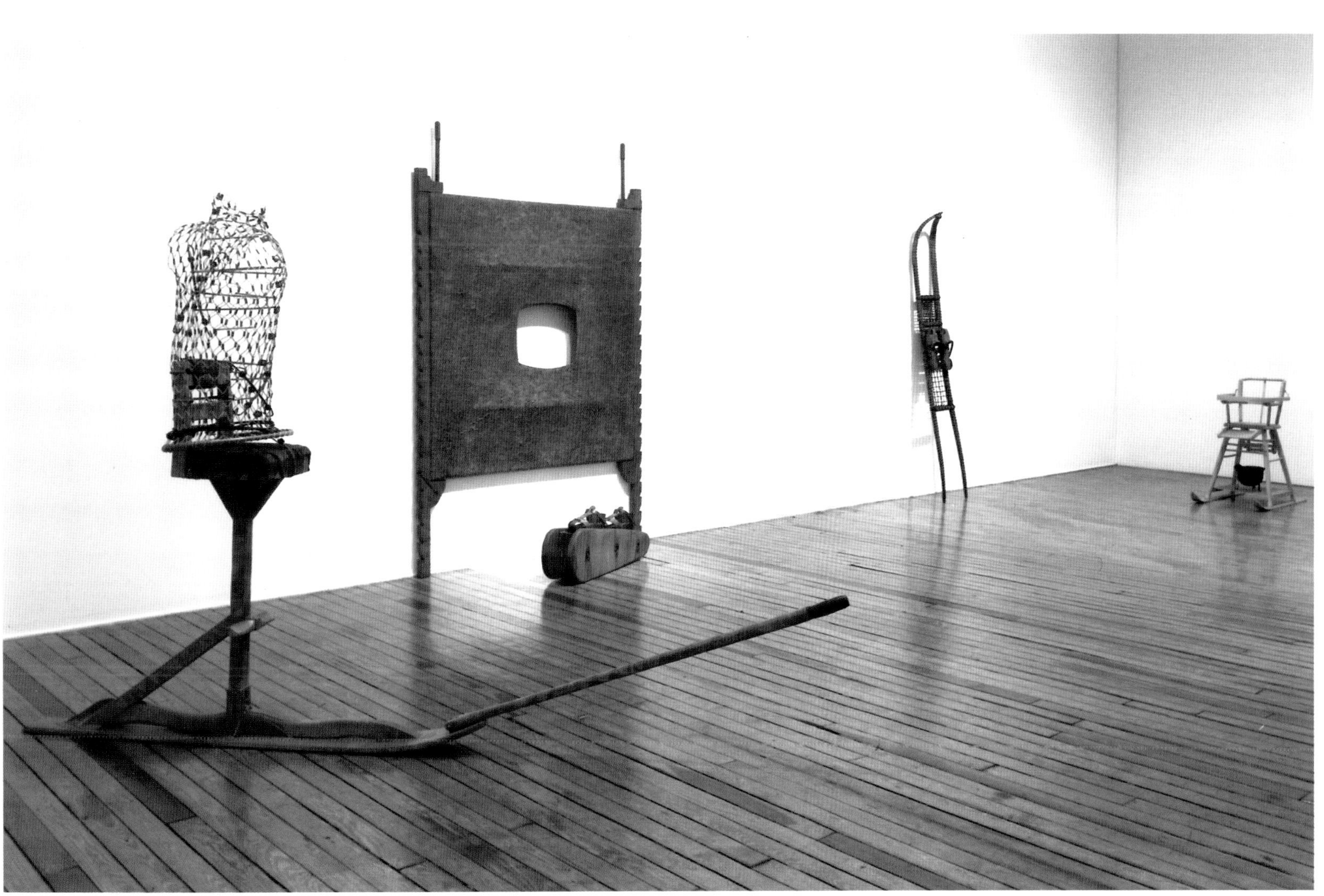

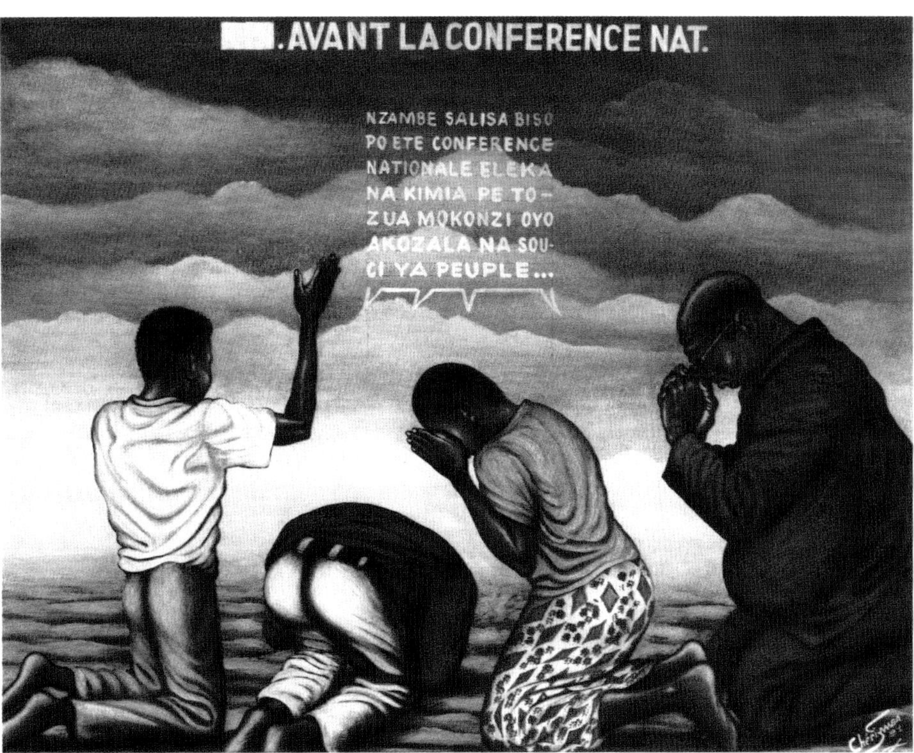

on that exhibition.

RL: Were there other instances in which you showed artists that you'd chosen according to, let's say, particular criteria?

AN: Understanding and exhibiting Chéri Samba's paintings proved a particular experience. I'd seen his work in the exhibition *Magiciens de la Terre* in 1989, curated by Jean-Hubert Martin at the Beaubourg. I staged it in collaboration with Magnin and the gallery N.O.M.A.D.E.. I also organized various Samba exhibitions afterwards, even collaborating with some institutions.

RL: We've arrived in the nineties. The previous decade was inevitably behind you, you'd changed the location of the gallery and your artists had changed too. Was it in the late 1980s that you'd left the Prince Street space for the one in Chelsea?

AN: No, it was in 1995 that I moved from 100 Prince Street to 22nd Street. I'd received a great offer from Prada, who wanted to rent the space. So I started looking around Chelsea, where there were only a couple of galleries at the time. I found one that I liked at 530 West, on the second floor, and so I rented it.

RL: In Chelsea, did you work with new artists as opposed to the ones you'd exhibited on Prince Street?

AN: Well, some, yes, but I'd worked with many before, such as Guillermo Kuitca, Shirin Neshat, Graciela Hasper, Jenny Watson, Chéri Samba, Julio Galán, Stephen Mueller, and Tsibi Geva. I'd worked on various projects with many of them, on both solo and group exhibitions. Amongst the new

Chéri Samba, *Avant la Conference Nationale*, 1991. Annina Nosei Gallery, New York.

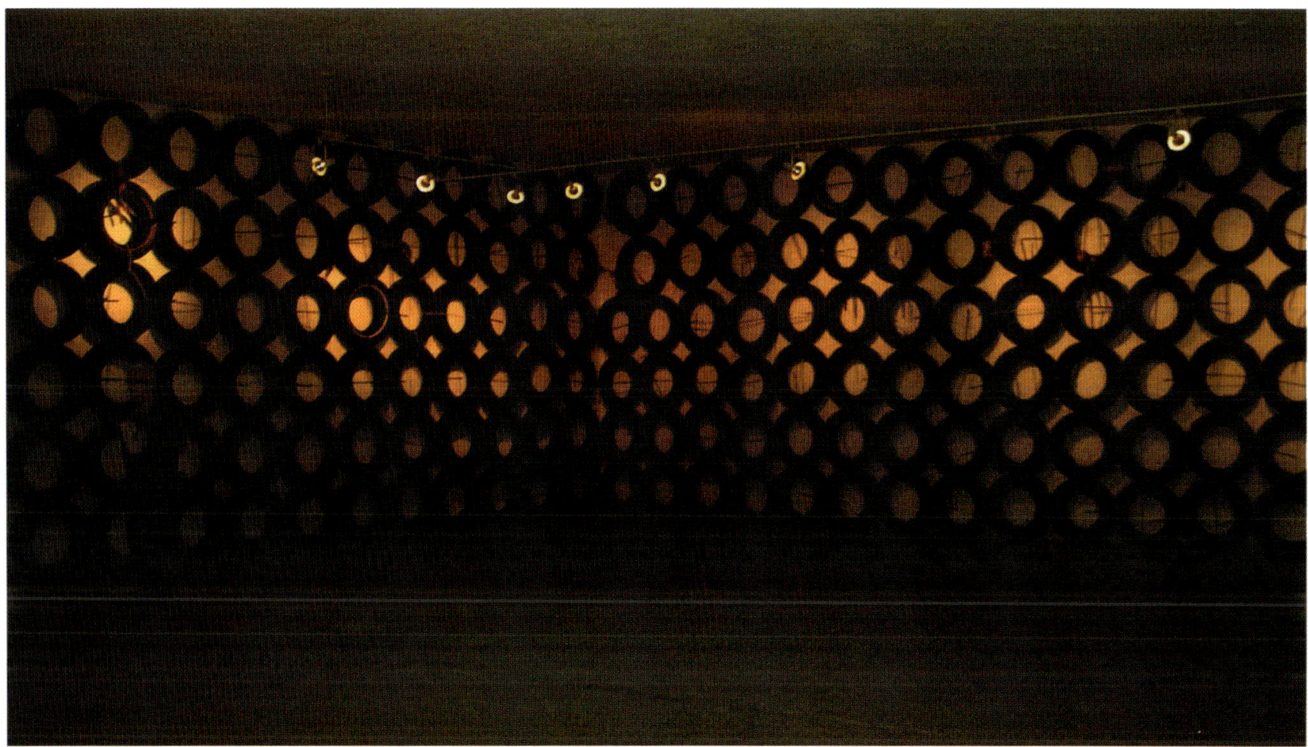

ones, there was Manuel Ocampo, for example.

RL: Did you also change the way you chose artists?

AN: I'd say no. What had always guided me continued to guide me. I continued to exhibit work that aroused my interest, I continued to seek out authenticity of expression and force of work. I was still fascinated by the fact that artists evinced an acute purposefulness, an awareness in the use of their own language, of their own iconography. Every artist I've worked with has always had a well-defined personality, distinct and potent.

RL: Earlier on we were reflecting on the fact that from the beginning of your career you've met with women in many ways exceptional, such as Ileana Sonnabend or Carla Panicali, such as Carmen Scarpitta or Carolee Schneemann, and then with figures like Mary Boone over the years that you ran the gallery or with the many female artists you've exhibited. A book on the subject has also been published recently. Tell me about your work surrounding the female world. What can you tell me, for example, about your relationship with Barbara Kruger? Her work was very different from Chia's or Paladino's or that of the other trendy New York artists of those years like Schnabel or Salle. Basically Barbara Kruger took other positions.

AN: Yes, you're right, I've always worked with women. The most important of them was undoubtedly Barbara Kruger, whom I exhibited for the first time in the group exhibition *Public Address*, which we've mentioned several times. The poet and critic David Shapiro had pointed her out to me. But I can't say that I had a specific agenda in that connection; I liked the artists – all of them, women and men. I've never been interested in issues of that sort. As I was telling you, I'd already presented Barbara in 1981. Obviously she was very important to me. Her works were sociopolitical statements.

Installation view of Tsibi Geva's exhibition, Annina Nosei Gallery, September 2001.

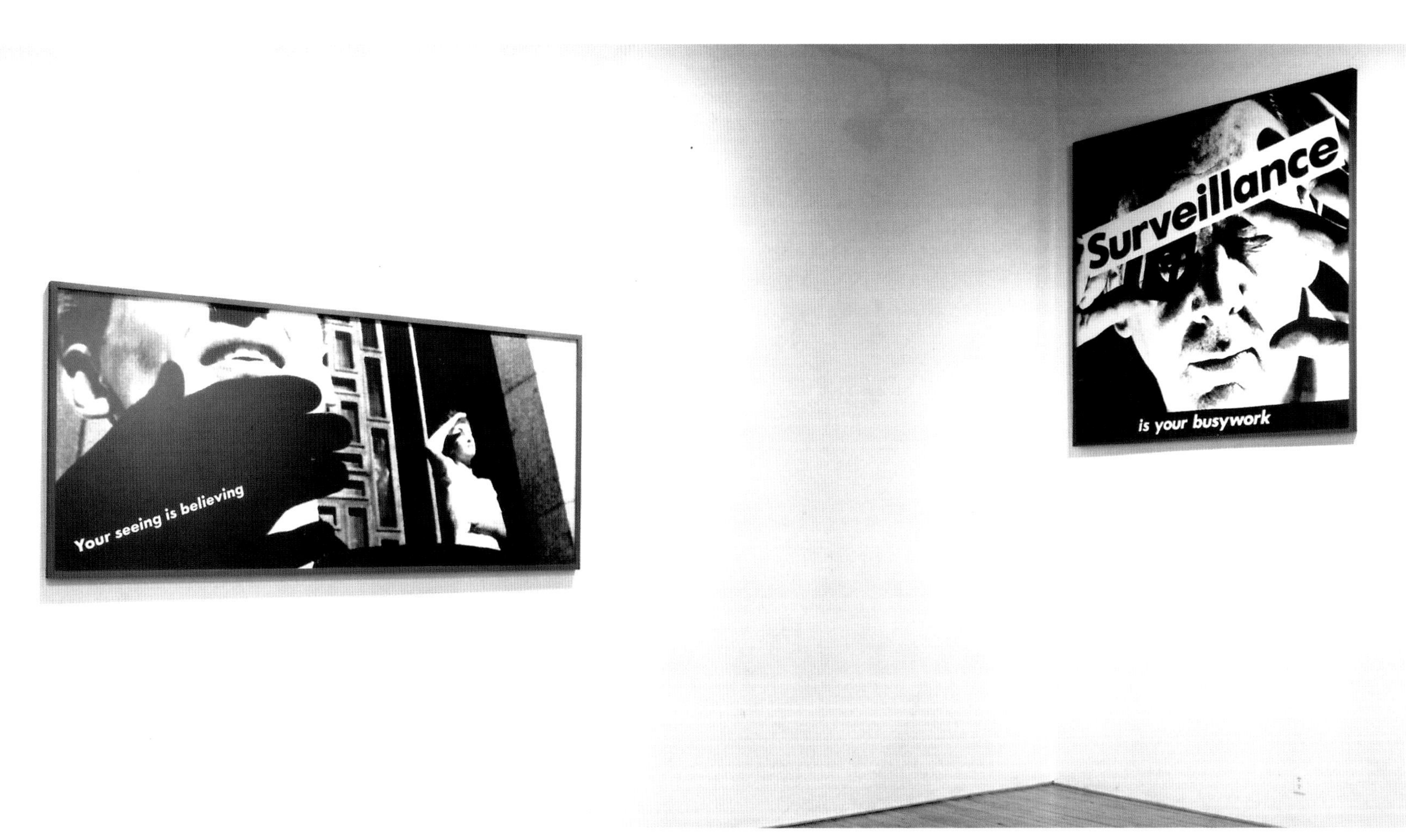

INSTALLATION VIEW OF BARBARA KRUGER'S
SOLO EXHIBITION, ANNINA NOSEI GALLERY,
MARCH 1984

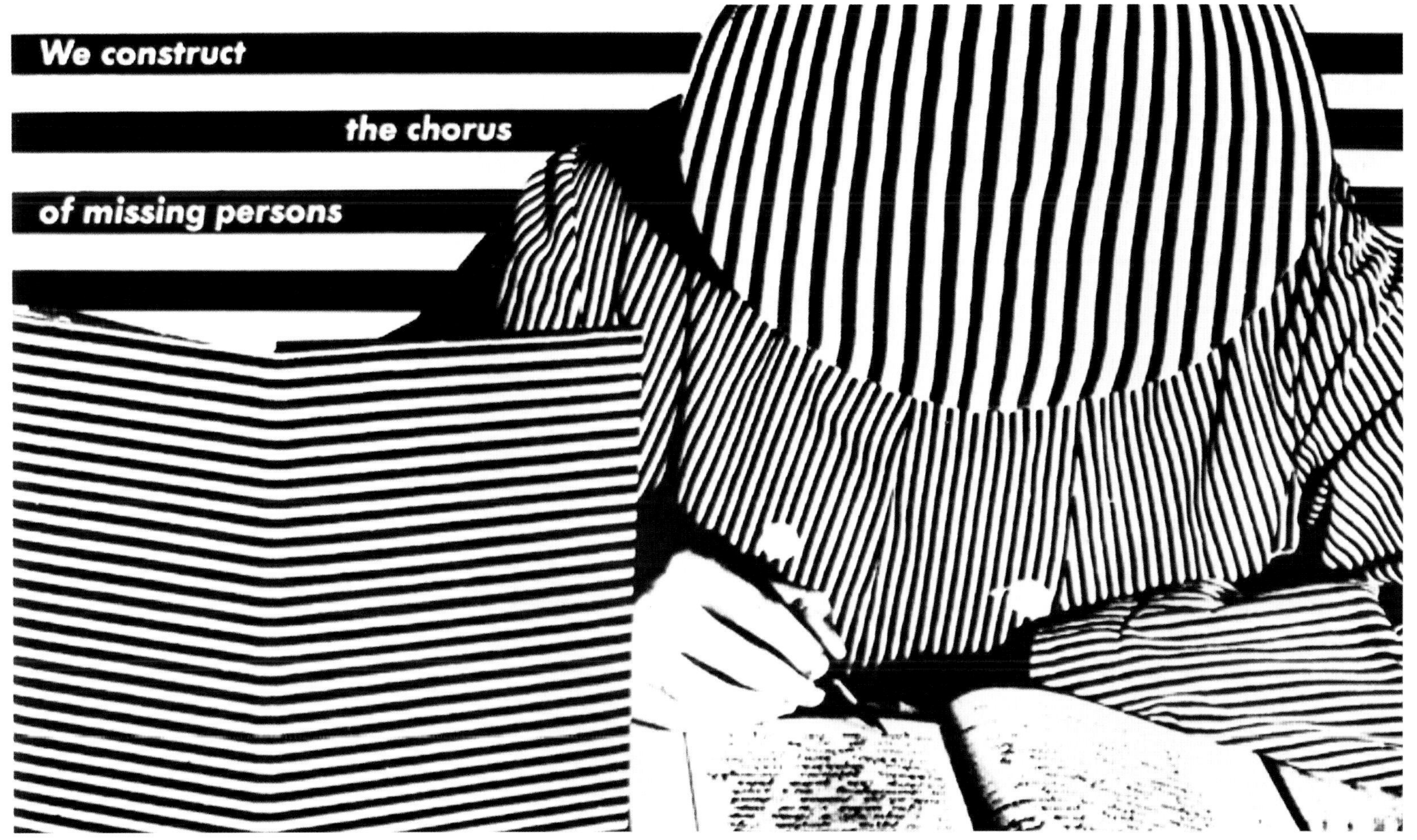

INVITATION CARD TO BARBARA KRUGER'S
SOLO EXHIBITION, ANNINA NOSEI GALLERY,
MARCH 1983

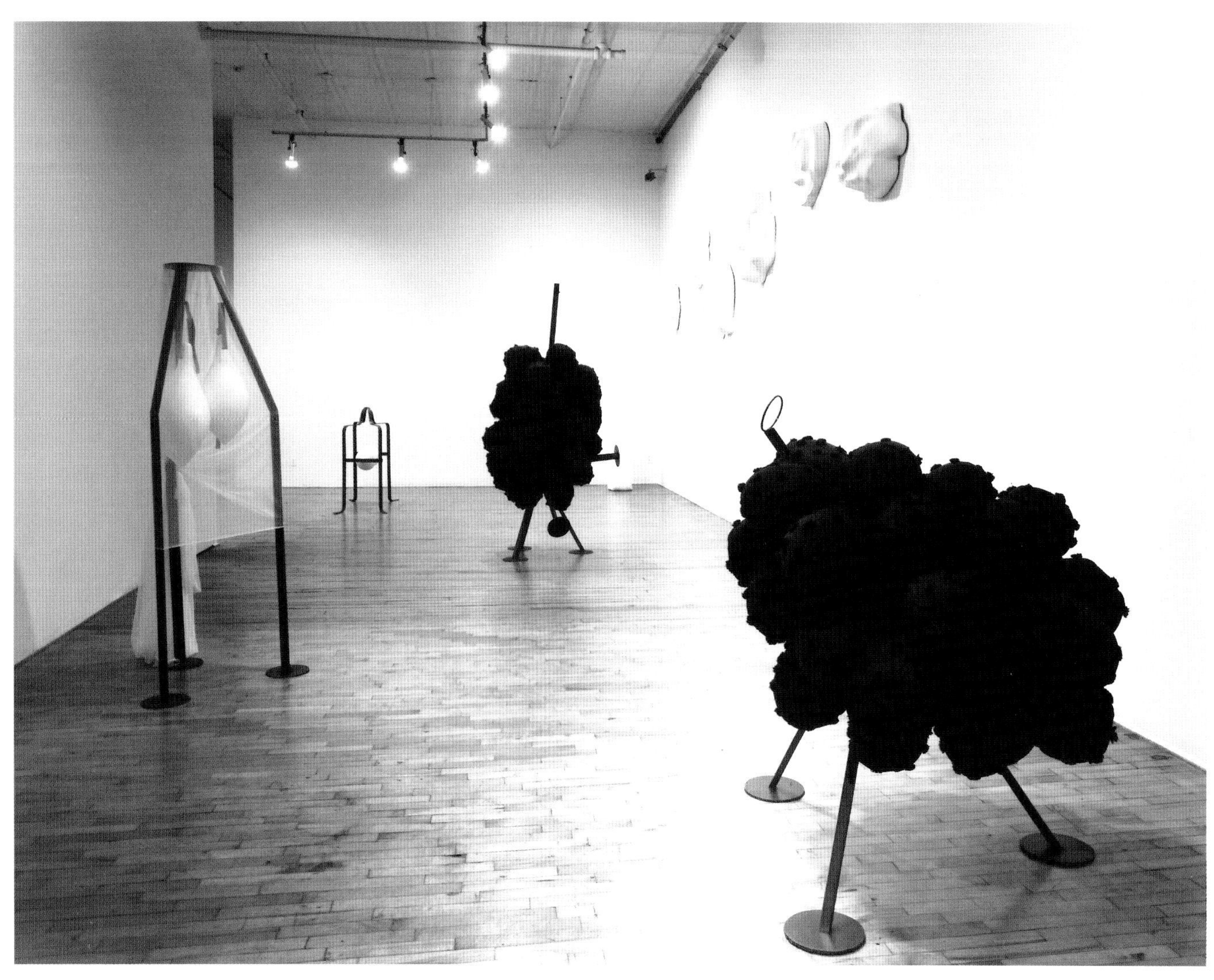

INSTALLATION VIEW OF TERESA SERRANO'S ARTWORKS AT
THE JUNE 1994 GROUP SHOW AT ANNINA NOSEI GALLERY, NEW YORK

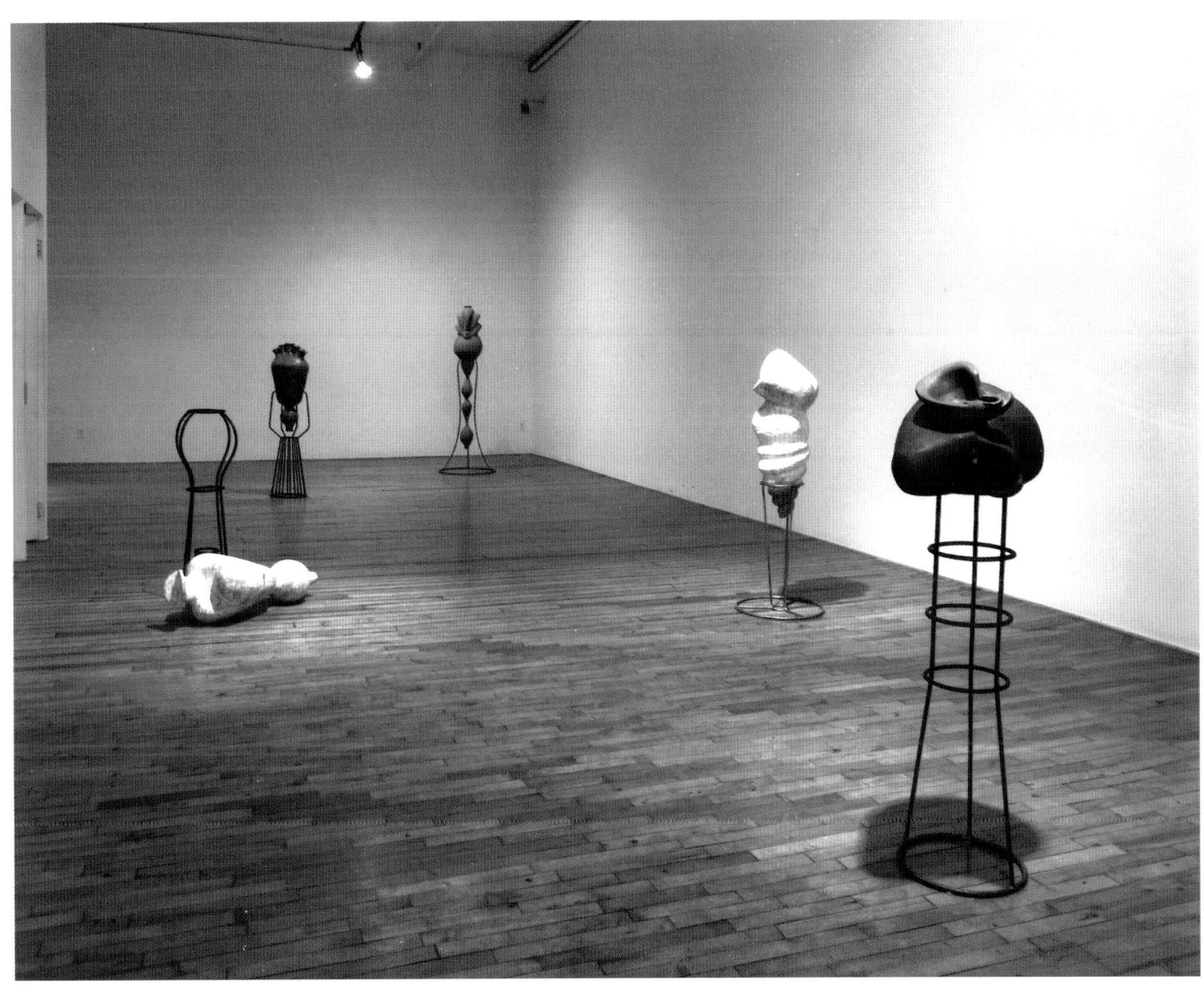

INSTALLATION VIEW OF NANCY BOWEN'S
SOLO EXHIBITION, ANNINA NOSEI GALLERY, NEW YORK
MARCH 1990

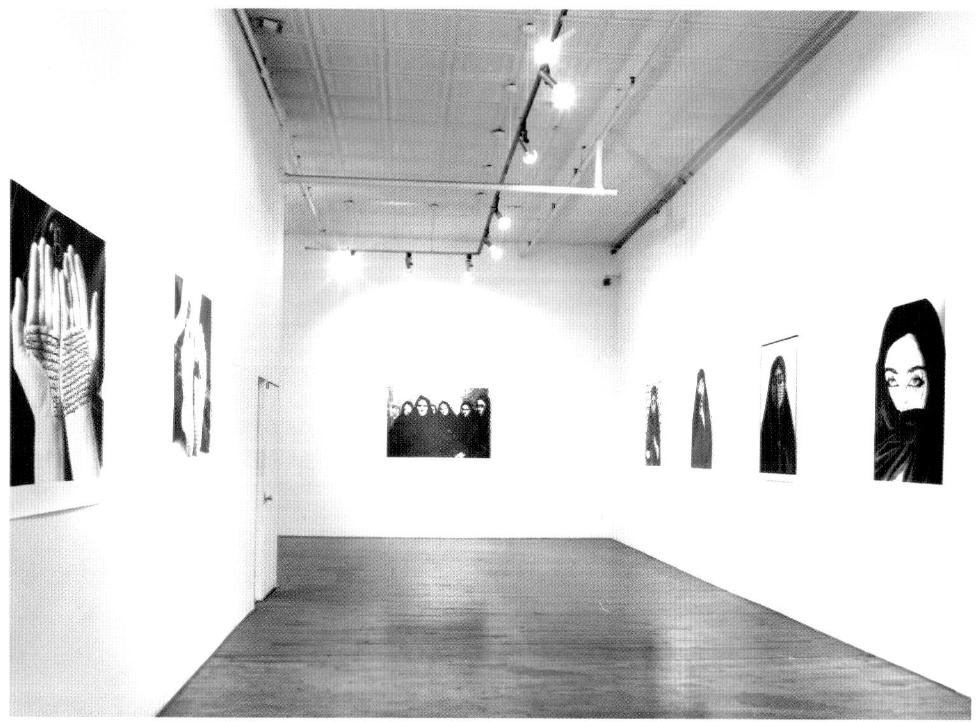

I'd also included Jenny Holzer in that exhibition too. They were different from each other, but both were busy crafting public statements out of their ideas. Kruger did so through certain phrases or statements. I even teased her a bit, saying that her works were essentially jokes, that they evidently stemmed from her background in advertising.

RL: From the point of view of personality, what were those artists like?

AN: Barbara Kruger was very lucid in laying out her ideas. She'd previously worked in advertising, so as far as I was concerned she was a little different from other artists. Her ideas weren't poetic; rather, they were quite political. They were suited to their period, but from my point of view they didn't have all that much to do with art. She insisted that she wanted us to do the exhibition – she was well aware that she'd then be recruited to a larger gallery through me. And so that was how she then showed with Mary Boone.

RL: What other artists did you encounter along your way?

AN: In 1983 I put on the group exhibition *European Expressions*, in which, after a series of Americans, I wanted to show Europeans. Among them was Sabina Mirri, whom I also included in two other group exhibitions and then in a solo show in 1985. In 1987 I worked with Beth Brenner and Ellen Brooks, two very interesting artists. In due course I collaborated with Mary Obering, Nancy Bowen, and then with the Australian Jenny Watson in 1991. I'd seen her work at the Madrid art fair and I'd loved it. I gave her several exhibitions.
Then I exhibited Teresa Serrano, a Mexican artist. We did several things with her as well. In 1994 I showed Anna Paparatti. In 1995, very important, I organized one of the first solo exhibitions of Shirin Neshat from Iran,

Installation view of Shirin Neshat's solo exhibition, Annina Nosei Gallery, September 1995.

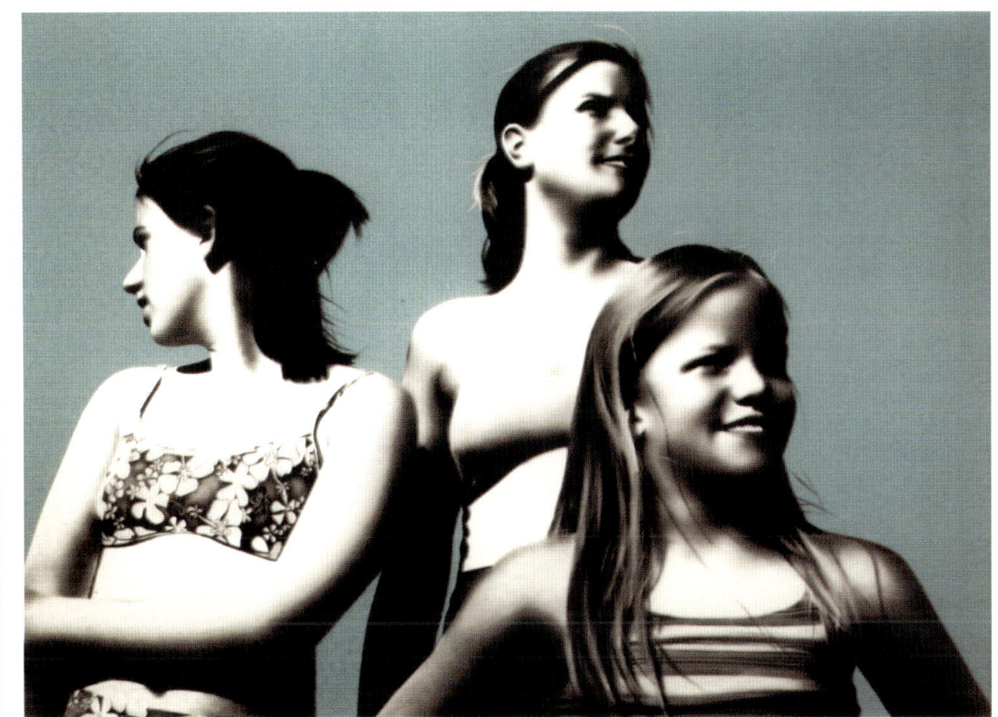

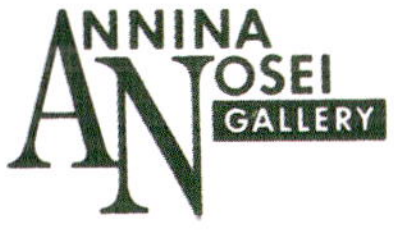

Left: Invitation card to *European Expressions*,
Annina Nosei Gallery, December 1983;
Right: Invitation card to Heidi McFall's solo
exhibition, Annina Nosei Gallery, May 2005.

whom I'd seen in a collateral event at the Venice Biennale. And that same year I worked with Ghada Amer. I liked her a lot. I'd been introduced to her work by my gallery director, Elizabeth Fiore. Ghada Amer, Egyptian, had already exhibited in Paris and I'd seen her work in a catalogue that my director had brought me. So first I included her in a summer exhibition called *Summer Invitational* and then in another group exhibition, *Inaugural Exhibition of New Address*, which I organized to celebrate the new gallery. Finally I dedicated a notable solo exhibition to her in 1996 at the new space in Chelsea. I especially appreciated the fact about her that there was a potent subversive aspect to her work both in religious and political terms.

RL: Do you have any works by these artists left?

AN: Yes, I have something by Ghada Amer and Shirin Neshat, but nothing by Barbara Kruger. I sold everything of hers. But I'd like to go on... I looked to South America at a certain point, with Graciela Hasper, for example, who won a great reception.

RL: You also worked with Kuitca – how did you come into contact with the South American scene?

AN: I'd met them through Josefina Ayerza, a Lacanian psychoanalyst from Buenos Aires. She introduced me to Guillermo Kuitca and Graciela Hasper.

RL: And to return to women?

AN: It comes to mind that, for example, I staged a Liliana Porter exhibition in 1998. She's from Argentina. A few years ago I saw a very funny theatre piece of hers. In her work there's always an ironic glance at the uselessness

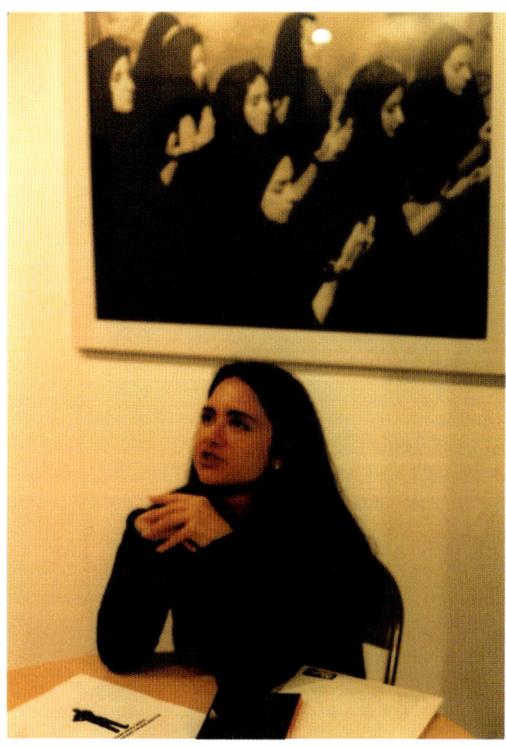

of certain aspects of the male world. If I looked at the gallery's resumé I'd find many other women with whom I've worked but who escape me in this moment.

Myriam Laplante, for example, or Heidi McFall. I saw the latter's work for the first time thanks to a collector of drawings. I'd been struck by a drawing placed on the ground, leaning against the wall. I remember turning it around to see the author's name and the title, and from the label I saw that she was working with a gallery in Santa Fe, so I contacted her and I put on the exhibition.

I set myself to it because I'd seen her work and I liked it. Anyway, many women. In some group exhibitions there were more female artists than male artists. What I particularly liked was their way of expressing femininity as a public fact. It's a dimension of their work that has always attracted me. Above all, though, the thing that most struck me was the authenticity and awareness with which they approached their concerns, not the concerns in and of themselves.

RL: One last question before saying goodbye. After so many years of experience, what advice would you give to a young collector?

AN: Collecting has to be an individual experience. I'd advise that they try to buy works of art that show extreme imagination and sensitivity. I've always enjoyed working with younger collectors; they're more open and more willing to spend money on the best works.

RL: And finally, what might a show of yours be today?

AN: If I still had the gallery or if I reopened it for an exhibition?

RL: Well, what would you exhibit in either scenario?

Lee Ortega in the office of Annina Nosei Gallery in 1997 with Shirin Neshat's *Prayer for a Miracle* (1995) in the background.

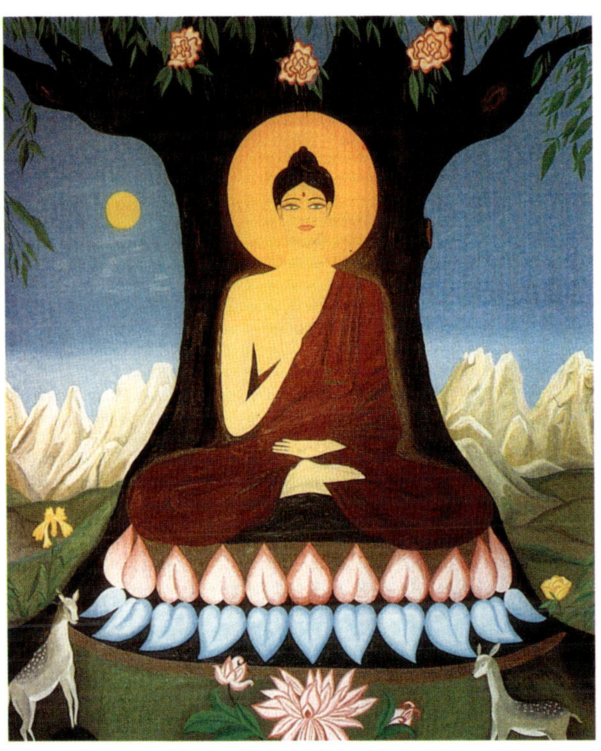

AN: One of the later exhibitions that I organized was the Filipino artist Manuel Ocampo. Ocampo's work represents another cultural point of view in the contemporary situation. There are some younger artists whom I've exhibited in the past, though, whose work I still like a lot and whose progress I continue to watch with enthusiasm. One of these is Ieva Mediodia, who comes from Lithuania and many of whose paintings I showed in the gallery. Another is Leemour Pelli, who uses painting to tackle highly pressing issues; and finally Alejandra Seeber. There. If I had to mount an exhibition in a gallery, I'd show those three artists.

RL: Well then, three women. So, with your permission, I'd like to conclude our conversation by recalling, in no particular order, the long list of women artists you've known and shown throughout the long period of your operation, coming from the most disparate parts of the world. You've already mentioned some of them, but I'd like to remember them all together: Teresa Serrano, Shirin Neshat, Heidi McFall, Myriam Laplante, Liliana Porter, Marta María Pérez Bravo, Graciela Hasper, Ghada Amer, Jenny Watson, Natalia Benedetti, Beatriz Monteavaro, Janieta Eyre, Sandra Bermudez, Deborah Turbeville, Leemour Pelli, Barbara Kruger, Sabina Mirri, Christiane Richter, Mary Obering, Ellen Brooks, Nancy Bowen, Donna Moylan, Anna Paparatti, Suzan Etkin, Beth Brenner, Veronique Bellavista, Carole Benzaken, Lucia Warck-Meister, and Ieva Mediodia.

Anna Paparatti, *Il Buddha Gautama*, 1994.

A
COSMO
POLITAN
STORY

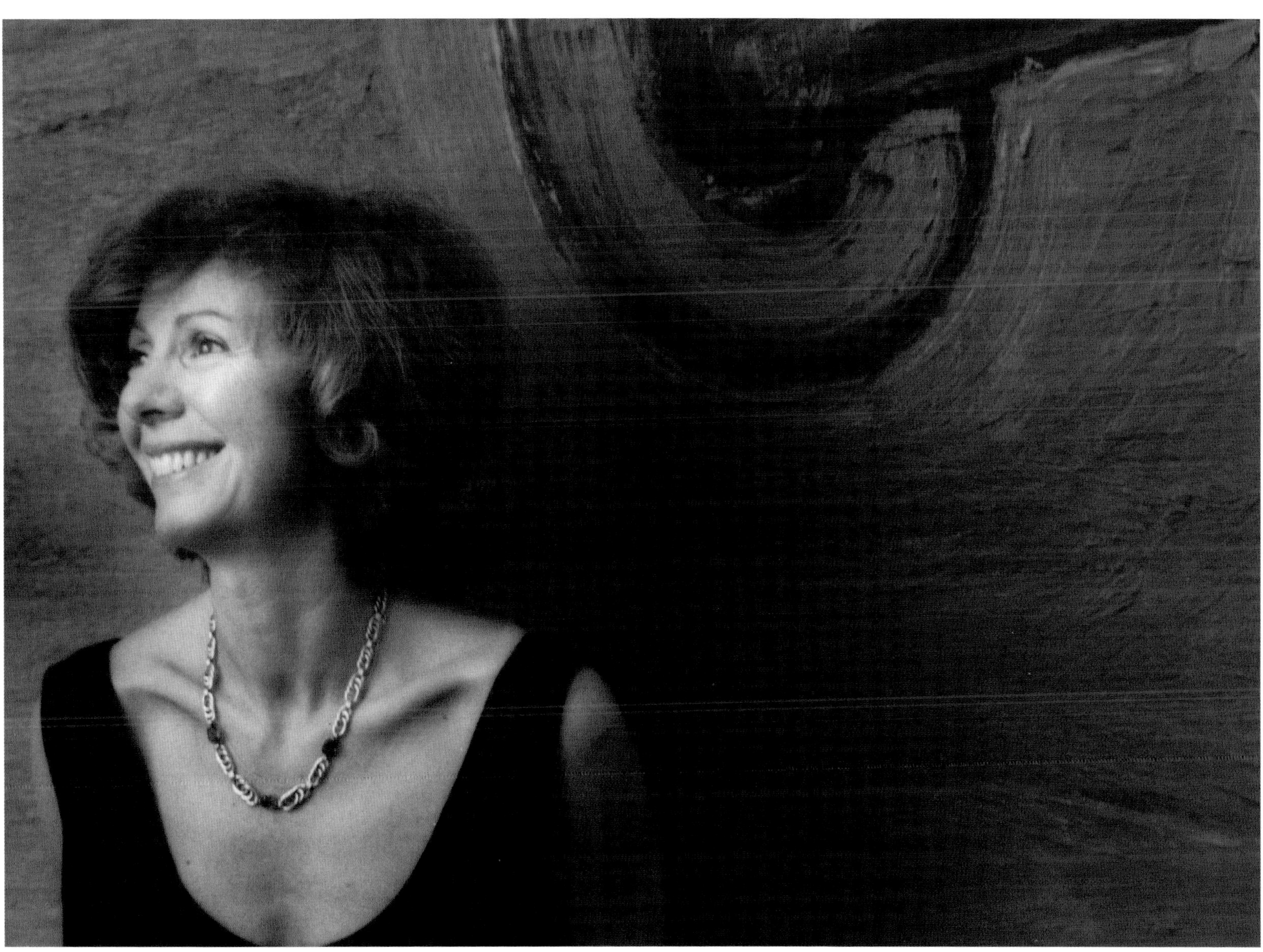

A COSMO POLITAN STORY

The name Annina Nosei is inextricably linked to the New York art scene of the 1980s, but her relationship with the art world dates back much further, to the period of her university studies, undertaken in her hometown of Rome as the 1950s yielded to the 1960s, a significant transition that marked a crucial moment in the history of Italian art. The Rome of the fifties was dominated by a proto-industrial culture that continued to follow rhythms dictated by the overlapping seasons. At the same time, however, there remained a sense of the ineluctability of the Futurist mandate, which had been smoldering in the ashes for around half a century, heralding a society profoundly renewed not only in its systems of production but also in its social structures and morals. The early 1960s were then witness to the proliferation of a great desire for change. The most receptive circles soon aspired to forge an international and interdisciplinary koinè that could unite the myriad forms of creativity in a unitary and thoroughly modern cultural ferment, modern both in its art and its way of life. Having successfully traversed the delicate phase of post-war reconstruction, that generation beheld the world with different ambitions, with a will to construct a secular and avant-garde culture that would derive encouragement and energy from the country's progressive industrialization.[1] The city boasted no shortage of artists of an international profile; suffice to mention only one name, Giorgio de Chirico, to convey the reach of the talents present and active in the Rome of that period, although art's leading light continued to be Picasso. Italian artists still looked to Paris and to an art understood as an expression of freedom and outspoken anti-fascism. And yet, this widespread "Picassianism", on one hand, and emergent scholarly study of Futurism, on the other, were both perceived by the younger generation as outdated tangents, in contrast to abstract currents – the most innovative art of the time – that answered a need for broader horizons and laid the foundations for true modernization. For all the progressive rediscovery of Futurism's important role within the continuum of European avant-gardes, young artists' interest was in fact turned toward America, even before the definitive transfer of artistic leadership from Paris to New York. This attitude was favored, moreover, by the overseas attention then being devoted to the *Bel Paese*.[2]

1. A valuable indication of the spirit fueling the 1950s can be found in the publications of the magazine *Civiltà delle Macchine*, established in 1953 and edited by Leonardo Sinisgalli until 1958. Financed by Finmeccanica, a subsidiary of the IRI (Institute for Industrial Reconstruction), it aimed to bring art and humanistic culture into dialogue with technology, an approach that, albeit superficially, echoed certain impulses of the Futurist cultural project. The theme of the relationship between art and industry, or art and technology, was extensively reprised in the 1960s, as further demonstrated by the activities later associated with the American group E.A.T. (Experiments in Art and Technology), a collective founded in New York in 1967 by engineers Billy Klüver and Fred Waldhauer and artists Robert Rauschenberg and Robert Whitman.
2. From the postwar era on, Europe became the key travel destination for many American artists. Popular venues included Paris, Peggy Guggenheim's Venice, and Rome. It was there that Leo Castelli would meet the young Americans Salvatore Scarpitta and Cy Twombly, whom he would duly recruit to his gallery, a fact that underscores the relationship between the two countries. Also significant in this sense are episodes surrounding Robert Rauschenberg, who, during his long stay with Twombly in Rome, met Alberto Burri while the latter was intent on making his first Sacks. This fact allows Burri a legitimate claim to having preceded Rauschenberg in the use of the extra-pictorial materials that would lead to the *Combine paintings*, a fact never acknowledged by Rauschenberg. These were intense but not always easy relationships, then, such as that between Leo Castelli and Plinio De Martiis, owner of the Roman gallery La Tartaruga, for years one of busiest and liveliest European venues for US artists, along with Beatrice Monti's gallery in Milan.

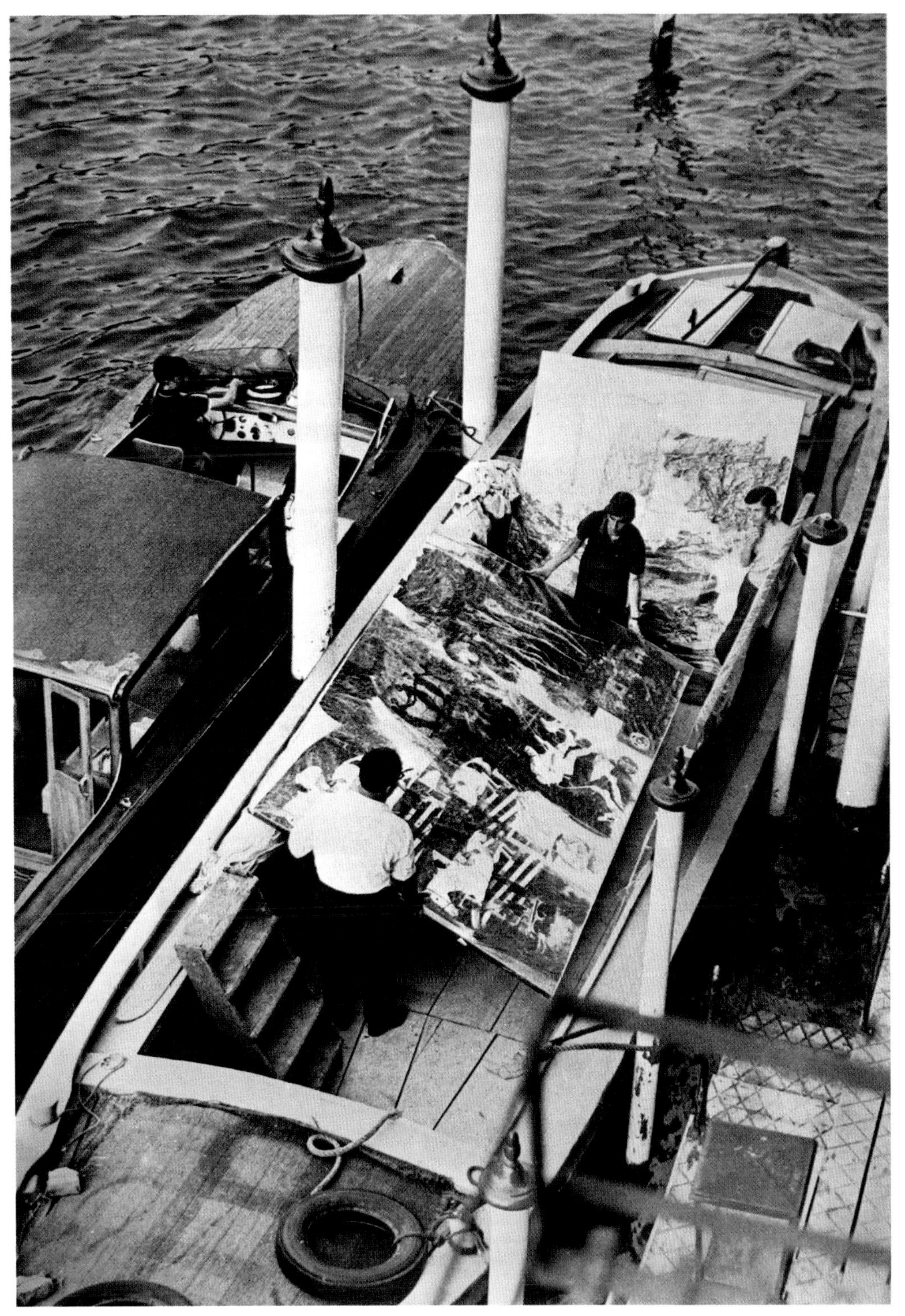

ACTION THEATRE

In those Roman years, Annina was friendly with artists and theatrical figures, including Claudio Cintoli and Franco Angeli amongst the former and Carmelo Bene amongst the latter, and she participated with her friends Carmen Scarpitta and Richard Robert "Rospo" Pallenberg in the Action Theatre group ACT. These were exponents of a youth that clamored for the onset of that *renewal* which took form in the extemporaneity of Happenings, imported directly from America. Rome's ACT group, an offshoot of the San Francisco group directed by Ken Dewey, not only represented an intermediary between the United States and Europe but was also the most progressive response to the need to overcome old turn-of-the-century avant-garde formulae. The culture underpinning Happenings came, it is true, from the legacy of those avant-gardes – but metabolized, reinterpreted according to a pragmatism that removed it from all ideological influences, or so it seemed. Happenings were cloaked in a neutrality that persisted throughout their pioneering of a new and complex linguistic code.

Annina was strongly attracted to the innovative form of theatre proposed by Dewey, with which he paved the way for a distinct vernacular; she adhered wholeheartedly to that idea. At that moment, many were uncertain how to approach that novel sector of the discipline, which embraced notably diverse approaches. ACT's work represents a turning point in theatrical practice; its reliance on the competition of different disciplines exalted spectacle at the expense of the spoken word, which implicitly announced the obsolescence of traditional media in the field of visual arts as well. It was in this particular context that Annina, together with her friends, conducted her first artistic experiments, motivated by her studies in art history and further incentivized by her knowledge of the work of Marcel Duchamp, acquired during the preparation of her final thesis.

The experiences that she forged within the ACT group catapulted her into the furthest regions of art while also giving her a certain visibility in the press. It was a great thrill for her, at only 20 years old, to see herself named alongside with her friends Carmen and Rospo in an article by Vito Pandolfi. She had been mentioned in relation to her part in the theatre pieces staged in Palermo as part of the Teatro *Gruppo 63* showcase, also featuring actors John A. Coe and Jamil Zakkai, freshly arrived from the Living Theatre.

In Pandolfi's words: "Our host among the evening's performers was Carmen Scarpitta, an Italian-American with a Parisian theatrical education, who was joined on stage, in close collaboration, by elements who come to the theatre for the sole consolation of their love for risqué undertakings."[3] This is a reference, not without a trace of sarcasm, to the rest of ACT's young cast members, who staged several of the 11 pieces that constituted the evening's entertainment (the others had been entrusted to the more traditional direction of Luigi Gozzi's Centro Teatrale di Bologna). But despite the "sole consolation of their love of hazardous undertakings," the spirit with which Annina partook in those performances was in fact exactly suited to them: spontaneous, light-hearted and deliberately ironic.

Of that evening, Annina particularly remembers *Povera Juliet*, written by Alfredo Giuliani, perhaps the only one in which she took part. She still has her costume, made of the same fabric as the armchair in which, by sitting, she camouflaged herself.

To Giuliani himself we owe a significant account of ACT's work, including Ken Dewey's function in the renewal of theatrical conventions and of Italian culture more generally. Ken Dewey had studied with Anna Halprin in San Francisco and he had frequented the Living Theatre and off-Broadway theatres; with ACT, he brought new trends to Italy and Europe at a time in which the "tradition of the new" – as Harold Rosenberg put it – was plunging into crisis, expanding that same culture to which Allan Kaprow had referred in discussing the legacy of Jackson Pollock. "He staged," Alfredo Giuliani wrote, "the central segment of the Palermo show according to the criteria of Action Theatre."[4] This was his innovation, which concerned not only theatre but the subdisciplines from which the principles of stage action derived and to which they were addressed. Giuliani also left us some methodological notes, beginning with the personal relationship that Dewey himself established with the actors: the director "allows the actors to stutter and stumble over their lines, wearing the lines thin by inverting them and reinverting them in every possible tone."[5] Dewey's goal was that of dismantling preconfigured models, of stripping the mask from canonical tropes, of deconstructing the text, even at risk of "tampering" or of "some happy transposition that the author (of the text) had not foreseen."[6]

In light of this spirit of renewal – which, were there no historical distance and contemporary climate to redefine its tone, one might be inclined to call a subversive spirit – Pandolfi's aforementioned remark concerning a "love for risqué undertakings" can be interpreted according to the alternate frame of reference implied by Giuliani when, at the conclusion of his account, he emphasized that Dewey's *Povera Juliet* brought "to its apex the progression from theatre to the dissolution of theatre."[7] A dissolution that no longer concerned only the relationship between director and actor, insofar as Action Theatre also overwhelms the environment and the space in which the performance comes to life. Giuliani, again, recounted its conclusion: "With *Povera Juliet* the exit from the theatre occurred literally: there was almost no separation between actors and audience, and everyone was drawn into a surprise that touched even me, I must admit, pleasantly."[8]

It is necessary to mention at this point that a key contributor to the set design for *Povera Juliet* was Achille Perilli, one of the young abstractionists who had been campaigning for the rejuvenation of Italian culture since the outset of the post-war era. From this point of view he was surely one of the most dedicated of those who pressed the stage toward the creation of a total theatre, and in any case the most resilient over time.

In writing of figures "who come to the theatre for the sole consolation of their love for risqué undertakings," Pandolfi demonstrated his inability to grasp the significance of the innovation that Ken Dewey championed, which depended precisely on the personal contribution of individual participants according to their training, their sensibilities and the artistic experiences behind them, just as it depended on the construction of an epic dimension through group bonding and the creation of art. Or perhaps, in fact, Pandolfi so well understood the effects of braving such risqué undertakings that he feared their consequences. But by no means did everyone take such a view; many recognized the outset of a new era in ACT's initiatives.

Nearly a year after Gruppo 63's Palermo showcase, an article by Giuliano Zincone took stock of the new Italian theatre's state of affairs.[9] He firmly acknowledged the role played by ACT, praising its approach in general terms, along with the fact that it had laid the foundations for a conception of total theatre based on the relationships interwoven on the stage: between music, acting and dance, between painting and architecture. Zincone also accentuated the group's personalities; of Annina he underlined her only occasional forays into acting, referring above all to her contribution to the organization of numerous "avant-garde shows" and her interest in new artistic phenomena linked to Action Painting and Pop Art. He then recalled her involvement in *Meat Joy*, the Happening that Carolee Schneemann had presented in Paris the May previous during the Festival de la Libre Expression.

The profile outlined by Zincone clearly indicated how deeply Annina was immersed in the experimentations of that moment, which sought answers to the anomalies produced by a society of unprecedented opulence. It was an attempt – a last gesture of modernism – to build a *new avant-garde* that could spawn a proliferation of images, sounds and information within a space common to different disciplines. It was thus that Annina found herself participating in the 1960s' historic project of transforming art.

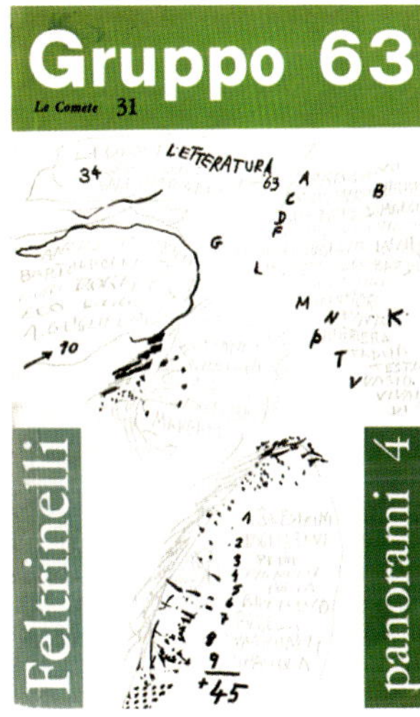

Cover of the book *Gruppo 63*, published by Feltrinelli in 1964, edited by Nanni Balestrini and Alfredo Giuliani.

3. Vito Pandolfi, "La nuova avanguardia," *Il Punto*, no. 37 (21 September 1963).
4. Alfredo Giuliani, "Il teatro d'azione di Ken Dewey," in *Gruppo 63*, ed. Nanni Balestrini and Alfredo Giuliani (Milan: Feltrinelli, 1964), 426.
5. Ibid., 426.
6. Ibid., 427.
7. Ibid., 431.
8. Ibid., 429.
9. Giuliano Zincone, "L'avanguardia teatrale in Italia," *Elsinore* 1, nos. 8-9 (September–October 1964).

IN PARIS

The year before *Meat Joy*, the same year as Group 63's Palermo showcase, Annina went to Paris with ACT to take part in the show *The Gift*, as part of the 10th instalment of the Festival du Théâtre des Nations.

To Annina, a trip to Paris was hardly a novelty. She had already visited on many other occasions, but this time she was at the center of events that clearly signaled changing times.

At that turn of Paris' new decade, Yves Klein's first *Anthropométries* had been given body, it must be said, while the first object-based *tableaux* of the Nouveaux Réalistes appeared; actions and works that demonstrated an evident continuity of the Dada spirit that had animated the city between the two wars and which was now reanimating the renewed international art scene, understood as a dialogical unity of Europe and America.

The Paris of those very early 1960s still boasted vigorous vital signs. The renowned stripper Rita Renoir could happen to contribute to a workshop conducted by Carolee Schneemann while the couple Michael and Ileana Sonnabend could happen to attend a Ken Dewey show. The cultural life of the French capital held up solidly against the ideas emanating from the United States, for which Annina would soon depart.

Added to her involvement in avant-garde theatre and her interest in American art of the preceding decades, both recalled by Zincone, was her dedication to writing. This plurality of interests was as expressive of the zeitgeist as it was of her personal sensitivity and vivacity. Writing on art, managing the organization of Happenings and other forms of interdisciplinary – or intermedia – events as well as participating in them was emblematic of the liberty that her generation so dearly sought.

From Paris Annina penned a chronicle, subsequently sent by telex to the editorial office of Rome's *Le Ore* magazine, containing a summary of the preparatory work for the show *The Gift*. She lent a certain brilliance of style to her account of the events surrounding the occasion, emphasising the sense of belonging to an international community spawned from young people's desire to be together. Hailing from America, France, Italy, and elsewhere in Europe, they dedicated themselves to building an artistic and cultural interface that shortened distances, overcame differences and allowed for the negotiation of disagreements. Annina also described the distinctive location chosen for the show's rehearsals, "An old villa, now completely in ruins, which the few inhabitants of Valmondois (a suburb 30 kilometers from Paris) refer to as 'Le Vieux Château', [rented] for a few thousand francs, to the delight of some bankrupt old landlord."[10] It was in these surrounds that the group's activities took place. They only went to the city rarely, she explained, "Indifferent to the comments of the no-longer tranquil villagers, who are now resigned to anything."[11]

That very heterogeneous group, 20 or so "actors, musicians [...], sculptors, painters and dancers, mostly Americans from San Francisco," had "gathered from all over Europe, where they were already to be found on various tours, akin to a form of pilgrimage."[12] This retelling underscores the show's defining elements, lending an immediacy to its evocation of the optimistic mood within which the overall artistic premise – which combined dance, mime, jazz and acrobatics – was interwoven with all manner of personal initiative from the participants, leaving the utmost room for both the unexpected and the improvisation of all involved. By that time, Annina had already accumulated ample experience in the arena of such occasions, which, again, represented the best that the new avant-garde could offer. Above all, she had developed an awareness that art needed to break with cultural norms bound to hidebound European bourgeois culture. In short, she had become acutely aware of the change in the air, building towards the climate of upheaval of 1968. Her collaboration with Ken Dewey, as well as her involvement in that international milieu, had given her the chance to sample an alternative way of living and had equipped her with cultural tools vital to confronting the choices to come.

10. Annina Nosei, "Avanguardia americana a Parigi," telex sent to the editors of *Le Ore* in Rome, Paris, 11 July 1963, 185 in this volume.
11. Ibid.
12. Ibid.

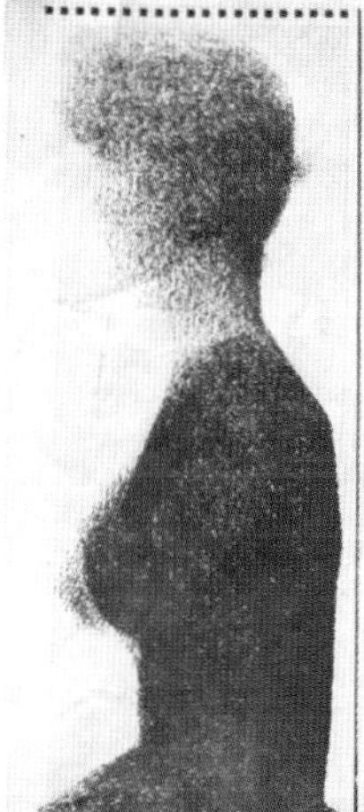

P. M. Pasinetti

La confusione

Una rappresentazione di tutta la realtà presa in blocco (Carlo Bo)
Volume di 320 pagine - rilegato - L. 1800

Libero Bigiaretti

Disamore

Il senso caldo, animale, diciamo pure volgare della vita (G. Gramigna)
Volume di 240 pagine - rilegato - L. 1800

Laudomia Bonanni

L'adultera

La distruzione della mitologia dell'adulterio
Volume di 204 pagine - rilegato - L. 1500

Enzo Marangolo

Un posto tranquillo

Il Marangolo è scrittore bell'e formato: chiaro, liscio, nudo
(Franco Antonicelli)
Volume di 172 pagine - rilegato - L. 1200

Ottiero Ottieri

L'impagliatore di sedie

Una storia d'amore o un esaurimento nervoso?
Volume di 216 pagine - rilegato - L. 1500

BOMPIANI

Tre ragazze nel pollaio d'avanguardia

PARIGI. Quinta serata del programma del "Workshop de la libre expression" (laboratorio della libera espressione) all'"American Center for Students and Artists" di Parigi, ovvero una manifestazione d'avanguardia organizzata dal giovane pittore Jean-Jacques Lebel assieme a qualche beatnik della riva sinistra. Quindi un festival a base di "jam session", mostre di quadri e oggetti "pop-art", "happenings" e altre attività escogitate da un gruppo d'artisti di tutti i paesi che da anni cerca d'imporsi, e in parte c'è riuscito, con argomenti provocatori e mezzi violenti, come già s'imposero, quarant'anni fa nella stessa Parigi, i surrealisti, i dadaisti.

Sembra una mummia

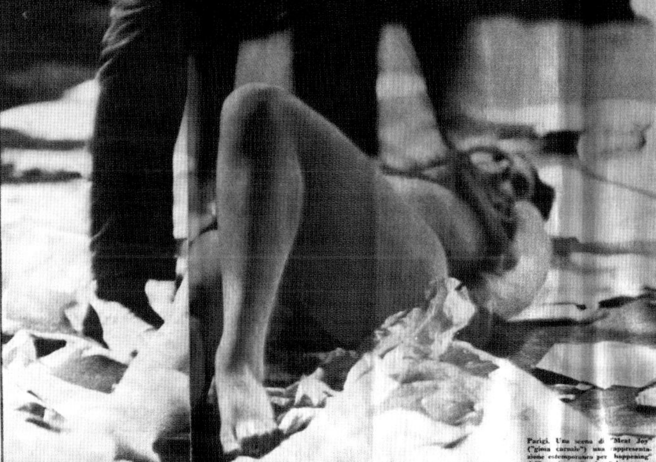

Parigi. Una scena di "Meat Joy" ("gioia carnale") una rappresentazione estemporanea per "happening" dell'americana Carolee Schneemann.

Schiaffi e baci

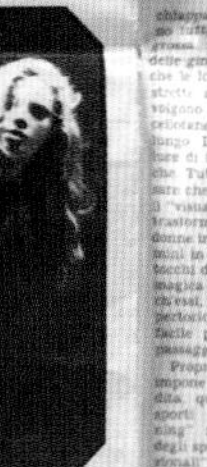

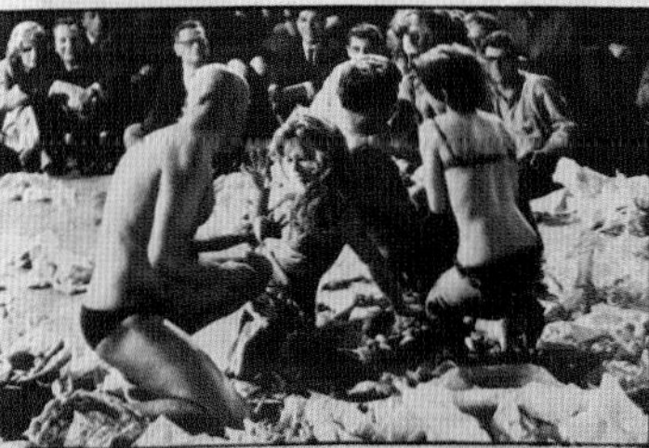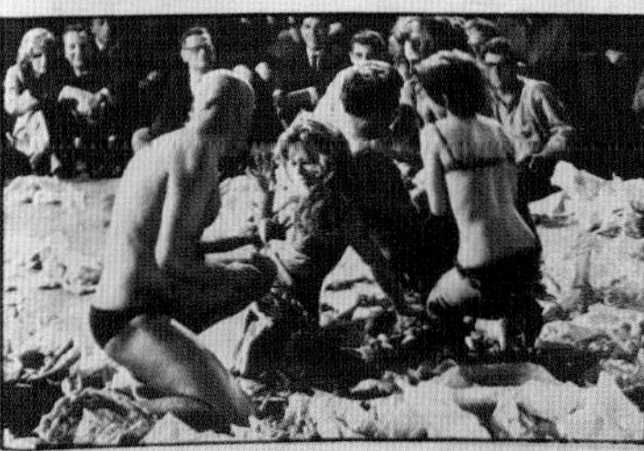

▲ Parigi. Una scena di "Ondulation" con l'attore di teatro Jacques Seiler e la strip-teaseuse Rita Renoir. Nell'ovale a destra Parigi. Le "happening" e il suo pubblico.

▼ Parigi. La scena finale di "Meat Joy" un "visual drama" di Carolee Schneemann. In primo piano Jacques Seiler e Rita Renoir si rotolano nella carta straccia.

In bikini e reggiseno

Svevo è caro come il Chianti

LONDRA. Questa settimana la regina Elisabetta ha inaugurato nel grande padiglione per esposizioni del quartiere londinese di Earls Court la prima Fiera internazionale del libro che sia mai stata allestita in Inghilterra: non grande come quella di Francoforte, ma pur sempre imponente. Una ventina di nazioni, oltre alla Gran Bretagna, espongono su un'area di 14.000 metri quadra. L'Italia ha la rappresentanza più forte.

Assurda ecatombe

ARTICLE IN *L'ESPRESSO* (14 JUNE 1964) DEDICATED TO CAROLEE SCHNEEMANN'S HAPPENING *MEAT JOY*, PERFORMED DURING THE FESTIVAL DE LA LIBRE EXPRESSION, PARIS, 1964

THE MURDER OF A CAULIFLOWER

In the creation of her first Happening, *Assassinio di un cavolfiore*, which she staged in 1962 or perhaps early the following year, Annina already captured the essence of the new artistic spirit pervading the West. All that remains of this "installative collage" – as this manner of performance was dubbed – is the statement she penned, which appeared as part of a dossier in the magazine *ABC* devoted to young European artists born into the prosperity of the economic boom, cast in the lingering light of a culture both romantic and rebellious. An imposing full-page photo of Annina and a pre-title headline, "24-year-old Roman Annina Nosei," accompanied her singular statement, which expressed the new context in no uncertain terms: "My theatrical debut, if it can be so described, accompanied my participation in a Happening at the American Embassy in Rome [...]. The theme was: murder of a cauliflower. How did it occur? Oh, with a knife and a cauliflower, of course."[13]

Ironic and paradoxical at once, she further wrote, "There was a wonderful audience that reacted magnificently by throwing steaks. A success that long occupied the American newspapers."[14] A kind of dramaturgy of the absurd emerges from the account, recalling illustrious auteurs; Annina lived it wholeheartedly and with provocative simplicity, but also consciously: "The secret to our performance is that of abandoning ourselves completely, arriving at a freedom of our own selves that allows us to feel as children do, open to everything. Only thus can we reach that heightened state that then allows us to perform."[15]

A few lines that reveal her personality, in which a natural humor is combined with an awareness of a new approach to reality. In those same pages a statement from her friend Carmen also appears, of which the formula is the same: a title, "Non credo nelle parole," and the pre-title headline, "28-year-old Carmen Berth [Carmen Scarpitta's nom de guerre at the time] from Los Angeles, California." The text consists of a brief profile and a final declaration of Scarpitta's future plans. As one reads it, an impression forms of the bond uniting the two: "We are presently hard at work at the Teatro dei Satiri and we are members of ACT in Rome (Annina Nosei, myself, Richard Robert Pallenberg and Ciro Formichella)." Carmen shared Annina's self-awareness: "I have never believed in words, in the possibility of expressing thought in words, which is why I didn't want to be involved in theatre." She duly continued, "I believed in gestures more than in language. But I have since discovered that it is possible to create a relationship between ourselves and the audience by arriving at a universal language, which eliminates language." As if still unsure her point was clear, she added, "I think, still and always, that words are useless."[16]

Annina had met Carmen through Franco Angeli and immediately became her closest friend of those years. She was the sister of the noted artist Salvatore Scarpitta, he too born in the United States and based in Rome at the time. From Los Angeles, Carmen had gone to Paris, where she had studied ballet for two years. Perhaps it was from these studies that she learned that the power of gesture, mime and action can carry more weight than words.

13. Annina Nosei, "Assassinio di un cavolfiore," *ABC* 4, no. 38 (22 September 1963).
14. Ibid.
15. Ibid.
16. Carmen Scarpitta, "Non credo nelle parole," *ABC* 4, no. 38 (22 September 1963).

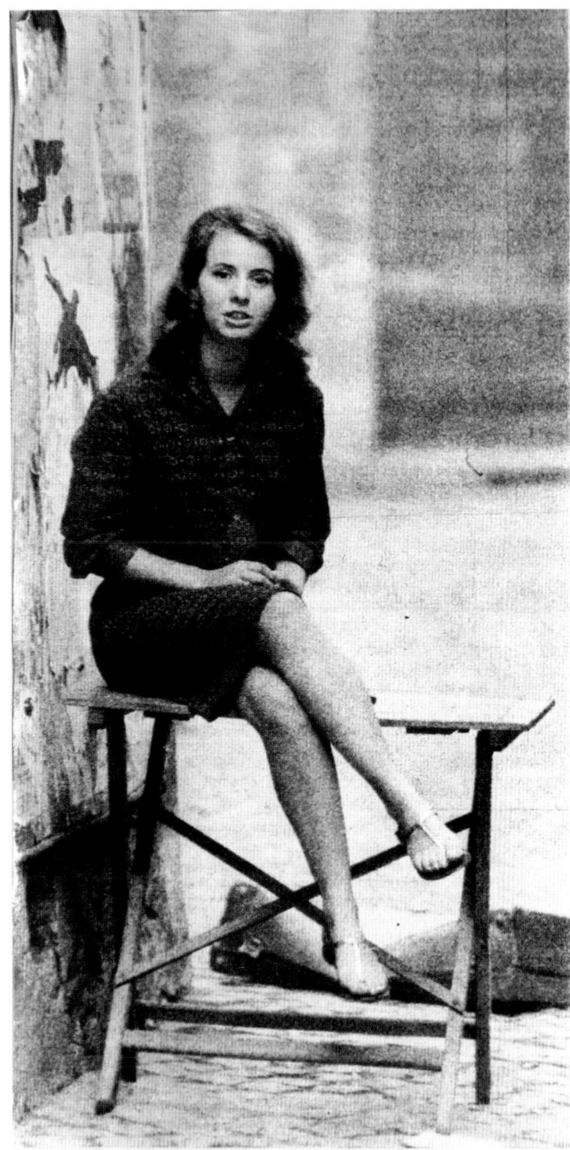

ASSASSINIO DI UN CAVOLFIORE

ANNINA NOSEI 24 ANNI ROMANA

Mio padre è italiano, è il professor Nosei. Mia madre polacca. La mamma era venuta in Italia con un biglietto aereo di andata e ritorno, poi incontrò papà... Non credo che abbia ottenuto il rimborso del biglietto.

Ho fatto l'università e mi sono laureata in lettere moderne con la tesi « Pittura d'avanguardia ».

Il mio debutto teatrale, se si può definire così, è avvenuto con la mia partecipazione a un « happening » all'ambasciata americana di Roma, uno di quegli spettacoli definiti « collages ambientali ». Il tema era: assassinio di un cavolfiore. Come avvenne? Ma, con un coltello e un cavolfiore, naturalmente. C'era un pubblico meraviglioso che reagì in modo magnifico con lancio di bistecche. Un successo di cui si occuparono a lungo i giornali americani. Sì, papà è molto contento.

Spero di ottenere una borsa di studio per Harvard. Ora ho le prove al « Teatro dei Satiri ». Il segreto della nostra recitazione è quello di abbandonarsi completamente, di arrivare a una libertà di noi stessi che porta a sentirsi come bambini, aperti a tutto. Solo così si raggiunge quello stato di tensione che ci permette poi di recitare.

20 - ABC

Clipping from the magazine *ABC* (22 September 1963) with a photo of Annina and her statement relating to the Happening *Assassinio di un cavolfiore*.

IN THE EMPLOY OF ILEANA SONNABEND

Participation in the Paris-staged *The Gift* had unforeseen consequences for Annina. Indeed, during the course of the Happening an episode occurred that, besides testifying to her verve and determination, gave her access to experience that would prove useful in the future. Annina has recalled that, in order to create a fluid and seamless performance, Ken Dewey asked her and another young actress to perform during one of the pauses in the dramatic action: they were to approach the audience and improvise something. At the agreed time, therefore, Annina closed ranks with the audience, stopping in front of a certain couple. In a stentorian voice, she declared more or less what she had also said to the weekly magazine ABC. She said her name, her father's name and his profession, further outlining her formal education and her aspirations, etc.

The couple in question were the spouses Michael and Ileana Sonnabend, who at the end of the performance invited her to join the staff of their Paris gallery. So it was that from the end of the summer of 1963 to the summer of '64, Annina remained in Paris to work for Ileana Sonnabend. A highly intense year. Paris still boasted all its appeal as a cultural capital equipped to attract artists, writers, and poets from every corner of the globe. Although the adjustments had already begun that would duly allow New York to claim Paris' place, no one in that moment would yet have wagered on it.

Upon her arrival in Paris, Annina took up a small apartment left to her by Christo, who was then leaving for America. The few items of essential furniture in the flat were covered with raw canvas. To Annina it was as though she inhabited one of his 'wrapped' works. As in this case, many of her other memories of that period relate to artists, such as Andy Warhol or Robert Rauschenberg – her favorite – but she often met Italians also, such as Michelangelo Pistoletto, Piero Manzoni, or Toti Scialoja: relationships and acquaintances that invigorated her on an existential as well as a cultural level. After all, in Rome she had already had ample opportunity to associate with artists, a circumstance with which she found herself very comfortable.

IN VENICE WITH ROBERT RAUSCHENBERG

Early in the summer of 1964, Annina went to Venice in the service of Sonnabend. She was to monitor the selection of Rauschenberg's works due to be exhibited at the 32nd Biennale by invitation of Alan Solomon, director of the Jewish Museum and curator of the American pavilion in the Giardini. Annina also supervised the transit of the works from the American Consulate, where they were initially installed, to a small building summarily erected beside the American pavilion. She undertook the trip to Venice in the company of Carolee Schneemann, whom she had befriended after taking part in her performance of *Meat Joy* in Paris a few months earlier. An endearing note has survived that the artist sent to the musician James Tenney: "Off tonight with Annina on the train and marvelously so I can return to Paris next Friday."[17]

That year's Biennale was to assume particular importance insofar as Robert Rauschenberg was awarded the Venice's prestigious Golden Lion, a gesture that ratified the acknowledgement of American art in Europe.

During the same sojourn, Annina also contributed to the show staged by Merce Cunningham at the Teatro La Fenice, in which John Cage and Rauschenberg himself also participated: an undertaking that once again confirmed Annina's insertion in that distinctive artistic and cultural climate. All the more reason, then, to persist on the course that she had plotted.

Before her trip to Venice, Sonnabend had asked her to stay with the gallery for at least another year. Annina, however, had won a Fulbright scholarship and preferred to follow that plan through. She therefore left for the United States soon after, bringing an already considerable professional background with her.

17. Kristine Stiles, ed., *Correspondence Course: An Epistolary History of Carolee Schneemann and Her Circle* (Duke University Press, 2010), 88.

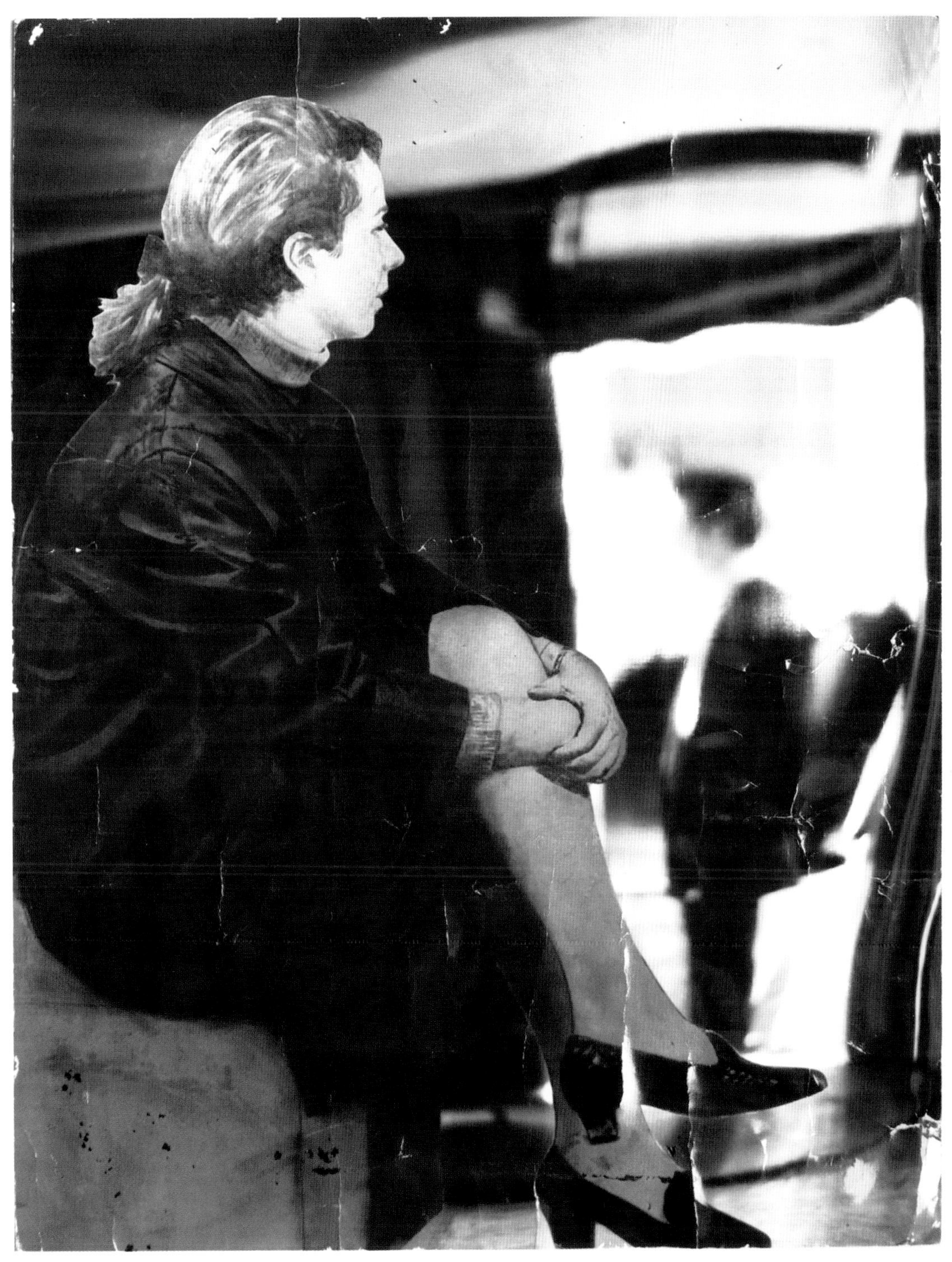

MICHELANGELO PISTOLETTO,
ANNINA SEDUTA - *L'ATTESA*, 1964

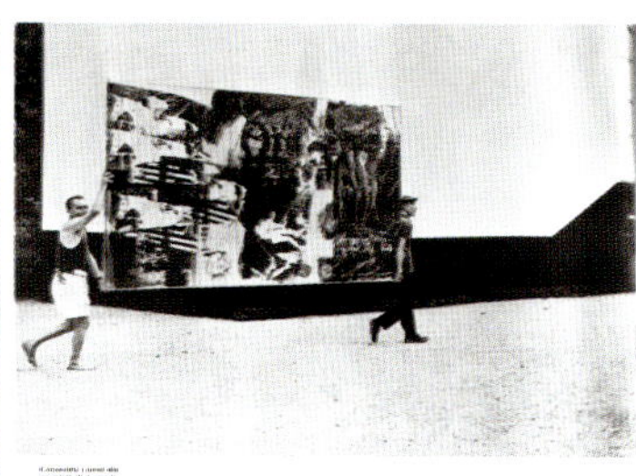
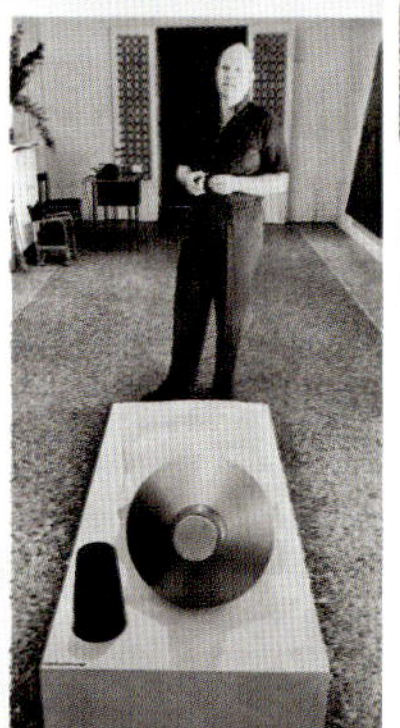
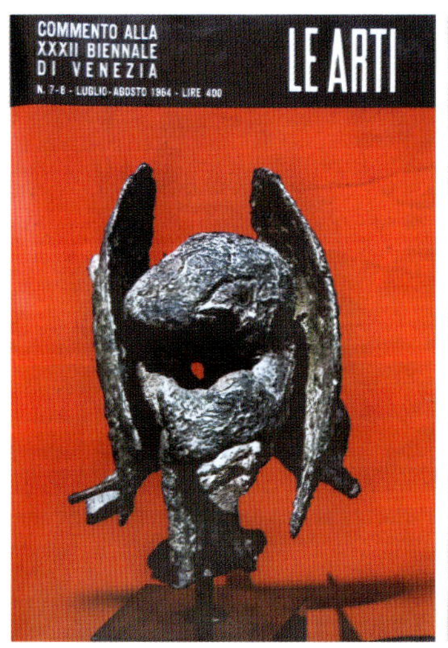
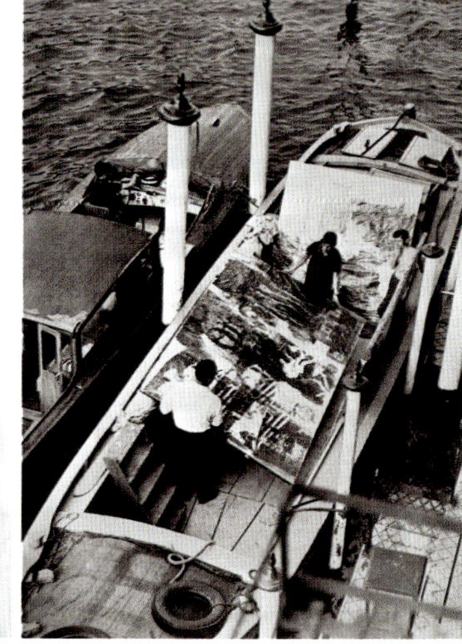
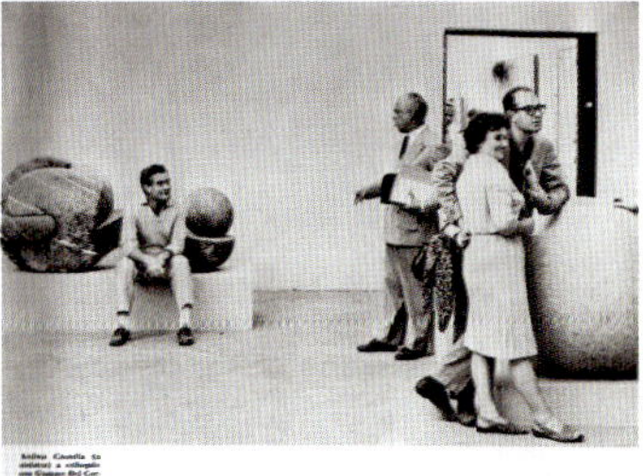
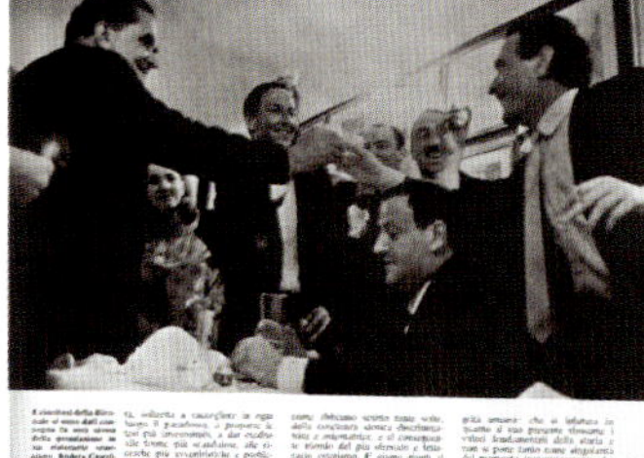
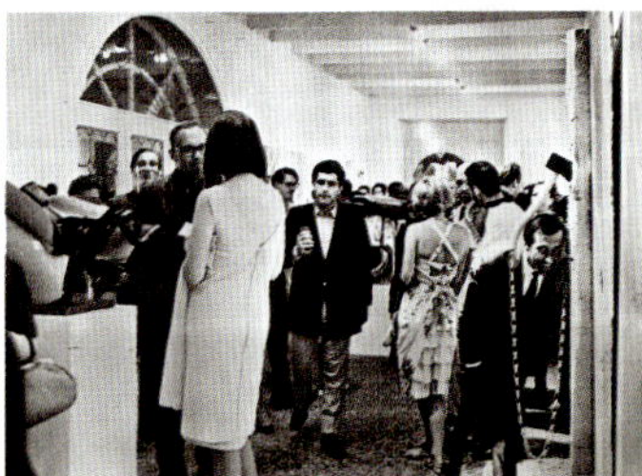

In the summer of 1964, the magazine *Le Arti* published a special entitled *Commento alla XXXII Biennale di Venezia*, which featured contributions from authoritative figures accompanied by images of significant moments, including the transfer of Robert Rauschenberg's works from the Consulate to the American Pavilion at the Giardini.

DEPARTURE FOR AMERICA

Annina left for the States buttressed by her education and the friendships that she had made in Paris. She arrived in New York full of enthusiasm, bearing the names of various people to whom Rauschenberg had suggested she might turn. To her, this meant ripe opportunities ahead. It was the ideal setting at that moment, amidst an era of heightened euphoria in American art, which was finally reaping the fruits of a 20 year battle to assert its independence from European culture, from painting as it was understood in Paris. The prime target of American polemics had long been Picasso, as New York artists strove to demolish his reputation and, with it, the prestige of European painting. "Picasso is the man to beat," had been Willem de Kooning's mantra throughout the 1940s, until, in the company of the other action painters, he had succeeded in attracting the attention of New York and America.[18]

Annina had experienced that transition's salient moments. In 1958, the same year that Mark Tobey won the Biennale's Golden Lion, she and her friend Claudio Cintoli had visited Jackson Pollock's exhibition at the Galleria Nazionale d'Arte Moderna in Rome, conscious of the event's importance, fraught as it was with consequence. That fact was reinforced by, among others, Giulio Carlo Argan, an outstanding figure on the Italian critical scene – and shortly thereafter one of Annina's university professors – who would write of the exhibition: "The event occurred at the most opportune moment: after the common experience of the war, strong was the desire for a dialectical rapport between European and American culture."[19]

Annina's employment with Sonnabend had also allowed her to bear witness to the transition's crucial stages, culminating in its crowning occasion: Rauschenberg's award ceremony, which announced the primacy of American art. In leaving the old continent, Annina also abandoned its way of thinking about art as a prefiguration of new forms, new patterns of behavior and alternative social relations; arriving in the new world, she found an art that grew out of the dynamics of a young and evolving society.

A STEP BACK: FAMILY AND STUDIES IN ART HISTORY

If every person's destiny is at least partially dictated by their place and date of birth, it was by Annina's own initiative that she invested her efforts in the study of art history. How did she arrive at such a choice? Born to Angiolo Nosei and Paolina Frydman, Annina attended the customary lower middle school, *ginnasio* (classical junior high) and lyceum at the Terenzio Mamiani State School, following the example of her uncle Giorgio Pasquali, who had married her aunt Maria Nosei in the early twenties. Pasquali (1885-1952) was professor of Classical Philology at the University of Florence and, partly by merit of his relationship with Giovanni Gentile, lectured on Greek and Latin philology at Pisa's Scuola Normale Superiore for many years. Of formidable cultural depth, Pasquali debated with Croce on idealist historicism, advocating the German philological method, but did not fail to sign Croce's own *Manifesto of the Anti-Fascist Intellectuals*. Over the course of his career he published extensive research on philology, on the history of philology and on linguistics, proving himself a worthy interpreter of antiquity. In the margins of these activities, he also published the book *Socialisti tedeschi*, in which he openly expressed his advocacy of a moderate socialism – or, as some have observed, a liberalism with social democratic leanings.

All this to say that Annina's uncle Giorgio was an important figure whom her family could not but take into account. Nonetheless, Annina did not follow in his footsteps, nor in those of her father Angiolo, he too a philologist, professor of Latin and Greek and associate of the Treccani Encyclopedia Institute; nor those of her uncle by marriage, Gennarino Perrotta (husband to her aunt Adele, Annina's father's sister), philologist and the incumbent chair of Greek Literature at Rome's Sapienza University. Instead she elected, after graduating in 1958, to enroll in the faculty of Letters and Philosophy, where she was to study Art History.

One influence contributing to that choice was her fascination with the Roman art world, with which she had already become acquainted during her lyceum years through her friendship with Claudio Cintoli. The two had habitually visited such shows as the eternal city had to offer, some of which were of notable cogency, such as the aforementioned Pollock exhibition, held at the most important institution of its kind, the Galleria Nazionale d'Arte Moderna, precisely in the year that Annina was to sit her final exams prior to enrolling at university. That exhibition provoked uproar within the Italian art scene, marking an about-turn into an anti-realistic – or rather, anti representative – vein, steering the course of events for years to come. It also sparked public debate between artists and critics and between supporters and detractors.

This was certainly not the motive for which Annina undertook her studies in art history, even if she could hardly remain oblivious to the exhibition's call to arms, which had important repercussions for cultural debate and the evolution of Italian painting.

Also contributing to the path that she chose were the activities of her mother Paolina. Born in Poland, she had disembarked at Venice at

18. This statement comes from Harry F. Gaugh's interview of Rudy Burckhardt (24 November 1982) published in Harry F. Gaugh, *Willem de Kooning* (Abbeville Press, 1983), 122, quoted in https://www.dekooning.org/the-artist/biography. Accounts of this battle have reached an increasingly wide audience. To give just one example: early in Ed Harris' film *Pollock*, the young artist trudges drunkenly up the stairs to his home supported by his brother. Falling on the landing, he exclaims, "Fuck Picasso."
19. Giulio Carlo Argan, "I suoi colori cadono dall'alto," article quoted on the website of the Galleria Nazionale, with no indication of source, on the page devoted to Pollock's 1958 exhibition: https://lagallerianazionale.com/blog/dripping-jackson-pollock.

AN IMPORTANT FRIENDSHIP

the age of 20 to study at Ca' Foscari University. After her relocation to Rome, she had continued to maintain close contact with her place of birth and to cultivate friendships with her compatriots.

Paolina spoke five languages and had served as editor for publications of the International Institute of Agriculture, from which the FAO would subsequently be born. She had also occupied an important post at Warsaw's Italian Embassy from the end of the war until 1947, on the invitation of Ambassador Eugenio Reale.

Annina still remembers the evening in late 1951 that the two went to the Teatro Argentina for a concert featuring Arthur Rubinstein. It was to her utter delight that the virtuoso stayed after the performance to play a few pieces for the Polish friends gathered around the piano; a memory that also conveys Rome's cultural vibrancy in those years. During that concert season, to keep to this one example, in addition to Rubinstein and the Santa Cecilia Orchestra conducted by Paul Klecki, concertgoers could attend a performance of the music of Igor Stravinsky conducted by the composer himself.

Among Paolina's friendships, one of particular note was that with Joseph Jarema, another Pole and a well-connected painter in Roman circles. Indeed, Jarema had co-founded the Art Club with Enrico Prampolini and Gino Severini in 1945; for some years, at least until 1958, the Club was to remain a city institution, with an intense turnover of exhibitions and debates. Achille Perilli later recounted that the Art Club "was installed in a space borrowed from the picture-framer Pierangeli. With its walls upholstered in jute, it was at once an art gallery, a tavern, a venue for conferences and debates, and a meeting place for all the scattered people that the war had deposited in Rome: Poles, Yugoslavs, Jews, Austrians, and Americans, whether white or black."[20]

Claudio Cintoli was Annina's senior by three years. When they met, she was still at lyceum and he attended Cipriano Efisio Oppo's painting classes at the Academy of Fine Arts in Via di Ripetta. Cintoli himself painted and had already exhibited a little; Annina also took to painting somewhat during the same period, precisely on account of the sympathetic appeal of Cintoli's personality. With his quiet presence and the constant appearances and disappearances that made him a brotherly, affable and discreet personage – as Filiberto Menna once recalled him – Cintoli succeeded in endearing himself to all.[21]

Cintoli was a talented artist and had a nose for people and situations; a personality sufficiently *à la page* to be invited, in 1964 (the year of Rauschenberg and Johns' Biennale) to decorate the walls of Rome's Piper Club, the first Italian nightclub to categorically endorse young people's new form of socializing.

In 1958, the same year as Pollock's exhibition and Annina's enrollment at University, Cintoli staged his first solo show at one of the city's most highly esteemed galleries, La Medusa, belonging to Claudio Bruni Sakraischik, known for its important shows of foreign artists and its discerning attention to the younger generation.

To pen the critical texts for Cintoli's exhibition was Eugenio Battisti, a singular figure who, having graduated in philosophy before the war, had followed theatre for a time before, in 1953, undertaking postgraduate study with Lionello Venturi, Argan's acknowledged mentor. He then followed the work of contemporary artists with ever-closer attention until founding the Museo Sperimentale d'Arte Contemporanea in 1963 as well as launching *Marcatré*, an interdisciplinary magazine featuring contributions from those of the era's major intellectuals who sided with the positions of Gruppo 63. Cintoli's exhibition did not go unnoticed. It was immediately reviewed by Lorenza Trucchi, who in her customary, somewhat grouchy, manner wrote all-but encouraging words in *La fiera letteraria*: "An up-to-date but superficial sampling of contemporary painting." Such harsh judgment proved a stimulus for the young artist, to the extent that Trucchi herself duly provided the texts for his solo show at the gallery Il Segno (January 23, 1962), in which he exhibited a series of studies drawn from the work of Leonardo and Picasso.

Il Segno had been opened a couple of years earlier by Carla Panicali, a capable and confident woman for whom Annina had briefly worked; her first professional, non-academic experience, which had helped her feel connected to that world. Shortly afterward, Panicali opened the Roman branch of the Marlborough Gallery – an offshoot of the London gallery – where Rome's second Pollock exhibition would be held, after its predecessor at the GNAM. All this conveys something of the morass of interests that had formed in the city, revolving around its most prestigious local institutions.

To write Pollock's exhibition notes for the Marlborough was Carla Lonzi, future activist and founder of the group Rivolta Femminile, at that time still active as an art critic. For the occasion, she wrote: "The salient characteristic of his work, which reveals an entirely American

20. Achille Perilli, *Forma 1* (Corraini, 1989), 10.

peculiarity in approaching artistic production, is that it reaches beyond any inhibitions relative to the conception of that activity by association with an ideal category of preconceived dimensions, the category of painting, precisely."[22] Lonzi wrote these words in 1963, a few months before the Pop artists' debut at the Venice Biennale, while the phenomenon of Happenings was spreading like wildfire.

21. Filiberto Menna, "Claudio Cintoli, un performer inventivo e sconvolgente," *Paese Sera*, 28 March 1984.
22. Carla Lonzi, "Una mostra di Jackson Pollock a Roma," text reproduced on the page dedicated to the Pollock exhibition on the Galleria Nazionale's website: https://lagallerianazionale.com/blog/dripping-jackson-pollock.

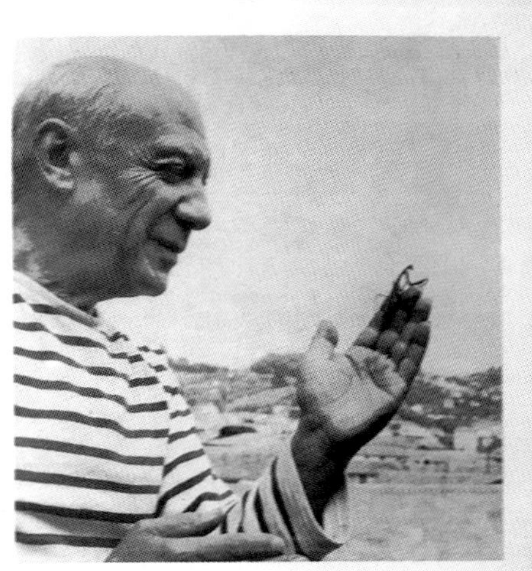

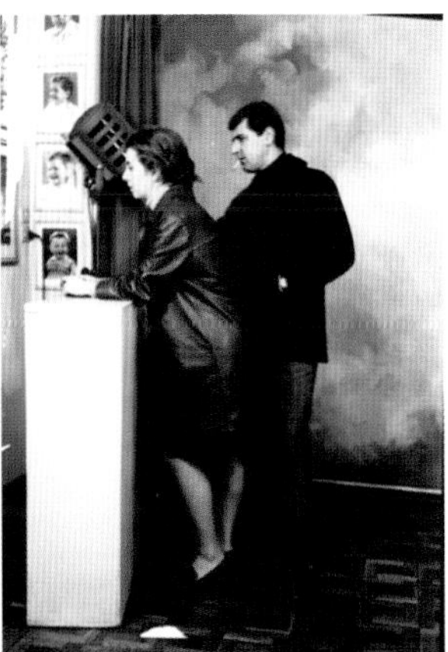

Left: Back cover of the catalogue for the exhibition of Picasso lithographs at the gallery Il Segno, Rome, 1960.

Top: Annina and Michelangelo Pistoletto during a photo session in Paolo Bressano's studio in Turin. Photo used for the realization of the mirror work *L'Annunciazione* (1968).

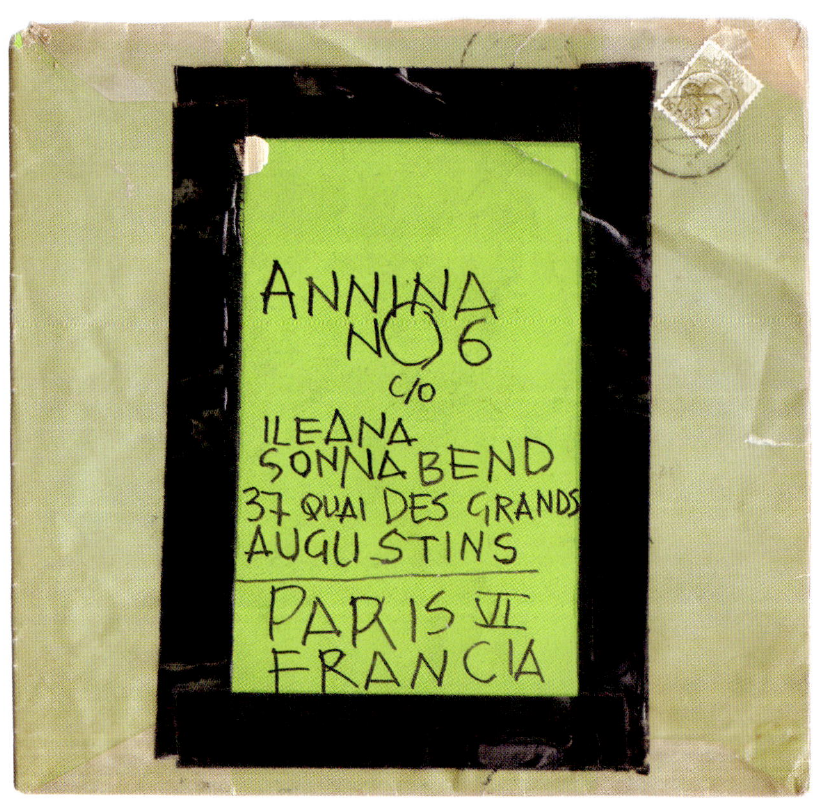

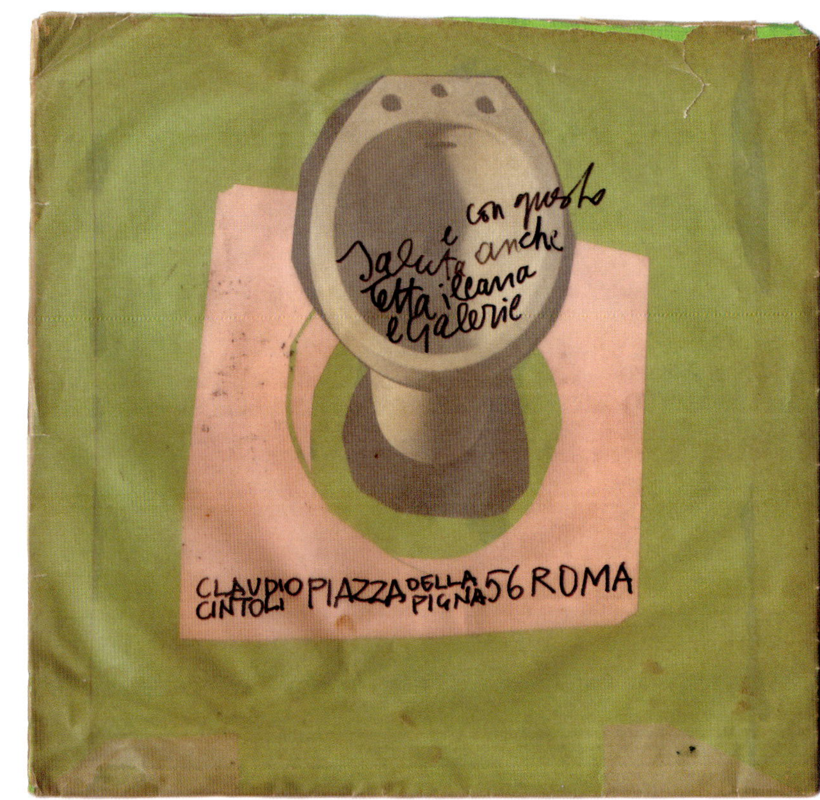

HANDMADE ENVELOPE FOR A LETTER TO ANNINA
FROM CLAUDIO CINTOLI, SENT WHILE SHE WORKED
AT GALERIE ILEANA SONNABEND IN PARIS

ARTISTIC LIFE IN ROME

It was thanks to Cintoli that Annina earned her first work experience at Il Segno; employment of which she remembers, with the irony that so characterizes her, the time she spent writing addresses and mailing invitations for an exhibition of Picasso lithographs.

Her friendship with Claudio Cintoli was important, but it was not unique. Apart from her already-mentioned friends Franco Angeli, Carmelo Bene, Rospo Pallenberg, and Carmen Scarpitta, there were many others who contributed to her electing to take an active part in the art world.

Roman artistic life in that period was decidedly intense and quick to change, but not so much as to exclude certain clichés and old habits. Many artists, along with their friends and supporters, still populated the city's venerable *Rioni*. New neighborhoods sprang up, it is true, and the city continued to expand, but its historic centre remained its main attraction.

Annina lived with her father at the foot of Via Flaminia, barely past the Porta del Popolo, which interrupts the circuit of the Aurelian Walls and from which the three channels of the "Trident" are clearly visible: Via del Babuino, Via del Corso, and Via di Ripetta, which fan out into an urban area in which artists have long kept their studios – at least since the seventeenth century, when the district's layout was established, making it one of the Grand Tour's foremost destinations. The Rome art scene still circulated against the same backdrop during the years in which Annina frequented it.

The last to undertake the Grand Tour, albeit incorrectly, since he had other reasons for doing so, had been Picasso. Ignoring some friends' efforts to dissuade him from the radical changes in his cultural allegiances, the artist came to Rome to join Olga Khokhlova, who herself had arrived on the heels of Diaghilev and the Ballets Russes, present for their performance at the Teatro Costanzi. It was 1917. Picasso was struck by the energy radiating from the Eternal City. He portrayed the artists' models who traditionally loitered on the Spanish Steps, at the end of Via del Babuino, and it was in that atmosphere that he sealed the transition from his Cubist manner to his so-called Neoclassical Period.

When Picasso returned to Rome for the second time, for his major exhibition at the Galleria Nazionale d'Arte Moderna in 1953, this episode seemed ancient history. It had been a brief interlude, but one that had left a deep impression. To promote the Galleria Nazionale show had been Lionello Venturi, a passionate supporter of French painting, particularly the Impressionists and Cézanne. A significant project, it reinvigorated the last glimmers of the debate that pitted figurative and abstract artists against each other: a debate that perished only a few years later with the extensive Pollock exhibition, opening a channel for the emerging young defenders of Abstraction, the members of Gruppo Forma 1 above all, who had held their first exhibition at Jarema and Prampolini's Art Club a decade earlier.

Close to Annina's home was the Fratelli Menghi tavern. It was not alone in its popularity among that milieu of painters, writers, poets, filmmakers, and thespians. There were also other haunts in the Trident where that motley assortment of artists gathered. They could be found, for example, at Cesaretto's on Via della Croce or at the Rosati bar in Piazza del Popolo.

Angiolo, Annina's father, habitually ate at some of those trattorias, and Annina often accompanied him. The most notable amongst them was none other than Fratelli Menghi, the success of which was largely due to the fact that it paid tribute to artists.[23]

By then, a regular presence at those hubs had perhaps lost its primary function of signaling membership in a group or trend – a phenomenon whereby one had been able to meet figurative artists at the tavern in Piazza Nicosia while younger, penniless abstractionists awaited at its counterpart on Via Flaminia. But while it was true that they no longer served so heraldic a function, they still constituted sites of exchange nonetheless, spaces for variably animated discussion.

Annina remembers that on one occasion in Paris in 1961, her father had insisted she visit Mark Tobey's exhibition at the Musée des Arts décoratifs. At first she was surprised at his insistence, until learning that Angiolo had heard the name quoted by the young patrons of Fratelli Menghi; she duly recognized that the American painter's works effectively provided the basis for the pictorial style of Carla Accardi, one of the core members of Forma 1.

23. Amongst various such Roman taverns, the Fratelli Menghi was the best known, immortalized in a long story by Ugo Pirro, writer and screenwriter, who frequented the Fratelli Menghi in those years: Ugo Pirro, *Osteria dei pittori* (Sellerio, 1994).

THE THESIS WITH GIULIO CARLO ARGAN AND THE ENCOUNTER WITH MARCEL DUCHAMP

When Annina embraced the proposal to dedicate her thesis to Marcel Duchamp, her interests had already become evident. All the same, it was that very decision which would allow her to apply an appropriate historical and theoretical awareness to the Happenings and the other artistic enterprises in which she would shortly take part.

Concluding an outstanding student career, Annina graduated in the summer of 1962. Her supervisor was Giulio Carlo Argan, professor of Renaissance and Baroque Art History and internationally acclaimed art critic. In the Europe of that time, Duchamp was a reputable artist who had served in the ranks of Dadaism and Surrealism, to whom Breton had referred as "the smartest man on Earth", and who in the 1950s was considered the most important pioneer of the American revival channeled through Cage, Cunningham, and Rauschenberg. The work that Annina undertook for her thesis had the merit of braving complex research on a cryptic and, despite everything, still little-known figure. To contemplate studies on Duchamp today is to be confronted with an interminable list of articles, essays, and books motivated by ever-increasing recognition of the artist's virtues, but few were the publications devoted to him at the dawn of the 1960s. A monograph had appeared in France in 1959, written by Robert Lebel and immediately translated into English, and *Marchand du Sel*, a collection of the artist's writings edited and introduced by Michel Sanouillet, had gone to print the same year. For that matter, even his best-known works still had little circulation, to the extent that a number of replicas of the famous urinal of 1917, *Fontaine*, had indeed been made with the artist's consent (the first in 1950, the second in 1953 and yet another in 1963) but it was only in 1964 that Duchamp authorized Arturo Schwarz, art historian and critic as well as collector and owner of a Milan gallery, to make 12 replicas (eight, plus four artist's proofs) of each of his most important Readymades, including the urinal.[24]

A mercantile operation? Perhaps. The fact remains that Schwarz accompanied the replicas with a critical volume that greatly contributed to the dissemination and understanding of the artist's ideas. If Annina's acceptance of her thesis subject was laudable by merit of her having perceived Duchamp's exceptional qualities with a certain punctuality – that is, before he became one of art history's storied names – Argan should certainly be credited, were there ever need, with great breadth of vision and genuine love of culture in choosing to entrust her with a thesis on a figure so far removed from his interests. In any case, Annina's encounter with Duchamp was of far-ranging consequences. In fact, some time later she translated his collected writings *Marchand du Sel* into Italian. She subsequently pitched her translation to Marcello Rumma, who published it in 1969 with an introduction by Alberto Boatto.

The acumen with which Annina conducted her work on Duchamp granted her an extensive understanding of the French artist's personality and his relations with Delaunay and the Cubists, but also with Futurism and Surrealism, his ideas regarding the great thinkers of the time – Bergson first and foremost – and also his relationship with contemporary currents. The further Annina delved into the origins of the avant-garde, the better she understood the historical reasons for her own present. The closer she came to the heart of the meaning of Duchamp's thought, the more sense it made to participate in Happenings. After all, Duchamp's conceptions had cleared the way for the new generation. "Everything seen – every object, that is, plus the process of looking at it – is a Duchamp," John Cage once said.[25]

24. Regarding the present location of the earlier replicas of the urinal, the first replica is in the Philadelphia Museum of Art, which holds the most important collection of the artist's work, the whereabouts of the second is unknown and the third is held in the Moderna Museet in Stockholm.

25. Sally Banes, *Greenwich Village 1963: Avant-Garde Performance and the Effervescent Body* (Duke University Press, 1993), 124.

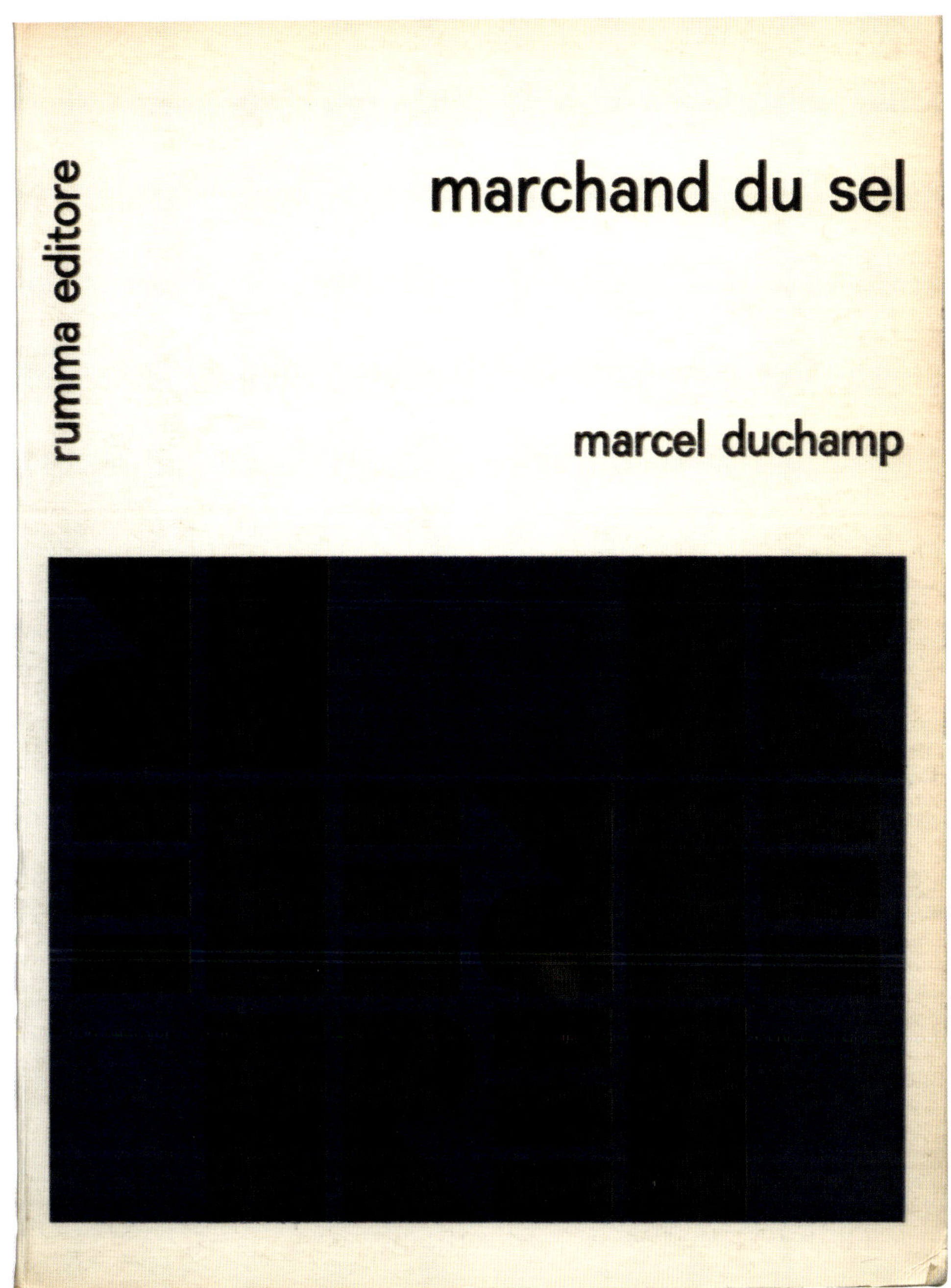

COVER OF MARCEL DUCHAMP'S BOOK
MARCHAND DU SEL (RUMMA EDITORE, 1969),
TRANSLATED BY ANNINA

by the ONCE Group

KITTYHAWK is composed of any number of developing episodes con-
concerned with flight, elevation, levitation, or exploration of the
three-dimensional performance space. Each episode has as its subject
a woman --- a single, performer-object p-- who is in some manner raised
above the performance area surface throught the actions of a man or men.
Each episode states that the woman could not achieve the elevated position by herself. Any mechanical or "magical" device for raising the
woman-object can become the basis of an episode, but no mechanical
principle or magical illusion should be used more than once.

Episodes can have any duration, and all episodes are performed simultaneously. (In some instances, the conditions for the appearance
and manipulation of the woman-object will have to be prepared in
performance prior to her appearance.)

Each episode should have a quasi-culminated or quasi-consummated
character. That is, the episode should end while the woman-object
is elevated or in motion, or before the consequences of a sequence
of actions are fully explicit. The quasi-culminative points in various
episodes can be coordinated or left indeterminate in performance.

Six episodes for KITTYHAWK:

I....Prior to the performance each member of the audience is given a sheet
     of paper, on two sides of which is a mechanical drawing whose function
     is not obvious. A girl appears riding en a hydralic hoist dolly pushed
     into the performance space by a man; she is holding a piece of paper
     like those the audience has. A voice from a loudspeaker begins reading
     instructions for folding the paper. She follows the instructions, and
     at the same time she is lifted very gradually (inshort, aperiodic, abrupt
     bursts) by the hoist. Sudden darkness (and the noise of airplanes from
     the loudspeakers): the girl and hoist disappear. Voice re-enters reading
     instructions for flying a paper airplane. Instructions end with
     "countdown" that leads to popular music from the loudspeakers.

II...A girl walking through the performance space is attacked and slammed
     against a wall by two men. Another man appears with a suitcase, from
     which he takes (first) masking tape. The firl is taped to the wall
     (completely covered). The two mem attackers leave and the man with
     the suitcase ravages the wall fixture, cutting away tape, pulling out
     articles of clothing, exposing parts of the girl's body. Sudden
     darkness: the man disappears. A dim light comes on, exposing the
     girl-fixture to the audience. Sudden darkness: the girl disappears.

III..A girl appears following instructions (a man's voice) from a walkie-
     talkie radio. She triangulates the performance area according to
     instructions, fixing the position of various properties obtained from
     a trunk brought into the space by two men; these include: a number
     of bowling balls, a block and tackle fixture, and a huge bag. She
     receives the bowling balls into the bag according to instructions

ARRIVAL IN THE UNITED STATES

At the end of the summer of 1964, Annina boarded the liner *Independence* for New York. Waiting for her upon her arrival was Carolee Schneemann, who would house her for the first few days, although her destination was the University of Michigan in Ann Arbor, where she was scheduled to take up a teaching position, as stipulated by her Fulbright scholarship.

She arrived eager, reinforced with important experience. The most significant of her previous activities had also been those that had most involved her culturally and emotionally: firstly her participation in the ACT group's shows, then the Happenings, including that with Carolee Schneemann. Then, naturally, her employment with Ileana Sonnabend, but above all her relationships with artists, with Duchamp in particular – even if, as she freely admits, that relationship had at first made little impression on her.

To a young European, the atmosphere in America proved particularly stimulating. She was offered many opportunities for new acquaintances and also for experiences of a curatorial character. In one of the first of these, she took advice that John Cage had given her in Venice and sought out exponents of the legendary ONCE Group. Indeed, she began collaborating with ONCE immediately, producing Happenings of her own conception and participating in the New York-staged version of the famous *Kittyhawk*, which later travelled to several other cities.

Her Fulbright commitments continued at the University of Los Angeles in 1965, where she gave a seminar on Duchamp that helped fulfil the requirements of her PhD.

In Venice once again, Rauschenberg had suggested that she meet John Weber in Los Angeles. He was director of the acclaimed Dwan Gallery, where Abstract Expressionists, Neo-Dadaists, Pop artists, and Nouveaux Réalistes exhibited, and where Minimal Art would soon spring to life. If her encounter with the ONCE Group had brought her fine opportunities, meeting John Weber would prove somewhat more consequential. The two married in October 1966 in New York, where Weber concurrently directed the Dwan Gallery's second location. He would continue to do so until 1971, when the gallery closed and Weber decided to open his own space.

ANNINA AND JOHN WEBER

Annina and John shared no professional relationship, and Annina still downplays their supposed partnership today. She does so mainly to refute a misunderstanding unintentionally provoked by Leo Castelli, who stated, "Annina Nosei worked with John Weber for a long time."[26] Annina was not directly involved in the management of the gallery, but she was certainly involved on the level of its relationships. An emblematic example is that of Mario Merz and his 1973 exhibition organized by John Weber – in cooperation, incidentally, with the Sonnabend Gallery. Annina's friendship with Merz dated back to the time of her employment at the Paris gallery and had been reaffirmed by the artist's attendance at her wedding in New York.

Even before he opened his gallery, John Weber had a significant career behind him. Before directing the Dwan Gallery, he had helmed the Martha Jackson Gallery in New York, while toward the end of the 1960s he became active in promoting American art in Italy, where he fostered relationships with several galleries, Lucio Amelio's not least. He was to achieve excellent results, such as his collaboration with Fabio Sargentini's L'Attico for Robert Smithson's sculptural event *Asphalt Rundown* in 1969. Not to be forgotten was his relationship with Giuseppe Panza di Biumo, nor his decisive contribution to the character of the latter's collection.

Through Weber, Annina came into contact with the sector of the art world – composed of galleries, collections and museums – that forms the backbone of its financial system, which in America has always been central to all its developments; much more so than in Europe. This acquaintance had no immediate consequence except on the level of an increased awareness, although in the succeeding years she would apply it to her unfolding activity as an organizer of independent exhibitions.

26. Alan Jones, *Leo Castelli: L'italiano che inventò l'arte in America* (Castelvecchi, 2007), 325. Translator's note: quotations from this book, originally written in English but only published in Italian translation, are therefore retranslations from Italian.

AN INTEREST IN EUROPEAN ARTISTS

Thanks to Annina, John Weber intensified his dealings with Italy and acquired an ever-clearer idea of what was taking place in Europe. In a statement that he made a couple of years before his death, he said, "I also had all of these Italian Arte Povera people, which was great, whom I met when I was married to Annina Nosei."[27] Indeed, Annina and John habitually spent much of the summer in Italy – in Rome, but especially at their house in Ansedonia, Tuscany. Many art personalities, whether American or European, passed through there. For example, it was there that John met Pino Pascali, for whom he would gladly have arranged an exhibition if not for the tragic motorcycle accident that cut his life short: "So I went there a lot, and I really got in with the Italian artists – also those – like, Pino Pascali from Rome [...] He died, tragically, early on, poor one."[28] The house in Ansedonia was a place of encounter and cultural ferment, a hothouse that allowed Weber to establish more tangible relations with European artists; in all likelihood, it was there that the idea for the exhibition *De Europa*, held in 1972, was born. From it, the gallery derived a measure of its program for the following years.[29]

Regarding *De Europa*, a hypothesis has been hazarded that this choice of name was linked to the thesis that common linguistic roots form a prerequisite for the existence of a shared visual culture. This hypothesis was reflected in Weber's choice of exhibits, attached to conceptual artists and their reflections on language. Supporting this interpretation is the presumed influence exerted by Annina, her father and her uncles, all of whom were engaged in the field of philology.[30] I find the latter surmise especially plausible, not only because of the role played by those eminent scholars in Annina's education, but especially on account of her father Angiolo's constant and loving attention, which enabled her to claim the fundamental method of that discipline as her own – a discipline founded not only on the intrinsic value of historical culture but also on recognition of the importance of formal values. Annina was to demonstrate this faculty in the exhibitions that she would later organize, beginning with *Memory*, which will be discussed in due course.

In any case, the couple were united in their objective of supporting European artists. This represented a considerable change of trend for Weber's gallery, especially when considered in relation to its earlier work in supporting American artists, whom it had striven to promote in Europe.

27. James McElhinney, interview with John Weber for the Smithsonian Archives of American Art, conducted at Weber's home in Chatham, New York, March 21 and April 4 2006: https://www.aaa.si.edu/download_pdf_transcript/ajax?record_id=edan-mdm-AAADCD_oh_257024.
28. Ibid.
29. *De Europa* was held at the John Weber Gallery in New York from 29 April to 24 May 1972. On show were: Giovanni Anselmo, Art & Language, Alighiero Boetti, Daniel Buren, Hanne Darboven, Jan Dibbets, Hamish Fulton, Richard Long, Mario Merz, Giulio Paolini, Reiner Ruthenbeck, Salvo and Gilberto Zorio, a broad and timely sampling of cutting-edge European positions. The gallery's successive exhibitions would reaffirm the same orientation.
30. Fabio Cafagna, "Artisti italiani alla John Weber Gallery: Strategie commerciali e curatoriali (1971-1975)," in Conceptual Art/Arte povera: Politiche e mercato negli anni Settanta, *Ricerche di Storia dell'arte*, no. 132 (2020): 42-43.

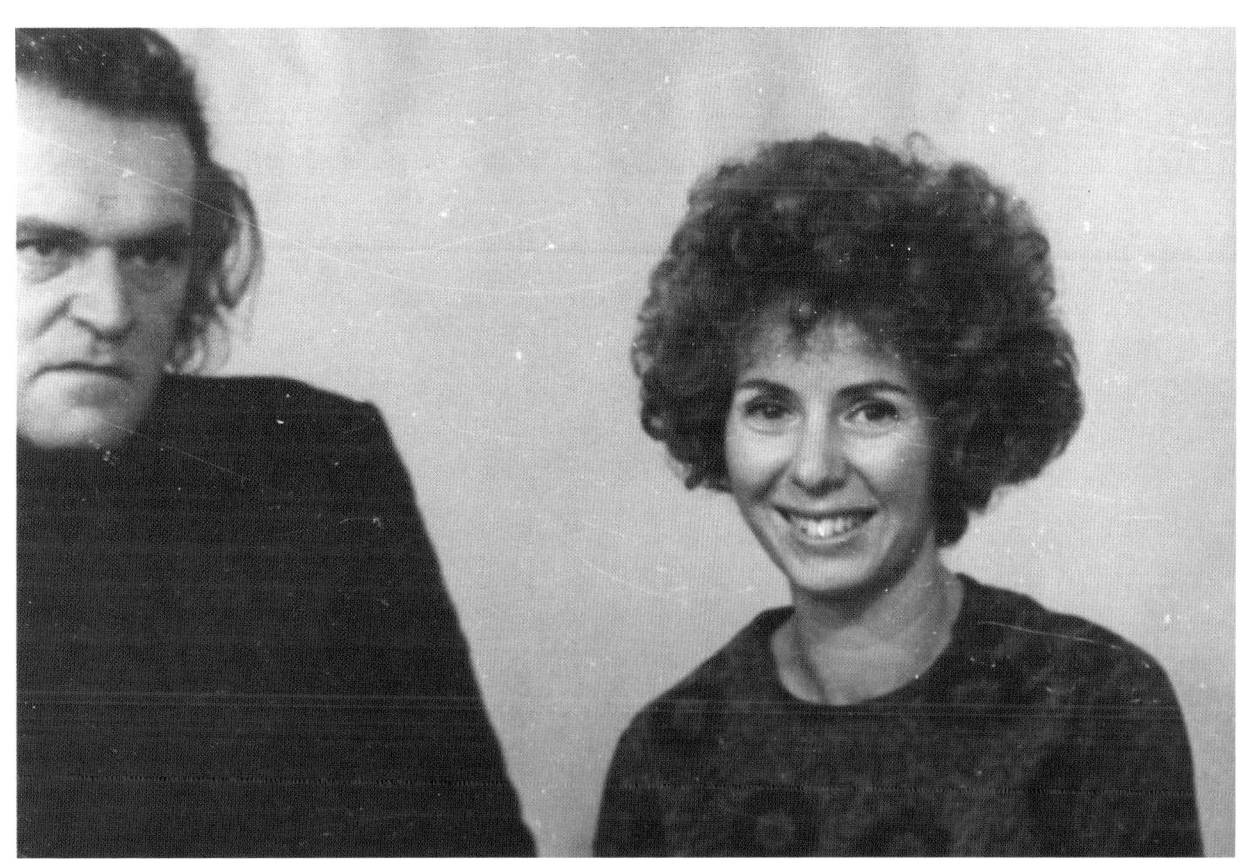

ANNINA WITH MARIO MERZ IN 1966

THE SURVEY FOR METRO MAGAZINE

This discussion has continued to make general reference to European artists, which is true to its subject, but it should be clarified that international attention was primarily geared toward French artists even in the late sixties; the preeminent axis reached between the United States and Paris, not to Rome and nor to Berlin. Reflecting this were the activities of the Dwan Gallery, which exhibited the Nouveaux Réalistes in Los Angeles or those that Sonnabend pursued in the French capital, despite the interest that she had shown in Italian artists.

Annina was not immune to such an attitude either, as demonstrated by an article-survey that she conducted with Otto Hahn for the magazine *Metro*. She was charged with procuring and commenting on a series of statements from American artists, while Hahn dedicated himself to their French counterparts.

It was 1968. The developments that distinguished that year also made of it a symbol: a year of protest. There was no longer simply the question of renewing art forms. The challenge, which had become global, was no longer directed only at cultural traditions but was brashly pitched against all institutions.

Already the opening gambit of Annina's survey left no room for confusion. She asked the artists, "Can the current language of artistic expression in the U.S. be said to challenge the system?" A query that left no loopholes, placing language – that is, the new forms that art had taken over the decade – directly at the heart of the question, and placing it in direct connection to "a challenge to the system". It therefore addressed artists and their awareness of being called to perform an important function for society, which was to construct an ideological vision that departed from art and included aesthetics, politics, and social concerns.[31]

The events associated with 1968 decidedly sharpened the tone of the debate. Americans campaigned against the war in Vietnam, against racial discrimination and for the recognition of women's rights; the French rebelled against the conditions dictated by the Gaullist regime. Young people everywhere sought a radical transformation of society, fighting their fiercest battles for freedom, beginning with free love and liberation from cultural mores, perceived as prerequisites for real renewal. Art had to reckon with the winds of change already betokened by avant-garde art and rekindled by the culture from which Happenings were born.

1968, then, made the taking of positions unavoidable, and it was on this theme that Annina questioned her chosen artists, inquiring whether art could constitute a form and a standpoint from which to challenge the system. Her questionnaire arose amidst a climate of suspicion towards the art system – which is to say, those artists who still responded to market demands. To remain within that system and languish in the rut of tradition, however modern that tradition might have been, was to give a weak, morally indefensible response. If the *Metro* survey still fell within the prism of Franco-American relations, the circumstances gradually asserting themselves in fact soon eclipsed the question. It was no longer to be a question of subverting the primacy of Paris, which by that date the Americans had largely achieved through their setting of new worldwide trends (Pop, Op, and Minimal Art), but of facing new balances of power. With 1968, art acquired a greater political and social charge, which reinvigorated European culture and artistic expression. Although, as previously observed, "The end of the old Paris-New York feud resolved itself into a form of internationalism centered on New York but with intense peripheral activity in Germany, Italy, England, and the rest of France," in practice the American scene opened up to Europeans, who had an edge in terms of ideological rigor.[32]

31. Annina Nosei Weber e Otto Hahn, "La sfida del sistema: Inchiesta sulla situazione artistica attuale negli Stati Uniti e in Francia," *Metro*, n.s., no. 14 (1968): page numbers, 232 in this volume. The artists whom Annina consulted were: Allan Kaprow, Donald Judd, Sol LeWitt, Robert Smithson, Dan Graham, Billy Klüver, and E.A.T.
32. Grégoire Müller, *La nuova avanguardia: Introduzione all'arte degli anni Settanta* (Alfieri, 1972), 5.

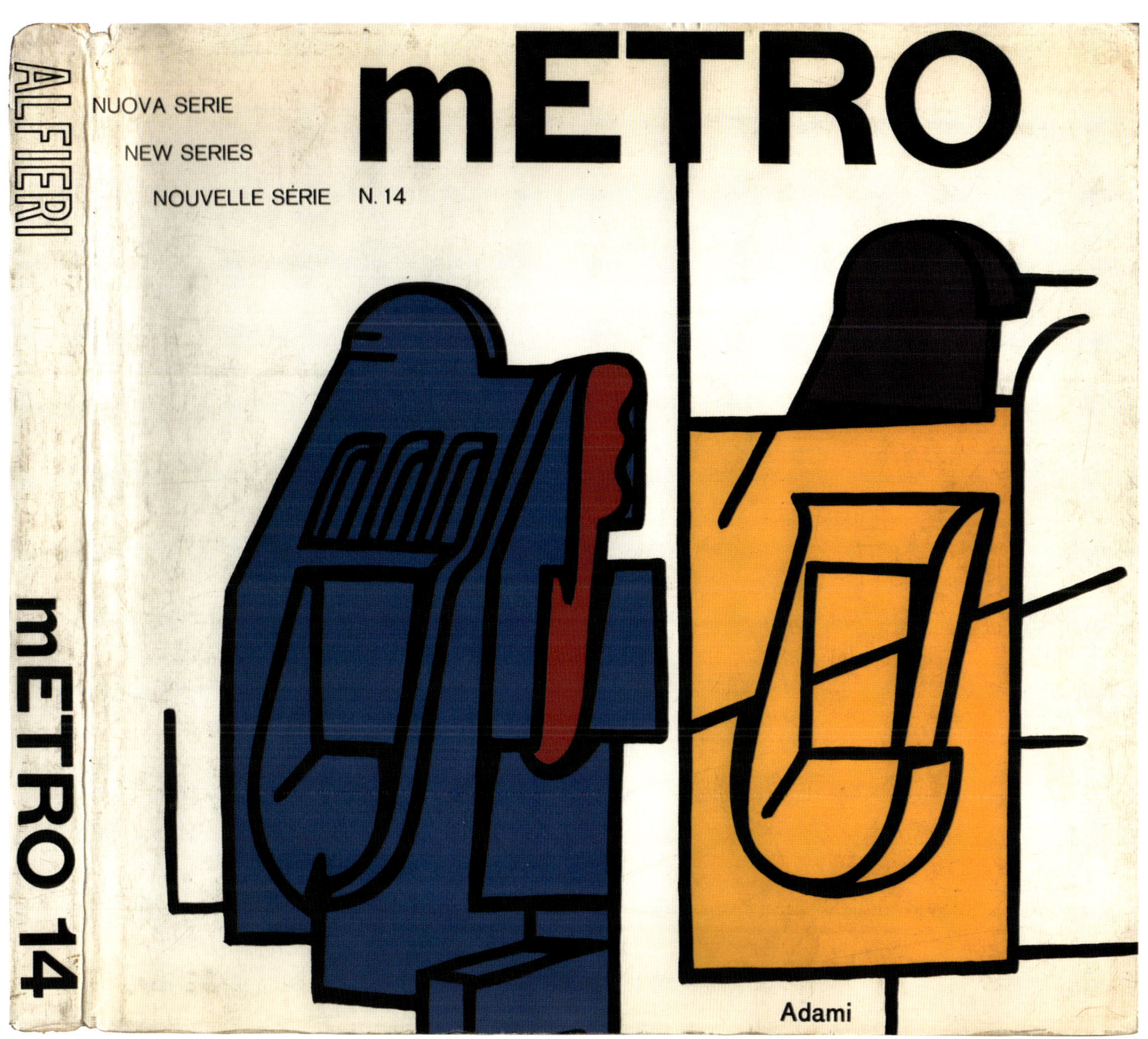

COVER OF ISSUE 14 (NEW SERIES) OF THE MAGAZINE *METRO* (1968),
IN WHICH ANNINA AND OTTO HAHN'S INQUIRY WAS PUBLISHED

STILL ON THE SUBJECT OF DE EUROPA

According to John Weber, "I think I was probably the first gallery to really make a commitment to European art as well as American art."[33] Perhaps it is reductive to treat the two camps as equivalent, but such was symptomatic of the context of the seventies.

With his receptiveness to European artists, and to Italian artists in particular, Weber responded to several prompts. The first and most immediate was attributable to sentimental motives; it related to Annina, to what she represented as an Italian and European woman – and, no less importantly, to their intellectual consensus and common appreciation for the work of the artists concerned. Weber made no lack of rapturously enthusiastic declarations on their account, even if on several occasions he lamented the difficulty of integrating them into American collections, stating that "there has always has been a certain chauvinistic resistance in America toward contemporary European art."[34]

Weber's second motive, which might be described as tactical, concerned the prospect of differentiating his role both from that which he had previously performed at the Dwan Gallery and from those performed by the galleries of Leo Castelli, Ileana Sonnabend, and André Emmerich, whose building he shared: 420 West Broadway. Finally, by favoring Europeans Weber responded to a strategic incentive, which compensated for dynamics mentioned earlier. In the early 1970s, in reality, American art found itself in difficulty. Although over the 20 years previous it had achieved the goals it had set for itself – namely, to overcome French dominance and to assert new home-grown trends – from 1968 onwards the bulk of the younger generation's resources were mobilized toward political and social engagement. On one hand, this fact precipitated an impasse in artistic creativity due to a lack of new input. On the other, increasingly widespread gestures of opposition to and defiance of institutional power could only rekindle interest in European art, which was decidedly more politicized.

33. Weber.
34. Alan Jones, Laura De Coppet, *The Art Dealers: The Powers behind the Scene Tell How the Art World Really Works* (Clarkson N. Potter, 1984), 201. Weber added an additional observation in relation to the difficulty of selling European artists, which makes an indirect virtue of his cultural adhesion to those preferences: "Of the three or four one-man exhibitions I did of the Italian artist Mario Merz, I sold one piece, to The Museum of Modern Art. I have never sold one piece by Boetti; I have never sold an Anselmo. I've never sold one Daniel Buren in America to anybody, institution or private collector."

A TRILOGY: PAINTING, MEMORY AND DISCUSSIONS

Annina divorced Weber in 1973, although she and her ex-husband remained on excellent terms. After all, they had exemplary role models near at hand in the form of Leo Castelli and Ileana Sonnabend, who had maintained an intimate understanding despite their separation. In those New York years, Annina taught at St. John's University and then at Kingsborough Community College. In the mid-seventies, however, the latter institution found it necessary to reduce staff numbers due to mounting financial difficulties and elected not to reappoint female teachers. Annina therefore decamped to teach at the School of Visual Arts.

Between 1976 and 1977, she organized three exhibitions as an independent curator: *Painting, Memory,* and *Discussions*. Although each took a distinct approach, all three were reduceable to a common objective, that of investigating, beyond the exhibitions' individual artists (and even while necessarily driven by their work), certain problematic areas that constituted foci of attention at the time.

Painting focused on the question of painting. A practice contested from all sides insofar as it was too deeply embedded in tradition and for that very reason seemed obsolete or simply unfit for grasping the transformations taking place; *Memory* explored the function and value of memory as presented both from a theoretical point of view, citing certain historical interpretations, and from an immediate one bound to the artists' own interests; finally, Discussions highlighted radical uses of formal debate, of speech, whereby discussion became a new form of art.

The shows constituted a three-phase inquiry into ways of making and thinking about art at a time when the activities of the avant-garde, having reached a zenith in the questioning of expressive languages and their communicability, were directing themselves at the pioneering of alternate systems. Hers was a trilogy built on a single plotline that, by way of quip, could be summarized as a broad discussion of the condensation of "memory" in the meaning of "painting". The debate that would take place over the course of the decade, incidentally, revolved to a considerable degree upon the question of painting, for all that it was ever-further displaced by new practices. For the exhibition *Painting*, Annina invited a dozen artists both male and female, including Daniel Buren, Carolee Schneemann, and Ralston Farina – a performance artist who focused his work on the manipulation of time and the unexpected in everyday events: "I use stylistic tendencies as a painter would color. Every show I do is different and of the time."[35] This obvious inversion of codes well summarized the discussion at hand.

The invited artists radicalized their ideas to the point of paradox. Their behavior marshalled the effects produced by the shock of 1968, increasingly embodying the trend toward contesting incumbent artistic thought and culture.

Discussions took its cue from the work of Ian Wilson and the international recognition that he had attracted during that period. In 1977 the Banco Gallery in Brescia, to give an Italian example, presented

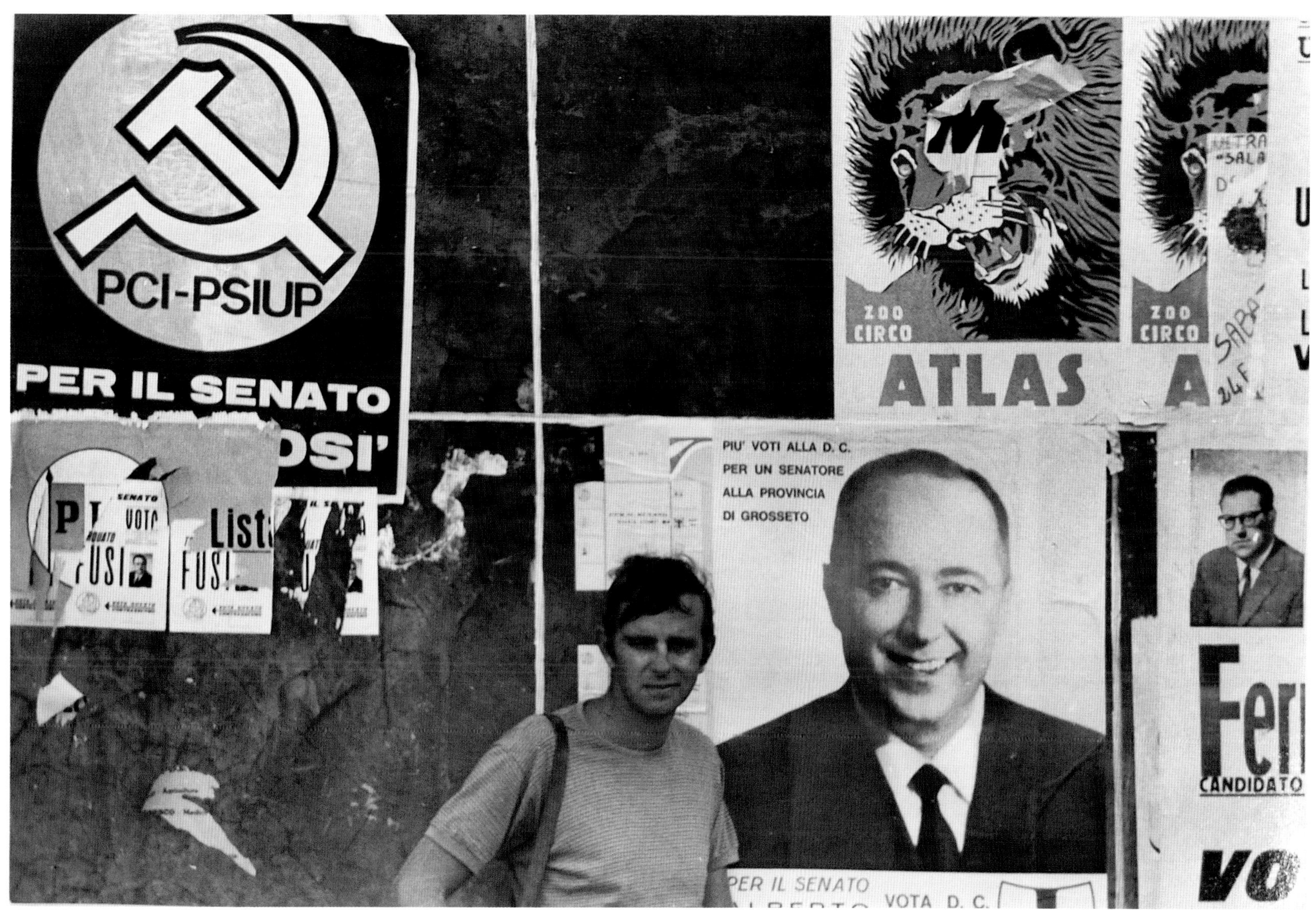

JOHN WEBER IN ROME, 1968

one of his *Discussions* – as all of the artist's post-1968 exhibitions were called, after which he ceased executing object-based works in favor of exploring the aesthetic potential of spoken language.

All the artists invited to *Discussions* were called upon to express themselves (though not exclusively) through speech, discourse, and dialogue – at any rate, through verbal communication.[36] The exhibition presented installations, audio recordings, videotapes, and conferences in the form of encounters between artists and the public. The use of spoken and also written language as sole artistic medium was at that time the furthest frontier of avant-garde escalation. *Discussions* foregrounded the final destination of the battle against the idea of the work as artifact, as object; in short, the work of art had dematerialized, making room for metalinguistic analyses of the making and thinking of art.

Annina circulated within that sphere, recording its aspirations, tensions, and outcomes. The same is true of *Memory*, held a short time previous, which stemmed from an invitation from Marina Urbach, director and founder of C Space, to curate one of the three exhibitions that she intended to devote to the theme of memory, one to be curated by Urbach herself and the other by Marcia Tucker.[37] Each of the three curators was to develop the theme of memory according to her own vision. Annina conducted research on the origins of the function of memory; she reflected on mnemonic traditions, beginning from that of ancient Greece, which associated memory and the soul; she referred to the four Pythagorean virtues (courage, temperance, justice, and wisdom) and to the Christian concept of love, also emphasizing Apollonius' assertion that the glorification of memory represented the highest virtue of the intellect. She further addressed the theme of Giulio Camillo's 16th-century Theatre of Memory, which represented (in addition to exemplifying the relationship between memory and mnemonics), as its author explained it, "All that the mind can conceive and all that is hidden in the soul – all of which could be perceived at one glance by the inspection of [its] images."[38] This was precisely the nodal point from which to derive, perhaps even by opposition, the work of contemporary artists. Indeed, having begun from the aspect of memory evoked through history, Annina segued into one of its decidedly more pressing manifestations. She borrowed a passage of Beckett, the master of the absurd, drawn from his essay on Proust: "The man with a good memory does not remember anything, because he does not forget anything. His memory is uniform, a creature of routine, at once a condition and function of his impeccable habit, an instrument of reference instead of an instrument of discovery. The pæan of his memory: 'I remember as well as I remember yesterday…' is also its epitaph, and gives the precise expression of its value. He cannot *remember* yesterday any more than he can remember tomorrow."[39]

This was the motif onto which the exhibition *Memory* was grafted, transferred to the sandpit of current art, where Annina's interest, free from schemes and preconceptions, remained fixed.

Annina's intellectual verve and her background left her substantially free from prejudice against the contemporary. True to that persuasion, she curated another group show at C Space toward the end of the following year, in 1978, to which she invited Sandro Chia, Paolo Colombo, and Suzanne Santoro: three artists in their 30s who, though all representing the novelties of the moment, developed them along radically different lines. Once again, Annina demonstrated her interest in rendering the different souls of contemporary artistic inquiry.

35. Ralston Farina, *Mission Statement*, The Museum of Modern Art Library.
36. Annina's guest artists for *Discussions* were Joseph Beuys, David Antin, Carolee Schneemann, Giuseppe Chiari, the group International Local (Sarah Charlesworth, Joseph Kosuth, Anthony McCall), Victor Burgin, Robert Ashley, Lucio Pozzi, and of course Ian Wilson.
37. In a recent private exchange with Annina, Marina Urbach reminded her that Marcia Tucker had just left the Whitney Museum at the time and was working toward establishing the New Museum, on account of which, at the opening of her exhibition at C Space, she had the staff wear t-shirts emblazoned with the phrase NEW MUSEUM, considering it the new institution's debut.
38. Frances Yates, *Selected Works Volume III: The Art of Memory* (Ark, 1984), 158.
39. Annina Nosei, "Memory," 1977, typewritten text accompanying the exhibition of the same name (C Space, New York, April 1977), collection of Annina Nosei. See also Samuel Beckett, *Proust* (Grove Press, 1957), 17, 192 in this volume.

the John Weber Gallery
at 420 West Broadway
New York. Structures &
wall-drawings. Sol LeWitt.
Opens September 25, 1971

INVITATION CARDS TO A
JOHN WEBER GALLERY EXHIBITION, NEW YORK

NOVEMBER 27 — DECEMBER 9

CARL ANDRE

DAN FLAVIN

RICHARD HAAS

DALE HENRY

JEFFREY LEW

SOL LEWITT

ROBERT OVERBY

ROBERT RYMAN

FRED SANDBACK

KENNETH SNELSON

ROBERT SMITHSON

JOHN WEBER GALLERY

420 WEST BROADWAY
NEW YORK 10012
(212) 966-6115

INVITATION CARDS TO A
JOHN WEBER GALLERY EXHIBITION, NEW YORK

C Space
96 Chambers Street
New York, N.Y. 10007

Sandro Chia
Paolo Colombo
Suzanne Santoro

Organized by
Annina Nosei Weber

October 29-November 11   Gallery Hours
Opening, October 29 6-8 p.m.   3-6 p.m.

INVITATION CARD TO THE EXHIBITION *SANDRO CHIA, PAOLO COLOMBO, SUZANNE SANTORO*, CURATED BY ANNINA FOR C SPACE, NEW YORK, OCTOBER 1978

PAINTING, IN PARTICULAR

Annina's interests were always drawn to the most hotly-debated topics of their moment. With *Painting*, she addressed a question of primary importance. Even its title's concluding comma – *Painting*, –framed the theme of painting in a manner that left the way open to other vernaculars, which she knew well from personal experience. She confronted the issue of painting without either siding with it or rejecting it. She did not intend to cast doubt on the fields of object-based and conceptual art from which severe attacks on painting had often originated, painting having borne the accusation of being too burdened with memory, too entangled in tradition. Rather, she sought to identify common ground, complementary sectors of creative terrain. In counterpoint to Daniel Buren's inclusion in the exhibition, for example (Buren being engaged in an art practice beyond any pictorial function) she opposed – or rather, juxtaposed – that of Carolee Schneemann. Although Schneemann used different media (Happenings, video), she defined herself a painter.

Faced with the evolution of artistic vernaculars whose very newness seemed tailored to faithful renderings of the changes in contemporary society, *Painting* emphasized the persistence of painting and stressed the energy unleashed from the confrontation of different means of expression.

This exhibition was held at C Space also, in the Fine Arts Building, a highly active and dynamic environment indicative of the ambitions of a time marked by the search for a new, alternative and collaborative spirit.

THE FINE ARTS BUILDING

Between 1974 and 1978, the Fine Arts Building, which represented an alternative to commercial galleries and museum institutions, was a major meeting point for artists and the world that revolved around art's more radical incarnations. Because of the open and interdisciplinary nature of the activities it hosted, including many exhibitions and pop-up events, it received a great deal of attention from Annina's generation.

Among the many initiatives that took place within its walls, one of significant scale and organizational scope was the exhibition *Lives*, Jeffrey Deitch's first curatorial project. Deitch had previously worked as an assistant at the John Weber Gallery. The exhibition's agenda was spelled out in the subtitle "Artists Who Deal with Peoples' Lives (Including Their Own) as the Subject and/or the Medium of Their Work," an obvious extension of new trends and their search for a connection between art and other fields of experience, whether existential, social, or political.

Introducing *Lives*, Deitch wrote. "Several of the artists in the exhibition have made an effort to totally integrate their political and philosophic beliefs with their lifestyle and with their art."[40]

Lives responded to a spirit distinguished by utmost freedom. In addition to addressing contrasts of ideas, of forms of self-expression, it was also based on participation and collective being, consistent with the peculiarities of its venue. In this regard, the Fine Arts Building was the place that, more than any other, channeled the climate of that moment, the watchword of which was "alternative," a moment calling for the rejection of every form of constraint while at the same time expressing a desire for collectivity and for art-making in keeping with a continuous existential flux. Even personal relationships – such as that between the director of the Fine Arts Building, Julian Pretto, and its habitués, for instance – were often oriented toward alternative formulae of exchange of goods and services as part of a reciprocal coexistence that fused art, creative acts and everyday life.

All this appears truly out of tune with the commercial structure of art, of which painting seemed the form to be most categorically repudiated. It was in this context that painting became the main target for those who sought to sever ties with everything that seemed to inhibit ongoing diversification.

40. Jeffrey Deitch (ed.), *Lives* (1975). Catalogue for the exhibition of the same name at the Fine Arts Building, New York, 29 November – 20 December 1975.

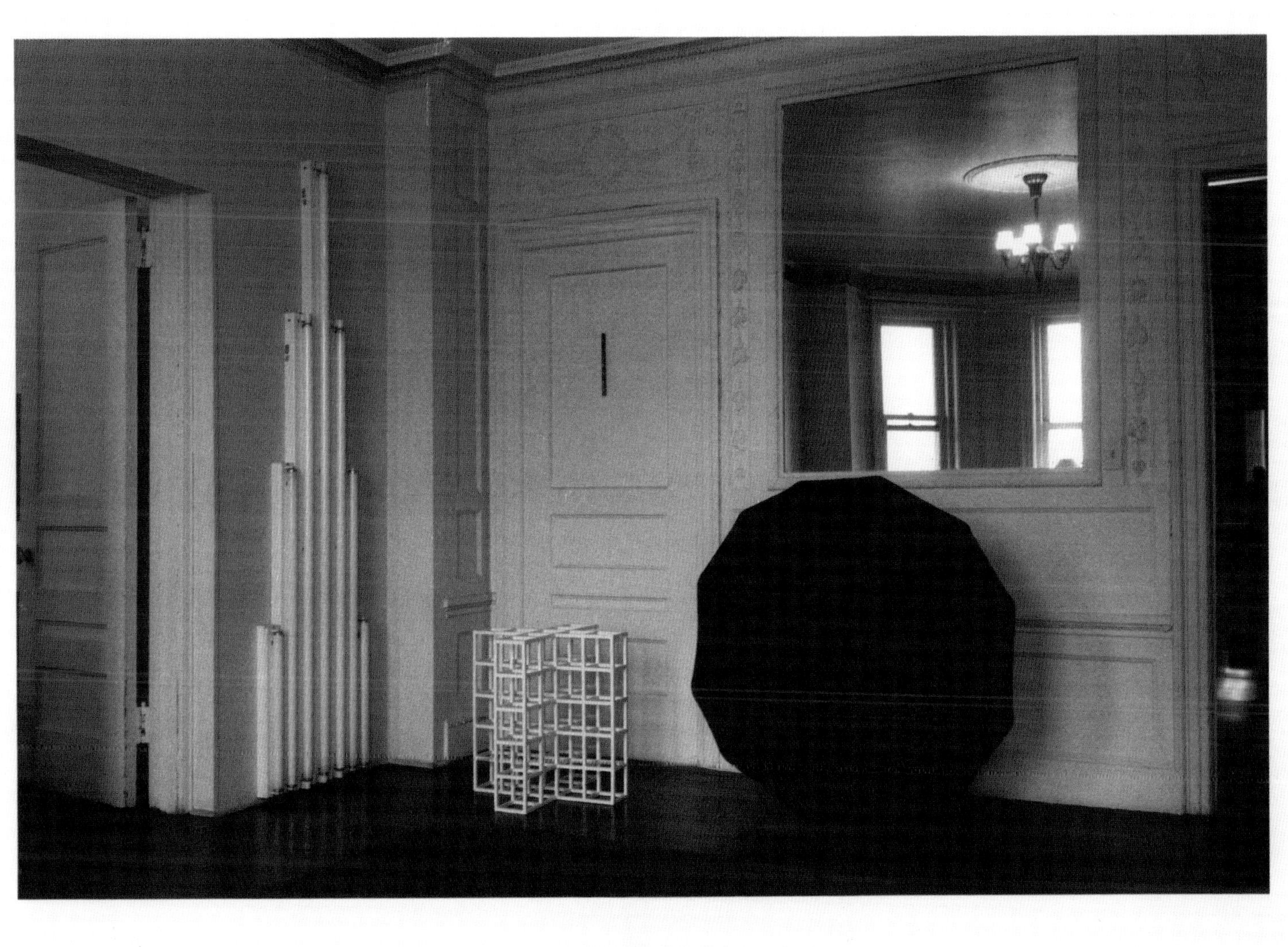

ANNINA'S APARTMENT IN 1973, WITH WORKS BY
(FROM LEFT) DAN FLAVIN, SOL LEWITT, AND ELLEN PHELAN

THE END OF PAINTING

Of the three exhibitions that Annina organized, *Painting* touched on the most sensitive issue. As with *Memory* or *Discussions*, *Painting* approached its topic with both historical and critical awareness. Above all, though, it braved an old dispute that had reclaimed utmost relevance at that time, as further evidenced by *Artforum*'s publication of a special monograph devoted to painting.[41]

The crisis of painting had begun long before. In order to understand it, however, there was no need to return to the birth of photography, which had produced the first cracks in the reasons for painting's existence; nor was there need to refer to the great flowering of abstract painting, which, even as it had given painting new vitality, had in many ways indicated its limits, as in the case of Malevich or Rodchenko, who had carried painting to extremes of spirituality or tautological objectivity. To understand the centrality of the theme of painting, one need only look at the debate spawned from certain positions of Allan Kaprow, which linked the works of Pollock to Happenings in the spirit of the Duchampian readymade.

Of the artists invited to *Painting*, some practiced painting with a conceptual attitude – that is, while reflecting on its means and function – whereas others used an object-oriented or behavioral vernacular even as they continued to construct images in pictorial terms. Thus Annina remained within a dialectical opposition that also contemplated possible solutions. It is to this that the title's comma alludes, following the noun "Painting".

With *Painting*, then, she touched upon a far-from-resolved issue that indeed would continue to stimulate controversy such as that deliberately provoked by the 1979 exhibition entitled *American Painting: The Eighties*, which took a drastic stance in favor of painting, presented as the singular medium that would define the future of American art.[42] Writing in the catalogue, the curator supported this hypothesis by the negative example of the Museum of Modern Art's 1974 exhibition *Eight Contemporary Artists* and the work of its eight protagonists, whom she accused of addressing artistic problems through extra-artistic media.[43] This was a denunciation of the incongruity between a set of goals and the means used to achieve them, but it was also an attack on approaches that deconstructed artistic values and the modernist tradition: deconstruction as exemplified by the work of Daniel Buren, the single artist most committed to the critique of art institutions.

A few years after *Painting*, therefore, the debate still thrived. To remain in the New York sphere, in 1981 (and subsequent to articles appearing in *Artforum* that addressed the question of painting), *October* published an article by Douglas Crimp with the more-than-eloquent title "The End of Painting".[44] Crimp's was at once a reaction to positions taken in favor of painting and a defense of the work of the *Eight Contemporary Artists* and all that they represented, exemplified by such exhibitions as *Lives* (1975) and *Rooms* (1976); it was the latter exhibition that inaugurated PS1, which focused on the same deconstructive tendencies. Despite the variety of approaches involved in that arena and the diversity of techniques that it deployed,

Crimp unhesitatingly considered it a homogeneous field, identifying none other than Buren as its most representative example. "I take Buren's work to be exemplary," he wrote, defending the latter against negative judgments of his work and accusations of sabotage.[45] Buren's contributions to the MoMA's 1974 *Eight Contemporary Artists* were consistent with those he made for *Painting*, aimed at creating a short circuit in the separation of what was considered art and what was not, or what constituted an (institutional) exhibition venue and what constituted "real" space. The metaphorical significance with which the artist invested his work, which sought to unravel the mechanisms underlying value-formation, indeed made it emblematic of that contested era. William Rubin himself, director of the MoMA's Painting and Sculpture department, appeared in an *Artforum* interview during the course of *Eight Contemporary Artists* in which he expressed the need to transform the museum, including its organization and function in relation to the meanings and implications that artists were then imposing on art.[46]

In this conflicted context, it is not that Annina was not attuned to bolder experimentation, to which important youthful experiences had bound her, but that she also contemplated the modernist tradition. Her background enabled her to outstrip contingency, to overcome schematisms of the "new vs. traditional", "aesthetic vs. artistic", "politicization vs. art-for-art's-sake" variety, allowing her to seek the artistic fact beyond the stylistic language, beyond the ideology. She could compare apparently unrelated works and identify their affinities, trace their similarities; she could find correlations and indicate potential lines of continuity between artists even of different generations.

Painting, in fact, broached an issue still limited to the generation at work at the turn of the 1960s and 1970s, yet which would erupt at the beginning of the following decade. Broad swathes of young people, members of the second generation born into mass culture, began to aspire to the conquest of the art scene – until then the exclusive prerogative of the most radical artists and their supporters – and found a new *raison d'être* in the recovery of painterly means.

41. "Special Painting Issue." *Artforum* 14, no. 1 (September 1975).
42. *American Painting: The Eighties*, curated by Barbara Rose, Grey Art Gallery, New York University, 5 September – 13 October 1979. The exhibition presented the work of more than forty artists, all working in the field of painting.
43. *Eight Contemporary Artists*, curated by Associate Curator of Painting and Sculpture Jennifer Licht, The Museum of Modern Art (MoMA), New York, 9 October 1974 – 5 January 1975. The artists were: Vito Acconci, Alighiero Boetti, Daniel Buren, Hanne Darboven, Jan Dibbets, Robert Hunter, Brice Marden, and Dorothea Rockburne. The exhibition marked the official recognition of the new trend undermining the modernist tradition.
44. Douglas Crimp, "The End of Painting", *October*, no. 16 (spring 1981): 69-86.
45. Ibid.
46. Lawrence Alloway and John Coplans, interview with William Rubin, "Talking with William Rubin: 'The Museum Concept Is Not Infinitely Expandable'," *Artforum* 13, no. 2 (October 1974): 51-57. *Eight Contemporary Artists* was defined in its press release as constituting "the largest exhibition of contemporary art to be presented at the Museum since 1970." *Eight Contemporary Artists on View at Museum*, press release no. 101, MoMA, released 9 October 1974.

THE ARRANGEMENT WITH LARRY GAGOSIAN

Alongside her independent activity, Annina occasionally sold artworks. After all, her experiences previous to that point had served to illustrate that artistic practice, even of the most radical variety, needed never conflict with other activities. She had already gained this awareness before she met Larry Gagosian, with whom she went on to share a New York loft in the late 1970s. The crisis of that decade was progressively on the wane and the art market had begun to show signs of recovery.

The new generation of artists was coming into its own; after difficult years, collectors had begun to reappear in galleries, eager to purchase younger artists' works. Furthermore, as the months went by, the number and enthusiasm of collectors increased exponentially. Annina had learned by firsthand experience that the curator's role was the weakest link in the artist-curator-gallery-collector-museum chain. Unlike in Europe, where money was always regarded with a certain moral suspicion, a decidedly more pragmatic attitude prevailed in America. This is not to forget, however, John Weber's words to the effect that: "At its best, art dealing has another mission that comes before profit."[47] Castelli expressed himself more trenchantly: "It's ridiculous to talk about galleries as places where somebody simply goes to buy paintings. Firstly, we all have to support artists, and secondly, we have to make our living by it too."[48] In looking for a space, Annina and Gagosian settled on 421 West Broadway, right across the street from the legendary 420, the building that housed the galleries of John Weber, Leo Castelli, Ileana Sonnabend, and André Emmerich, which made the location particularly appealing. It was Hague, of Hague Art Deliveries, who had located the site, perhaps only by chance; his warehouse at 108a, which he shared with the Dwan Gallery and Leo Castelli, had been earmarked by the city for demolition. John Weber recalled that, on the day of the joint opening of the galleries at 420 West Broadway, "12 or 13,000 people came through like a swarm of locusts, stopping traffic all up the street."[49]

For Annina, choosing 421 West Broadway inevitably meant entering into dialogue with a pool of galleries that had significantly defined the New York art scene.

Her partnership with Gagosian was oriented around selling works, but Annina soon thought of using the loft to stage exhibitions; one in particular, David Salle's November 1979 show, hinted at the energy of the situation. The show was well-received, opening up an important future for the artist. Mary Boone, who in the meantime had opened her own gallery at 420, decided to work with Salle. After all, as Boone herself has recalled, Annina did not yet know that she would open her own gallery soon after.

It was rather a compact scenario, for all that there could have been rivalry between them, there is an organic quality to the picture that emerges of the group of personalities perched at 420 West Broadway. There was healthy competition rather than rivalry between them, which spurred each to further exertions, functioning as a stimulus toward the assertion of individual gallery identities. As previously observed on others' accounts, Mary Boone wanted to belong to that milieu, she needed to represent something new. David Salle or Julian Schnabel, artists of the emerging generation who outlined a different argument, were exactly what she needed. With her exhibition of David Salle, Annina had shown her faculty for grasping the moment's ferment ahead of time, for readily embracing the offerings of the advancing art scene without ceasing to distinguish the threads that wove the fabric of art. In this connection, she remembers an episode that seems significant to me: namely when, with Salle's paintings hung in the loft, she glanced out of the window and saw works by Robert Mangold displayed in John Weber's gallery across the street. The works were obviously very different, but the harmony of that dialogue-at-a-distance surprised her, testifying to her interest in detecting possible correspondences between even very distinct authors.

She may already have been contemplating establishing her gallery when, thanks to Richard Milazzo, the book *Discussion* was published, collecting the documentation, recordings, and photographs of the exhibition *Discussions*, held exactly three years earlier in May 1977.[50] The book concisely rendered the conceptual extremes spanning a decade that had seen the victory of ephemeral experience over the physical work, and the written or spoken word victorious over all. Now, almost without warning, another situation had unfolded, the distinguishing feature of which was its interest in painting. What caused it? Was Christopher Lasch justified in writing, in *The Minimal Self*, that each new generation differentiates itself by opposition to the generation preceding it? Is this the reason for the sudden shift from conceptual formulae to the resurgence of painting and sculpture? This motivation was undoubtedly a factor, but not one adequate to singly account for a phenomenon that defined much of the eighties. The change worked by the new generation, that generation's success with the public and especially its success with collectors – primed for euphoria at a streak of paint, a tangle of brushstrokes or even a scrawled autograph – bemused the artists of the previous generation, who in the face of that phenomenon began to speak of "reflux": of a recycling of fin-de-siècle tropes, of supine acquiescence to the reigning system and so forth.

The transition into the eighties was anything but painless, while the new decade's sudden upheaval was probably attributable to fatigue generated by the repetition of certain post-minimalist and post-conceptual formulae; tropes that, albeit with variable intensity for each individual artist or group, had been identified with resistance to the system, or indeed with the outermost fringes of anti-establishment rebellion.

It was surely no coincidence that interest in painting, replete with panegyrics of the painterly hand and rapture at the epiphany of images, resurfaced concurrent with the neoliberal turn. And if it was no coincidence, it was certainly paradoxical. Perhaps it was natural that, just as opposition to the establishment – to use a protest-era expression – began to wane, the effects of neoliberalism began to be

THE SOHO GALLERY OPENS

felt. Yet it was paradoxical that an economic policy based on deregulation coincided with a return to the orthodoxies of painting. The twentieth-century avant-garde, from its two transatlantic hubs, had initiated a process of transformation that affected the whole cultural sphere: historically, artistically, aesthetically, and economically. The avant-garde had deconstructed the forms and norms that attributed value, meaning and significance to art. Latter-day painting, even as it recovered the forms and taste inherent to the modernist tradition, was in fact no longer able to recover its values. As the art world increasingly eschewed ideology, creative choices were progressively decided by the more traditional criteria of "artistry". Institutions were reevaluated also; the art market, eager to enjoy the surplus generated by that wave of success, liberated itself from the moral censure to which it had previously been subjected. A surge of energy resulted, pressing inexorably toward another horizon.

At the threshold of the new decade, Annina contemplated opening her own gallery. She had no uncertainty about the program that it would pursue; it would conform to her sensibilities and her affinity for the youthful zeitgeist, with which she was also in contact through teaching at the School of Visual Arts.

She chose a venue at 100 Prince Street in SoHo, a few minutes' walk from 421 West Broadway. She did so knowing what she was up against, the difficulties involved. Running a gallery meant many things: it meant, for example, choosing a side in a game that would have to be replayed over and over, knowing that there was also a business element. But she also knew very well that the gallery's activities could not be reduced to their commercial aspect alone; the examples of John Weber and Leo Castelli, already quoted in relation to their respective perceptions of their trade, were cases in point. And then, there are those who insist that buying an artwork is already a critical act – by extension, so is choosing which show to hang, or selecting which artist to exhibit and promote. Insofar as it offered a means of continuing to maintain a close relationship with artists, there was little difference between staging an exhibition as a curator or doing so in the capacity of a gallerist. The difference was in the relative autonomy at one's disposal.

Her decision to open a gallery can also be interpreted as the natural conclusion to her two decades of artistic experience. Although the notion of becoming an art dealer had never occurred to her before – neither while she worked for Sonnabend in Paris nor during her very brief, first-ever experience with Carla Panicali at Rome's Il Segno gallery – entertaining close contact with artists had, in both cases, sufficiently fascinated her that she had decided to devote her life to art. Even during her years married to John Weber, when it might have seemed only natural, the thought of opening a gallery had not crossed her mind. Yet perhaps it is precisely this fact that marks the decision as the direct consequence of a journey all her own. After all, there was nothing particularly alarming about the desire to have her own exhibition space; such things happened every day. There were so many figures who had established galleries after studying art history, working as critics or teaching. She would surely have been in good company.

In her particular case, she may have been encouraged by the excellent response to the exhibitions that she had organized in the loft at 421 West Broadway. They had sold well, a fact that could not fail to move her to a certain enthusiasm, perhaps even some excitement, especially in light of the difficulties of the previous decade.

So it was that on 20 September 1980, she opened the Annina Nosei Gallery.

47. Jones and De Coppet, 202.
48. Jones, 385.
49. Jones and De Coppet, 199.
50. Annina Nosei Weber, *Discussion* (Out of London Press, 1980), 194 in this volume.

THE NEW DECADE

The moment was favorable. A new generation was emerging into the limelight and the market was recovering, with perceptibly beneficial effects. Annina would not have to face the challenges of which John Weber would later speak, recalling the difficulties of convincing American collectors to buy European artists' works in the 1970s, a period in which – as Annina herself recalls – even Warhols were hardly selling. Nor, in Italy, was Mario Schifano, the Italian Warhol, as Annina likes to call him.

A growing enthusiasm was now pervading the art world. The economic recovery was mirrored by collectors' declared appreciation for younger artists' work, including their return to painting and other traditional techniques.

As the seventies' economic woes were steadily overcome, therefore, so too faded the ideological polemics that had characterized the decade.

The awakening market was a powerful stimulus that also energized public galleries and museums. Within two or three exhibition seasons, artists of the new scene had commanded a level of attention, in many cases a veritable notoriety, unknown to the protagonists of past years. There was no precedent for the speed with which works sold and with which prices rose. Annina's circumstances improved dramatically, adding apparent substance to the phrase that Duchamp had addressed to her in Rome in the early 1960s, at the home of Gianfranco Baruchello: *Il faut que tu te transforme en argent*." She knew perfectly well that the master was not to be interpreted literally; such was not his manner. Although he had produced works that lent irony and a little sarcasm to the question of art's relationship to money – as Yves Klein or Warhol himself had done after him – she knew that his statement had to be framed in Duchamp's own thoroughly different context: one symbolic and alchemical. Yet the sixties seemed to have returned. The same enthusiasm greeted this wave of boom-year prosperity, as it had in the years of her youth when she had participated in the work of Ken Dewey, Ileana Sonnabend, and others.

THE GALLERY

The Annina Nosei Gallery's inaugural exhibition was a group show. It was not indicative of her agenda, nor was it a foreshadowing of the exhibitions to follow. Nor indeed was it a designated shortlist of names to promote in the near future. Rather, it was the expression of a method, a way of working. If the exhibition was indicative of anything, it was of a business model that preceded even the choice of authors; so much so that in subsequent seasons Annina would schedule one, two or often even three group shows a year. They were a means of establishing first contact with a greater range of artists and of fostering relationships with those she found most interesting. It was a characteristic of her exhibition program that corresponded to her character and her need to operate with utmost freedom. Staging group exhibitions was hardly an oddity, but Annina did so with a rhythm and in a manner that instrumentalized the group show, yielding results that would duly be widely acknowledged. Annina proved a natural talent scout, with an ever-keen eye for the right artist. Castelli conveyed this image perfectly: "Make a detailed list of what Annina has done: she has pretty much had every artist, at one time or another, no matter how briefly: the same artists who are now in my gallery, or at Mary Boone, or even at Metro Pictures, at Sperone Westwater or even at Blum Helman – God knows where, at Barbara Gladstone: anyway, everywhere you look, you'll find someone who started with Annina Nosei [...]. And she's still doing it, with the new Roman painters."[51]

To be clear, Annina's method was not to the detriment of the names to whom she dedicated solo exhibitions, far from it. Her judgements were consistently timely and corresponded to a well-defined project. The inaugural group show was followed by two solo shows, the first dedicated to Mimmo Paladino and the second to David Salle, two artists on the rise who would soon establish themselves as major players on the international stage.

One of the cornerstones of the gallery's exhibition program was the presentation of American artists (not only New Yorkers), Italians, and Europeans more generally. This conformed to the interests that had already become fully apparent during Annina's years with Weber, consistent with the international spirit by which she was strongly animated.

In December 1980, exactly three months since opening her space, she mounted a second group show. Its title, *Drawings and Paintings on Paper*, perhaps says little today; it might seem overly explanatory, perhaps even banal, but at that moment it bore emphatic implications, representing solidarity with the nascent, still-developing scene. To offer a space to drawing and painting once again meant rehabilitating suppressed practices. It meant a counterreaction to the phase preceding it, during which the rethinking of art had given birth to such daring conceptualizations. It meant once more placing the relationship between creativity and historical formats at center stage. It was from this perspective that Annina turned her attention to the younger generation. But she had always approached art from that same fundamental perspective, as previously demonstrated in the case of *Memory*, for example.

Inherent in the idea of exhibiting works on paper was a principle that had always guided her selection of artists. Works on paper, precisely because of their support, are often considered minor pieces. Yet it is for this very reason that works on paper allow artists to express themselves with utmost freedom, to experiment and to reveal a more authentic self.

Drawings and Paintings on Paper featured the works of artists such as David Deutsch, Julian Schnabel, Francesco Clemente, Sandro Chia, and Enzo Cucchi, among others. These were some of the most outstanding of up-and-coming names, which reaffirmed Annina's readiness to embrace the most significant developments of any given moment. She then decanted her chosen artists into solo exhibitions, which inevitably defined her program.

Although her sensibilities led her to embrace the work of younger artists, she did not repudiate her own past. Disavowing nothing, she did not risk self-contradiction; rather, she sensed the many correlations between the artists then rising to prominence and those who had preceded them. She distinctly understood the interlinking continuities that resided in artistic creation. After all, the appearance of the book/catalogue *Discussion*, which had been published a few months before the gallery's opening, had already indicated that there would be no about-turns in her interests – and, consequently, in her art dealership.

In the mid-eighties she staged *The Door*. This was an unmistakable homage to Duchamp and his famous *Door: 11, Rue Larrey*, while at the same time recalling her own academic background: another potent hint to better elucidate her agenda. She would reassert the same direction some years later with the 1992 exhibition *Who's Afraid of Duchamp, Minimalism, and Passport Photography?*, curated by Collins & Milazzo.[52]

With *The Door* Annina reaffirmed her preferred approach, exhibiting the works of leading young artists such as Jean-Michel Basquiat, Mike Bidlo, Julian Schnabel, Mimmo Paladino and Piero Pizzi Cannella alongside recognized masters such as the Americans Robert Rauschenberg and Sol LeWitt or the Europeans Antoni Tàpies and Karel Appel.

This was the character that Annina wanted to give to her gallery. A character in keeping with her manner of juxtaposing artists' work, much as on the occasion that, having hung Salle's works in the showroom-loft that she had opened with Gagosian, she had been surprised to notice their colours harmonizing with Mangold's. Annina preferred to identify formal interconnections rather than to highlight differences or stoke conflict, as had so often been the tendency of the 1970s.

51. Jones, 323.
52. *The Door*, 7 June – 7 July 1985, Annina Nosei Gallery, New York. Invited artists: Karel Appel, Jean-Michel Basquiat, Mike Bidlo, Chuck Connelly, Vincent Gallo, Sol LeWitt, Mimmo Paladino, Pizzi Cannella, Robert Rauschenberg, Doug Sanderson, Julian Schnabel, and Antoni Tàpies. Tricia Collins and Richard Milazzo (eds.), *Who's Afraid of Duchamp, Minimalism and Passport Photography?*. Catalogue for the exhibition of the same name at Annina Nosei Gallery, 3 – 31 October 1992. Invited artists: Ford Beckman, Lawrence Carroll, Stephen Ellis, Suzan Etkin, Peter Halley, Nicholas Howey, James Hyde, Jonathan Lasker, Annette Lemieux, Fabian Marcaccio, Donna Moylan, and Philip Taaffe.

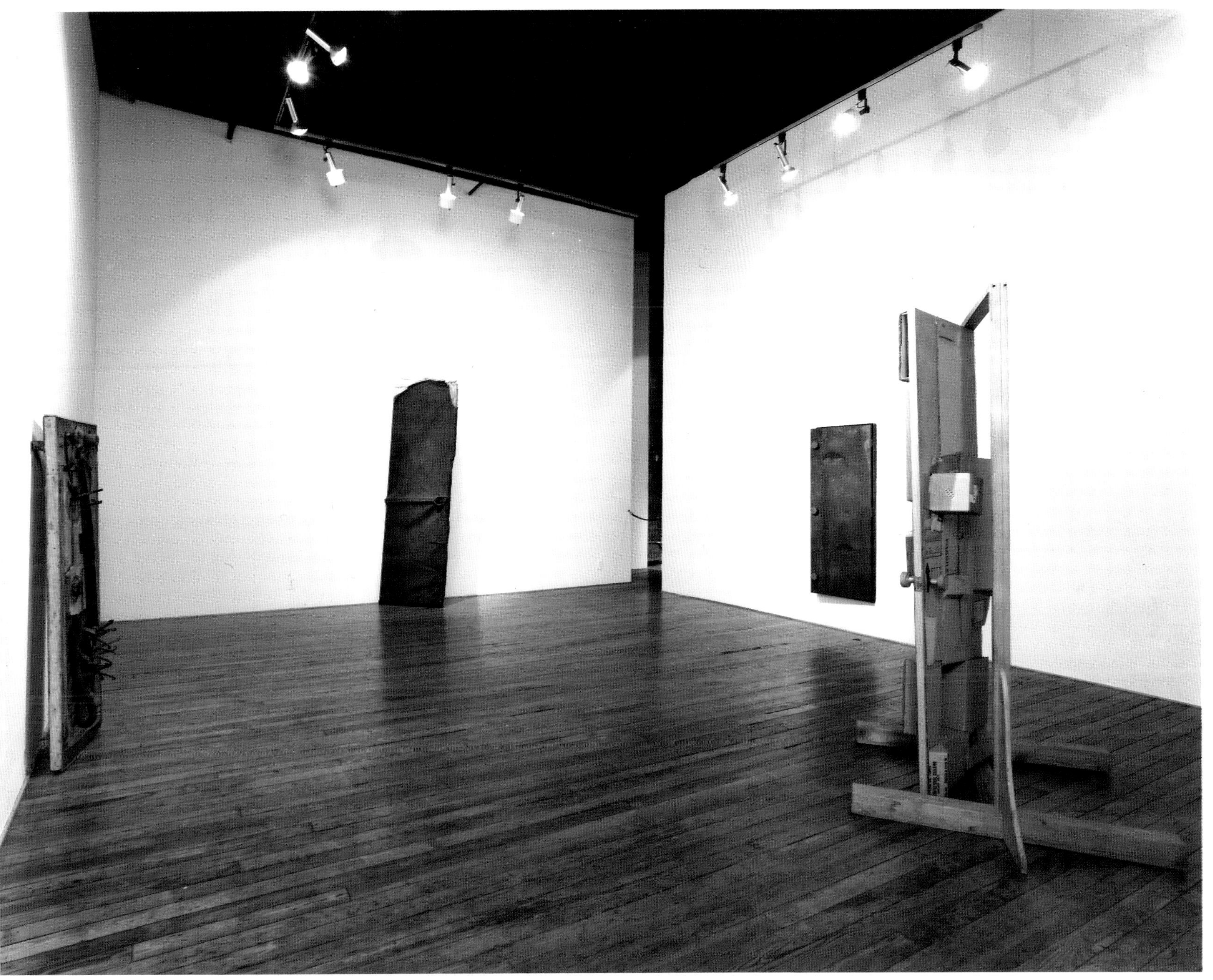

INSTALLATION VIEW OF *THE DOOR*,
ANNINA NOSEI GALLERY, JUNE 1985
From left, artworks by:
Karel Appel, Mimmo Paladino, Vincent Gallo, and Robert Rauschenberg

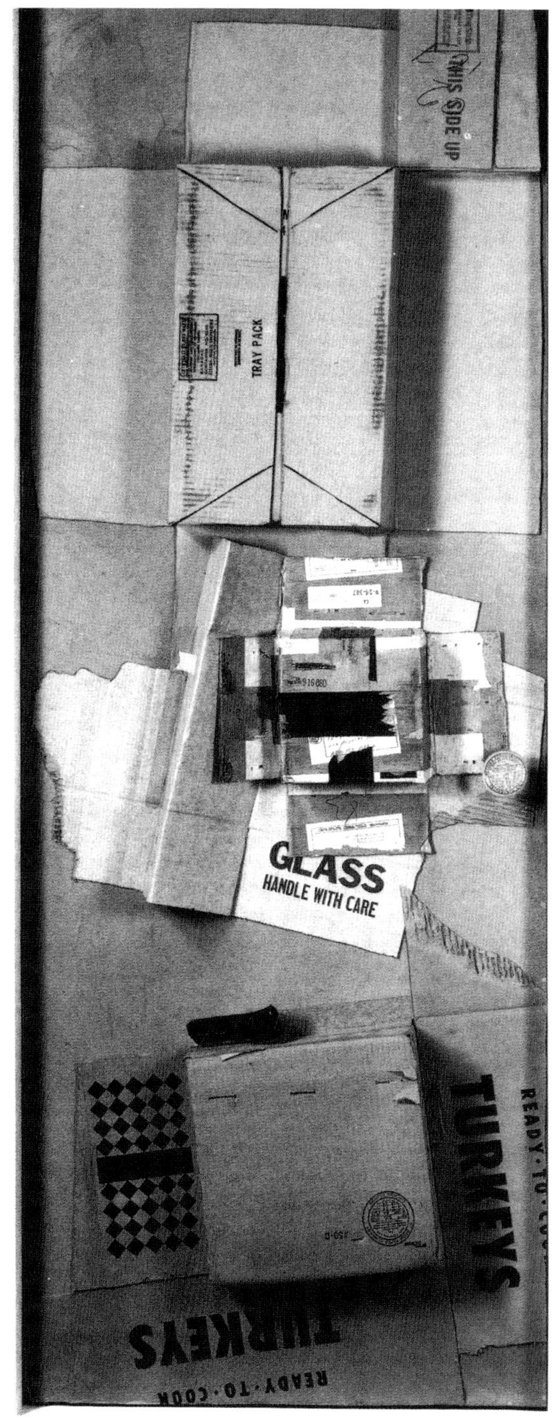

ROBERT RAUSCHENBERG, *CARDBIRD DOOR*, 1970-71
ARTWORK FROM THE EXHIBITION *THE DOOR*, ANNINA NOSEI GALLERY,
JUNE 1985

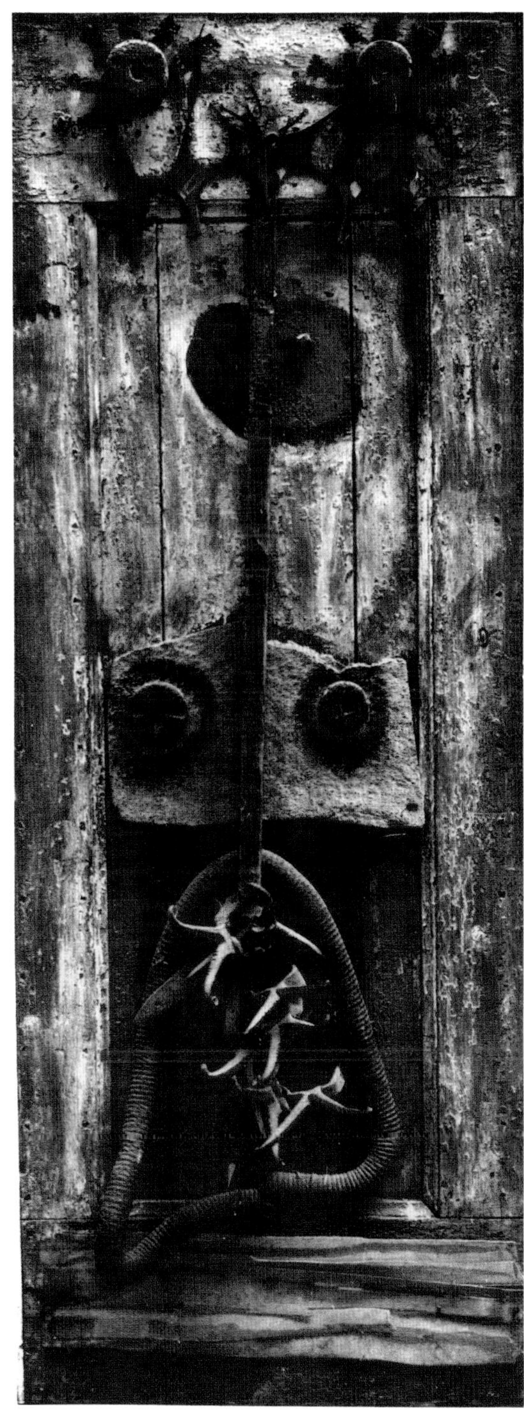

KAREL APPEL, *DRIFT OP ZOLDER*, 1985
FROM THE EXHIBITION *THE DOOR*, ANNINA NOSEI GALLERY,
JUNE 1985

SUCCESSFUL YOUTH

Between 1979 and the following year, when Annina opened her gallery, few were yet aware of the change underway. An earthquake was soon to strike the already-restive art world, and few yet had the resolve to put their weight behind new players. The same was still more true of museums and other public institutions.

Annina, as already established, welcomed new experiences. She took a conciliatory stance toward the young artists who had once more set themselves to paint and canvas, which, by contrast, aroused the suspicion of many of her fellow veterans of the tempestuous years previous.

Public institutions' slowness to take account of such developments remained, as ever, proportional to the time required for headlines to filter into history. Soon this would no longer be the case. Since William Rubin's provocative exhibition *Eight Contemporary Artists*, a debate had simmered concerning the imperative for structural change in museums, necessary to keep in step with the times, a debate that now began to bear fruit.[53] Yet the apparent need was no longer for modification of the spatial and conceptual structures of the museum in order to accommodate new works, as it had seemed throughout the years of debate that the exhibition had generated. That problem had at least momentarily resolved itself with the return to the traditional media of painting and sculpture. What now disoriented public institutions was the speed and scale at which the phenomenon imposed itself, highlighting the gap that still persisted between any cultural moment and its public recognition. Nonetheless, some high-profile institutional episodes began to betray the first hints of change.

In the same year that Annina opened her gallery, the Venice Biennale introduced a generous section devoted to young artists, *Aperto '80*, which won sufficiently tremendous international attention as to remain a highly-regarded fixture for more than a decade.[54] Like *Aperto '80*, PS1's exhibition *New York/New Wave* also enjoyed a worldwide resonance. Featuring more than 100 artists, largely drawn from the fledgling Lower East Side scene, the exhibition charted the transformation underway in presiding artistic formats.[55] Both events chronicled the arc of the 1970s while simultaneously foreshadowing the immediate future.

Both initiatives, on the part of respectively Harald Szeemann and Diego Cortez, attempted to surpass the ideological vision that had marked the decade just ended. The approaching scene promised a kaleidoscopic variety of artists working in different vernaculars and with different media, unburdened by hierarchical distinctions. Such were the new developments then gathering momentum, further stimulating the still-open debate around the meaning of postmodernism in art.

Participants in *New York/New Wave* included visual artists, writers, musicians, photographers, and filmmakers demonstrating the existence of manifold currents in search of a common identity – a melting pot that in New York could boast a historical *raison d'être*. It was a generation that wanted to make a spontaneous art, outside the strictures dictated by the academy. They swarmed the streets and clubs, they enlivened both the nightlife and the galleries of SoHo, known as an exclusive gateway to the inner sanctum of high society.

53. Alloway and Coplans.
54. The *Aperto* section, inaugurated with the 39th Venice Biennale and primarily the creation of Harald Szeemann in collaboration with Achille Bonito Oliva, would be suspended in 1995 on the occasion of the Biennale's centenary, to which Jean Clair wanted to give a more historicist imprint. For the 48th Venice Biennale in 1999, Szeemann, who was called upon to curate the international exhibition that served to retire the Biennale's organization by sections, created *dAPERTutto/APERTO overALL/Aperto parTOUT/Aperto über all*, reaffirming the principle behind *Aperto '80*, namely the transcending of any distinction between artists and expressive strategies.
55. *New York/New Wave*, curated by Diego Cortez, PS1, Long Island City, 15 February – 5 April 1981. The exhibition formalized an existing trend already manifest in two previous exhibitions, *The Real Estate Show*, which opened on New Year's Eve 1980 and was closed by the police two days later, and *Times Square Show* (June 1980), both organized by a group of artists working under the auspices of New York Colab.

"PUBLIC ADDRESS"

GROUP SHOW

JEAN MICHEL BASQUIAT   MIKE GLIER

BILL BECKLEY   BARBARA KRUGER

KEITH HARING   JENNY HOLZER

PETER NADIN

OCTOBER 31 - NOVEMBER 19
OPENING OCTOBER 30, 5-7

ANNINA NOSEI GALLERY   100 PRINCE ST. NEW YORK   431-9253

INVITATION CARD FOR THE SHOW *PUBLIC ADDRESS*,
ANNINA NOSEI GALLERY, NEW YORK
OCTOBER 1981

THE MYTH OF JEAN-MICHEL BASQUIAT

Jean-Michel Basquiat's biography recounts his involvement in the latter milieu: the formation of his band Gray, which performed in 1979 at Diego Cortez and associates' Mudd Club, his immersion in nightlife and his aimless wandering through the byways of New York, his graffiti signed SAMO (Same Old Shit), his participation in the *Times Square Show* and in *New York/New Wave*.[56] And then the new phase that unfolded from meeting Annina, through whom the young firebrand came into contact with the upper echelons of the New York art scene.

As recorded elsewhere, Annina first encountered Basquiat's early works while visiting *New York/New Wave*. Suitably impressed, she arranged to meet him in his studio. The artist displayed a certain self-awareness regarding various aspects of his own work and conveyed a fierce determination to show in her gallery, which convinced Annina to include him in her October 1981 group show *Public Address* alongside Bill Beckley, Mike Glier, Keith Haring, Barbara Kruger, Jenny Holzer, and Peter Nadin.[57]

Public Address proved an important exhibition, through which Annina sought to underscore the social character of such younger artists' work. It was another of her so-cherished sites of interlinking continuities. She duly organized a solo exhibition of Basquiat's work for a few months later, in March 1982. *Public Address* constituted his first serious chance to introduce himself to Lower Manhattan society. The artist had to exert himself to earn the opportunity, since Annina – for all that she had immediately recognized the excellence of his work, sufficient to warrant seeking him out so as to know it better – was not entirely convinced that he belonged to the socially-engaged climate by which she wanted to define the exhibition. But, by her account, the artist's arguments and his stubborn insistence persuaded her.

Basquiat was highly motivated but he had yet to understand the sacrifices that his ambitions required. He was strongly attracted to the East Village atmosphere and to everything inherent in the self-managed and provocatively rebellious *Times Square Show*, in which he had exhibited a few months earlier. His affinity with that world was such that in due course, after he had already exhibited with Annina, he felt compelled to show in a November 1982 exhibition at Fun Gallery: one of the essential points of reference for graffiti artists such as Fab 5 Freddy, Lady Pink, or Futura 2000 as well as for the punk music scene. It was no coincidence that in February 1983, a few months later and under thoroughly similar circumstances, his friend Keith Haring also showed there.

Annina opposed Basquiat's involvement in the exhibition, which belonged to a milieu that openly opposed the SoHo galleries. Only afterward did Basquiat begin to understand that such circles could be irreconcilable. Annina continued to support him nonetheless, to the limit of her ability. First she housed him in the gallery's basement, a large, windowed space that served as a studio, then found him an apartment to rent in which he could also work. She introduced him to collectors, presented his work to critics – in short, she did everything required to promote an artist.

She knew that a part of Basquiat was still fascinated by that world, but she also knew of a part of him that gravitated toward a more sophisticated culture. Basquiat commanded a solid knowledge of art history and of the city's museums, which he had often visited with his mother as a boy; he held Rauschenberg in high esteem, he liked Franz Kline and admired Cy Twombly, whom he knew through Annina herself. Indeed her high opinion of Basquiat related precisely to the coexistence of his two souls.

Despite some misunderstandings, the two enjoyed an excellent rapport. Then the unexpected occurred: Basquiat met the prominent Swiss art dealer Bruno Bischofberger, who took it upon himself to promote him. Bischofberger proposed a collaboration with the incomparable Andy Warhol. Basquiat had already met him; there was a natural affinity between them that could have developed into something more. Their relationship worked well on a communicative level, if perhaps slightly less so on a creative one, particularly bearing in mind the works created for Tony Shafrazi's September 1985 exhibition *Warhol Basquiat*, Bischofberger's brainchild. In any case, their partnership sparked conversation: an established master mentoring a rising talent – for that matter, the first African American artist in such a remarkable position – and then rumors of their alleged affair, amongst various other amusements. In short, their pairing had everything required to set the press alight.

Only three years since the East Village exhibition, Basquiat's prices had leaped impressively; he now belonged to a completely different world. He had lost contact with the part of his soul that bound him to his old friends. It is difficult, if not impossible, to say how the transition affected him, but one episode might offer some hint: Annina has recounted that, on hearing the news of Warhol's death, Jean-Michel remained silent for a moment. Then, shaking his head, he said softly, "Who am I going to talk to now?"

Those who knew Warhol knew that he was a person of few words, which is to say that Basquiat's problem was evidently not a need for someone with whom to talk. Rather, he most likely needed someone with whom to share the isolation that greets all those who rise into the pantheon of celebrity.

Annina played a complicated role in her relationship with Basquiat. She attempted to curb some of his waywardness during those crucial years, within the limits of their mutual independence. There was a unitary art world, but within it each gallery constituted a microcosm in its own right and it was not always easy for artists to determine what was best for them and for their work.

Annina had never wanted to manipulate artists, to bind them to contractual obligations, it was not part of her character. One incident, concerning Jeff Koons' career beginnings, is symptomatic of her working method. In early 1981, Annina had invited Koons to participate in one of her first group shows, along with two other artists, Neil Jenney and Ronnie Cutrone. Koons exhibited *The New*, a work that

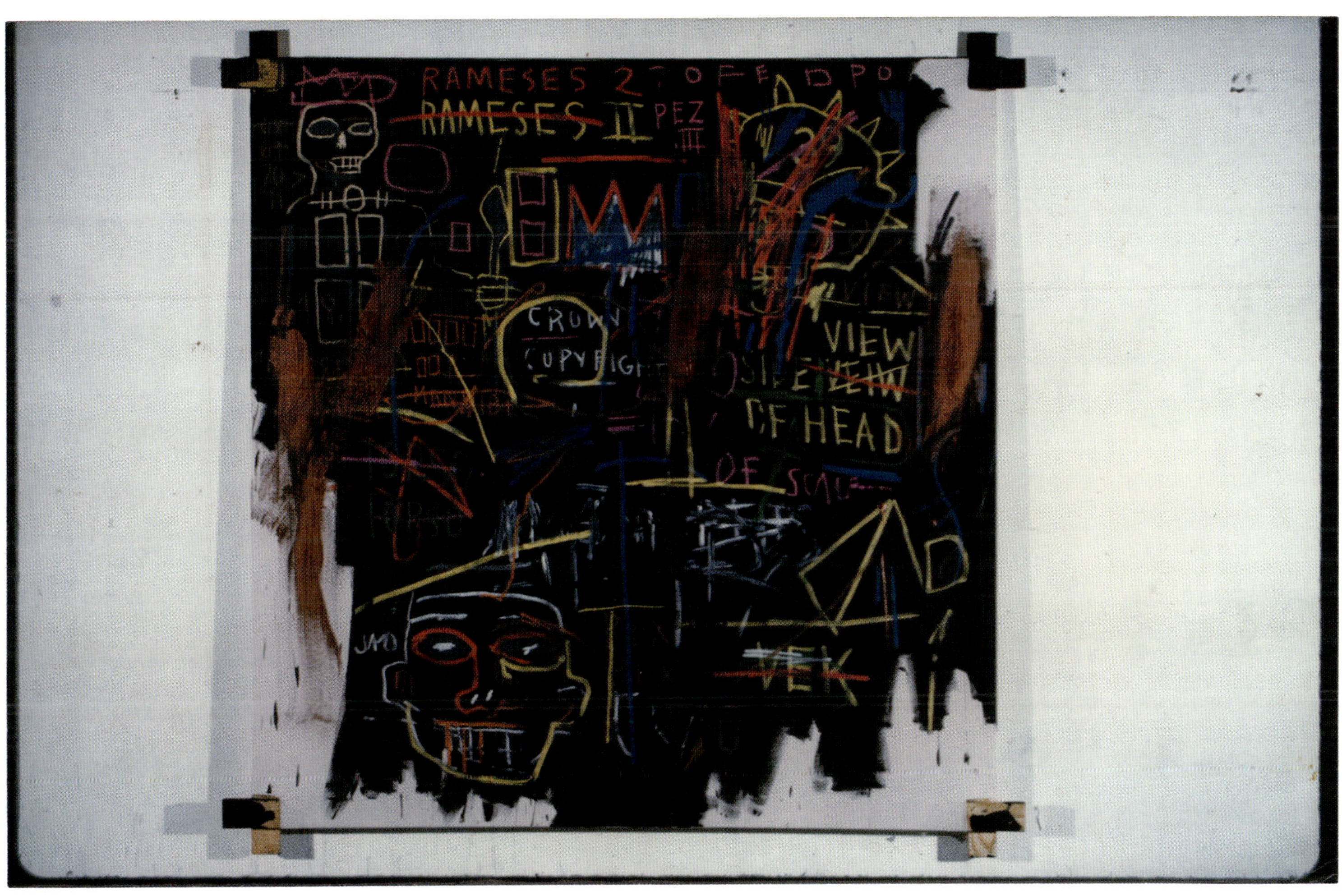

POLAROID OF JEAN-MICHEL BASQUIAT'S
KINGS OF EGYPT, 1983

ATTUNED TO THE LATEST FASHION

would subsequently become famous: two vacuum cleaners resting on a base of neon tubes and housed in two Plexiglas cases, one stacked atop the other. A few days after the opening, Annina received a letter in which the artist enquired what she planned to do for his career. Her answer was succinct but eloquent: she had never been concerned about her own career, so how could she concern herself with his?

56. *Times Square Show*, curated by New York Colab (Collaborative Projects, Inc.), June 1980. More than 100 creatives and artmakers participated in the self-organized event. Aside from Basquiat, many other subsequently prominent artists also exhibited including Keith Haring, Jenny Holzer, Mike Kelley, and Kenny Scharf.
57. *Public Address*, Annina Nosei Gallery, 31 October – 19 November 1981. Artists invited: Jean-Michel Basquiat, Bill Beckley, Mike Glier, Keith Haring, Jenny Holzer, Barbara Kruger, and Peter Nadin.

Annina's notoriety would be linked in part to Basquiat's fame and to the art scene from which, of all its protagonists, he most completely emerged. That scene aroused an enthusiasm sufficient to attract elevated numbers of collectors, reinvigorated by works that recalled the most well-trodden attributes of the modernist tradition. That enthusiasm also inspired collecting on an unprecedented scale, typified by the yuppie mentality forming at that time. Among the many definitions that abound of the term "yuppie," one particularly fitting summary reads: "Yuppie (short for Young Urban Professional) is an English term widely used internationally since the 1980s, denoting a young, 'upwardly mobile' professional or entrepreneur who embraces the capitalist business community and finds self-fulfillment therein [...]. Many young Yale, Harvard, or Princeton graduates pursued the dream of fast money in New York City and Manhattan in particular, places that [...] promised much to those who invested and worked in the stock market [...]. They frequented exclusive restaurants and nightclubs such as Manhattan's famous Studio 54, they worked in downtown New York skyscrapers and they appeared at parties organized by their peers, by players [...]. Many of them used cocaine recreationally, they dressed in designer clothes [...] and they bought paintings by the artist Jean-Michel Basquiat."[58]

The fact that young, upwardly mobile professionals bought works by up-and-coming artists, amongst whom Basquiat was evidently the best-known name, was an unheard-of phenomenon. From it was born a form of profit-oriented collecting that capitalized on the rapid escalation of artworks' prices, triggering unprecedented speculative processes in a market now fully unshackled from the crisis of the previous years.

Of course, there was no lack of collectors in the classic mold, who derived their own euphoria from the new works – painting and sculpture based on decidedly commonplace models – and who were further spurred by the meagre fare that conceptual polemics had imposed upon them.

The new artists had attained success on a grand scale and nor was recognition long in coming from the world's leading museums. The ensuing economic benefits rebounded onto the entire art system, instituting the radical transformation that would mark the postmodern era. *Public Address*, the first of Annina's exhibitions in which Basquiat had participated, had focused on the enduring politically-engaged themes so dear to 1970s debate. Annina sought to maintain that trajectory out of personal conviction, even if her own somewhat rebellious nature ensured her readiness for change. She perceived the advance of the new in the young artists with whom she dealt, while also recognizing that, contrary to Christopher Lasch's intimations of generational conflict, they bore a certain admiration for their predecessors. Their attitude interrupted the old dynamic: a perennial succession of new trends, each of which declared its precursor outdated in the name of the avant-garde.

These artists expressed no aspiration toward the new, nor interest in claiming to have mothballed the old. There was no longer any question of finding new forms or new languages; rather, they felt the need to construct a more vigorous subjectivity, fueled by a heady mix of the avant-garde, the tradition of the new and mass communication. It was precisely in this that Annina perceived the peculiarity that they represented, and it was on the same account that she felt she could put greater trust in them.

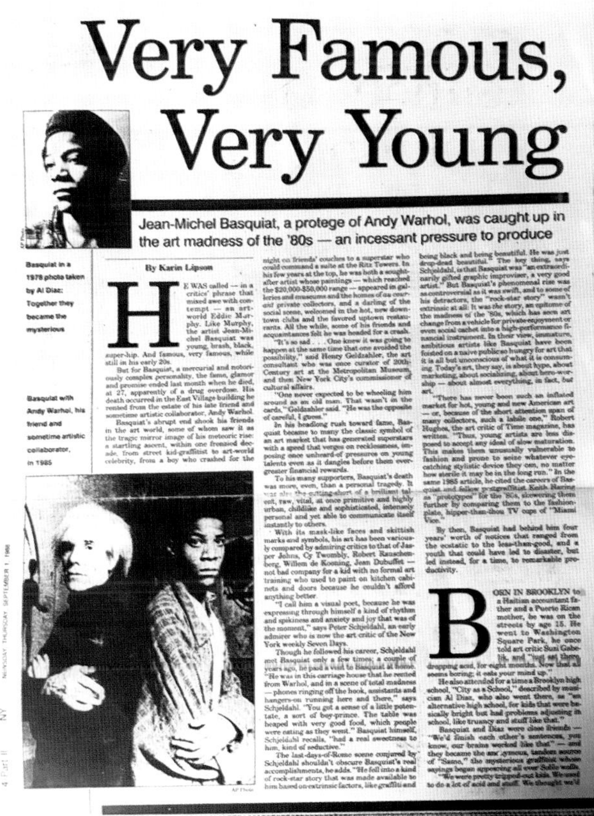

Article dedicated to Jean-Michel Basquiat in *Newsday* (1 September 1988).

58. https://it.wikipedia.org/wiki/Yuppie.

A vitality and effervescence issued from the artistic affairs of this period that harked back, in many ways, to those of the 1960s. The East Village recalled a onetime Greenwich Village, when artists filled the local bars and clubs, enlivening the night.

Also evoking that resemblance was the Warhol-Basquiat relationship – which, while constituting a unicum in the general scheme of artists' relationships, in some ways signaled continuities that were not limited to New York. The same phenomenon occurred in Rome, where younger artists' work and their success put the older artists of the Piazza del Popolo School back on the map. Annina's January 1983 exhibition of Mario Schifano reflects this context perfectly.

As previously noted, Annina often recalls the difficulty with which Warhol's works had sold during the crisis of the 1970s before finding new vigor in the 1980s with the recovery of the market surrounding young artists. The same was true of Schifano.

All told, those who had embraced the climate of the sixties now found themselves at ease in the early eighties; there was a sense of breathing a familiar air, one charged with an enthusiasm that became only more conspicuous in contrast with the decade between, the difficult seventies. Moreover, many of the artists then working had come of age in that post-postwar context and had undertaken a similar journey to that of Annina, who, having left her homeland in the early sixties, was now poised to write the greatest pages of her story. With *Public Address* she attempted to give visible form to that continuity, harking conceptually back to a time in which all things, including private matters, had been political. With *The Door*, which was to sing the praises of Duchamp, she would seek continuity once more, this time by demonstrating and comparing the links between artists of different generations. The continuity that concerned her was not limited to theme, it often lay in artists' respective approaches to their work or to formal consonances between the works themselves. In turn it could relate to questions of cultural frameworks, including her own relationship with Italy and with Rome – her city – to which she had never ceased to return and for which she served an important function as a liaison with New York.

It is duly no coincidence that, for one of her first exhibitions (in December 1980), Annina elected to include the most successful young artists in Roman circles – Francesco Clemente, Sandro Chia, and Enzo Cucchi – whom she therefore exhibited ahead of the other New York galleries. Nor is it any coincidence that she later (in December 1983) exhibited Bruno Ceccobelli and Giuseppe Gallo, once again a good two years prior to their solo show at Sperone Westwater Gallery in SoHo (although, to be precise, she had already invited Sandro Chia to join a 1978 exhibition at C Space, and it was she who had introduced him to Julian Schnabel).

Overall, in the first period of her gallery's operation (and in addition to the aforementioned), Annina included an ample selection of Roman artists in group and solo shows, from Mario Schifano, Carlo Maria Mariani, and Luigi Ontani to the younger artists Marco Tirelli, Piero

Pizzi Cannella, Nunzio, Sabina Mirri, Claudio Palmieri, Pietro Fortuna, and Alfredo Zelli.

New York's warm reception of these artists was immediately reflected in Roman artistic affairs; a significant achievement, reaffirming the service that Annina performed for the city of her birth. Rome was a hotbed at this point. The revival of painting had found fertile ground, spawning several hubs in which fresh young artists' offerings could be sampled: Ugo Ferranti's gallery, those of Mario Diacono and Giuliana De Crescenzo, or Gian Tomaso Liverani's La Salita – not forgetting Plinio De Martiis' La Tartaruga. It was at the latter gallery that, courtesy of the critic Maurizio Calvesi, *Anacronismo* (Anachronism) took form: a trend that drew its inspiration from pre-modern painting. Thus, plentiful names were in circulation at the time, also due to the exertions of independent spaces. Two new factors then intervened to further enliven the scene. The first was attached to Gian Enzo Sperone, who, having already represented the artists of Arte Povera and having exhibited Chia and Clemente before Transavanguardia had come into being, saw fit to continue working with up-and-comers, recruiting artists who had previously exhibited with Ugo Ferranti (Domenico Bianchi, Bruno Ceccobelli, Gianni Dessì, and Giuseppe Gallo). The second factor arose with the reopening, after several years of inactivity, of Fabio Sargentini's gallery, L'Attico. A renewal of the pair's previous rivalry, which dated back to the years of Arte Povera, was inevitable. That rivalry now overflowed into the latest generation of artists. If Sperone preferred young artists who already had a gallery behind them, Sargentini, who for some years had devoted himself exclusively to theatre, struck out on another path. In collaboration with this writer, he constructed a program from scratch. L'Attico reopened in December 1983 with an exhibition of Maurizio Corona, a young artist in the circle of Mario Merz, whose solo show at Franz Paludetto's gallery in Turin, LP/220, I myself had curated the year before. Three solo shows followed, featuring respectively Pizzi Cannella, Nunzio, and Marco Tirelli: the core around whom the new phase of L'Attico was built. At this point, as Leo Castelli was to duly acknowledge, Annina's role acquired particular value, with benefits for the Roman scene. If she included Bruno Ceccobelli and Giuseppe Gallo in 1983's *European Expressions*, then in the following season she focused instead on solo shows of Marco Tirelli, Pizzi Cannella, and Nunzio.[59] So doing, she restored a balance between the two groups while, and above all, actually condensing them into a single trend by merit of the exposure that she gave them within the New York scene.[60] Then, in late 1986, she exhibited Bruno Ceccobelli, Pietro Fortuna, Nunzio, Claudio Palmieri, Pizzi Cannella, Marco Tirelli, and Alfredo Zelli, reaffirming her position in relation to the Roman situation.

59. *European Expressions*, Annina Nosei Gallery, 13 December 1983 – 11 January 1984. The exhibition presented works by Jean-Michel Alberola, Miquel Barceló, François Boisrond, Bruno Ceccobelli, Peter Chevalier, Giuseppe Gallo, Karl Horst Hödicke, Helmut Middendorf, Sabina Mirri, Luigi Ontani, and Mimmo Paladino.
60. In his exhibition text for Bruno Ceccobelli's 2009 show at L'Attico in Rome, Fabio Sargentini reaffirmed the role that Annina performed, if from his particular point of view: "In the meantime I had evened the odds by opening an international conduit for Nunzio, Pizzi Cannella, Tirelli and in due course Palmieri, represented by Annina Nosei's New York gallery."

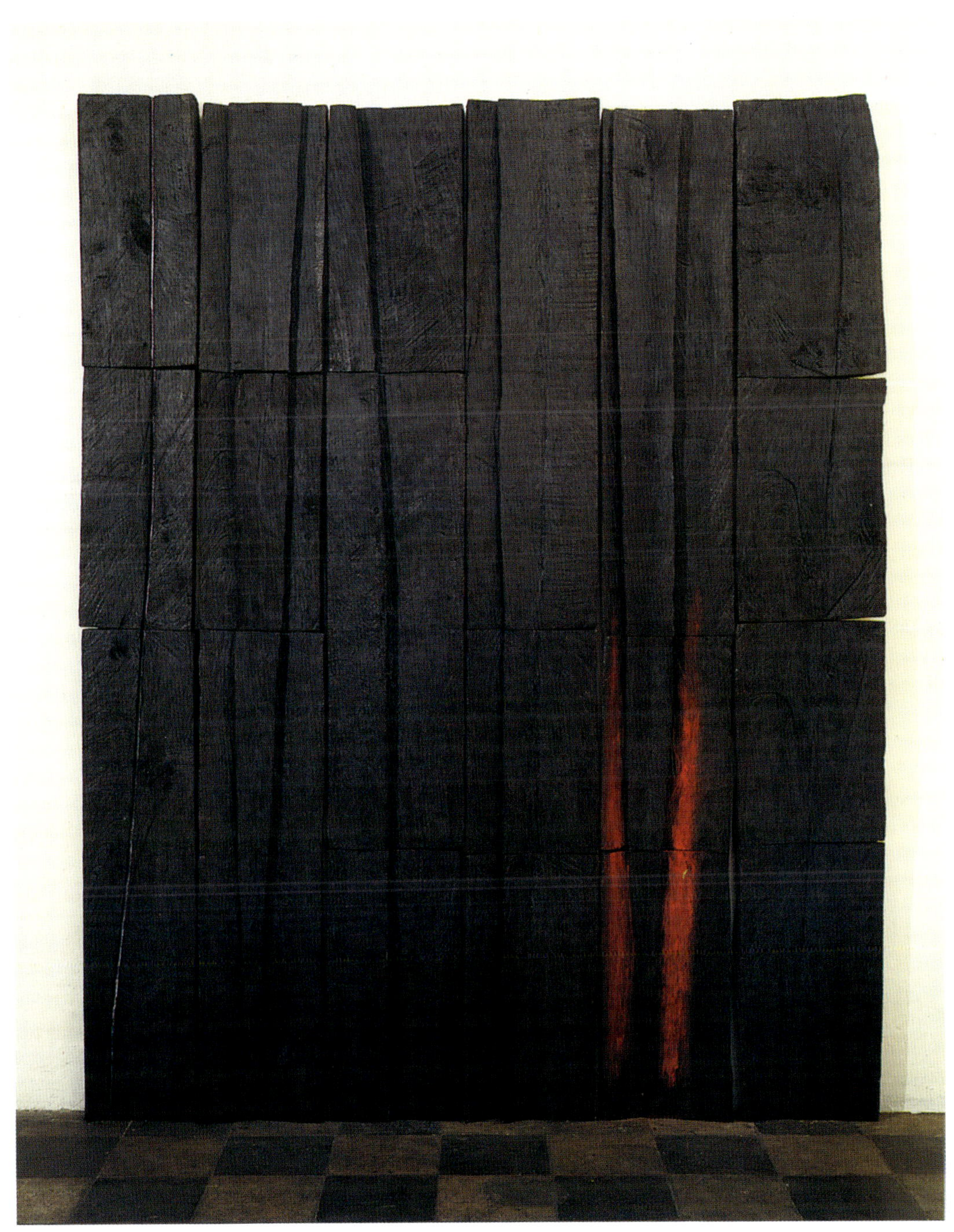

NUNZIO, *NOTTE*, 1986.
ANNINA NOSEI GALLERY, NEW YORK

A COSMOPOLITAN SPIRIT

The show *European Expressions* was perfectly in tune with Annina's program and was conceived with the express intention of devoting an exhibition to European artists, she having most recently dealt with Americans. In this way, she contributed to a broader process of building an international model helmed from New York. After all, most of her activity, whether as an independent curator or as a gallerist, had taken place there: in the place best equipped to fulfill the international aspirations of modern art, which therefore could only be American-led.

Vivid echoes of Weber's words still resounded, noting the difficulty of endearing European artists to American collectors, yet Annina's gallery was patronized not only by important collectors but also by film stars and musicians, who bought her artists' works regardless of their nationality, be it European or American (here Richard Gere comes to mind, who collected photography and purchased a large painting by Claudio Palmieri, as does Mick Jagger, who opted for a work by Carlo Maria Mariani). This was an indicator both of her personal success and of the consolidation of an identity: that of Western art culture. This was an achievement toward which artists and galleries had labored for more than two decades, which made it somewhat paradoxical that it was fully accomplished precisely as younger artists, for whom Annina had advocated, reclaimed historical forms and cultural precedents through their associated pictorial practices.

By this point, the search for the new had exhausted its deconstructive momentum. Artists had taken to experimentation with the various available languages, then to the pursuit of extra-artistic goals or indeed ideological ones. On the other hand, concurrent with the rehabilitation of painting, a different archetypal artist also surfaced: individuals who found the constitutive elements of their behavioral models in themselves, in their own search for a personal rubric and in mass media. Most importantly, however, the same elements served to frame a landscape of meaning.

As Annina has recalled, there was in that period "an actuality, an atmosphere, that represented the culture of New York City [...]. I believed that it had a palpable connection to the island culture of the Caribbean. I felt that in the music in those days, in the people in the streets and in the fashion magazines, all in one way or another mirroring the city's youthful energy."[61] Such recollections regard the work of Basquiat, but it remains evident that, at that time, the Western world's most international metropolis displayed an unprecedented interest in phenomena originating from outside. That connection with given cultures of origin – which, in the case of Basquiat and Wifredo Lam, Annina traced to those of the Caribbean – manifested the *genius loci* that had insinuated itself into the New York metropolitan cultural model.

Even if, to Annina's mind, younger artists' practice recalled the same spirit of collective participation typical of the 1970s, such as the vitality that had surrounded the Fine Arts Building, she felt that

times had changed nonetheless. Artistic paradigms had changed with them, now revolving upon rising new sensations' search for their own identitarian origins.

Annina therefore broadened her discourse. She reframed her horizons, turning her attention first to Afro-Cuban culture, then to Mexican and more generally Latin American culture. Her interests began to betray the formation of a new worldview.

On that note, during an interview of some time ago, I asked her to comment on her work with Roman artists in the 1980s, recalling the period in which I had occasion to write the texts for some of the shows in question: an Italian introducing Italians. To me, this approach had seemed connected to a desire to assert her own originality and the independence of her program, such that she duly asked me to write for American artists as well.[62] She replied only curtly, however. An explanation for this reluctance, I believe, is to be found in the fact that such decisions, while relevant to Italian discourse, do not lend themselves to a particularistic reading. They fall, rather, within the broader dialogical vision that has characterized her entire journey. Annina has never looked at art according to ostensible Italian or German, Iranian or Egyptian, Caribbean or Mexican declinations, but has always sought to identify the cultural substrate upon which artistic forms are erected.

In her oft-noted and aforementioned visit to PS1, whereupon she first saw Basquiat's work, Annina was also drawn to the works of another artist, Roberto Juarez. In both cases, what most impressed her was their authenticity, which stemmed, as she herself attests, from the application of an exemplary sense of painting to Caribbean iconography, in the one case, and to Mexican iconography in the other.[63] Considering the fact that during the same period she encountered the same magnetism before Paladino's works – which she credits with an Italic spirit – one might imagine that such an interest were new to her as well, had she not always been distinguished by her cosmopolitan spirit, albeit one *sui generis*, insofar as it has never inhibited her constant homecomings to Italy.

61. Annina Nosei, "Common Ground. Wifredo Lam and Jean-Michel Basquiat," in Krystyna Gmurzynska, Mathias Rastorfer and Mitchell Anderson (eds.), *Lam/Basquiat* (Galerie Gmurzynska, 2015), 44, 203 in this volume.
62. My professional involvement with Annina Nosei dates from the mid-1980s. Aside from introducing the exhibitions of Pizzi Cannella and Claudio Palmieri, I curated those of Vincent Gallo and Stephen Mueller.
63. Roberto Lambarelli, conversation with Annina Nosei, "Il Faut que tu te transforme en argent" in this volume, 77.

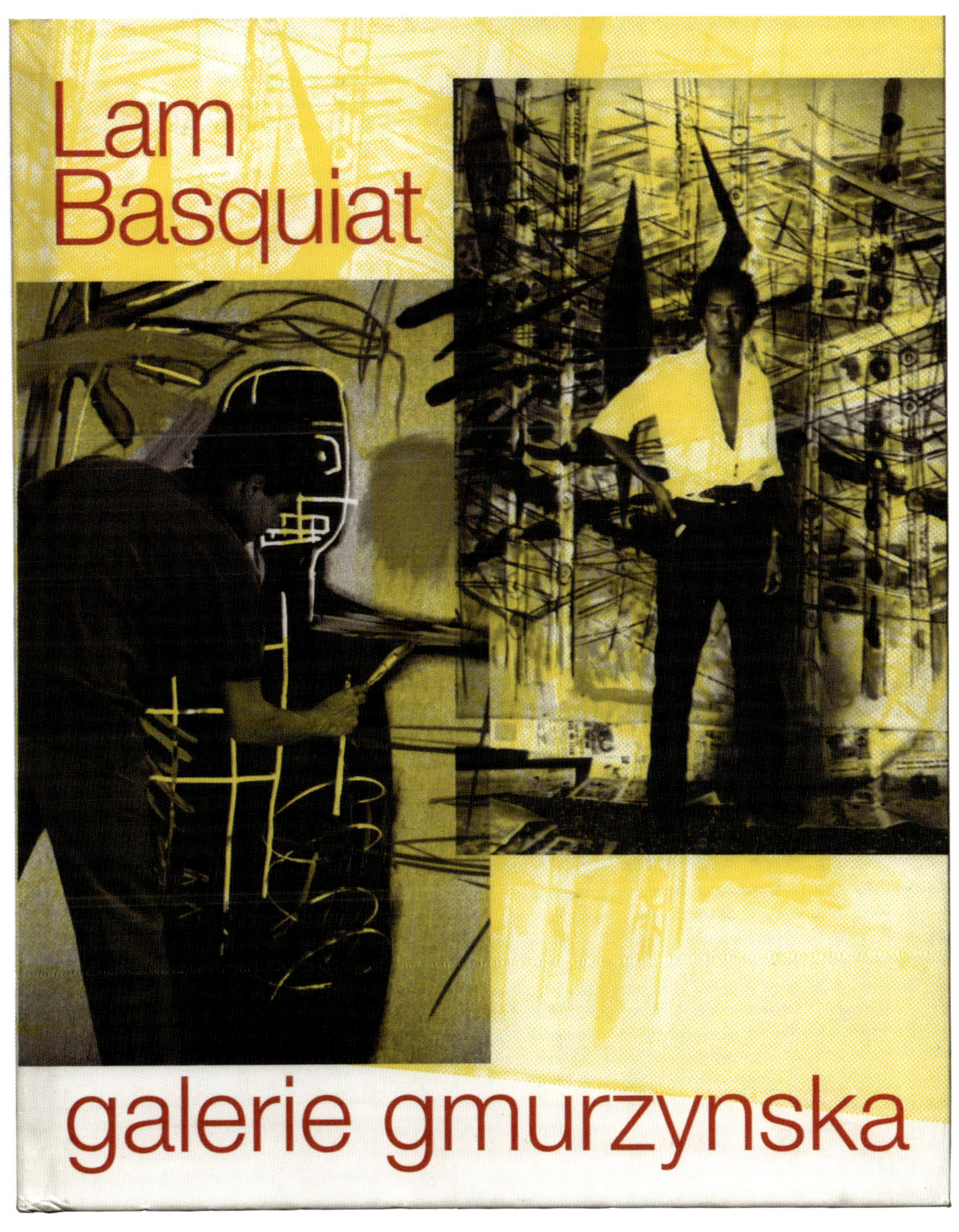

COVER OF THE CATALOGUE *LAM/BASQUIAT* (GALERIE GMURZYNSKA, 2015), WHICH INCLUDES ANNINA'S ESSAY "COMMON GROUND: WIFREDO LAM AND JEAN-MICHEL BASQUIAT"

A WORLD RECONSIDERED

In the late 1980s, with the aim of locating artists of palpable authenticity, in terms of a fusion or contrast of modern forms and artists' cultural roots, and while continuing to work with both European and American artists, Annina began to turn her attention to artists who engaged more fully with themes surrounding the cultural changes taking place.

Once again, her recruitment of Basquiat, accomplished years earlier with the stated intention of addressing the evolving New York scene, returns as a case in point. Basquiat, more than other artists, personifies a complexity that might be described as intersectional, to use a term that became widespread at the end of that decade and which has only more recently found a place in the vocabulary of art criticism, indicating the overlapping or intersection of different identities. Basquiat, born in New York and of Haitian descent, has often been reduced *tout-court* to that metropolitan landscape in which graffiti artists remain pigeonholed – this despite Annina's frequent efforts to demonstrate his intimate acquaintance with modern art. As she has written: "The compositional strength, the structure, and the harmony found in his work [place] his visual language in the context of the classic art of Western Modernism. A painting such as his *Untitled* from 1981 with its basic architectural and multi-perspective organization of space is reminiscent of Matisse's painting, *The Moroccans* (1915/16), at MoMA. A similar correspondence can be detected between Basquiat's works and some of the paintings of the CoBrA movement. For example, Jean-Michel's *Dust Heads* from 1982 could easily be compared to a painting by Asger Jorn."[64]

In light of these words, Basquiat might be said to constitute a bridge between "high" and "low" culture, and it is in this way that, up to a point, his work has been read. But Annina has also indicated another frame of reference in stating that "Jean-Michel's visual language meanwhile – his magical and spiritual signs – produced a special aura of sacrality. [...] His visual emblems had a natural, logical association with Afro-Caribbean ritualistic traditions and syncretic folklore, such as Vodou and Santería or the islands' artifacts such as pagan masks, all of which partly derived from Western Africa."[65] If Paladino's reference to Italic culture, as Annina has described it, can be understood as part of this search for such anthropological roots as might invoke individuals' ostensible territorial identities, in Basquiat's case the matter is decidedly more layered. There is no simple resolution in recalling his African-American origins – that is, by clinging to his immediate historical context. It is necessary to go back much further in time, furnished with perspectives introduced into artistic debate through the influence of Area Studies and postcolonial research.

It was with the same awareness, even if it may not have been so structured at the time, that Annina felt the need to work with what she herself has called "a voice of the minorities."[66]

Without addressing too closely the interweaving of vernaculars attached to different cultures – in relation to which, again, a significant theoretical discussion was only later to evolve – it might be said that Annina, at a certain point, intuited new directions for her exhibitions that would lead her to hold a solo show of Chéri Samba in 1990, succeeded by shows of Shirin Neshat and then Ghada Amer: figures who, in light of the non-Western modernist cultures to which they belong, address different social and identitarian issues, including, in the case of Shirin Neshat and Ghada Amer, questions related to the female experience. In this regard Annina states, "What I particularly liked was their way of expressing femininity as a public fact. It's a dimension of their work that has always attracted me... Above all, though, the thing that most struck me was the authenticity and awareness with which they approached their concerns, not the concerns in and of themselves."[67]

It is widely recognized that other parameters have infiltrated the value-scale of art since 1989, sufficient to produce a different body of meanings. This was the year in which the Berlin Wall fell, an event symbolic of the moment that Western culture began to lean toward globalization. At the same time, there were many developments that signaled the same shift on an intimate scale. Reference cannot but be made to *Magiciens de la Terre*, the exhibition that heralded another way of understanding relations between the West and the rest of the world and in which many recognized the influence of Global Art History and World Art Studies as well as the premises for a new museology.[68] Several years later, in 1998, Annina staged an exhibition of the same title, *Magiciens de la Terre*, exhibiting six artists who had also participated in the Paris event: Chéri Samba, Bowa Devi, R. B. Sharma, Singh Shyam, Vyakul, and Yang Jiechang. The fact that nine years had passed since the original exhibition should not imply a delay or a nostalgic retread. Rather, Annina expressed the need for a different relationship with time – different to the reigning customs of progress-oriented and modernist Western art – and reaffirmed her adherence to the defining spirit of the new situation.

More comprehensively, Annina broadened her purview by contemplating artists who emphasized their belonging to non-Western cultural environments, an objective that she had demonstrated in timely fashion in 1990 by mounting the first of three solo shows dedicated to Chéri Samba.

64. Nosei, "Common Ground," 45, 203 in this volume.
65. Ibid.
66. Ibid., 44, 203 in this volume.
67. Roberto Lambarelli, "Il Faut que tu te transforme en argent,", 128. On Nosei's work with women artists, see Graziano Menolascina (ed.), *Annina Nosei: The Difference Is Woman* (Stamen Editore, 2021).
68. *Magiciens de la Terre*, curated by Jean-Hubert Martin, Centre Georges Pompidou / La Grande Halle – La Villette, Paris, 18 May – 14 August 1989.

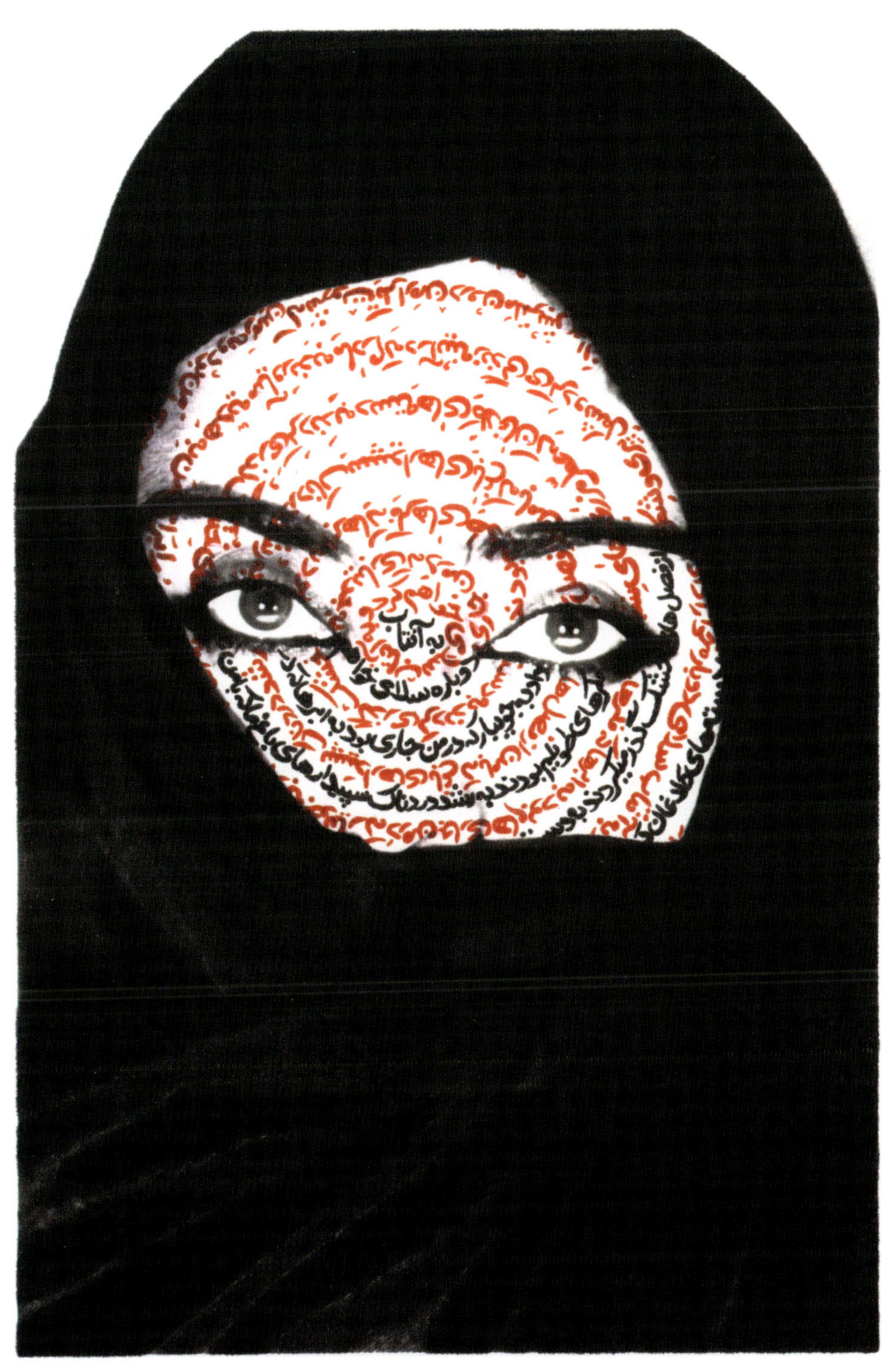

SHIRIN NESHAT, *I AM ITS SECRET,* 1993
ANNINA NOSEI GALLERY, NEW YORK

THE LATIN AMERICANS

In 1993, reaffirming her adherence to such globalist and post-Eurocentric perspectives, Annina hosted a group show that testified to the expansion of her concept: *7 Latin American Artists*.[69] Among the factors motivating her to focus on the work of Latin American artists, apart from personal taste, which had always occupied a prominent place in her decision-making, was the relaying of a cultural vision that had begun to cement itself in those years, at a moment in which the historical condition of Latin American countries received increasing attention. Amongst many possible indicators, a particularly significant example is provided by the exhibition *Art from Latin America: La cita transcultural*, held at Sydney's Museum of Contemporary Art in March 1993, a few months before *7 Latin American Artists*. The exhibition encapsulated many of the issues in the relationship between Latin American countries and the West, challenging the stereotypical and somewhat nostalgic conception of Hispanic culture as exotic and somewhat primitive. It also gestured toward the larger project of cultivating a postcolonial sensibility, emphasizing the diversity of cultural contexts, each with a unique indigenous and colonial history, while recognizing the complex relationships between center and periphery. In the exhibition's catalogue, an essay by its co-curator Nelly Richard – very explicitly entitled *Postmodern Decentrednesses and Cultural Periphery: The Disalignments and Realignments of Cultural Power* – starkly outlined the most difficult issues underlying the dominance of rationality and the machinations of the Western Logos. Richard accomplished this, essentially, by denouncing the equation of modernity = progress, which produces an absolutization and exaltation of the new at the expense of the historical dignity of "minorities."[70] Annina's interest in Latin American artists did not appear out of nowhere: it had accumulated over time. Among the first to attract her attention was, as previously intimated, Roberto Juarez, but she had always esteemed Wifredo Lam also, although it has been only in recent years, on the occasion of Galerie Gmurzynska's show dedicated to Lam and Basquiat at 2015's Art Basel, that she has had cause to express specific reflections on his work.

Among the first artists featured in the gallery's lineup, for example, was Tom Wudl, whose Austrian heritage distracts from a more attentive interpretation of his work, which I believe is significantly influenced by the place of his birth (in 1948), Cochabamba, Bolivia, where he was raised until the age of 10, at which point he emigrated to Los Angeles. But the figure in whom she invested the most effort was Julio Galán, whose first solo show with her took place in March 1989, a couple of months before he exhibited in the Parisian *Magiciens de la Terre*. The following year it was Guillermo Kuitca's turn for a solo show, followed, significantly, by *7 Latin American Artists*, in which the questions on the agenda were addressed directly. Foremost of these, the question of identity, was explicitly stated in Meyer R. Rubinstein's catalogue text, in which he wrote: "It is refreshing to have arrived at a moment when there can be a show of Latin American artists in New York that is not intent on promoting any image of ethnic authenticity or mysterious otherness (nor even of countering such clichés by insisting on some thorough assimilation of European/North American practices)."[71] The latter statement also clarified the direction in which Annina was headed, which fundamentally distanced itself from the assumptions of Global Art, from the reduction of grass-roots cultures to exotic attractions and from more polemical positions concerning Latin American culture.

69. *7 Latin American Artists*, Annina Nosei Gallery, 21 May – 30 July 1993. Artists invited: Arturo Duclos, Julio Galán, Guillermo Kuitca, Miguel Ríos, Teresa Serrano, Jorge Tacla, and Meyer Vaisman; catalogue essay by Meyer Raphael Rubinstein.

70. Nelly Richard and Bernice Murphy (eds.), *Art from Latin America: La cita transcultural* (Museum of Contemporary Art, 1993). Catalogue for the exhibition of the same name at the MCA – Museum of Contemporary Art Australia, Sydney, 10 March – 13 June 1993. Essays by: Néstor García Canclini, Ticio Escobar, Celeste Olalquiaga, Nelly Richard, and Osvaldo Sanchez. Artists exhibiting: Luis F. Benedit, Juan Davila, Eugenio Dittborn, Arturo Duclos, and Flavio Garciandía.

71. Meyer Raphael Rubinstein, "500 + 1", in *7 Latin American Artists*. Catalogue accompanying the exhibition of the same name.

IN CONCLUSION

After running her gallery in SoHo for 15 years, in the mid-1990s Annina moved her business to Chelsea, prior to the area becoming New York's famed Arts District. Perhaps it is not mere happenstance that this move coincided with an emerging shift in cultural and artistic models; rather, it could be interpreted as a further sign of the abandonment of a certain way of understanding art within US and European practice, which gave way to a more inclusive vision, oriented toward embracing non-Western contexts.

For years now, to speak of Annina Nosei is to acknowledge her as a pioneer, courtesy of her early recognition of outstanding artists in the likes of Jean-Michel Basquiat, Barbara Kruger, Shirin Neshat, Ghada Amer, and many others.

As previously noted, Leo Castelli himself observed that her discoveries perpetually went on to exhibit in the most important New York galleries. But while this facet of her activities is undeniable, it proves reductive in the face of the wealth of offerings and the complexity of content marking her approach over more than 20 years of operation. Moreover, her activities in the art world date back much further and span a wider gamut than such reductions allow, ranging from political engagement to scholarship, through writing and teaching to curating. She remained at the forefront of her field throughout complex decades in which art passed from an avant-garde paradigm to a postmodern condition, from political idealism to the neoliberal dismantling of modernist values.

One often reads that the Annina Nosei Gallery has specialized in painting, photography, and sculpture from the United States, Europe and Latin America, but this also is a drastic reduction of the real breadth of the directions she has taken, which, as I have attempted to demonstrate, are never traceable to facile schematisms and trivial categorizations. Rather, they derive from a cultural consciousness that forms a part of her family inheritance, they derive from her personal background, from her participation in the most radical enterprises of avant-garde groups and, above all, from her passionate and assiduous association with artists and their poetic worlds.

TEXTS

ANNINA NOSEI

The following article concerning Ken Dewey's Happening *The Gift*, held at the Théâtre Récamier on 8-10 July, was sent by Annina to the editorial staff of *Le Ore* on 11 July 1963.

THE AMERICAN AVANT-GARDE IN PARIS

In an old villa, now completely in ruins, which the few inhabitants of Valmondois (a suburb 30 kilometers from Paris) refer to as "Le Vieux Château," a group of approximately 20 artists has gathered from all over Europe, where they were already to be found on various tours, akin to a form of pilgrimage. There are actors, musicians (one addition to the group, for example, is Chet Baker, who plays in Paris these days, at the Chat Qui Pêche, the Huchette and the Blue Note), sculptors, painters and dancers, mostly Americans from San Francisco. The group has rented the estate for a few thousand francs, to the delight of some bankrupt old landlord; its walls are now in ruins and its forest is sumberged in nettles and weeds. Here, the artists carry out their esoteric activities with fierce intensity, going only rarely into the city. They remain indifferent to the comments of the no-longer tranquil villagers, who are now resigned to anything. This is the ACT group from San Francisco. On this, the occasion of the 10th session of the Théâtre des Nations Festival in Paris – together with the cycle of American avant-garde art that includes: Hawkins' ballets and Jean Erdman's *The Coach with the Six Insides*, already presented at the Spoleto Festival and next at the upcoming Allan Kaprow Happening – ACT will present Ken Dewey's piece entitled *The Gift*; previously presented in San Francisco in a different version by the dancers Lynn Palmer and John Graham – both of whom will also participate in this performance. The show, which fits seamlessly amongst the most recent expressions of avant-garde theater, includes and entwines dance, action, mime, jazz, acrobatics, and all sorts of personal initiatives from the group's participants. The stage required for the show could be any other place besides the Récamier Theater, where it officially took place on the 8th, 9th, and 10th of July. Over the course of about three weeks, in a huge and dusty barn of the villa – where there is enough junk stacked to keep an entire *marché aux puces* contented (and from which the group has stocked up on their costumes) and which can be reached only by unsteady stairs – the group holds its "rehearsals". The script, extremely vague and open to any improvisation on the part of the actors, concerns a symbolic and metaphorical "gift" that someone gives to a girl. The gift is a candle. However, the gift-giver, after giving it, wants to burn it. The girl, who becomes one with the candle itself, is frightened by this. The action does not develop following any apparent logic, but rather according to a series of numerous rites, allusions, and symbols whose meanings and rules have been misplaced.

The text has, in fact, lost every characteristic of a traditional theatrical script. Instead, it presents itself as a list of actions free to improvisation and alludes only in part to the movements that the actors and all the participants in the show or "rehearsals", including the public, may or may not do.

During the time spent wait before the presentation of all this to the *blasé* Parisian public – who (despite all the indifference with which it is now accustomed to welcome every most extravagant thing) was perhaps this time mildly surprised – strange rituals took place within the large room suspended in midair, with its creaking floor and its uneven walls.

The director Ken Dewey, chronometer in hand, directed the actors using a language that even the most skilled in American theatrical jargon would find abstruse. They instinctively obeyed him: rolling on the ground, jumping on ramshackle beds, sitting on broken chairs and employing all manner of tools.

In the middle of the cavernous space, suspended from a huge roof beam that somehow still endures, a mobile sculpture by the sculptor Jerry Walter sways menacingly. The sculpture is a huge iron skeleton. It is made up of approximately 100 kilos of iron piping in two sections respectively five and seven meters long.

The actors climb upon it. From high above they let themselves alarmingly fall; they slip between the cross-links of the iron bird; they seem to be fighting the huge mechanical monster.

There are those who try to conquer it by throwing themselves upon it and invoking help. There are those who lash out against it, making it sway frightfully.

(I would not want to be amongst the audience in the front rows of an evening's performance). They say that they want to sell it or leave it as a "gift" to the city of Paris after the show, or perhaps to hang it under the Eiffel Tower and organize another outdoor show there. Indeed, during the afternoon before the show, the company organized Happenings on the sidewalks of the Champs-Élysées and at Saint-Germain. The various moments of the performance were further underlined by the perfect music of Chet Baker, who had already played on the sidewalk in front of the theater for about half an hour before the show, surrounded by curious onlookers illuminated by the technicolor lights of the floodlights.

Chet Baker participated in the rehearsals and the show not only in the role of musician but also as an actor. His presence was extremely effective. He attended the rehearsals accompanied by his wife and by his huge blond toddler, who looks strikingly like him. The cries of birds entered through the ramshackle windows of the barn, as did the branches of the trees in the garden, where countless children of unknown nationality played and cried to the rhythm of jazz amidst the beating hammer of the French workmen who labored while grumbling against all and sundry, the chiming bells of the country churches and the roar of the two great motorcycles that the troupe used as a connection to the civilian world. While every one of the actors was completely engaged with the full gamut of theatrical activities, the music was further complemented by tapes recorded by Terry Riley. Thus, we witnessed Jamil Zakkai, actor-realist of New York's Living Theatre, participate in the abstractions of *The Gift*; as well as Carmen Scarpitta, an Italian actress of an international theater background, who – after having braved Gassman's monster, the big top – was now attacking Jerry Walter's monster. Walter himself, equipped with an iron mask and in the guise of a welder, also appeared on stage. But even the teddy boy of the company, Kit Goldsmith, the kid motorcyclist who rides with his tailpipe open, seemed to bear the same artistic responsibility as John Coe, the intellectual and refined professional actor.

To accompany her article, Annina sent the editorial staff a number of photographs, now lost. We reproduce their captions, listed at the beginning of the comuniqué, for the evocative image that they lend to those days.

1. The San Franciscan dancer-actress Lynn Palmer during a rehearsal of *The Gift*. During an intense dialogue of looks and sounds with Chet Baker.
2. Lynn Palmer, creative modern dance teacher from San Francisco, on Jerry Walter's mobile sculpture, upon which various scenes of Ken Dewey's *The Gift* take place.
3. Chet Baker and the dancer-actress Lynn Palmer of San Francisco's ACT rehearsing a scene from Ken Dewey's *The Gift*, presented at the Théâtre des Nations Festival in Paris as part of a cycle of USA Avant-garde Theater.
4. Jamil Zakkai of the Living Theatre in New York, who joined San Francisco's ACT while in Rome.
5. John Graham, a member of Anna Halprin's troupe from San Francisco, who came to Rome the previous May, and Lynn Palmer during an improvisation.
6. Chet Baker joined the group of San Franciscan actors in Paris. The show is accompanied by the music of the well-known jazz player.
7. Chet Baker during a break between rehearsals in the barn in Valmondois, located 30 km from Paris.
8. Patrick Hickey, the lighting designer of San Francisco's ACT company, appears onstage with the actors during the show.
9. Chet Baker at one of the barn windows in the ruined villa in Valmondois, during a break from the musical séances.
10. Carmen Scarpitta and John Graham in one of their improvisations, which follow each other in the manner of variations similar to those in jazz.
11. Jamil Zakkai, New York actor recently resident in Rome, where he joined Ken Dewey's ACT.
12. Lynn Palmer and John Graham on the mobile sculpture of Jerry Walter, a sculptor who collaborates with ACT and who has had various exhibitions on the Californian coast.
13. One of the production's most intense scenes of mime, dance, acrobatics and drama, staged on Jerry Walter's mechanical monster in the barn of the villa in Valmondois, located 30 km from Paris.
14. Chet Baker and the orchestra; in the foreground, Lynn Palmer.

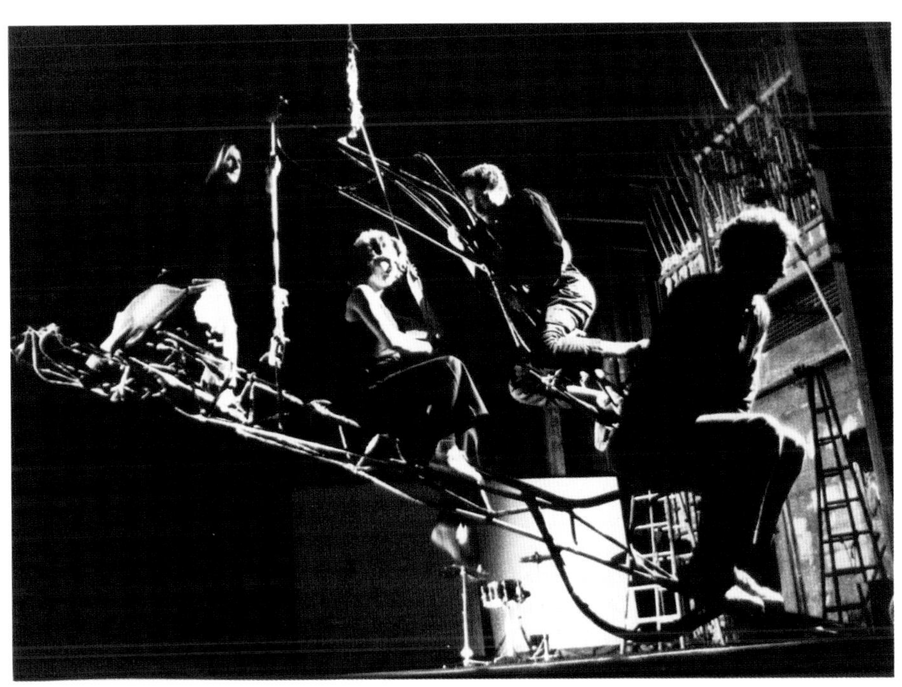

AN IMAGE OF KEN DEWEY'S SHOW *THE GIFT*
AT THÉÂTRE DES NATIONS, PARIS, JULY 1963

PISTOLETTO

Annina Nosei, "Pistoletto," *Collage*, no.2, Palermo, March 1964. Reproduced in the catalogue to the exhibition *Pistoletto* at the Forte del Belvedere, Florence, 1984. Transcription of the text reproduced in Florence, 1984.

Our every experience, considered in a moment isolated from our lives, in the present, constitutes a point of reference for the past and the future. This point of reference, utterly denuded of all that fills it, is a filter through which to sift through memory and the present. It is in this way that Pistoletto, in the specular surface of his artworks, traps an instant of our vision of the present: an instant that eludes our empirical vision and yet is here frozen, precisely so as to metaphorically embody the visual sieve that corresponds to the fixed mirror of awareness. His works present themselves as naked panels of stainless steel, polished to a mirror-shine. Carefully drawn and finished silhouettes have then been glued to these mirrors, apparently serving the sole function of adapting them to our eye and distinguishing spatial reality from the reality that they reflect. Before this naked visual sieve, we cannot but see our own presence, yet our present is one both unreal and real at once; which is part of a judgement and a narrative. It is through the total sacrifice of every pictorial measure, the abandonment of every pretense at execution (color, gesture, expression) that the painter, trained for an excessive attention to such pictorial means (having begun as a restorer under his father), has succeeded in making his works into that "visual sieve through which to measure past, present and future."

Here the complete sacrifice of painting has been carried to a metaphysical extent (while it is probably to the *Scuola Metafisica* that Pistoletto, who lives in Turin, has referred).

It is with extreme austerity that this rejection of every expressive device has been accomplished, if the enterprise is compared to the efforts of other painters who have shared his pursuit of objectivity. In Pistoletto's case, the revelation is wrought through the simple veil of vision, and the vision in question is that of reality. The most obscure of allegories is rendered transparent though the simplest of stratagems: reality is unraveled from its mirrored identity. The artist repudiates himself as artist and denies the public every projection of artistry; all that remains to us is the reality of ourselves. Ourselves reflected in the artwork, condemned to form a part of it, to be purified and judged through the mirror of our awareness. In observing ourselves and our reality, our metric is necessarily the void. Its silence and freedom cannot be stripped from the dialogue underway, on account of which, space – modified and mystified in the mirror – loses its dimensions, multiplies itself infinitely and catches itself in time. Time within these works thus becomes a dimension of consciousness.

In Luigi Carluccio's words: "It is possible to convince ourselves that the machination enacted by Pistoletto is a bid for the accomplishment of an absolute example of that commingling of space and time dreamed of by so many of today's aesthetes." The point of departure, before giving way to utter reality, is necessarily the void, the naked mirror. All that remains, the qualifying necessity, is the image of a person or an object, attained by the careful pasting onto the panel of a silhouette

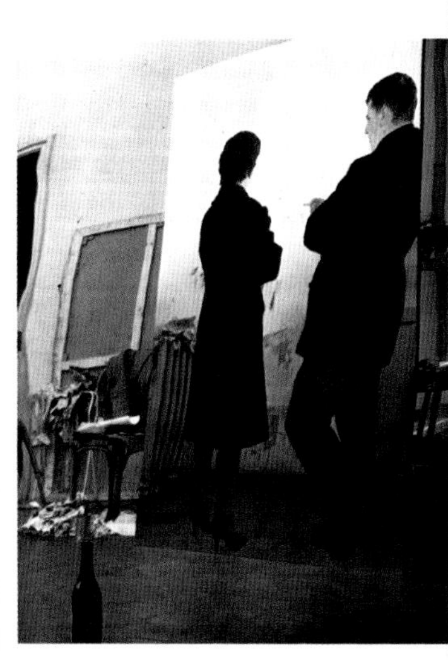
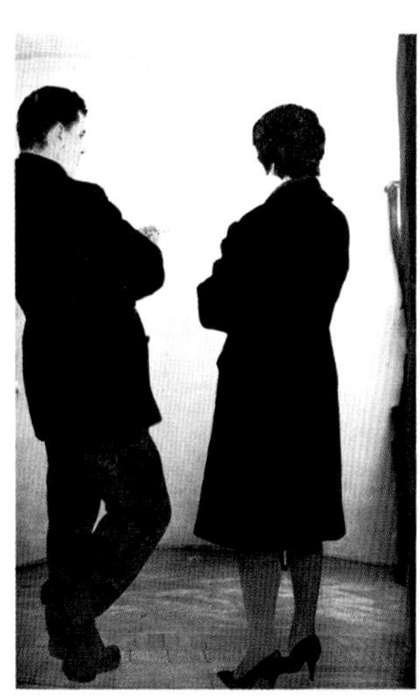
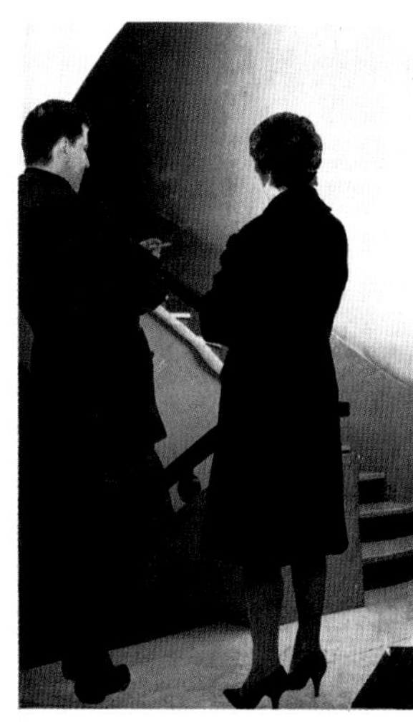

Three pages from the catalogue for Michelangelo Pistoletto's solo exhibition, Galerie Ileana Sonnabend, Paris 1964.

of outlines derived from photographic enlargements at life scale. The two planes (that of the collage and that of the panel) become fused; they are no more than an initial plane, an unreal division, something between "a simulacrum and the simulacrum of a simulacrum" (in the words of Alain Jouffroy, from his essay for Pistoletto's March 1964 exhibition at the Sonnabend Gallery in Paris). The pasted silhouettes, however, give the impression of being in the foreground; their life-scale dimensions, their somewhat shadowed, monochrome execution and their opaque radiance all project them outward, beyond the gleaming surfaces. And these surfaces, fixed in the figures, vary continuously elsewhere, reflecting continuously mobile space. The figures become a balance of mobility and spatiality. It is surprising to consider that there can never be a definitive vision of these artworks. Duchamp's *La Mariée* comes to mind, the piece that summarizes the artist's work, constructed from glass, transparent, open to the fluctuations of reality. But a work of Pistoletto is not "a lunar projection of an invisible form, its dimensions necessarily reduced a step, just as a shadow is the projection of a three-dimensional object" (as is the *Large Glass*). They are a projection of the visible real – of which, however, the difference, the variation in dimensions, casts a veil of allegorical mystification. In Duchamp's *Mariée*, painting invades real space; Duchamp, too, worked through transparency. Here it is the world that invades painting. Alice's greeting in the mirror remains suspended at the margins of the anonymous, quotidian, aleatoric figures whom Pistoletto presents. Destroying every possibility of Surrealism, he delivers us to the ordinary once more, to our "voie habituelle." And that is the truest message of the works of Pistoletto, who does not want us to contemplate but the objectivity of the real world. The objectivity of the random present, of fleeting reality, of naked reality, stripped of its uniform (to cite Duchamp's *Large Glass*: the "cemetery of uniforms and liveries"). It is this pursuit of absolute objectivity and this complete immersion in the reality of objects that situates Pistoletto's works in the same ambit as pop art. Reflected, objects reintroduce themselves as such, in all their banality and vulgarity. As he himself has said: "I cannot make a critical comparison between my work and Pop Art, because the process that I followed to arrive at these works is independent of that followed by the American painters. However, when their work was brought to my attention I was surprised and satisfied to find that their work and that "objectivity" interested me [...]. This objectivity is the consequence of the needs of current art [...]. I do not believe in any form of invention or use of the imagination [...]. An art that expresses personal sentiment does not exist. I am more interested in understanding what I see when I first get up in the morning: my things... a bottle... the things that make me up, the reality around me, rather than to continue my dream of that night [...]. I owe the mirror in my works not merely to my own needs but to a specific position. It is the void in which the entirety of reality dwells... It is the form and the boundary to which I am confined."

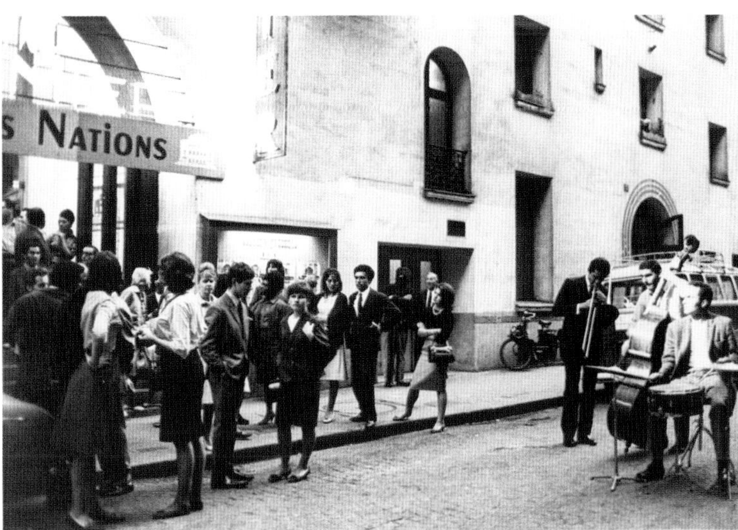

Crowd outside *The Gift*, New York, 1963.

CHALLENGE TO THE SYSTEM
INQUIRY INTO THE CURRENT ARTISTIC SITUATION IN THE UNITED STATES AND FRANCE

In 1968 Annina, together with Otto Hahn, edited an inquiry for the magazine *Metro* (no. 14, 1968, new series). Annina addressed her questions to American artists (Allan Kaprow, Donald Judd, Sol LeWitt, Robert Smithson, Dan Graham, Billy Klüver, and E.A.T.) and Otto Hahn to French artists.

QUESTIONS

Can the present language of artistic research in the United States be said to contest the system? In which way and to what extent? Considering the present ideological situation (political, aesthetic, social) is it possible for the function of art to occur to its full extent and not be compromised by the establishment even though it may be in opposition of it? Or can the hypothesis of a revolutionary outlet as being the vital condition of art outside and against the establishment, be verified in a symptomatic situation in the United States?

COMMENT BY ANNINA NOSEI ON THE ANSWERS

The reaction of many American artists when confronted with the problem of the relationships between their work, society and their function as artists — or confronted by the possibility of a dialectic between the meaning of their practice and the current ideological context — is generally to object that their art has nothing directly to do with the conditions and consequences created by society. Concerning the connection between art/esthetics and *system/ideology*, many American artists, whose language is more immediate, answer by sidestepping any comprehensive analysis of the problem, taking refuge in more detailed positions, in more pragmatic attitudes; they seem to refuse to take general critical stances. Indeed they profess, on one hand, an "implicit" morality; from a personal point of view, everyone naturally has human, political, cultural, and esthetic sympathies; but with regard to analyses of the ideological and social conditions in which their work is produced, on the other hand, their preferences and personal situations correspond not so much to indifference as to a realization that their work has nothing to do with anything more than itself.

An explicit dialectic of art is negated and the esthetic underlying the more recent American art, of Minimal art, for example, is silent on dialectical problems that are not necessary to the definition of that same esthetic.

Barbara Rose declares that a particular American critic — Rosenberg and his notion of "Action Painting", with "the vocabulary and polemical tone he used as a political writer in the thirties" — shows that "a disappointed political idealism, without hope for outlet in action, has been displaced to the sphere of esthetics, with the result that for some, art has become the surrogate for the revolution."

On the other hand, this "displacement of political ideals into the area of esthetics" corresponds to the criticism of Michael Fried, for whom the modern period is characterized by "the alienation of the artist from the general preoccupations of the culture in which he is embedded, and the prizing loose of art itself from the concerns, aims and ideals of that culture."

With regard to the criticism of Fried and also Greenberg, Barbara Rose recognizes "their necessity to purge art of all social and political meaning as issuing from a frustrating inability to come to terms with a political position calling for action in a situation in which action is virtually impossible." Rose further elaborates: "That this purgation of subject content from art takes place at exactly the moment when a vocabulary of politically charged terms is adapted to a discussion of art is no accident [...] We have indeed come full circle from David: from a concept of art in the service of the revolution to one of art instead of the revolution."

Barbara Rose believes that, given the complexity of the current artistic situation, a more appropriate criticism would approach art on a general level; an a posteriori criticism for which evaluation commences such as that of William Rubin, Robert Rosenblum, and Leo Steinberg.

In reality, everyone realizes that in the United States ideologies do not exist, just as there is no "system" with which artists and intellectuals are directly preoccupied. Contemporary American society is perceived as an amalgam of varied systems (Allan Kaprow speaks of a pluralistic society, where various cycles of closed systems coexist, creating not "black and white" contrasting structures, but a general "grayness" that gathers everything in without distinction), identifiable as a uniform "middle class." Artists are part of the middle class, like everyone, and in spite of being absorbed into this social structure, being an artist puts them in a category that is in reality a dead weight for the machinery of American society, which gratifies only those who give it something in return, though nothing that is not a confirmation of society itself.

In reality, for society, art is not necessary. The sculptor Sol LeWitt says, "Sometimes someone says: we have to decorate a building, let's get an artist. So an artist is called who decorates the building and goes away. If the building had not been decorated it would have stayed up just the same. The artist spends the money they gave him and isn't any better or worse off than before." What happens to artistic production, once it has been embraced by society in the form of cultural dissemination, public or private collection, of speculation or anything else, does not interest the artist. The American artist does not refuse to conform to the standards of society, but as an artist has the freedom not to reinforce them. Within the structure of American society everything ought to be used to validate the "American Way of Life," not only religion, recreation, not only education — university and various systems of dissemination of culture — but culture itself and therefore also art. Culture, art, in order to be deployed in validation of the American Way of Life, has to become educational. To make culture serve an educational role, the American system "conquers" one "cultural trophy" after another, states the sculptor Carl Andre: "American museums are the storehouses and warehouses of banners, flags, armor and memorabilia of battles won over culture... a Rodin, a Manet, $85,000, a private collection of Assyrian art..." With the same drive and enthusiasm as for an attractive economic investment, works of art are acquired, ideas are spread, as signs that the American system has conquered this or that cultural phenomenon. "Instant culture" says the sculptor Christo (who, having lived until the age of 21 in Eastern Europe, followed by Paris, has been based in New York for the past five years), speaking of the methods of American society, which evades various stages of cultural formation in order to arrive at instant diffusion, just as powdered coffee means skipping the filtering of water, rotating the coffee pot, etc.

Behaving in a way similar to the mechanics of political and economic advertising, American society spurs a process of transition, a mutation of ideas into the use of their corresponding images, to the advantage of the "American Way of Life."

In the United States there are no ideologies, there is iconology. Carl Andre: "Art becomes the iconology of conquest." This was evident in the motivations of Pop art.

The United States' mode of operation is revolutionary. The American attitude is always one of action, compared to its European counterpart. Pop art was revolutionary. The same voracity, avidity, speed in capturing, of seizing the various parts of life, of commerce, the vulgarity and vital enthusiasm of America, are demonstrated by Pop art. Pop art was the art of American iconology.

The necessary ingredient for transitioning from culture to education is itself imposed by the American system: faith in the "American Way of Life." The sculptor Christo identified this agent, ever present in sustaining the American Way of Life, with its optimism, "goodwill," etc. as "an act of civic loyalty" called for in every social function: a decision to believe and support the vague idea of morality, goodness and democracy that, just so, the "American Way of Life" is meant to represent. Such American loyalism wins over any intellectual and idealistic speculation, and proposes an art that integrates itself into society: "un art de croyance," in Christo's words. Art, in any case, is "incroyable," reactionary with respect to society, with which it is not engaged, due to the fact that the prerogatives of art are based on a complete concentration on itself.

The artist doesn't take part in any "conspiracy" involving culture on the part of society and individuals. In this regard, many contemporary American artists refuse to consider any direct relation between what happens in the world, or even previous artistic or European movements, and their work; they seem to defend the utmost "actuality" of their work: its "conditions of reality." Continued and complete focus on "conditions of reality" of artistic production, that is on what is inherent and indispensable to artistic expression, seems to have encouraged a climate of greater creativity.

Naturally, this is an opinion, but it is often borne out through the trend of imitation and manner found in Europe, where cultural conspiracy is more easily observable with specific reference to the so-called avant-garde.

The consideration of the actuality of a production has nothing to do with a search for expressive novelty or originality, instead it is a consideration that in America has to do with immediacy. It excludes any temporal relationship, whether with the past, with the real present, or with the future and it resides – from artist to artist, from work of art to work of art – in a personal dialectic that severs any possibility of dialogue. In a certain sense, it occasionally tends toward that "Focus Historicus" that Duchamp spoke of, referring to that timeless moment in which a work of art has its utmost power, its utmost expressive value.

MEMORY

Text written for the exhibition *Memory*, curated by Annina at C Space, New York (2-20 April, 1977).

The consciousness of memory responds to an elementary need: the need to recall.

The poetic tradition of the classical world celebrates the knowledge of its sources in the form of memory: memory joins the anthropological data with the atemporality of myth. For it is memory which in the classical myth, plays the same part played by mimesis in Greek art; memory relates to myth in the same way that mimesis relates to art. The Greek mnemonic tradition unfolds itself through the connection of memory with the soul, through the memory of the lived lives of the Pythagorean reincarnation and through the memory of perfect knowledge in the imperfect reality (outlined in the platonic myth of the cavern – a metaphor for human memory) to become an object of idealization in Apollonius (I-II cen. A.D.). Apollonius, as Philostratus recalls, was a Pythagorean, famous for his beauty and for his chastity. He travelled as far as the Ganges to meet with the great Indian wisemen, and, after a long life of example and inspiration for his disciples, ascended to Heaven.

His century and the centuries after him (until Saint Augustine's apologetical work for the affirmation of Christianity) regarded him a saint, opposing him to Jesus.

To the four virtues of Pythagoras – courage, temperance, justice, wisdom – and to the exaltation of love by Christianity, Apollonius responded with the glorification of memory as the highest virtue of the intellect.

To memory he dedicated a hymn (which was lost). This hymn, the *Hymn of Memory* (Mnemosyne the mother of all Muses) idealizes memory as knowledge and wisdom, and elevates history as the inheritance of tradition.

It is Apollonius who embodies the great pagan intellectual tradition of culture. In an age of action, his message pertains to the contemplative state of recollection, the meaning of the historical layers of human experience, wisdom which comes from memory.

The eventual distinction between memory and mnemotechniques is overcome by the Latin approach to mnemonics within the art of rhetoric, intended as a system of analytical knowledge and including mnemonics in the theoretical speculation about cognitive thought, so that, in fact, memory can be understood as an integral part of the classical logic.[1] The theoretical development of memory as the art of memory plays an important role in the Neoplatonic culture of the Renaissance, as is revealed by the running conceptual structure of the various "summas."[2]

Among these is the Theatre of Memory of Giulio Camillo, characterized by its particular connection with memory and for its realization in concrete form.

Giulio Camillo's "great work" consisted of a tridimensionally constructed '*summa*' which was to function as an embodiment of the total knowledge and tradition of his time.[3]

This object was a structure made of wood, a large filing cabinet, large enough to be entered by at least two people at once, "full of little boxes" containing "a mass of papers" – filed documents of a system of memory of "all things the human mind can conceive and which we cannot see with the corporeal eyes, (things) collected together by diligent meditation (which) may be expressed by certain corporeal signs in such a way that the beholder may at once perceive with his eyes everything which is otherwise hidden in the depths of the human mind. And it is because of this corporeal looking that (Camillo) calls it a theatre."[4]

When Viglius, a correspondent of Erasmus, asked Camillo the "secret" of the work, Camillo spoke of it as representing "all that mind can conceive and all that is hidden in the soul all of which could be perceived at one glance by the inspection of images."[5]

The structure had painted images referring to the Bible and to the Cabala as well as "locations" – '*loci*' of the classical art of memory. Camillo, learned in the neoplatonic philosophy and in the hermetic principles, with his Theatre of Memory had built a system of knowledge enriched by the combination of the mystical traditions with the classical rhetoric of Cicero.

It is evident that this "Theatre" is based on a theoretical perspective which does not correspond to the conventional idea of the art in Camillo's time, just as it does not represent the conventional idea we have of its official culture.

However, in the light of the connection that the Theatre of Memory of Giulio Camillo had with the rhetoric – the "linguistics" of classicism – and with the ethics, underlining the moral stance of the mystical doctrines, it is interesting to consider this work as a cultural product which, although unorthodox in relation to the usual request of the art patronage, met with acceptance and fame in his time.

The patron of Camillo, in fact, was Francis I, king of France, who gave him money periodically towards this work.

In 1559, a book, a guide to the villas surrounding Milan, describing the collections of that region, still mentioned Camillo's Theatre of Memory, listing it as part of the collection of a certain wealthy Pomponio Cotta; later we lose track of the theatre. The theatre itself was lost despite the fact that Camillo's fame remained alive in Italy and in France for at least two centuries after his death. A less prejudiced history of art, contemplating the production of conceptual dialectical "art works," consistent throughout the centuries despite its acritical discontinuity, could not help but recognize the value of Camillo's achievement.

(S. Beckett, *Proust*, 1931 (John Calder, 1965):

> [...] The laws of memory are subject to the more general laws of habit. Habit is a compromised effect between the individual and his environment or between the individual and his own organic eccentricities, the

guarantee of a dull inviolability, the lightning-conductor of his existence. Habit is the ballast that chains the dog to his vomit. Breathing is habit. Life is habit. Or rather life is a succession of habits, since the individual is a succession of individuals; the world being a projection of the individual consciousness.

[...] The man with a good memory does not remember anything because he does not forget anything. His memory is uniform, a creature of routine, at once a condition of his impeccable habit, an instrument of reference instead of an instrument of discovery. The paean of his memory: I remember as well as I remember yesterday... is also his epitaph, and gives the precise expression of its value. He cannot *remember* yesterday anymore than he can remember tomorrow.

[...] Strictly speaking, we can only remember what has been registered by our extreme inattention and stored in that ultimate and inaccessible dungeon of our being to which Habit does not possess the key, and does not need to, because it contains none of the hideous and useful paraphernalia of war.

[...] Memory a clinical laboratory stocked with poison and remedy, stimulant and sedative.

All art can stand as a registration of habits, sometimes even of obsessions and the time quality of art, only as a deception, is anticipating the contemporarity of the future; but this is already memory.
We construct for ourselves systems chaining us both to the past and to the future, filing cabinets to put in place the elements crowding our mind, but while we give the recollection of our experiences order, we also accept the menace of future conditioning.
In this industrialized culture the role of memory has been conditioned by the invention and the introduction of new tools for recording the reality around us; nature and all our experiences; tools supplying effective memories of images, sounds, speed, notions.
These mechanical means, by their very nature open to manipulation, have divested the individual memory of its responsibility at the social level, the level in which the individual experiences were identified with the cultural tradition of history, where memory was a collective factor. Memory, deresponsibilized, has abandoned the social realm; it has been relegated to the place of the individual experiences, the place of personal reliquaries.
Memory now is the memory of one's life, a place of contact with the uncertain reality and when it establishes connections with this culture of "decadence," then it is only at the level of intimate reflections. An added manipulation takes place, which focuses on single attuned moments, fragments, relics, memories of something in memory of something: traces. The relation is intimate, the nostalgia forgotten. The fragments of the individual *'iter'*, material for the now alienated memory, residue for an archeology of the present, denounce absence.

The spontaneity of Dada proclaimed its disgust for any hierarchy: Dada rejected history, prophets, future, theory, causes... Yet the opposites met and art as "a private thing" was planting new seeds.
To Dada's total abolition of memory, the Surrealist answer was the complete reverse: the assumption of memory not only as the very nature of the process of learning, but also of art.
Automatism was abolishing all barriers, the passage of conscience to reality was fluid; no distinctions existed between memory and present. Memory was floating from the past into the future, back and forth. In both Dada and Surrealism the rationalistic models were abandoned. There were no more obstacles. Free creativity could fill the vacancies.
A similar thoroughness characterizes current artistic processes. The current socio-cultural context sees the objectivation of memory both as an implement and as a process.
Memory then is adopted as an operational device. The objectivation of memory is apparent in those artistic operations where mechanical means of recording are used only at the extreme limit of their technical capabilities. As well as when the process of memory, or any process of learning, is itself the object towards which the artistic operation strives.
In the first case, the "present tense" of the "documents" shifts the artistic process to practices that are not only systems of learning but searches for truth. In the latter, the natural psycho-organic development of memory itself reveals memory's basic characteristic: a faculty which is liberatory inasmuch as it connects the mental field to sensual fields, a capacity for subverting the conventional structures of history, culture and rationalistic procedures, because of its plebeian strength of unselective course.
Memory does not explain, nor does it classify, it does not record: memory remembers.
Therefore memory at zero degree brings about much more than awareness of its mechanical products or of its bio-physical processes: memory singles itself out as the autonomous motor.
The radicalism of memory again illuminates art as learning and gives way to the identification of the public with the participatory phase of the art experience.

1. The texts Ad Herennium attributed in the Middle Ages to Cicero and De oratore by Cicero were the most famous treaties of rhetoric during the Middle Ages and Humanism.
2. Cfr. The Summas by Giordano Bruno, Marsilio Ficino, Pico della Mirandola, Giulio Camillo.
3. The 'Divine' Camillo was one of the most famous men of the sixteenth century, born in 1480, lived in Venice. For the description of his Theatre of Memory cfr. The Art of Memory, Frances A. Yates, The University of Chicago Press, 1966.
4. Erasmus, Epistolae, ed. P. S. Allen and others, XI, p. 479.
5. Op. cit.

DISCUSSION

This text was published as a foreword in the book *Discussion* (Out of London Press, 1980), which collected material produced during the exhibition *Discussions*, curated by Annina at New York University (9-20 May 1977).

The exhibition *Discussions* was held at New York University, Washington Square, May 9th to May 20th, 1977. It was comprised of artists who utilize the medium and technique of linguistic discourse in various ways.

The idea for the exhibition originated with the international recognition of the work of Ian Wilson, who has been active in the art world through his exclusive use of discussion as art.

The medium of discussion, the direct application of the oral faculty in conversation or argumentation as a basis of artistic activity, is a phenomenon accompanied by controversial and ambiguous factors concerning the use of spoken language. The confrontational aspects of dialogue are far too protean to allow for a simple definition of such activity in terms of the provincial formalisms of art literature. Given these conditions, the thesis that originally guided the organization of the exhibition and guides this collection of transcripts and photos from it suggests that the principle of mutual participation in discussion as art should not be confused with 'performance' or panel discussion *about* art.

In most of the artists' works for the show, the design of the discussion place, the structure of the talk, even its specific planned conceptions, were determined by the artists in a manner that discarded the conventional distinction between discussion (open in form and content) and art. The dialogue itself was the most important element; its cultural categorization was irrelevant. Reviewing the discussions as they occurred in chronological order, the exhibition commenced with the showing of Joseph Beuys' *Public Dialogue* on a videotape shot by Andy Mann at the New School for Social Research in 1974 and produced by Willoughby Sharp in collaboration with Ronald Feldman Fine Arts, NYC. Willoughby Sharp had announced that he would be present to discuss the videotape, but in fact spoke about his artistic relationship to Beuys, centering around the 'Dialogue'. In fact, Sharp's oratory overlapped the sound of the videotape.

Speaking on his work at the New School, Beuys had defined the event as a "social sculpture." This notion projected the idea of art as an ideological forum gaining expression in the form of a discussion with the public. Joseph Beuys declared that political and humanitarian concerns have been shared also with his more specific art world public as they have been the motivation behind the artist's various art activities: visual, recitative, sculptural, environmental, and philosophical. Beuys' metaphorical performances and graphic works have likewise demonstrated more general approaches to art and culture that the artist has sought to engage with public discussions. Lucio Pozzi fashioned his discussion as a strict contrast between a

secret, regimented subject code and a free participatory scheme. In this four hour long discussion, the involvement of the audience spanned a wide variety of issues, often demonstrating the difficulty of cohesive conversation in the face of an apparent free choice of subject matter and discursive method. Pozzi transformed the discussion into an experiential situation. His speech rhythm was, unknown to his audience, marked by changing his seat every half hour (timing determined by a kitchen clock) and the shifting from one subject to another was determined according to a secret code that was established previous to the public discussion (this fact was revealed to me in a letter received after the discussion was held). The code coordinated colors with corresponding topics. Having constructed this workshop-like situation for himself, and having afforded only an apparent freedom to the course of the discussion, Pozzi's relationship with the audience seemed remarkably democratic. Even though the discussion was theoretically "signed" by the artist as a product of his own work, an atmosphere of psychological freedom prevailed in which Pozzi was just another interlocutor. Leaving aside possible comparisons to political or psychological interactions between individual and group, a reference to Lucio Pozzi's other art activities could be made. The demonstration of a visual point — whether in drawings or paintings — is similarly produced by other Pozzi pieces. The effects of Pozzi's work impress not so much graphically or didactically but actually as a practical experience.

Sarah Charlesworth, Joseph Kosuth and Anthony McCall represented the group International Local with a video installation that presented a pre-recorded discussion among themselves concerning the political function of television and other media in American society. The installation consisted of four tv monitors placed in the lobby of New York University's Loeb Student Center. The images on three of the monitors focused upon each member of International Local in conversation. The remaining fourth monitor alternated between a long shot of the three participants in discussion and excerpts from network commercial television, namely *Chico and the Man* complete with advertising interruptions.

The topic of International Local's discussion was both abstract and self-referential. Charlesworth, Kosuth and McCall talked about the experience of video and the quality of its political uses and effects. Victor Burgin's discussion was presented through a video tape produced by Paul Tschinkel and Innertube Cable TV. It was a video interview with the artist conducted by the art historian Tom Wolf. In the interview, Burgin speaks of his analysis of the terms of the socio-economical "discussion" which is the undercurrent of his scholarly articles and art works. In the works of International Local and Burgin, audience participation was indirect and generalized. This format coincides with the ideological content which is the frame of these artists' general artistic activities. The International Local and Burgin discussions recognize their political structures. The subject matter of the talks inevitably involves a denunciation of the present political reality and suggests ideological and politically pragmatic goals. These works examine the identification of social feelings in an attempt to restore art's connections to historical facts. Such work gains its strength from the support of theory, explaining and constructing a system of political argumentation through art. It often criticizes social manipulation while using the very same methods in order to express a political discourse. The works' concern for the fact of manipulation at the hands of culture is ambiguous.

David Antin has been specifically using spoken language as an artistic medium for some time (see his *Talking at the Boundaries*, New Directions, 1974). In his discussion for the exhibition, Antin's poetic talk to the public was a direct speech following its course along a personal track and rhythm of thoughts. The delivery was spontaneous, yet the structure of the narrative related to the invention of a story; a metaphoric tale that seemed to grow by osmosis.

Carolee Schneemann's ABC – *We Print Anything – In the Cards* presented the artist sitting in front of the audience, reading sentences from a series of marked, colored cards that documented personal conversations from her past. The audience was simultaneously presented with a projection of slides that illustrated the spoken text. The cards' colors and their initials, announced with each sentence, indicated whose words were being read. The subject-matter of the text was autobiographical, referring to a sentimental situation among several people: a woman (Schneemann) and two unnamed men. The relationship among these people is articulated and expanded in time through the recollection of the spoken expression of feelings; this enunciation was further expanded in narrative participation since the many comments of friends relevant to the relationship between the woman and the two men (characters identified as A, B, and C) were incorporated into the reading.

The audience listened to the oral material and observed the text develop into a presentation of frames within frames, of removal and reattachment of contrasting and contradicting narrative layers of personal, sexual, political actuality in connection to a past interpersonal situation. Since the early seventies, Giuseppe Chiari's musical performances have been more and more paralleled or substituted with "discussions" as an aesthetic form. These discussions have been ideologically inspired using techniques that seek to liberate artistic possibilities from the constraints of conventional culture. The presentation of Chiari's work has become an identification with his aesthetic ideas; the direct approach to the public has been used as a method to efficiently and realistically convey the final issue of basic human needs and the aspirations of social culture.

Chiari's piece required an interpreter to translate his native Italian into English. With the installation of loudspeakers, conference table, audience seating and interpreter, the atmosphere was similar to that of a press conference. Chiari stipulated some rules for the work. The audience would address the artist with questions and he would try to answer them.

Near the conclusion of the discussion, Chiari decided to reverse the roles of interrogation, addressing questions to various individuals in the audience.

All participants in the discussion were free to inquire on any topic whatsoever. As a result, Chiari was exposed to a mixture of aggressive, sympathetic attacks and defenses against and for his project. The questioning and answering became a way of simplifying dialogue, delivering the new discourse as an artistic one, personal enough to be of real concern to all participants.

Ian Wilson's discussion took place in one of the classrooms of New York University. The discussion extended over two periods of several hours each. Wilson's discussions have an analytical form that tends to purify the talks from any manipulation of the situational dialogue. This absence of manipulation is achieved through the means of an ideally Socratic situation in which the interlocutors become teacher and student simultaneously and, by the mere fact of discussion, are open to a mutual learning process. The topic of Ian Wilson's discussion was philosophical and placed under such careful analysis that the analytical methodology itself often became the content of his long discussion. Wilson's method of analysis places the artist-teacher in a discursive position of ideal humility. A common subject of discussion is found to establish a humanist base for truth. The analytical techniques of Ian Wilson focus the participants' maximum attentions on a topic. Responses to an enlarged creativity concurrently impose a discipline of discussion — an assurance of movement of ideas toward the development of the polemical subject. In this dialogue, the listening and the talking are equalized; an order is established and the experience is one of rigorous concentration within the movement of idea.

Composer Robert Ashley directed the last discussion of the exhibition. Ashley's piece was installed in Lassman Hall of NYU. The place was emptied of its seats, the floor totally lined with South American newspapers positioned in a fashion to suggest the layout of urban streets and blocks. The space was dark with a spotlight aimed only on a telephone in the center of the empty floor. The phone was connected to a loudspeaker.

Ashley, who was not in the hall but in his apartment, was called on the telephone in the exhibition space. With the call, the discussion started; a long, monotonous conversation based on an undisclosed language-code. In the background of Ashley's voice, Latin American music and announcements from a radio or television could be heard. This discussion was obviously not a dialogue.

The political overtone of Ashley's exhibition reached levels of psychological lyricism. Yet after 40 minutes, the poet Jackson Mac Low became frustrated by the oneway nature of the discussion, walked to the telephone, picked up the receiver, and after declaring that the talk was "like a summer night in the Bronx" and asking why a two-way discussion was not possible, hung up the phone. This act concluded Robert Ashley's piece.

SAVELLI

In March 1978 Annina wrote a critical text for Angelo Savelli on the occasion of his solo exhibition at Max Hutchinson Gallery in New York.

Perhaps Savelli's daemon is the same one who frequently visited Socrates.

That spiritual voice, Socrates says, interrupted him since boyhood and always turned him away from any evil or superfluous act. The daemonic voice never uttered a positive command but rather spoke with prohibitions and warnings. The Platonic moral attitude with its humility and wisdom characterizes Savelli's art. Plato's Socrates, like the artist, speaks for reduction and purity.

Self-restraint in Savelli's art comes from the simplicity and the austerity of sincerity.

Relieving him of past artistic ties, self-restraint precedes a reduction in the sign-system of his artistic expression, while intensifying this system's presence.

La *rétention volontaire* gives birth to the discovery of a rich world of action within these strict self-imposed limitations.

Retention means direct contact with the core of his art. It means freedom from superfluity, from redundancy, from convention.

What is more, this questions art's efficiency in the struggle against materiality.

It implies the acceptance of the contingencies of the artifact and the contingencies of the artist who as a craftsman confronts metaphysics with the physical nature of his art work.

Involved with a similar dilemma - the charm and the malaise of materiality - artists have, in Savelli's words, "worked to free themselves from the object. Left with space, artists have tried to dispose of space itself. In this effort of liberation, they have often created new forms of space."

The idealist/materialist dichotomy, manifested throughout Western art history, is the locus of Savelli's work.

For Savelli, the content of art is obscured by the matrix of artistic signs. It cannot be revealed through only a dialectic of forms, but rather through the dialectic between art and reality.

The profusion and interplay of signs deprives art of its essential connection with spirituality as much as it impoverishes art of reality. Savelli's affluence of signs (his painterly language) loomed, after a time, as an obstacle to the purposes of art.

"Like a love letter which arrives empty of words, but is received with a full understanding of the feeling that motivated its reserved writer," Savelli's white silence is a way to bridge spirit and matter. Savelli's art reaches poetry through modesty.

In comparison with Savelli's principles, words and forms appear conventional, speaking only of their references; they are descriptive and just a supplementary discourse.

The silence Savelli has maintained also in regard to glib public art-world issues is autonomous, removed from the art forum of aesthetics.

The surfacing character of nearly all recent art has been that of a sustained dialogue with our present technology.

Savelli's resistance to such a contagious exchange might have placed him in a position of artistic solitude.

To a generation of works (Pop, Minimal, etc.) that exemplifies the dealing of art with technology, Savelli answered with a long-standing question: How valuable is the contingency of the artist's *techne*?

If his public dialogue with the artists of the sixties and seventies was suspended, Savelli's affinity to the art of a generation twice as young comes from that sensibility which reevaluates the quality of intimacy, of closeness, between the artist and the work.

Savelli's research proceeded in an archetypal mode, exploring an *a priori*, where the meaning of art and process occurs by itself - bare, irreducible, stubborn, actual.

In any period, artistic phenomena may become the paraphrase of the current orthodoxy in contemporary aesthetics, or art can try to initiate itself from a new point. Artists, with or without the burden of the past, can repeat the Promethean attempt to reinvent the original motivation of gesture, form, sound. Such a "start from the Zero line " opens up a world of circumstance and occurrence.

In traditional art, nothing is contingent. All is designed to conform mimetically with the established paradigm of art.

Conversely, Savelli's *tabula rasa* leaves him with a contradiction, an operation towards immateriality that must concede to the dispositions of materiality. Savelli's reduction allows causality to take its course, stripping it of its protective shields, disclosing the making, not making enclosures, allowing forms and signs to be verbs and art to resemble itself.

The artist is at once *homo sapiens* and *homo faber*.

What eases the conflict between a systematic reduction and Savelli's plurality of output is his spontaneous affinity between thinking and working.

The basic humanity of labor is innately moving in Savelli's art. His work reconciles the dualism of materiality and immateriality, in a polarized situation like a magnet in which reduction and plurality co-exist. Such a dynamism has a nearly religious sense of transcending materiality.

The moral atmosphere that appears through his practice is humane and vernacular. His art is poetry in colloquial language. His impulse towards spirituality travels not into a metaphysical desert, but to a humanized place, where ideals are shared with the simplicity of work. This dynamic combination of the abstract and the concrete established the contemplative aspect of Savelli's work.

Since the Fifties, Savelli has promoted a praxis of contemplation as an alternative to the expressionist pathos of American painting. Like the *grand respirateur* (as he calls Duchamp), Savelli found the retinal value of the artistic experience insufficient. With regard to the traditionally visual nature of art, Duchamp had apparently retreated

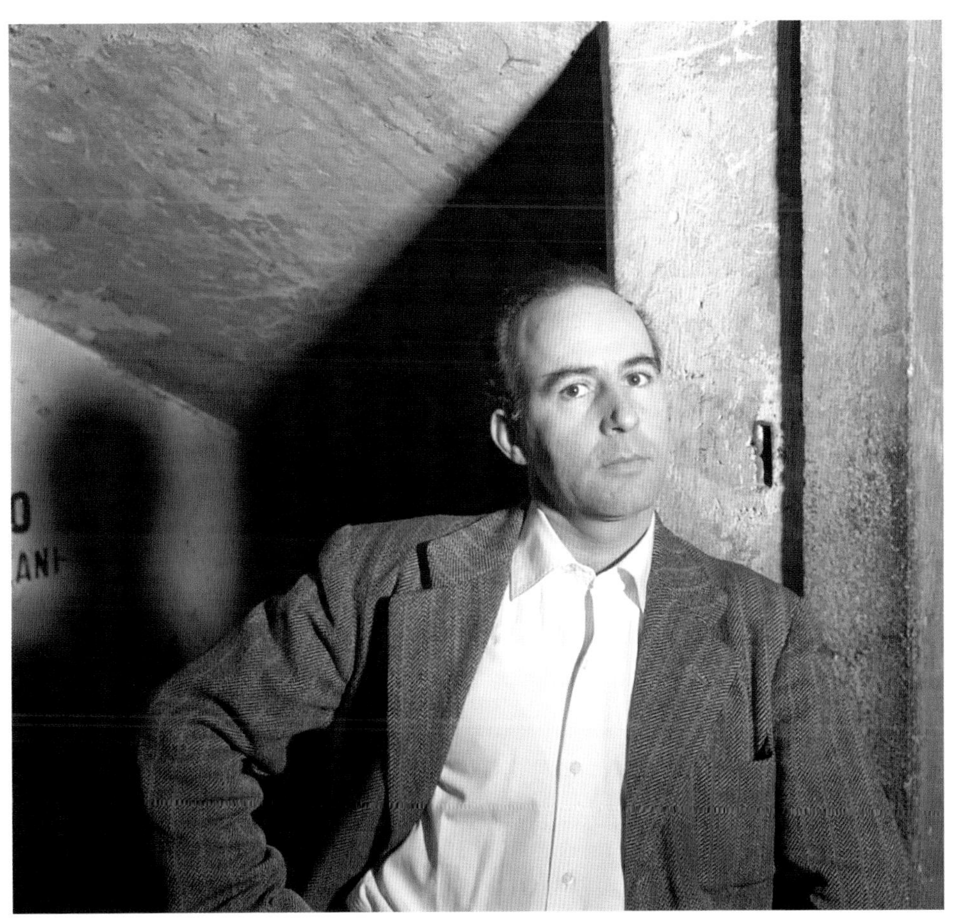

PORTRAIT OF A YOUNG
ANGELO SAVELLI

into a kind of aphasia which was, in fact, emphatic silence.
Savelli, instead, challenging redundance and defying all emphasis, undertook a radical rejection of all cosmetics in art.
Savelli's abandoning of color accompanied his opposition to extreme additive and juxtapositional methods in art. Savelli found "in a burning solar spectrum a persistence of white light."
The notion of persistence of content has been one of the gains of modern culture. The critical recognition of this concept has eliminated the hierarchy of expressive elements in favor of a uniformity.
In the 15th century Alberti formulated the fusion of the visual and the mental image. His *Prospecttiva* implies a unity of all possible ways of seeing. This also suggested a persistent content for art throughout the periods to follow.
In our industrialized culture, the artist's persistence has turned into an alienated, individual obsession.
The artist is left with an isolated, relative, solitary discourse.
Nevertheless, Savelli's work seeks a certain universality; though a single voice, the artist wants this utterance recognized as human.
For Savelli, Barnett Newman, more than any other New York artist, shared this concern with the universal.
Savelli, considering all colors as *lumi* (the neoplatonic, Renaissance interpretation of colors as symptomatic of materiality), adopted the exclusive use of white in his paintings, sculptures and environments.
Savelli's criticisms, like Alberti's against the Gothics, protest surfeit, worldliness, personal moods.
Monochrome having disappeared from Savelli's painting, only white was left to signify space.
White not as a play of light, but as clarity.
White as the place of the spatial *a priori*; white not to engage the eye, but to question the perception of space itself.
" ... quoting the authority of Plato and Cicero, Alberti advocated the use of plain white, as he was convinced that the divine power loved purity best in life and art and valued the white wall not only for what it is but for what it is not ... "
The sole counterparts of Savelli's procedure in painting have become white paint, canvas, silk, gauze, nails, rope, and - as supports - stretchers, plexiglass, walls.
These, together with any decision, any move, have been raised from an accessory state to a necessary role.
The pictorial means have been used for their technical properties: the canvas as support for the surface-paint; the nails as centers of animation from the surface towards the space, or as perforators of the skin-like plane; the ropes as divisions of the plane or as directional lines of the vibrations of the space; the pigment as traces of movement of the paint or as coated layers of the surface.
These elements have been accompanied or preceded by the artist's distinct and clear gestures: cuts and recompositions of the non-stretched canvas; pouring of the paint and directing its spreading or smearing; perforation or stitching of the area of the canvas; fraying of its edges or delineation of them on the stretchers.
All the results of the artist's operation on the canvas tend to reveal the nature of the paint and of painting, as well as to incite a passage from the plane towards space and a transposition of the physical experience into contemplation.
In the mid-sixties, Savelli used rope in his paintings as an additional element.
The rope, with its diagonal stitching, crosses the plane of the stretched canvas, animating it rhythmically. Its segments set in motion a directional impulse which extends the area of the canvas into a plane.
The twisted fibers of the rope, painted white, originate a continuing vibration. The use of the rope in these works, which Savelli continued for several years, recalls the artisan civilization of the Mediterranean.
The ropes are a memory of the past, a memory of Savelli's beaches of Calabria, where the ropes cut the surface and penetrate the body of the sand and of the sea.
They suggest a movement paraphrased in the title of these works - *Ascent*.
The conversion of place into space transposes both the naturalistic structure and the symbolic motivation of these paintings.
There is not a great difference between these paintings and the upward-reaching quality of the sculptures that also enclose the rope ('64-'69) entitled (by Barnett Newman) *Dante's Inferno*. These works contain the seed of a theme later developed in a variety of ways: the theme of continuity and the divisibility of space.
This theme is formulated in Savelli's paintings as one relative to the surface. In the Seventies, the ropes became thinner, the vibrations more acute; their original line, a rift.
The diagonal crossing the paintings is a precise tearing across a membrane which reveals, through that rip, the nature of the skin, the nature of the surface.
The edges of the skin, cut by the diagonal, respond to each other in an undulating rhythm, nearly touching at times, retracting, tending to cicatrize, to join their common substance. Layers of paint, as diagonal waves, arrive at the rift of the painting, building a surface which grows upon itself. To perceive this process, the eye, as in other Savelli works, does not only move around the skin-like surface, but actually penetrates it from above, looking down into it.
Beginning in 1972, the flow of the pigment on the surface moves very loosely. The skin is thinner, sometimes nearly transparent. The pigment leaves traces of its process and flow.
The heightening of this sensitivity is developed in a group of paintings where the autonomy of the surface increases and the canvas is left unstretched. This series of unstretched canvases (the *State College Series* of 1976 and the most recent group) are supportless and autonomous. The artist, cutting the canvases and recomposing them, combines geometric figures free in space. As Savelli says, "the form flies." It is the very property of buoyancy in the works that subverts the consideration of gravity, that defies the convention in

the placement of paintings in vertical space.

The ambiance of freedom in these works is due to the fact that the canvases physically elude, and therefore reorganize, the architectonic logic of their exhibition place. They hang, refusing to comply with the rigid legality of the common perpendicular site. The paintings, though retaining their tactile qualities, accumulate the empirical ambiguity of their whiteness with contingencies instigated from the very circumstances of display.

Another significant theme of Savelli's is the polemic of the Center. This theme was first dealt with in a group of early works still on stretchers, perforated in the center by a raised nail. In these, a piece of silk stretched over the painting's center (sometimes its off-center) with its moiré-like surface causes an expansion into space.

This subject is also manifested in a recent series of unstretched canvases. In these a centerpoint is marked just off the geometrically correct location within a slightly irregular square. Rethinking the notion of center as a *specific* place, but citing a center abnormal in terms of the laws of the formal square, Savelli, redefines the scope of perceptual focus, establishing an "imperfect square." These works summon a sensation of ambiguity if not sheer impossibility; they suggest an extension into space that tells us about something going beyond the specific physical experience, even in defiance of geometric logic.

In another group of works, Savelli examines the relation of the edge to the interior of the painting. In these pieces, the expansion outward from the picture's center has reached a maximum. The focal point has been pulled away from the center to the edges of the plane. The periphery is highlighted, and the perceptual functions and dynamic implications of the edges have taken over.

The movement has touched the limit of an inside-out point.

The emptiness of the surface has thrown all the activity at the edges of the cut-out canvas, now only supported by a transparent piece of plexiglass.

At first, a connection with Malevich could be seen, but Malevich, with his transfigurations, was reaching the static utopia of Suprematism. Savelli's interest is kept within the physical dynamism of his work.

The divisibility and continuity of space, the continuity of space and its expansion, the perceptibility of space, are also concerns of Savelli's environmental sculpture. Those contingencies of concreteness of his paintings are now substituted in his environmental sculptures by the themes that deal with the perceptual properties of space. Savelli's three-dimensional work presents a calm balance between those qualities and the "artistic design" of the author. This symmetry is constructed from the pairing of the visible and the invisible - the known and the unknown.

Steps Stepping Up the Wall (1972-78) consists of two rows of "steps," slabs running diagonally the length of the room; one of the two rows continues for a few steps from the ground up the wall. The "steps" are white slabs of elongated, rhomboidal, equal sections; each slab is cut diagonally, a few inches thick, and oriented obliquely. The oblique cuts of the slabs face each other in the two rows, symmetrically.

The slabs do not seem to rest on the floor; they are slightly raised from it so that they appear to float above the ground, freed from any gravity. Surface, color, shape make them look ethereal, as though an elongated projection of another form. What is more, their shape is unstable; it is dynamic, begin a transitional form in relationship to a rectangle or a Parallelpiped. The forms are cut in space, not as the surface of an object, but as the surface of a shape. Their succession plays with perspective by offering the profile point of view. They seem to be an elongated distortion of a square. The rows lead the viewer to travel along them expecting an ideal focal point in which the closest slab would be a square.

It takes a few further steps to realize the blatantness of this illusion: The artist has reversed the orientation of the slabs going up the wall so the corner of the 145 degrees is now at the place of the one at 45 degrees.

In the *Floor Sculpture Going Up The Wall* similar factors are again experienced. A series of I-beams runs along the floor connected by rods of the same dimension and length (a little shorter than two feet) as the central part of the beam.

This creates an effect of continuity. Given that the dimensions of the rods are equal to the I-beam for only two elements (length of the segments and thickness of the top section of the beam and thickness of the rods) and given the same white color, the eye establishes a strong desire for continuity, wanting it to be not only for those described two elements, but also for the body of the I-beam itself, so that the segments would appear to be all part of one stiff sculpture. It is not so. Instead, it is a series of dashes provoking the sense of suspension or, rather, pauses of suspension. As in all sequential situations, the rhythmical sensation serves as an element of abstraction and, similarly to music, the effect of the piece is in its repeated absences and in the connections as absences.

In other sculptural and environmental works Savelli always maintains the dynamic projection of the physical experience and its transfiguration. What results from what had and what had not been planned by the artist is a surprising, dynamic element. Savelli's art contains this idiosyncratic factor. It is with this personal component that the artist, as an innocent daemon, provokes the identification of the spectator, involving the audience and giving life to the perception of the work. There is a parallel with Cage's transposition of life into music. Cage said: "To obtain the value of a sound, a movement, measure from zero - pay attention to what it is. Just as it is ... a bird flies ... " (*Silence*, page 96). The flight of Cage's bird is a call to the infinity of possibilities; to the simplicity of transcendence. Savelli normalizes this call, tracing the reciprocal movement of the active spirit and the labor of art. cfr. "January 30, 1978: The birds are singing. There's grass on the ground and Kasimir Malevich is in my room. The conversation is likely to begin ... when Duchamp knocked at the door ... " (From Savelli's biography, 1978 catalog).

THE DOOR

UNTITLED
[TO JEAN-MICHEL BASQUIAT]

In 1985 Annina staged an exhibition at her gallery entitled *The Door*, exhibiting "doors" created by Karel Appel, Jean-Michel Basquiat, Mike Bidlo, Chuck Connelly, Vincent Gallo, Sol LeWitt, Mimmo Paladino, Pizzi Cannella, Robert Rauschenberg, Doug Sanderson, Julian Schnabel, and Antoni Tàpies. For the occasion she published a catalogue with some brief notes on the artists.

There can not be a better metaphor for art as the one of the door because the door is the ideal symbol for the function of art. What a metaphor does is invites the extension of meaning. The door, in its substitution of the painting or an object of art, illuminates the broader meaning of the fundamental of art. The work of art as door is a passage through which the artist travels to reach a position of ethical reality: it is a passage from reality to an inner life. But also the door is a symbol which opens the possibility for communication. In fact, doors are images of opening and enclosure.

The door has always assumed a symbolic function allusive to meanings other than that of immediate reality. This is also the function of art – to offer the extension of language. This way of thinking about art is the spiritual way of thinking about art.

In the door, *11 rue Larrey* – opened and closed at the same time – Duchamp embodied the coincidence of opposites.

The domestic allusion, the quotidian aspect of the piece, is the transcendency that we have at home. It is a paradigm and has an alchemic symbology.

It defies time that this archetype can be presented again in an artistic forgery by MIKE BIDLO.

For CHUCK CONNELLY this door is the entrance to a strange obsessed room in which the artist is held prisoner like a tied up child.

JEAN-MICHEL BASQUIAT's door is an old door from an apartment of a tenement building, smelling of a Latin kitchen, reminiscent of the immigrants and the villages from which they came and the saints to which they prayed.

Food and religion, which give shape to their day, remain a part of the family life of this group of people.

In the case of VINCENT GALLO, the door is an object of entrance and exit. His works on metal plates reveal nostalgic signs of past places and times evoking and erasing memories. They are layers of continuing processes which the artist fixes at once in a pure image. His door is a functional expression of his concept: in all the works of VINCENT GALLO there is this double current – the willful flux from the past to the present and back.

Sometimes there are trespassings of cultures. At times there are cultures of the past which can appear to be more advanced than those which are being replaced. Industrial detritus is transformed by VINCENT GALLO into still lifes which are perfect images, celebrations of purity.

This text was published in the catalogue *Jean-Michel Basquiat*, Galerie Enrico Navarra, Paris, 1996.

Damn you Jean-Michel! Why did you die? Didn't you know the hardest thing to shake is the banality of people. You can break their correctness, and mend their incorrectness, but no transgression or excessiveness will win against the paralytic commonplace.

Like Artaud or Manzoni, each drawing that you did, or each word you wrote has monumental solidity against which crash and break, instantly shattered the pretended good will of the insensitive.

That your extreme courage was blindly vulnerable, I knew the first time I met you. And it intoxicated me, the enthusiasm of being a small part of your *Public Address*.

That first show that you insisted on "fitting yourself into" certainly hit the public more than I would have liked. "The Philistines" were attracted to those same paintings that were "pointing the finger" at them. Did they find those paintings cathartic? Or are they using these paintings as trophies for those unconquered territories, truths, where you in fact kept your purity?...

(I think that necessity, that hunger to keep that purity, made him appear as eccentric, as selfish, or made him dissipated. Maybe sometimes he couldn't hold it. Some paintings might be routine, or of repertory, but the whole extraordinary body of work is remaining as a "Eucaristic" witness of his great artistic sacrifice).

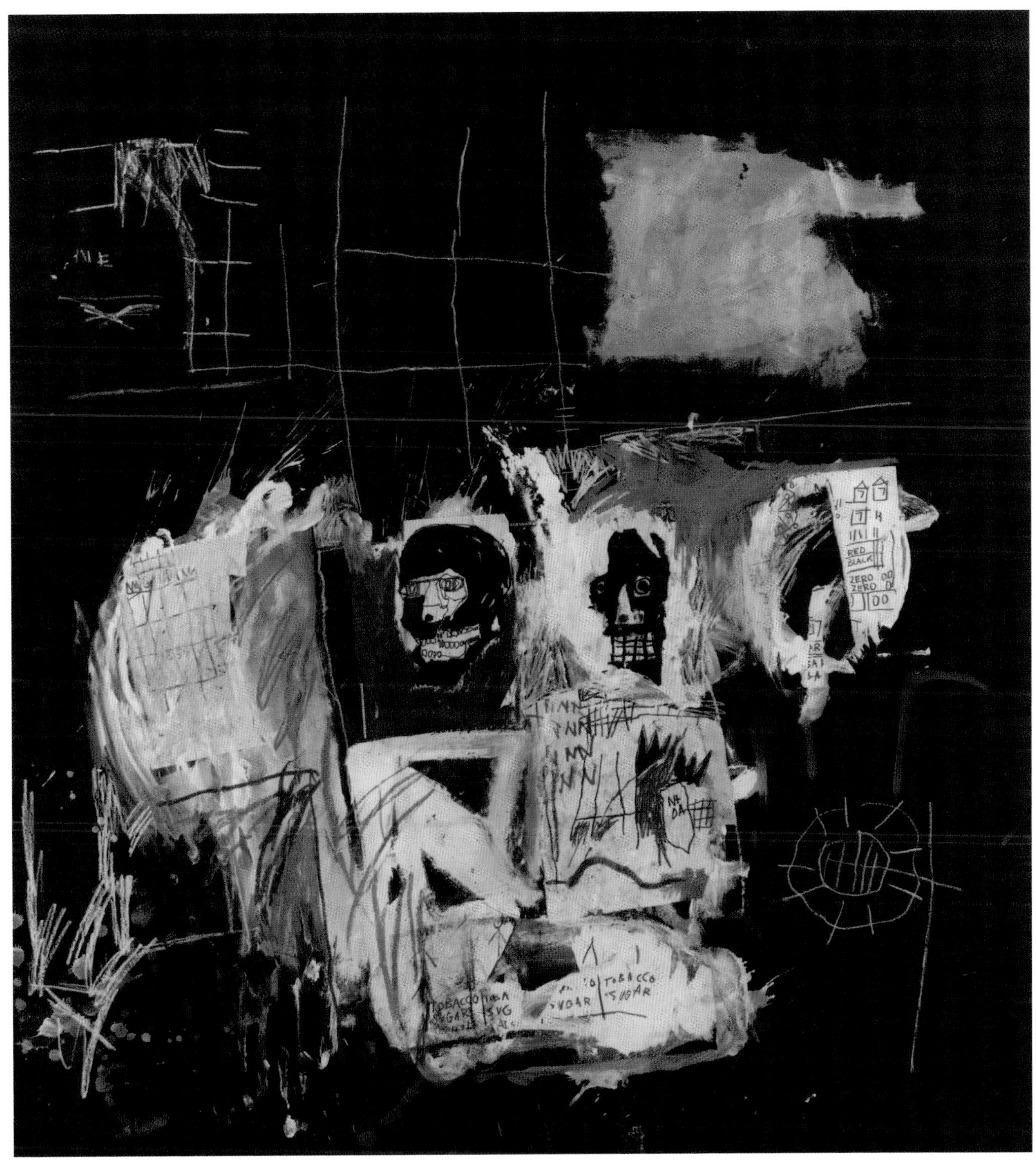

JEAN-MICHEL BASQUIAT,
UNTITLED, 1981

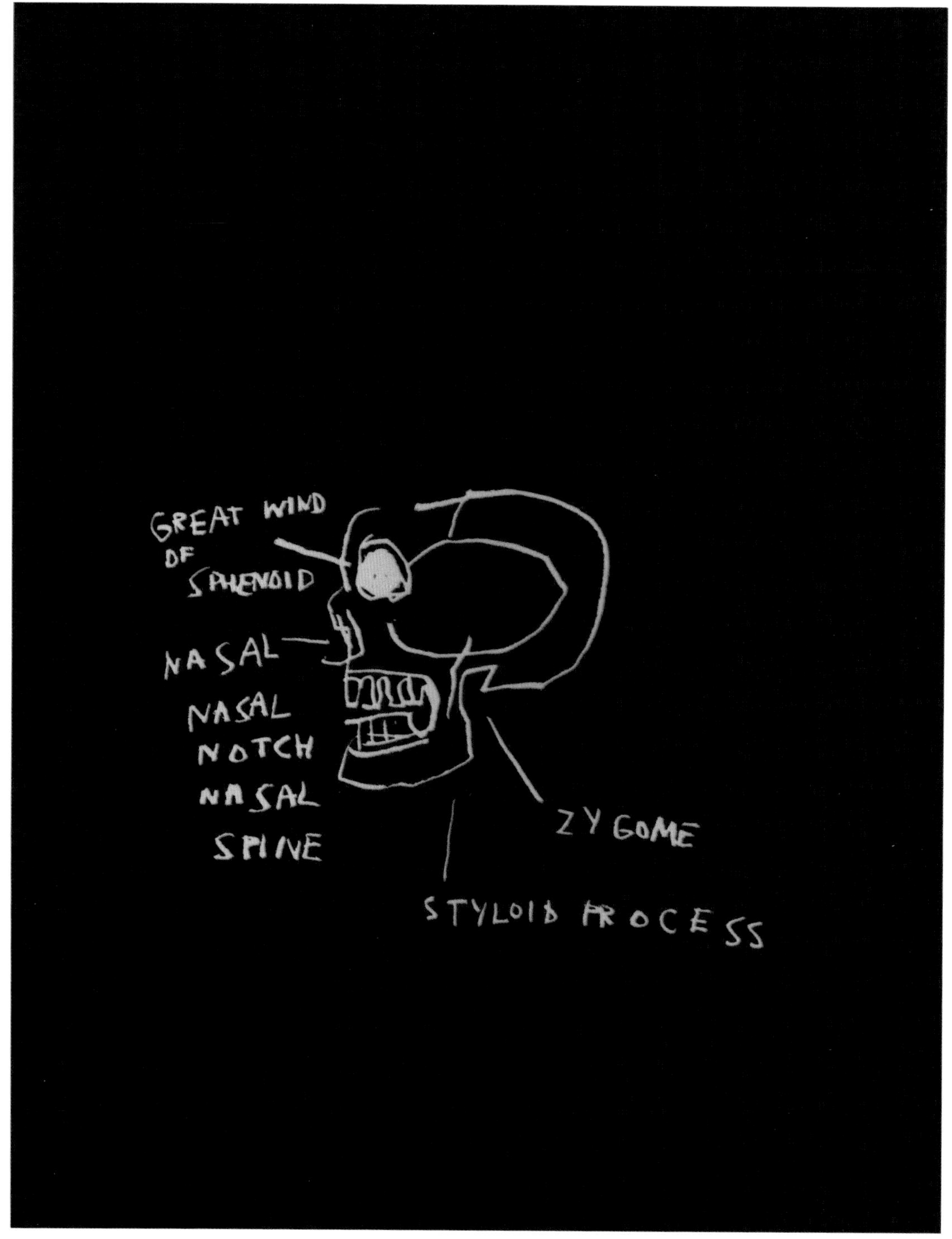

JEAN-MICHEL BASQUIAT,
ANATOMY, 1982

COMMON GROUND: WIFREDO LAM AND JEAN-MICHEL BASQUIAT

This text appeared in the catalogue *Lam Basquiat* published by Galerie Gmurzynska on the occasion of Art Basel 2015.

One day in 1981, when I had my gallery on Prince Street, I went to see an exhibition at PS1 entitled *New York/New Wave*. This was the much talkedabout show introducing the latest generation of upcoming New York artists. At that time, I had exhibited the work of Italian and German artists, but now I wanted to show American artists, living and working in New York. There was an actuality, an atmosphere, that represented the culture of New York City at that time, and I believed that it had a palpable connection to the island culture of the Caribbean. I felt that in the music in those days, in the people in the streets and in the fashion magazines, all in one way or another mirroring the city's youthful energy.

When I went to PS1, the two artists that I liked the most and that I wanted to have in my gallery, represented exactly that aspect of New York: open and connected to that urban aesthetic mirroring a tropical hybridity. One artist was Roberto Juarez, in whose paintings I sensed the affinity for this "tropicalism"; the flowers, the colors and the warmth were present in his imagery. I thought the paintings were fantastic and I wanted to show them in my gallery. As it turned out, he was already showing at the Robert Miller Gallery, so I could not sign him up, but I did put his work in some of my group shows. Juarez's work is still provoking that kind of enthusiasm after all these years. The other artist whose work had a similar feel to it albeit of a completely different nature, was in fact Jean-Michel Basquiat. His works I saw at PS1 were small paintings, "written" images on canvas, vignettes similar to the writings on the walls of lower Manhattan he had been known for. And so while these works were so different to Juarez's formally, they also communicated a distinctly Afro-American experience.

Several art writers at the time and later called his powerful works "iconic" or "magic signs" and "verbal images," while Jean-Michel however also inherited the graffiti stigma for his writing on the walls. But his was a quite different message. In fact those writings are concrete poetry and that mode of expression continued throughout his late works.

In 1981 I invited Jean-Michel to participate in my gallery group show *Public Address* for which he created large, spectacular canvases. In those works, there was also another element, which one could describe as a voice of the minorities. Their directness and unique vision presented a confrontational clarity. The paintings stated a social and innovative purpose, a clear agenda, together with a personal reflection, that further stressed the presence of the young Afro-American within society and cultural history at large. Jean-Michel's visual language meanwhile – his magical and spiritual signs – produced a special aura of sacrality. Because of this, his visual emblems had a natural, logical association with Afro-Caribbean ritualistic traditions and syncretic folklore such as Vodou and Santería or the islands' artifacts such as pagan masks, all of which partly derived from Western Africa.

The compositional strength, the structure, and the harmony found in his work places his visual language in the context of the classic art of Western Modernism. A painting such as his *Untitled* from 1981 with its basic architectural and multi-perspective organization of space is reminiscent of Matisse's painting, *The Moroccans* (1915/16), at MoMA. A similar correspondence can be detected between Basquiat's works and some of the paintings of the CoBrA movement. For example, Jean-Michel's *Dust Heads* from 1982 could easily be compared to a painting by Asger Jorn, in particular the raw and boldly colored heads facing the viewer, and the white band running through the center of the composition, bifurcating the space in each of these works.

Many art critics who have written about Basquiat discussed the obvious affinity his work has with preceding artists, such as Jean Dubuffet, Picasso, Pollock, Twombly, and Rauschenberg. Everyone underscored the strength that Jean-Michel's work possesses: his use of words, his images, his signs, were all written about and analyzed. But from the very beginning there was this other quality in the presentation of all these visual elements that went beyond the reproduction or imitation of any modernist style of painting, going beyond these immediate affinities or influences. His work was completely changing the course of art history, as his image making represented a direct reference to himself, yielding a subjectivism even in images reproducing vignettes or what may be considered a general description of life in New York or his paying homage to black athletes and jazz musicians. All this suggested a sociopolitical agenda that came from a deep personal awareness.

It was manifested in a strong spirituality, an inherent belief system, which again connects his work to the Afro-American spiritual tradition rooted in the culture of the Caribbean. For all these reasons I had early on mentioned and pointed out that one of the most striking parallels between Basquiat and his artistic forebears, is the work of Cuban modernist Wifredo Lam. Lam hailed from Cuba and was born to a Chinese father and an Afro-Cuban mother and thus his connection to Caribbean pagan-ritualistic culture was more autobiographically ingrained in his work. And yet, the aforementioned sacral radiance of Basquiat's paintings and his drawing's elaboration on imagery drawn from Haitian Vodou and Cuban Santería cults suggest a strong correspondence of mutual attitudes and themes. Although Basquiat, being a New York native, never had to emigrate from a non-Western locale to access the cosmopolitan artistic center as Lam did when leaving first for Madrid and subsequently Paris, Basquiat's multi-ethnic family background is not dissimilar, his father having been Haitian and his mother American of Puerto Rican ancestry. Due to these parallels, both of their practices follow a self-referential methodology to engage the modernist canon for a sometimes explicit and other times subtle socio-political agenda to express the hybridity inherent to culture.

Last winter I went to Havana, Cuba, to see the incredibly inspiring installation of Lam's work at the Museo Nacional de Bellas Artes. Of course I was already familiar with many of his paintings and drawings, such as the masterpiece *The Jungle* held at the Museum of Modern Art in New York, but those rooms in Havana dedicated to his work were simply spectacular. There was a series of paintings on black backgrounds. The angular and strident movement of these anthropomorphic figures, their mysterious presence, clearly demonstrated Lam's unique voice within postwar modern art. The theme of tropicalism, which runs through Lam's work, has a revolutionary spark that also speaks to minorities' struggle for freedom. It is that energy and flair of the tropics that permeates his signs and colors, in contrast to the work of Picasso, whose *négritude* is more forced. Picasso was re-inventing painting a generation or two before Lam, but Lam's take on *négritude* is more urgent and genuine than Picasso's more superficial approach famously exemplified by his *Les Demoiselles d'Avignon* (1907), a work inspired by the African masks Picasso saw at the Musée du Trocadéro in Paris. So Picasso's work is based on appropriation and quotation while Lam's work is an organically derived expression because his is rooted in personal first-hand experience and engagement with his cultural heritage, which is a quality one discerns in Basquiat as well. Exemplifying this dialogue is a late work by Basquiat entitled *Exu* from 1988, a large oil and acrylic canvas that exhibits several similarities with Lam's works from 1950s and 1960s. Exu is originally a demonic deity of the West African Yoruba religion, where it represents death as well as figuring as a trickster subverting boundaries and stirring chaos, overseeing the threshold to the afterlife. Also known as Eshu or Eleggua it is one of the deities that during the West African slave trade found its way into Afro-Caribbean culture, where it is a well-known character of the so-called Orisha spirits idolized in for example the Santería tradition of Lam's native Cuba, which also frequently populate Lam's paintings. (In fact Lam's grandmother was deeply immersed in this cultic tradition).

Several analogies can be distinguished here, most prominently of course in Lam's own numerous depictions of the horned Eleggua or in thematic works such as a major canvas from Lam's Cuban period, the 1944 *Autel pour Elegua* (Altar for Elegua). Here Lam revisits the classic Western genre of the still life rendered in a Pointillist manner, which however has been transposed to the local cultural context of Cuban pagan ritualism, the various goods depicted representing the offerings to Elegua. Lam here deploys Elegua allegorically, as an artistic device that adopts the deity's faculty of crossing specific realms whose boundaries thus become blurred and ambiguous – in this particular a classical motif of Western art and Cuban spiritual customs.

Basquiat, in his version, adopts this Elegua character by blending the creature's physiognomy with his own, including trademarks such as his dreadlocks, while the rolled cigars at the feet of Basquiat/ Exu represent devotional offerings. (In 1984, Jean-Michel wore the dreadlocks fashion of the Rastafari, which comes from Ras Tafari (Chief Tafari), the 255th monarch of Etiopia, Haile Selassie, who was perceived as a true god. Rastafari means the liberation and the coming back to Zion in the unity of all black people).

The agitated lines and scribbles radiating from the figure out to the canvas's edges meanwhile, along with the multitude of eyes that intensify the explosive energy of Basquiat's painting present yet another formal and thematic bridge to several pastels of Lam, such as his *Composition* from 1958 or *Composition* from 1962. Their energy and iconography are remarkably similar. Both Lam and Basquiat would further imaginatively tap into socially or ethnographically distinct sign systems. Lam particularly drew on the ideographs of the Afro-Cuban Abakuá cult, a coded sign system circulated within the group's male initiates who mostly came from the segment of the island's former slave community. This strategy of a creative appropriation is famously exemplified by a work like *Rumblings of the Earth* (1950), which today is in the collection of the Guggenheim Museum.

In rather similar fashion and approach Basquiat would study the coded sign systems used by hobos, representing the historical American outsider demographic, which he discovered in a book called *Symbol Sourcebook* by Henry Dreyfuss. Just like Lam had done some 30 years earlier, Basquiat studied these motifs and subsequently transformed them into novel visual elements to serve his individual artistic expression while introducing these non-orthodox motifs to the realm of fine art painting.

Another interesting work for this discussion is Jean-Michel's painting *Untitled* (1984) which I also refer to as *Ironworks*. It presents a seated male figure, his legs akimbo with his knees pointing outwards, and his right arm raised above his shoulder. The head is in partial profile, and we can see the mandibular, lower jawbone. His face is like a mask. An orange upper background is interrupted by white openings that are contiguous to the lower white half of the backdrop. Around the head something like a large halo is hinted at, while the figure's black dreadlocks are barely peeking out from a swath of red semi-transparent paint covering the face, dripping down the canvas onto the right leg. That leg is not human; it has a hoof, evoking the god Pan, or an African animal deity, part animal and part human. This is perhaps the most interesting aspect of the painting as it reveals the Caribbean source of the image. It reminds us of the frequently hoofed anthropomorphic figures populating Lam's canvases, notably one of his 1940s key works *La Réunion* (1942).

The masks of Jean-Michel's paintings distinctly remind us of the Caribbean and African masks that Lam also painted. We also find similar morphological elements like the bent knees. Yet, while in Basquiat's work feet point outwards, in Lam they frequently point inwards and create a diamond-like triangular shape. Another interesting detail is the set of ribs depicted in Basquiat's piece discussed above, which is similar to Lam's use of exposed ribs and other bone

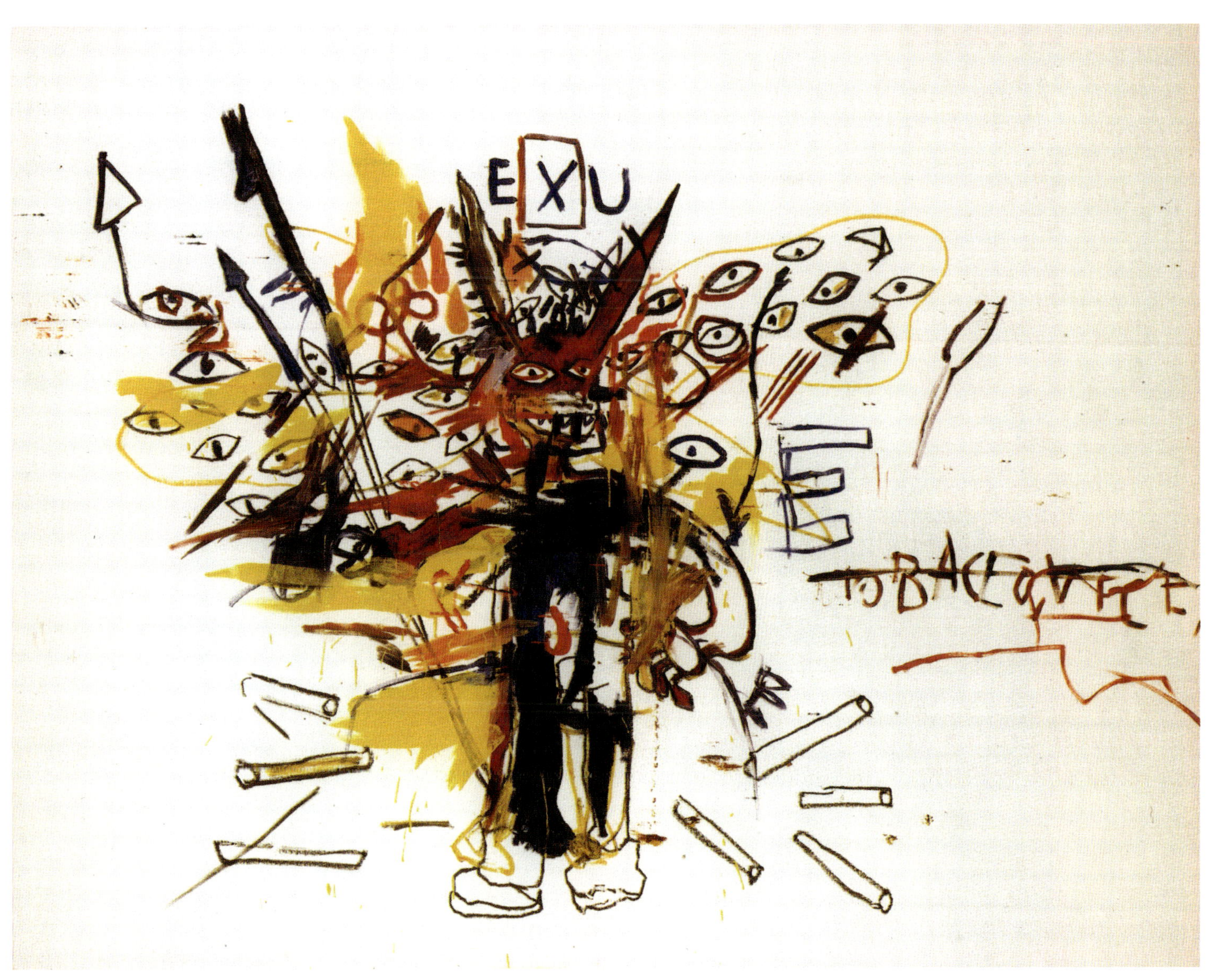

JEAN-MICHEL BASQUIAT,
EXU, 1988

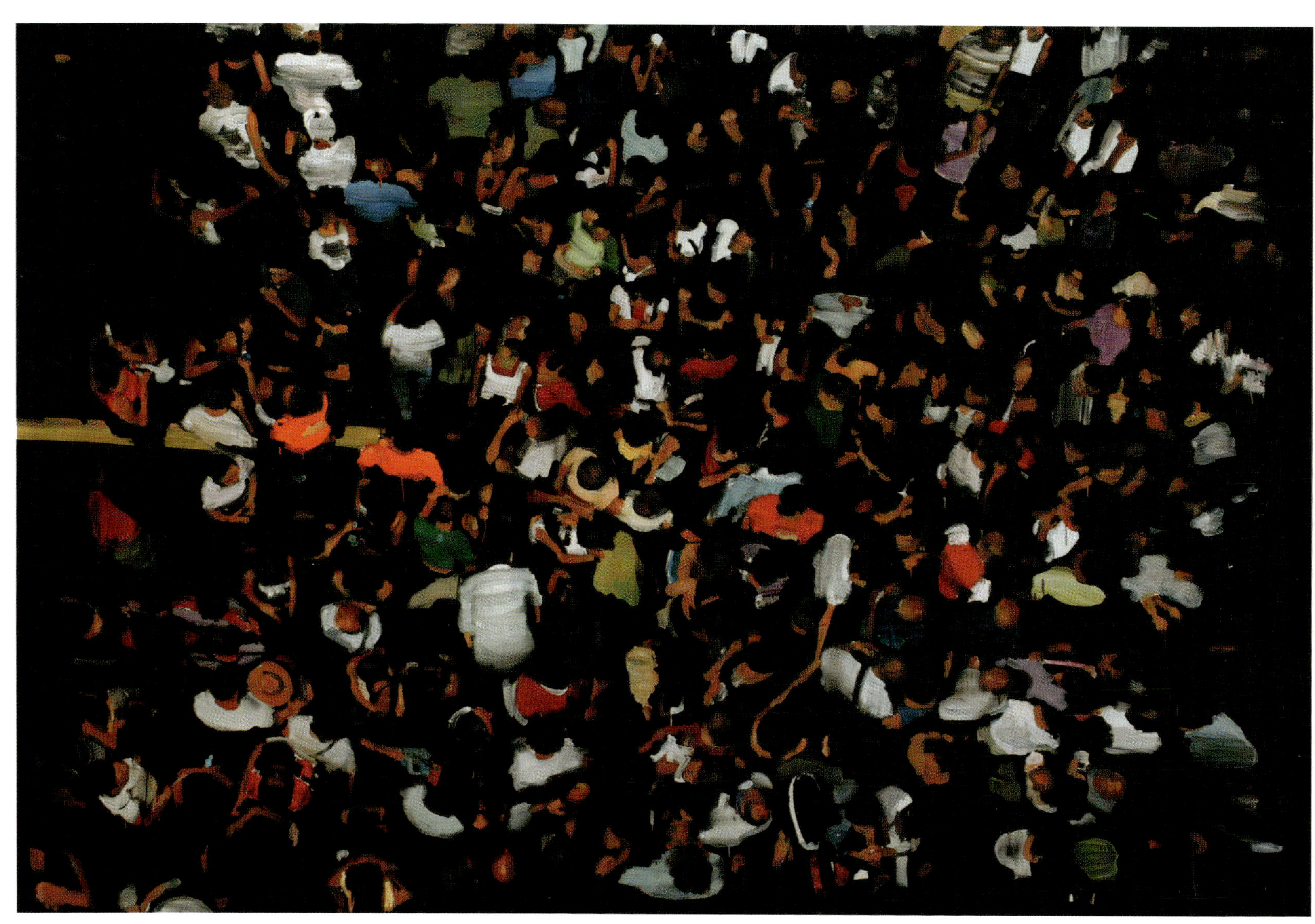

DANIELE GALLIANO
CONSTELLATIONS, 2010

AURELIA

forms in a number of his compositions. In Basquiat's painting, a nail appears to have penetrated the body and similarly the left foot of the figure has a broken chain behind it. Details like these evoke ironworks such as shackles and other torture tools endured by the slaves, which are also found in Vodou rites.

One of Jean-Michel's late paintings, *Riding With Death* from 1988, is comprised of a starkly empty background roughly painted in gold, surrounding a lone rider mounted on a skeletal creature. This looming solitude or sudden silence of pictorial space are present in some of the late paintings by Lam, and that economy of visual impact reflects a focus and a clarity that both artists had accomplished, one that most other artists of that time had not, including Picasso. Even in American modern and contemporary art of the time, except for Pop art in the manner of Warhol where there was just a graphic image, there was still a sense of a background that "housed" images or signs. This silence of space surrounding a solitary figure in the mature oeuvre of these two artists is unique to their work and distinguished their practice, now and then.

Over the years of our friendship, Jean-Michel gave me presents here and there; some of them were more meaningful than others.

For instance, in 1988 he gave me a cube that had collaged pictures on it, one of which was an image of a mother and child. Underneath it he wrote, "Thank you Anina," which was intended to show recognition and gratitude, because I had been sort of a mother figure to him. The last time I saw him, in 1988, he gave me a poster showing his portrait which he had signed "To Anina, with love 1988," which was unfortunately the last time I saw him. But at the very beginning of our working relationship, he gave me two presents, which are still meaningful to me. One was a little booklet on Duchamp, and for a 19 year-old to give me such a sophisticated present, was remarkable. Another present that he liked – and was so amused when giving it to me – was a little African statuette made from wood. It is similar to and perhaps a source for some of his drawings, while reminding us of Lam's own avid collecting of tribal artifacts such as the many statuettes and masks he gathered at his studio.

I will always remember Jean-Michel's generosity of spirit, his exceptional talent, and unique vision.

This text was published in the catalogue *unknown + Galliano: BAD TRIP*, Galleria In Arco, Turin, 2014.

My granddaughter Aurelia, when she was six years old, had to say something the first day of school. 14 children on a carpet, she raised her hand and said: "Art does not have to be about something, because there is abstract art." I guess that Daniele Galliano's work is not abstract art, it is about "something": that something is in a way foreign to me, but I found that – in the paintings of Daniele Galliano – instead that something was always strongly "present." I never was at a "rave" and I do not like pop music, I read Pavese, but I do not know Turin, the people of Daniele's paintings are probably those with whom I hope Aurelia will not spend time (I hope for more joyful times for her). But each time, in front of those paintings I found myself in a compelling and interesting reality. The actuality of the instant, the insistence of time has been projected into painting through Daniele Galliano's miraculous ability.

ANNINA NOSEI GALLERY EXHIBITION HISTORY

ANNINA NOSEI GALLERY
100 PRINCE STREET

1980

SEPTEMBER 20 / OCTOBER 7

GROUP SHOW
Jim Casebere, Mike Glier, Mike Kelley,
Kathryn Mish, Tom Sansone, and others

OCTOBER 11 / NOVEMBER 1

Mimmo Paladino

NOVEMBER 6 / 20

David Salle

NOVEMBER 22 / DECEMBER 31

Tom Wudl
Paolo Colombo

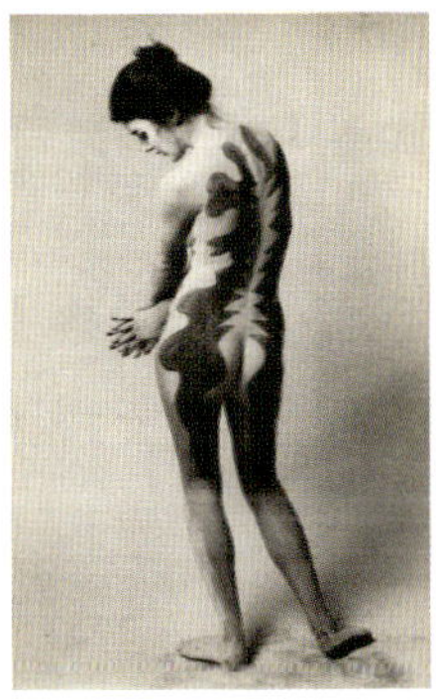

DECEMBER 20 / JANUARY 17

DRAWINGS AND PAINTINGS ON PAPER
Jack Barth, Troy Brauntuch, Francesco Clemente,
Sandro Chia, Enzo Cucchi, David Deutsch, Mike Glier,
Robert Longo, Mimmo Paladino, David Salle, Julian
Schnabel, Ernesto Tatafiore, Tom Wudl

1981

JANUARY 20 / FEBRUARY 8

Ernesto Tatafiore

FEBRUARY 10 / 28

Lynn Hershman
Michael Clegg and Martin Guttmann

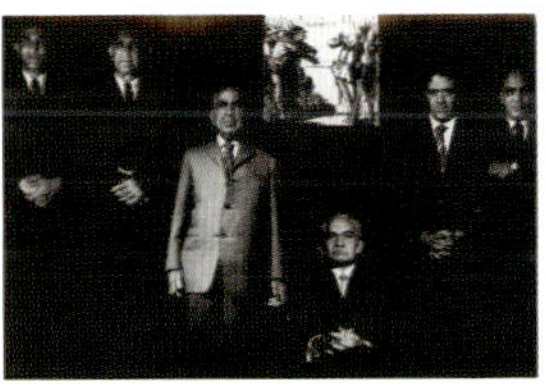

MARCH 3 / 21

Loren Calaway

MARCH 25 / APRIL 18

Mike Glier

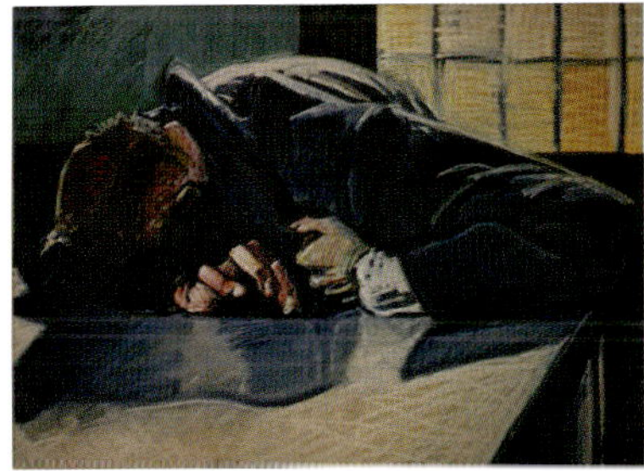

APRIL 21 / MAY 18

David Deutsch

MAY 19 / JUNE 4

Keith Milow, Salomé and Castelli

JUNE 5 / 30

Bill Beckley

1981

SEPTEMBER 19 / OCTOBER 29

K. H. Hödicke

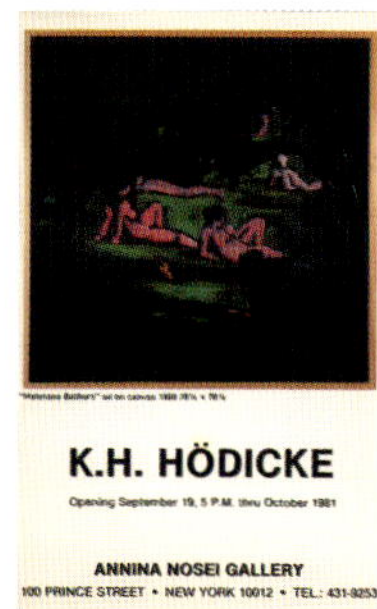

OCTOBER 31 / NOVEMBER 19

PUBLIC ADDRESS

Jean-Michel Basquiat, Bill Beckley, Mike Glier, Keith Haring, Jenny Holzer, Barbara Kruger, Peter Nadin

NOVEMBER 21 / DECEMBER 16

Salomé

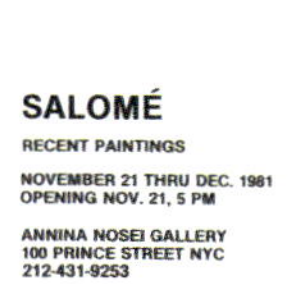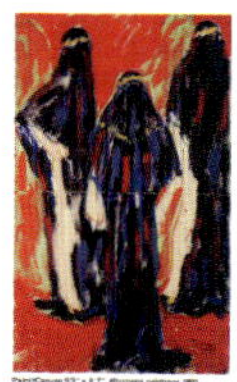

DECEMBER 19 / JANUARY 24

GROUP SHOW

Jack Barth, Loren Calaway, Paolo Colombo, David Deutsch, Carlo Maria Mariani, Ernesto Tatafiore, James Welling

1982

JANUARY 30 / FEBRUARY 28

Donald Newman

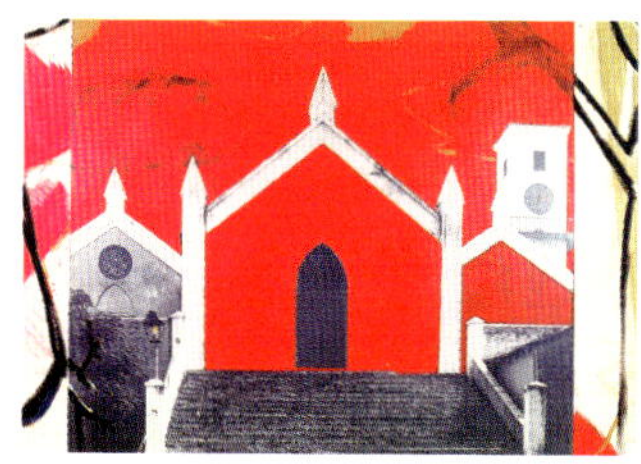

MARCH 6 / APRIL 1

Jean-Michel Basquiat

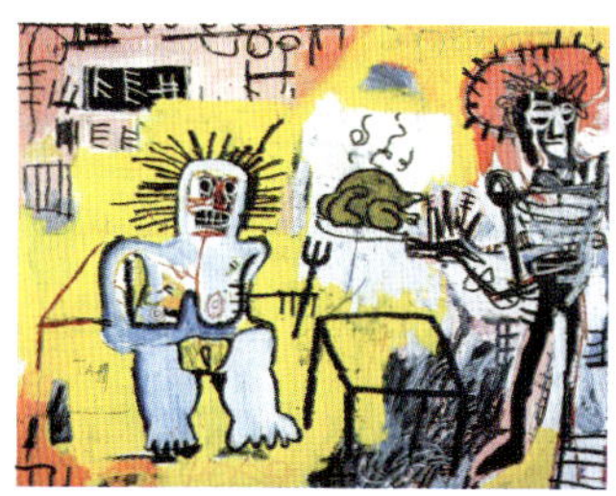

APRIL 3 / MAY 6

Bernd Koberling

MAY 8 / JUNE 3

Luciano Castelli

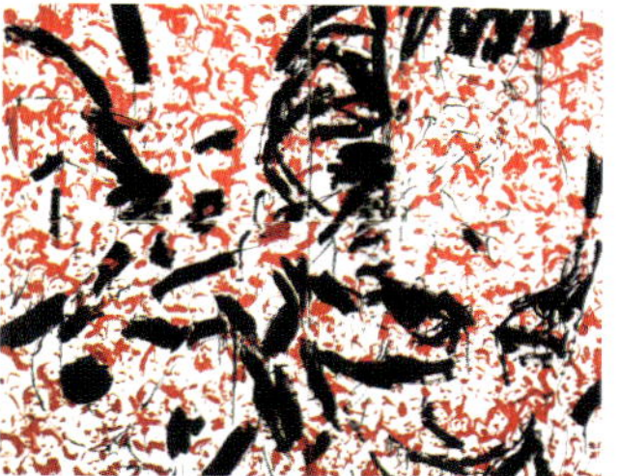

1982

JUNE 5 / 30

GROUP SHOW
Jean-Michel Basquiat, David Deutsch, Mike Glier, K. H. Hödicke, Bernd Koberling, Donald Newman, Mimmo Paladino, and others

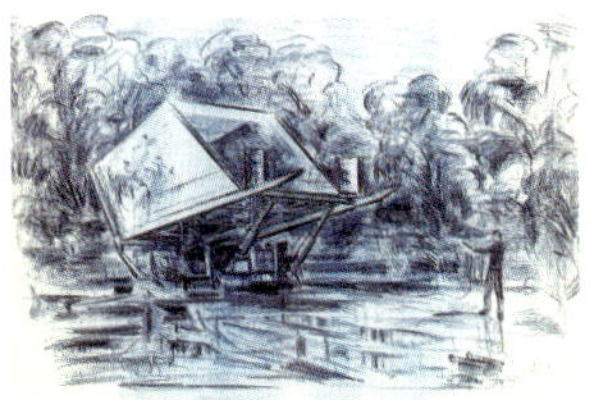

SEPTEMBER 11 / 30

Keith Milow

OCTOBER 2 / 30

Stephen Mueller

NOVEMBER 3 / 30

David Deutsch

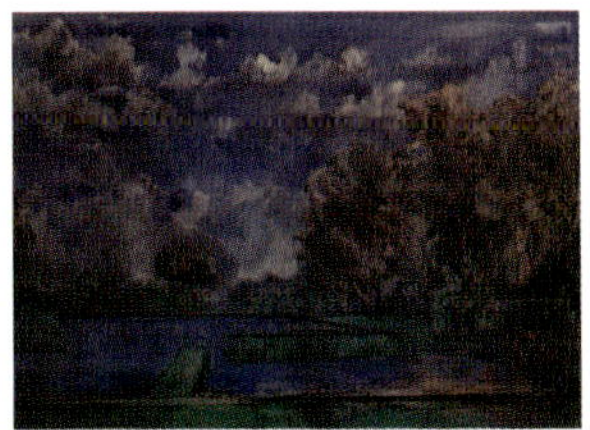

DECEMBER 18 / JANUARY 6

GROUP SHOW
John Ahearn, Jean-Michel Basquiat, Martin Disler, Mike Glier, Keith Haring, Roberto Juarez, Anselm Kiefer, Mimmo Paladino, Salomé & Castelli

1983

JANUARY 8 / FEBRUARY 1

Mario Schifano

FEBRUARY 12 / MARCH 3

Jean-Michel Basquiat

FEBRUARY 12 / MARCH 3

Rammellzee

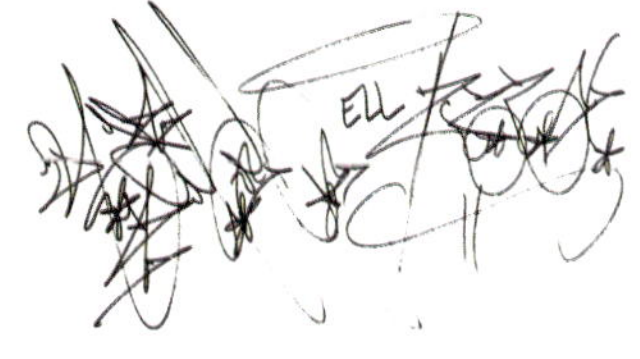

MARCH 5 / 24

Barbara Kruger

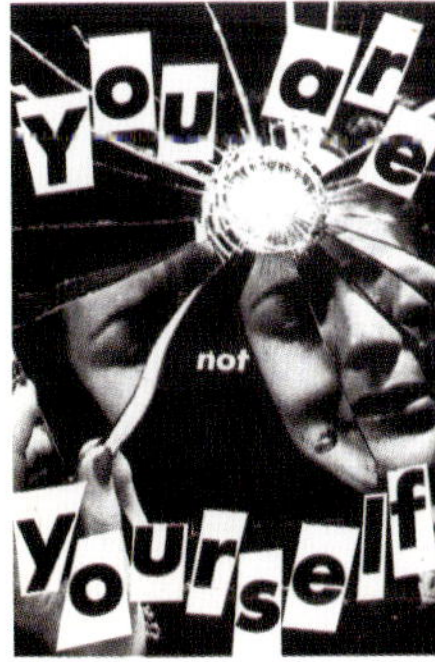

MARCH 25 / APRIL 9

François Boisrond

1983

APRIL 19 / MAY 7

Athos Ongaro

MAY 10 / JUNE 10

K. H. Hödicke

JUNE 11 / JULY 29

GROUP SHOW

Jack Barth, Jean-Michel Basquiat, François Boisrond,
David Bowes, David Deutsch, Jan Hashey, Angela Ho,
K. H. Hödicke, Barbara Kruger, Keith Milow, Sabina Mirri,
Stephen Mueller, Athos Ongaro, Mimmo Paladino, Ira
Richer, Mario Schifano

OCTOBER 1 / NOVEMBER 2

Ira Richer

NOVEMBER 5 / DECEMBER 3

GROUP SHOW

David Deutsch, Neil Jenney, Robert Mangold
Back Room: Keith Sonnier

DECEMBER 13 / JANUARY 11

EUROPEAN EXPRESSIONS

Jean-Michel Alberola, Miquel Barceló, François Bois-
rond, Bruno Ceccobelli, Peter Chevalier, Giuseppe
Gallo, K. H. Hödicke, Helmut Middendorf, Sabina Mirri,
Luigi Ontani, Mimmo Paladino

1984

JANUARY 14 / FEBRUARY 8

Sabina Mirri

FEBRUARY 11 / MARCH 8

David Bowes

MARCH 10 / APRIL 14

Barbara Kruger

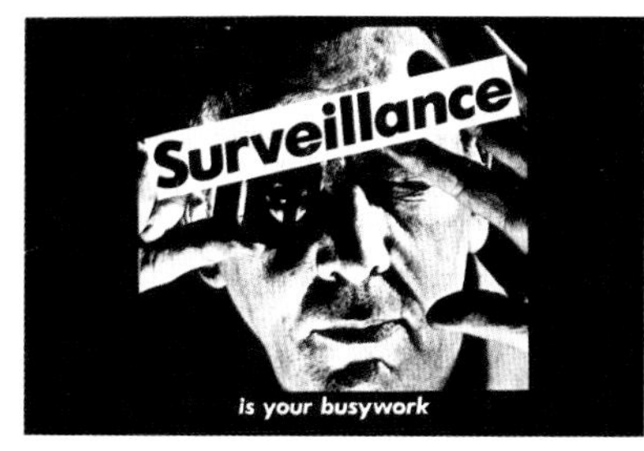

APRIL 14 / MAY 4

GROUP SHOW

David Shapiro (Poetry Reading) José María Bermejo,
David Bowes, George Condo, Sabina Mirri, Stephen
Mueller

MAY 5 / JUNE 2

Helmut Middendorf

1984

JUNE 5 / JULY 29

GROUP SHOW
Jean-Michel Alberola, David Bowes, K. H. Hödicke,
Helmut Middendorf, Keith Milow, Sabina Mirri, Ira Richer,
Marco Tirelli

SEPTEMBER 11 / OCTOBER 4

Georges Rousse
Back Room: K. H. Hödicke

OCTOBER 6 / 31

Chuck Connelly

NOVEMBER 3 / 30

Karel Appel

DECEMBER 1 / 31

Stephen Mueller

1985

JANUARY 5 / 31

Marco Tirelli

FEBRUARY 2 / 28

Pizzi Cannella

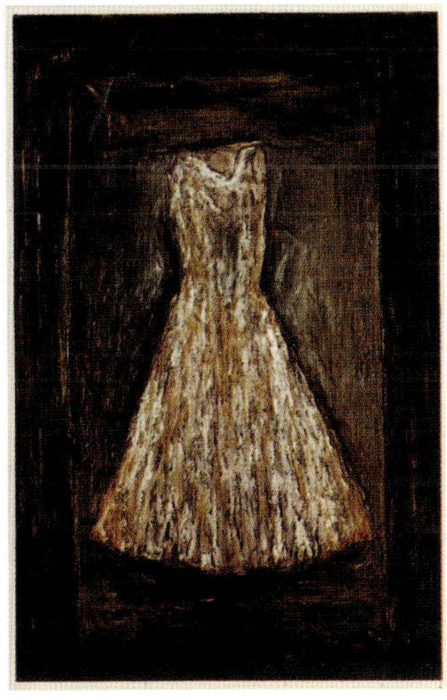

MARCH 2 / 28

Nunzio

MARCH 30 / APRIL 18

Ira Richer

APRIL 20 / MAY 9

François Boisrond

MAY 11 / JUNE 6

Sabina Mirri

JUNE 7 / JULY 7

THE DOOR
Karel Appel, Jean-Michel Basquiat, Mike Bidlo, Chuck
Connelly, Vincent Gallo, Sol LeWitt, Mimmo Paladino,
Pizzi Cannella, Robert Rauschenberg, Doug Sanderson,
Julian Schnabel, Antoni Tàpies

1985

SEPTEMBER 21 / OCTOBER 17

DRAWING THE LINE / PAINTING
Jean-Michel Basquiat, Mike Bidlo, Chuck Connelly,
Pizzi Cannella, David Salle, Mario Schifano, Cy Twombly

OCTOBER 19 / NOVEMBER 14

Vincent Gallo

NOVEMBER 16 / DECEMBER 12

Chuck Connelly

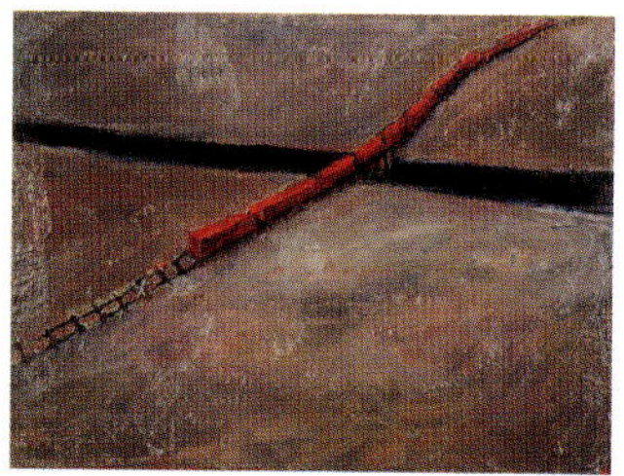

DECEMBER 14 / JANUARY 8

Jean-Michel Basquiat

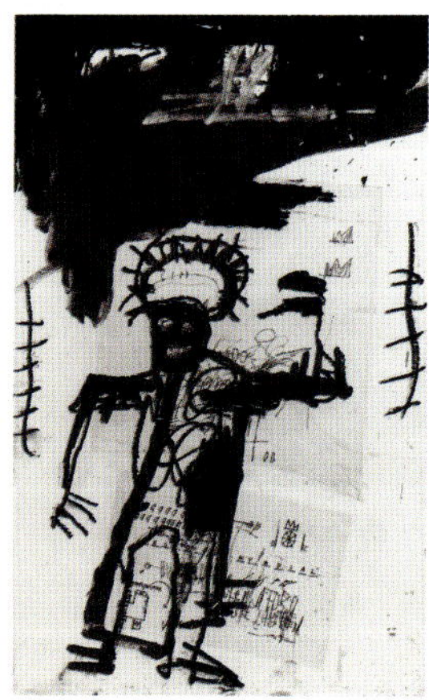

1986

JANUARY 11 / FEBRUARY 6

Helmut Middendorf

FEBRUARY 8 / MARCH 2

Barbara Kruger

MARCH 4 / APRIL 3

Claudio Palmieri

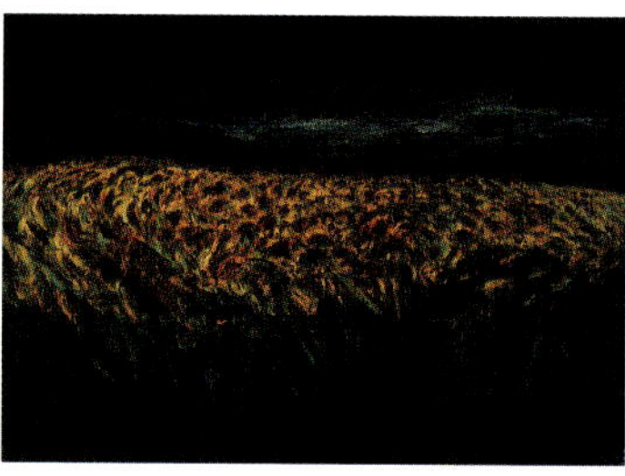

APRIL 5 / MAY 1

Pizzi Cannella

MAY 3 / 30

Pietro Fortuna

MAY 31 / JUNE 28

GROUP SHOW
Chuck Connelly, Vincent Gallo, Rayberry ©, Brigitta
Rohrbach, Sy Ross, Tod Wizon

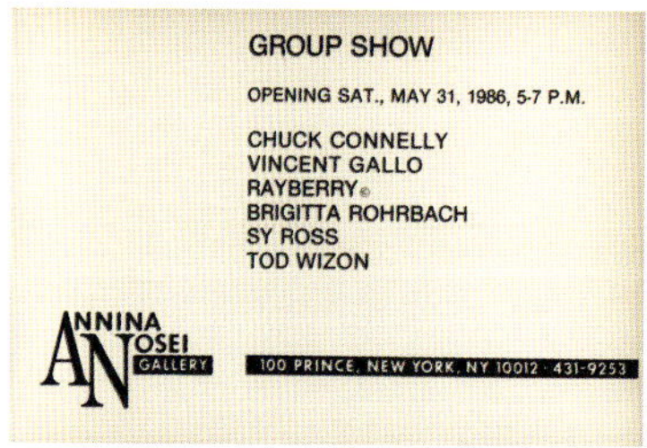

1986

OCTOBER 4 / 31

Vincent Gallo

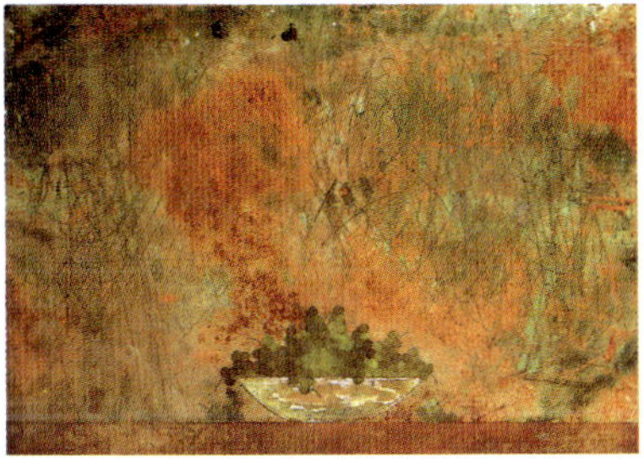

NOVEMBER 1 / 27

Stephen Mueller

NOVEMBER 1 / DECEMBER 31

GROUP SHOW

Bruno Ceccobelli, Pietro Fortuna, Nunzio, Claudio Palmieri, Pizzi Cannella, Marco Tirelli, Alfredo Zelli

1987

JANUARY 10 / 30

Group Show
Front Room: Barbara Kruger, Annette Lemieux, Peter Nagy, James Welling Back
Room: Ira Richer

FEBRUARY 7 / MARCH 4

Nunzio

MARCH 7 / 31

Tod Wizon

MARCH 7 / APRIL 2

Andy Moses

APRIL 4 / APRIL 30

Chuck Connelly

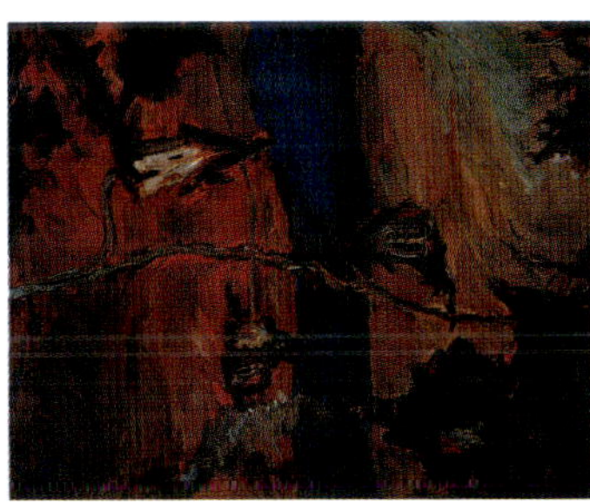

MAY 2 / 28

SPATIAL / FX
Vikky Alexander, Jack Barth, Beth Brenner, Tim Ebner, Steven Harvey, Andy Moses

1987

MAY 30 / SEPTEMBER 25
ROTATING PHOTOGRAPHY
Jennifer Bolande, Ellen Brooks, Victor Burgin, Vincent Gallo, Pierre et Gilles, Scott Gordon, Clegg & Guttmann, Steven Harvey, Larry Johnson, Karen Knorr, Richard Morrison, Richard Prince, Georges Rousse, Suzanne Santoro, Starn Twins, Lewis Stein, Sokhi Wagner, James Welling

OCTOBER 3 / 30
Beth Brenner

NOVEMBER 7 / DECEMBER 2
Ellen Brooks

DECEMBER 5 / JANUARY 6
FRAGMENTS
Nancy Bowen, Günther Förg, Jannis Kounellis, Nunzio

1988

JANUARY 12 / FEBRUARY 3
Vincent Gallo

FEBRUARY 6 / MARCH 3
Allan McCollum

MARCH 5 / 30
GROUP SHOW
Tamas Banovich, Beth Brenner, Jan Commandeur, Michael Corris, Marilyn Minter, Mary Obering, John Obuck

APRIL 9 / 30
Mary Obering

MAY 14 / SEPTEMBER 10
MUTATIONS
Vikky Alexander, Beth Brenner, Michael Byron, Steve DiBenedetto, Scott Gordon, Betsy Kaufman, Gary Lang, Marilyn Lerner, Steven Parrino, Alexis Rockman, Mark Stahl, Li Trincere, and others
Back Room: Michelangelo Tomarchio Levi

MAY 28
Massimo Kaufmann

1988

SEPTEMBER 17 / OCTOBER 1
Vincent Gallo

OCTOBER 8 / 31
Kristin Jones and Andrew Ginzel

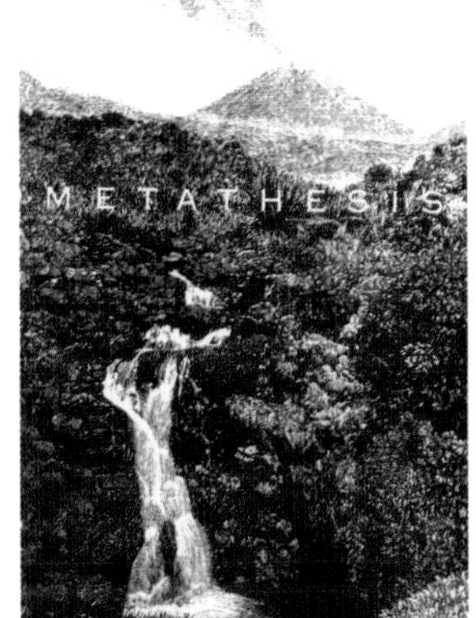

NOVEMBER 5 / 30
Stephen Mueller

DECEMBER 3 / JANUARY 15
MEMORIAL EXHIBITION
Jean-Michel Basquiat

1989

JANUARY 21 / FEBRUARY 15
Helmut Middendorf

FEBRUARY 18 / MARCH 11
Ellen Brooks

MARCH 18 / APRIL 9
Julio Galán

APRIL 15 / MAY 2
Gary Lang

MAY 9 / 30
Beth Brenner

JUNE 6 / 30
Christiane Richter
Back Room: Ronald Gault Jirado, Nunzio, Maurizio Pellegrin, Rini Tandon

---

JULY 6 / 28
GROUP EXHIBITION TO BENEFIT THE AIDS CRISIS
José María Bermejo, Beth Brenner, Stefano Castronovo, Mark DeMuro, Félix González-Torres, Willy Heeks, Gary Lang, Matthew McCaslin, Sabina Mirri, Olivier Mosset, Chuck Nanney, Rayberry ©, Sy Ross, Michael Zwack, and others

1989

SEPTEMBER 9 / 30
GROUP SHOW
Jean-Michel Basquiat, Beth Brenner, Ellen Brooks, Julio Galán, Bernd Koberling, Gary Lang, Helmut Middendorf, Stephen Mueller, Nunzio

OCTOBER 5 / 30
Ronald Gault Jirado

NOVEMBER 4 / 25
WORKS ON PAPER
Alice Aycock, Jack Barth, Jean-Michel Basquiat, Alighiero Boetti, Beth Brenner, Daniel Buren, Sandro Chia, George Condo, Vincent Desiderio, Eric Fischl, Lucio Fontana, Günther Förg, Julio Galán, Giuseppe Gallo, Ginzel and Jones, Jannis Kounellis, Julian Lethbridge, Sol LeWitt, Malcolm Morley, S. Mueller, Nunzio, R. Opałka, Pizzi Cannella, Lucas Samaras, Robert Smithson, M. Tirelli, L. Vinciarelli, F. E. Walther, Tom Wudl

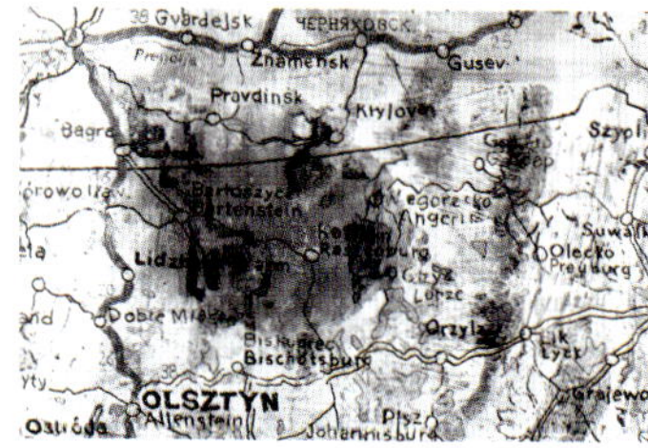

DECEMBER 2 / 30
Mary Obering

1990

JANUARY 3 / 24
GROUP SHOW
Jean-Michel Basquiat, Chuck Connelly, Julio Galán, Guillermo Kuitca, Gary Lang, Helmut Middendorf, Stephen Mueller, Marco Tirelli

JANUARY 27 / FEBRUARY 21
Guillermo Kuitca

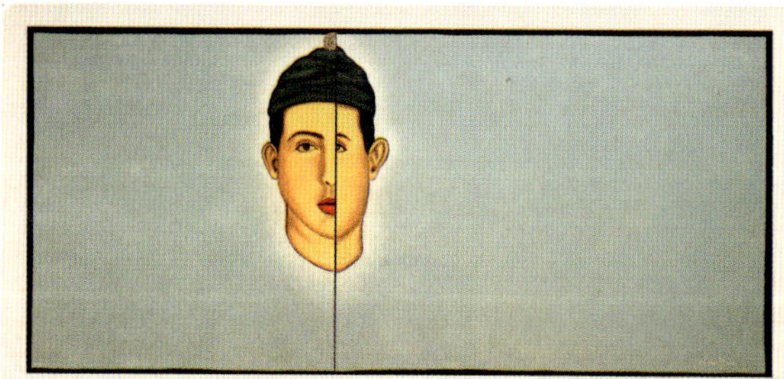

FEBRUARY 24 / MARCH 21
Gary Lang

MARCH 24 / APRIL 17
Nancy Bowen

APRIL 19 / MAY 15
Chéri Samba

MAY 17 / JUNE 30
Julio Galán

1990

1991

1991

SEPTEMBER 28 / NOVEMBER 6

Jenny Watson

NOVEMBER 9 / DECEMBER 7

Chéri Samba

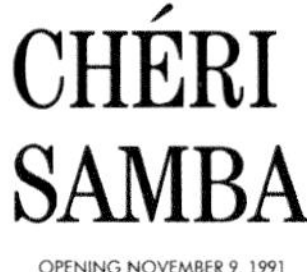

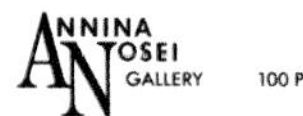

DECEMBER 10 / JANUARY 7

WORKS ON PAPER

Jean-Michel Basquiat, Nancy Bowen, Beth Brenner, Bruno Ceccobelli, Julio Galán, Tony Fitzpatrick, Anton Henning, Jacqueline Humphries, Guillermo Kuitca, Helmut Middendorf, Gian Marco Montesano, Stephen Mueller, Dennis Oppenheim, Nicolas Rule, Peter Schuyff, Ray Smith, Luiz Zerbini

1992

FEBRUARY 7 / MARCH 7

Sal Scarpitta
New Works 1990-1992 Curated by Collins & Milazzo in cooperation with Leo Castelli Gallery

MARCH 28 / APRIL 25

Julio Galán

MAY 2 / 30

Stephen Mueller

JUNE 5 / JULY 11

SPECS: PHOTOGRAPHY GROUP SHOW

Ellen Brooks, Carl Goldhagen, Elaine Reichek, Christiane Richter, Gary Schneider, Todd Watts, Roger Welch, James Welling

OCTOBER 3 / 31

WHO'S AFRAID OF DUCHAMP, MINIMALISM AND PASSPORT PHOTOGRAPHY?

Curated by Collins & Milazzo Ford Beckman, Lawrence Carroll, Stephen Ellis, Suzan Etkin, Peter Halley, Nicholas Howey, James Hyde, Jonathan Lasker, Annette Lemieux, Fabian Marcaccio, Donna Moylan, Philip Taaffe

NOVEMBER 4 / 30

Gian Marco Montesano

DECEMBER 4 / 31

Jenny Watson

1993

1993

JANUARY 6 / 30

GROUP EXHIBITION
Curated by Valerie Del-Sol John M. Armleder, Taro Chiezo, Mark Dion, Sylvie Fleury, Allan McCollum, Haim Steinbach

---

FEBRUARY 19 / MARCH 20

Pizzi Cannella

MARCH 27 / APRIL 22

Arturo Duclos

APRIL 23 / MAY 15

Tsibi Geva

MAY 21 / JULY 30

7 LATIN AMERICAN ARTISTS
Arturo Duclos, Julio Galán, Guillermo Kuitca, Miguel Ríos, Teresa Serrano, Jorge Tacla, Meyer Vaisman

---

SEPTEMBER 11 / OCTOBER 2

CONTINUING GENERATIONS
Curated by Paolina Weber René Pierre Allain, Carl Andre, Lawrence Carroll, Günther Förg, Donald Judd, Byron Kim, Paul Mittleman, Olivier Mosset, Daniel Terdo-slavich, Bettina Werner

---

OCTOBER 9 / NOVEMBER 6

Nancy Bowen

NOVEMBER 12 / DECEMBER 11

Kocheisen + Hullmann

DECEMBER 16 / JANUARY 29

GROUP EXHIBITION
Arturo Duclos, Flechemuller, Daniele Robbiani, Sara Sosnowy, Jenny Watson

1994

FEBRUARY 5 / MARCH 3

Stephen Mueller

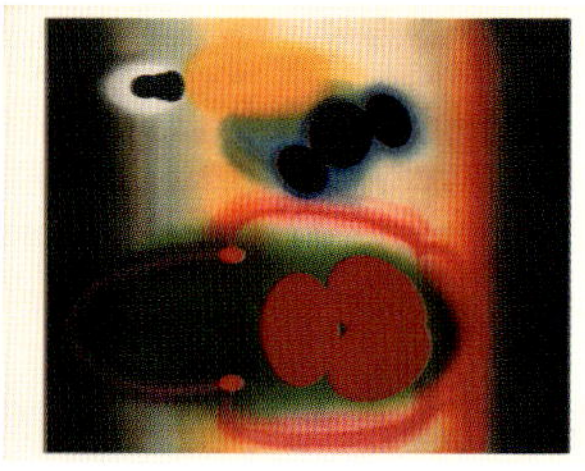

MARCH 5 / 31

Flechemuller

APRIL 6 / 30

Manuel Ocampo

MAY 7 / JUNE 4

Arturo Duclos

JUNE 7 / JULY 7

GROUP EXHIBITION
Flechemuller, Athos Ongaro, Teresa Serrano, Jenny Watson

SEPTEMBER 20 / OCTOBER 11

Jenny Watson

OCTOBER 12 / NOVEMBER 12

Teresa Serrano

NOVEMBER 16 / DECEMBER 15

Chéri Samba

DECEMBER 17 / FEBRUARY 8

Anna Paparatti

1995

FEBRUARY 10 / MARCH 2

Tsibi Geva

MARCH 4 / APRIL 5

Kocheisen + Hullmann

APRIL 7 / MAY 3

Flechemuller

MAY 5 / JUNE 1

Arturo Duclos

JUNE 3 / AUGUST 30

SUMMER INVITATIONAL
Ghada Amer, Arturo Elizondo, Gert Rappenecker, Amy Sillman

SEPTEMBER 30 / OCTOBER 28

Shirin Neshat

ANNINA NOSEI GALLERY
530 WEST 22ND STREET

1995 / 1996

NOVEMBER 18 / DECEMBER 12
INAUGURAL EXHIBITION OF NEW ADDRESS
Ghada Amer, Veronique Bellavista, Fernando Canovas, Arturo Duclos, Arturo Elizondo, Flechemuller, Julio Galán, Kocheisen + Hullmann, Gian Marco Montesano, Stephen Mueller, Shirin Neshat, Manuel Ocampo, Teresa Serrano

DECEMBER 16 / FEBRUARY 7
Athos Ongaro

FEBRUARY 10 / MARCH 14
Daniele Galliano

MARCH 16 / APRIL 10
Ghada Amer

APRIL 13 / MAY 12
Arturo Elizondo

MAY 18 / JUNE 30
Julio Galán

JUNE 3 / AUGUST 30
SUMMER GROUP EXHIBITION
Ghada Amer, Fernando Canovas, Arturo Duclos, Arturo Elizondo, Julio Galán, Daniele Galliano, Stephen Mueller, Shirin Neshat, Jenny Watson

1996

SEPTEMBER 14 / OCTOBER 9
DEATH IN LIGHT OF THE PHONOGRAPH: EXCURSIONS INTO THE PRE-LINGUISTIC
Paul D. Miller

OCTOBER 12 / NOVEMBER 7
Manuel Ocampo

NOVEMBER 9 / DECEMBER 9
Stephen Mueller

DECEMBER 14 / JANUARY 10
Helmut Middendorf

1997

1997

JANUARY 11 / FEBRUARY 5
GROUP DRAWING EXHIBITION
Ghada Amer, Veronique Bellavista, William Cotton, Arturo Duclos, Daniele Galliano, Manuel Ocampo, Joana Rosa

---

FEBRUARY 8 / MARCH 5
Teresa Serrano

MARCH 8 / APRIL 2
Fernando Canovas

APRIL 5 / MAY 1
Arturo Duclos

MAY 3 / JUNE 1
Shirin Neshat

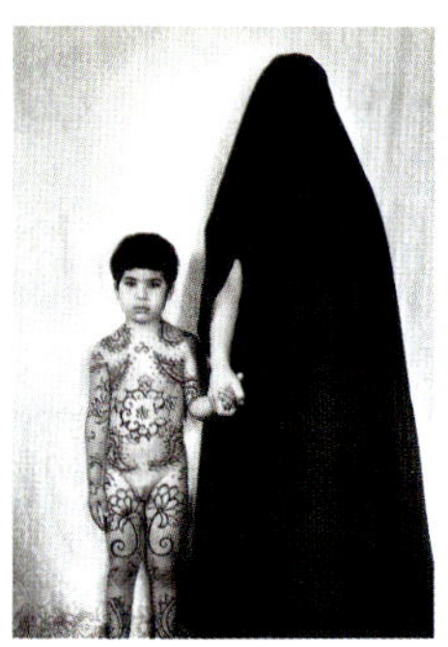

JUNE 3 / 13
Fabian Burgos

JULY 15 / AUGUST 18
GROUP DRAWING EXHIBITION
Ghada Amer, Veronique Bellavista, Fabian Burgos, Arturo Duclos, Arturo Elizondo, Daniele Galliano, Manuel Ocampo, Pablo Siquier

---

SEPTEMBER 20 / OCTOBER 16
Daniele Galliano

OCTOBER 18 / NOVEMBER 18
Pablo Siquier

NOVEMBER 20 / DECEMBER 18
WINTER GROUP EXHIBITION
Fabian Burgos, Alan Cheung, Arturo Elizondo, Daniele Galliano, Graciela Hasper, Martin Larralde, Stephen Mueller, Chéri Samba, Pablo Siquier

---

DECEMBER 20 / JANUARY 29
Graciela Hasper

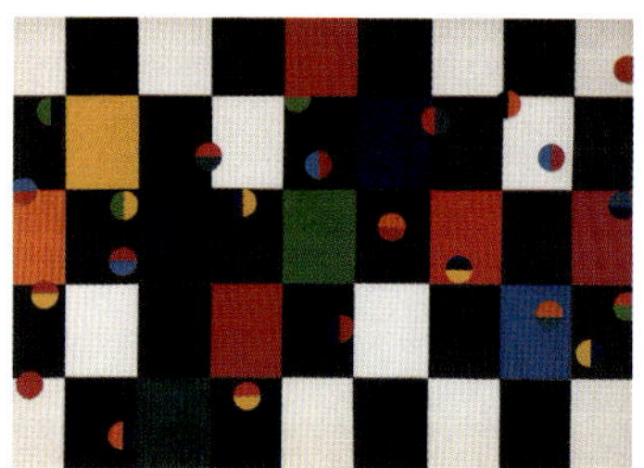

1998

JANUARY 31 / MARCH 14

Martin G. Larralde

MARCH 16 / APRIL 16

MAGICIENS DE LA TERRE WORKS FROM 1985
Bowa Devi, Yang Jiechang, Chéri Samba, R. B. Sharma,
Singh Shyam, Vyakul

APRIL 18 / MAY 20

GhadaAmer

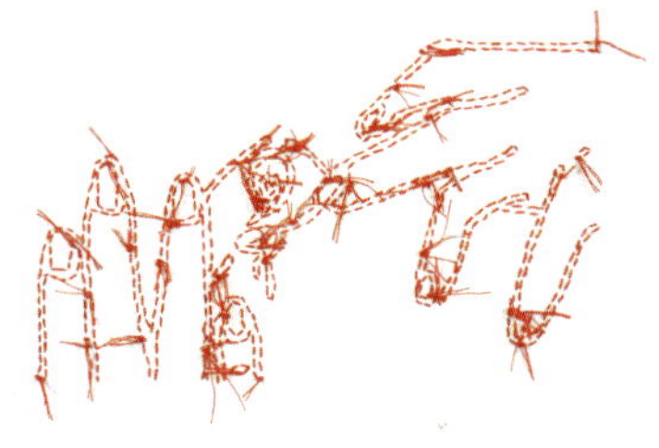

MAY 22 / JUNE 24

Fernando Canovas

JULY 10 / AUGUST 30

Jenny Watson

1998

SEPTEMBER 3 / OCTOBER 25

GALLERY ARTISTS
Ghada Amer, Veronique Bellavista, Fabian Burgos,
Arturo Elizondo, Graciela Hasper, Pablo Siquier, Jenny
Watson

OCTOBER 1 / 28

Deborah Turbeville

OCTOBER 29 / NOVEMBER 13

Santolo De Luca

NOVEMBER 14 / DECEMBER 10

Arturo Elizondo

DECEMBER 12 / JANUARY 14

Vincent Gallo

1999

1999

JANUARY 16 / FEBRUARY 14

FILTERED COMPONENTS
Curated by Paolina Weber
Chris Cunningham, Lucia Pearcey, David Perry

FEBRUARY 20 / MARCH 19

Liliana Porter

MARCH 20 / APRIL 22

Myriam Laplante

APRIL 23 / MAY 26

Abraham David Christian
Curated by Richard Milazzo

MAY 28 / JULY 17

José Bedia

JULY 19 / SEPTEMBER 28

GROUP EXHIBITION
Arturo Duclos, Arturo Elizondo, Gian Marco Montesano,
Cristiano Pintaldi, Andrea Salvino

SEPTEMBER 30 / NOVEMBER 9

Fernando Canovas

NOVEMBER 11 / DECEMBER 17

James Aldridge

DECEMBER 10 / FEBRUARY 4

GROUP PHOTOGRAPHY EXHIBITION
Janieta Eyre, Myriam Laplante, Martin Larralde, Shirin
Neshat, Luigi Ontani, Marta Maria Pérez Bravo, Liliana
Porter, Inez Van Lamsweerde

2000

FEBRUARY 5 / MARCH 8

Fabian Burgos

MARCH 11 / APRIL 6

Kocheisen + Hullmann

APRIL 8 / MAY 17

Marta Maria Pérez Bravo

MAY 19 / JUNE 30

Liliana Porter

JULY 5 / SEPTEMBER

SUMMER INVITATIONAL
Carole Benzaken, Fernando Canovas, Carlos Capelan,
Maki Na Kamura, Myriam Laplante, Gernot Lindner,
Federico Uribe, Jenny Watson

2000

SEPTEMBER 30 / NOVEMBER 1

Graciela Hasper

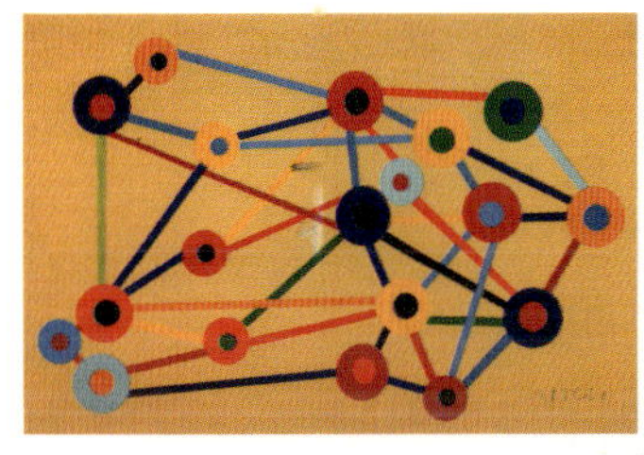

NOVEMBER 4 / DECEMBER 14

Federico Uribe

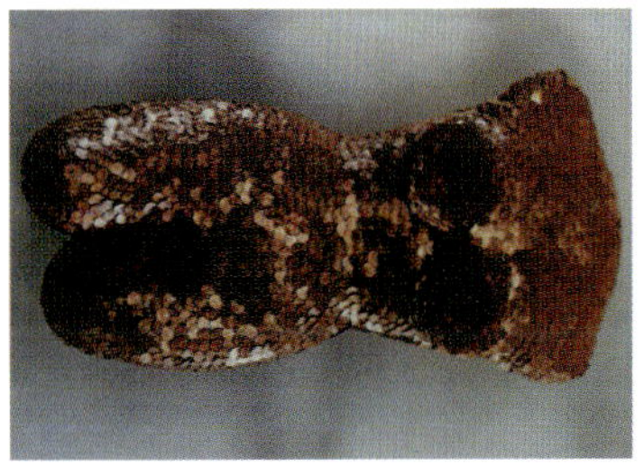

DECEMBER 16 / JANUARY 17

G. Lindner / C. Benzaken
22, rue Cauchy: Saint Clair Cemin, A. D. Christian, Elliot
Schwartz
Curated by Richard Milazzo

2001

JANUARY 19 / MARCH 3
Jenny Watson

MARCH 9 / APRIL 17
Tristano Di Robilant

APRIL 19 / MAY
Paolo W. Tamburella

JUNE / JULY
SUMMER GROUP SHOW
J. Bedia, H. McFall, S. Plumb, L. Porter, P. W. Tamburella, F. Uribe

SEPTEMBER 21 / OCTOBER 13
Tsibi Geva

OCTOBER 20 / NOVEMBER 25
José Bedia

NOVEMBER 30 / JANUARY 10
Arturo Elizondo

2002

JANUARY 12 / FEBRUARY 16
Liliana Porter

FEBRUARY 22 / APRIL 3
David Bowes

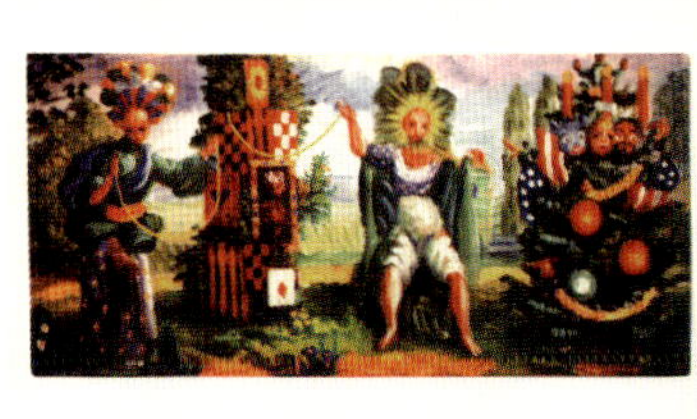

APRIL 5 / MAY 15
Heidi McFall

MAY 17 / JULY 6
Myriam Laplante

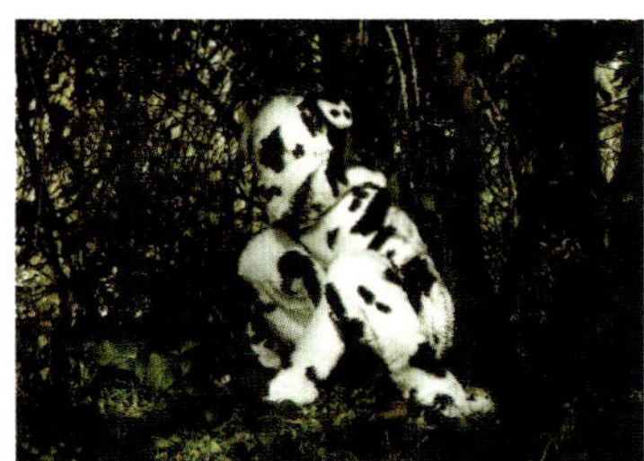

2002

JULY 9 / OCTOBER 15

SUMMER GROUP EXHIBITION
J.Bedia,I.Chiaraluce,M.Laplante, H. McFall, L. Porter,
F. Uribe, L. Warck-Meister

OCTOBER 18 / NOVEMBER

Federico Uribe

DECEMBER 10 / JANUARY 31

Paolo W. Tamburella

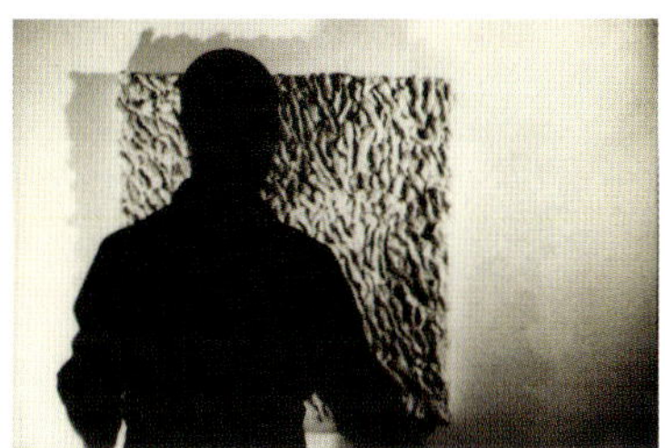

2003

FEBRUARY 26 / MARCH 31

GROUP EXHIBITION
José Bedia, Myriam Laplante, Ieva Mediodia, Liliana
Porter, Paolo W. Tamburella, Lucia Warck-Meister, Jenny
Watson

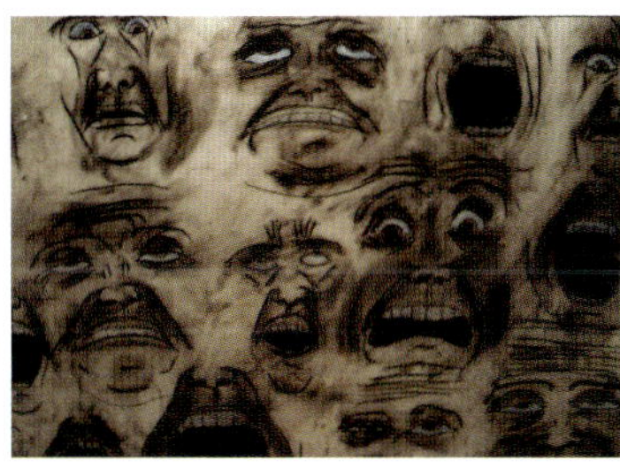

MAY 9 / JUNE 30

Heidi McFall

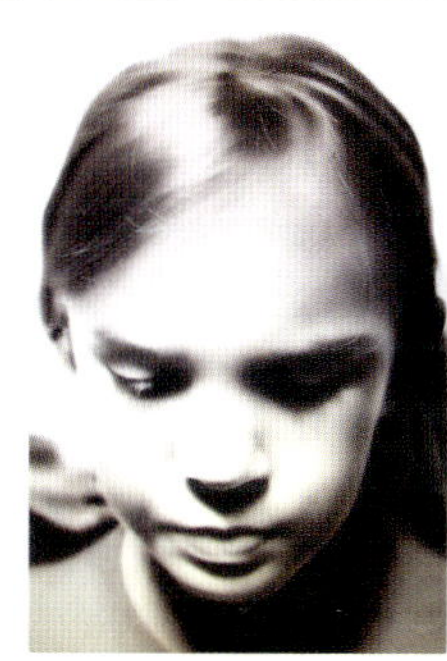

SEPTEMBER 10 / OCTOBER 15

GROUP EXHIBITION
Graciela Hasper, Heidi McFall, Ieva Mediodia, Liliana
Porter, Pablo Siquier, Paolo W. Tamburella, Federico
Uribe Second Room: Boaz Arad, Tsibi Geva, Miki
Kratsman

OCTOBER 14 / NOVEMBER 21

James Rosenquist
Curated by Robert Miller Gallery

NOVEMBER 28 / JANUARY 7

Federico Uribe

2004

JANUARY 9 / FEBRUARY 11

Michelle Mercurio

FEBRUARY 13 / APRIL 10

Ieva Mediodia

APRIL 16 / MAY 22

Jenny Watson

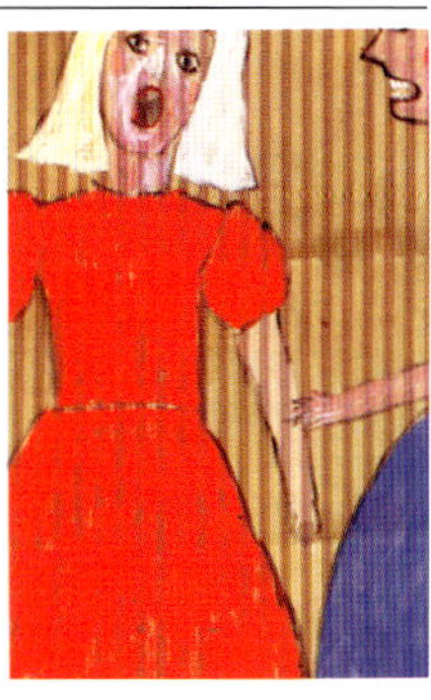

MAY 26 / JULY 14

Marta Maria Pérez Bravo
Second Room: Leemour Pelli

2004

JULY 16 / SEPTEMBER 6

GROUP SHOW
MyriamLaplante,Michelle Mercurio, Marta Maria Pérez Bravo, Liliana Porter

SEPTEMBER 9 / OCTOBER 5

YOUNG MIAMI
Natalia Benedetti, Pepe Mar, Beatriz Monteavaro, Cristina Lei Rodriguez, Leyden Rodriguez Casanova, Wendy Wischer, Brian Reedy. Curated by Dorit Arad

OCTOBER 9 / NOVEMBER 6

Liliana Porter

NOVEMBER 9 / DECEMBER 8

Arturo Elizondo

DECEMBER 10 / JANUARY 16

Lucia Warck-Meister

2005

JANUARY 18 / FEBRUARY 17
Tsibi Geva

FEBRUARY 18 / MARCH 30
Michelle Mercurio

APRIL 1 / MAY 5
Kocheisen + Hullmann

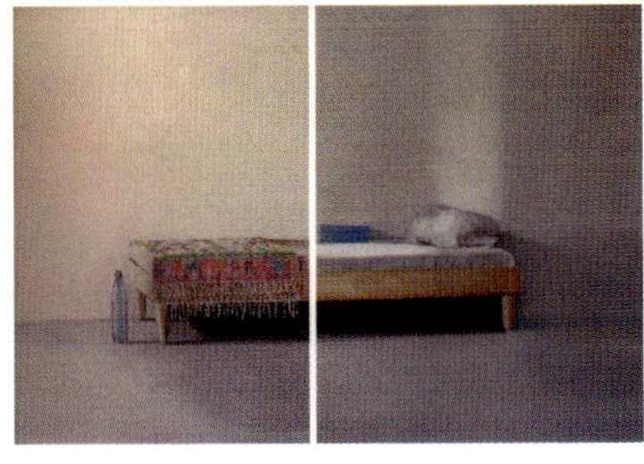

APRIL 11 / MAY 31
Leemour Pelli

MAY 6 / JUNE 6
Heidi McFall

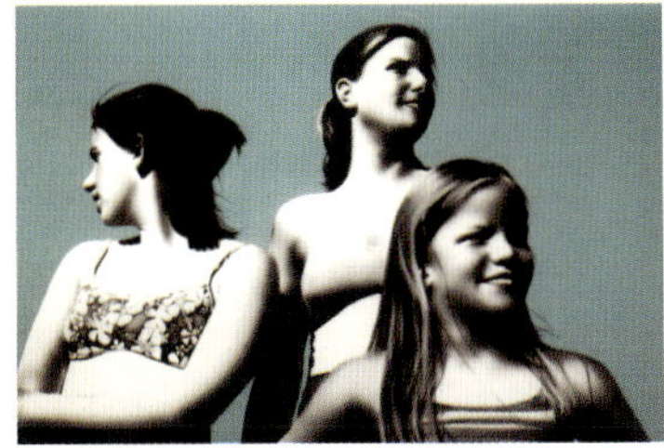

2005

JUNE 10 / JULY 23
EVERLAND
Curated by David Gibson Peggy Bates, Erik Benson,
Sandra Bermudez, Nancy Friedemann, Linda Ganjian,
Kim Keever, Dean Monogenis, Russell Nachman, Mark
Power, Raven Schlossberg, Ruth Waldman

JULY 24 / SEPTEMBER 27
SUMMER GROUP SHOW
Arturo Duclos, Heidi McFall, Ieva Mediodia

SEPTEMBER 28 / NOVEMBER 1
Myriam Laplante

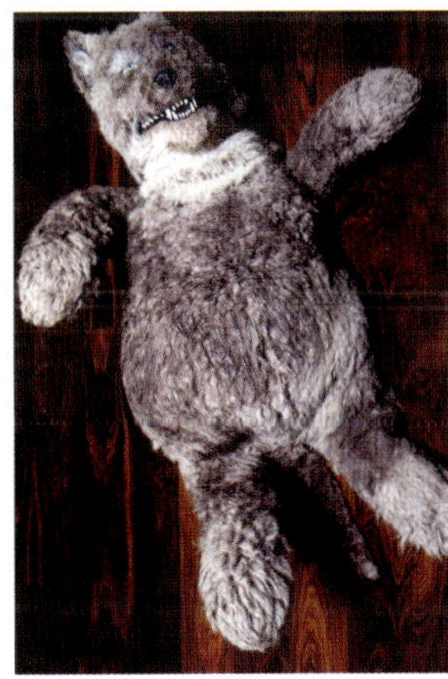

NOVEMBER 4 / 30
Gian Marco Montesano

ODE TO DOUGHNUTS

AURELIA WIGGINS

ODE TO DOUGHNUTS

With its infinite sides,
Along with infinite possibilities,
This godly object appears to have a mysterious
vast hole of infinite nothingness.
The silent sizzling of this newly crafted pastry
rests warmly in your shaking hands.
A sweet scent wafts into your nostrils along with
a violently creamy smell.
The deliciously crafted sweet continues to impatiently wait.
Although soft to the touch, this delicacy has a crunchy shell.
Your mouth fills with saliva as this godly thing raises itself to you.

For a moment you are in heaven.

But in the next, your doughnut is gone.

AURELIA WIGGINS
New York, 26 April 2018

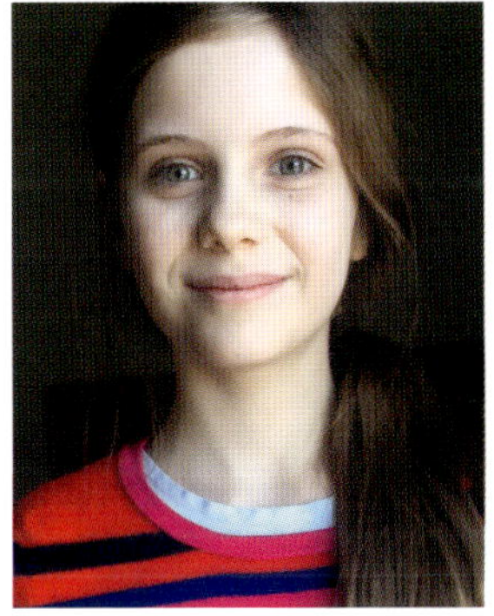

Aurelia Wiggins, Annina's granddaughter.